RENAY JORDAN

Happily Ever After

Secrets

For Mama and Daddy

You told me I could do anything I wanted. So, I did.

THE WOODLAWN FAMILY AND FRIENDS

THE TRENTONS AND FRIENDS

LILAH ANNE WINSTON TRENTON

(divorced from Eric Michael Trenton)
Their children (in order of birth):

Benjamin Winston Trenton

(biological father Mitchell McCain)
His girlfriend: Blair Loussant
(her father owns Lou's diner in Amityville)

Veronica Lauren Trenton – Vonnie

Her boyfriend: Hunter Alistair Montgomery
(the singer in their band)

Michael Todd Trenton

His girlfriend: Chantal Stephens

Maria Michelle Trenton

LILAH'S PARENTS

Alexander & Loretta Winston

THE LUNDS AND FRIENDS

ISABEL LORENE REYNOLDS LUND

(divorced from Thomas Ryland Lund)
Their children (in order of birth):

Isaac Reynolds Lund

His girlfriend: Tiffany Grace Bennett
(Adrian's twin sister)

Matthew Landon Lund

His girlfriend: Eden Victoria Wilson
(Vonnie's friend)

Abraham (Abe) Ryland Lund

ISABEL'S PARENTS

Robert & Eleanor (Ellie) Reynolds

TOM'S MOTHER

Mama Etta Lund

"TRISTAN" AND TIFFANY'S FOSTER PARENTS

Leon and Evelyn Jenkins

WOODLAWN POLICE DEPARTMENT

Nelson Reynolds, Police Chief (and Isabel's uncle)
Roy West, Deputy

DEA AGENTS - RICHMOND FIELD OFFICE

Marcus "Base" Johnston

Bettina "Tina" Evans

THE MCCAINS AND FRIENDS

James Mitchell "McCain"

Lilah's college boyfriend and Ben's biological father
Breton Russell McCain (Bret) - McCain's son
(mother unknown)

Desiree

McCain's next-door neighbor/girlfriend

THE AMITYVILLE FAMILIES AND FRIENDS

THE FAIRY TALE INN
THE SUTHERLAND FAMILY

MASON AND SICILY SUTHERLAND (NANA)

Their children (in order of birth):
Mason Carter Sutherland (Julie)
Jonathan Cabell Sutherland (Amy)
Thomas Colin Sutherland (Lisa)

Caris Anne Sutherland (married Raymond Bennett)

Her children (in order of birth):

Tiffany Grace Bennett, twin daughter (unmarried)

Adrian Cristiano Bennett, twin son (unmarried)

***PALAZZO CREMISI ***
(PRESENT DAY)

LORELEI ROSLYN ANASTASIO VALLARIO

Her children (in order of birth):

Stefan Antonio (Vallario) Bennett

(Adrian Cristiano Bennett)

Serena Michele Chevalier (Michel Chevalier)

Estela Herrera-Anastasio (adopted)

Adriana Grace Bennett (Adrian Cristiano Bennett)

Renaldo Thompson, Lorelei's butler

Ariana Acosta (Ari), Lorelei's best friend

Loren Acosta, Ari's brother

<u>DEA OFFICE – AMITYVILLE</u>

Jenny Stafford, Adrian's boss
Her son: William Wesley Stafford, III (Trey)
Terrence Mason (Adrian's co-worker)

His Fiancée, Sharla Johnston

THE EMPIRE HIERARCHY

****WHITE WILLOW MANSION****
THE CORLEONE FAMILY

THE SOVEREIGN
Samuel (Sam) and Valentina Corleone

Their children (in order of birth):
Saverina Corleone (married Roberto Benedetti)
Laura, daughter

Joseph (Joe) Corleone (unmarried)

PALAZZO CREMISI
THE ANASTASIO FAMILY

Francesco and Mary Angela Anastasio

Their children (in order of birth):

Mary Renata Anastasio (married Gabriel Lanza)

Sebastian & Roland, sons
Mary Lorraine 'Lorrie' Anastasio (married Darnell Giordano)
Adair, son
Mary Michelle 'Shelley' Anastasio
Leslie, son

Antonio 'Tony' Anastasio (married Roslyn Benedetti)

Lorelei Roslyn, daughter

ANGELIC MANOR
(Formerly Summerview Manor)
THE BENEDETTI FAMILY

MARCO AND ELENE BENEDETTI

Their children (in order of birth):

John 'Johnnie' Benedetti (married Elena Giordano)

Cavelora, daughter
Caterina, daughter
Roberto Benedetti (married Saverina Corleone)
Laura, daughter

Roslyn Elene Benedetti (married Antonio 'Tony' Anastasio)

Lorelei Roslyn Anastasio, daughter

LAKELAND
THE MONTENARI FAMILY

CRISTIANO AND LUCIA MONTENARI

Their children (in order of birth):

Mary Elizabeth Montenari (never married)

Giovanna Montenari (Ana)

Christoph Montenari (married Sylvia Vallario)
Alessandra, daughter

LONGHAVEN MANOR
THE GIORDANO FAMILY

MANCUSO AND CATENA GIORDANO

Their children in order of birth:
Darnell Giordano (married Mary Lorraine 'Lorrie' Anastasio)
Adair, son

Elena Giordano (married John 'Johnnie' Benedetti)

Cavelora, daughter
Caterina, daughter

Sergio Giordano (married Carlotta Lanza)

Thomaso, son
Cecilia, daughter

****FROST RIVER CHATEAU****
THE VALLARIO FAMILY

CHARLES VALLARIO AND ANGELINE LANZA

Their children in order of birth:

Gianni Vallario (married Lorelei Anastasio)

Sylvia Vallario (married Christoph Montenari)
Alessandra, daughter
Tessa Vallario (unmarried)

****CEDARVALE ESTATE****
THE LANZA FAMILY

JOEL LANZA AND CHRISTIANA LANZA

Their children in order of birth:

Angeline Lanza (married Charles Vallario)

Gianni, son

Sylvia, daughter
Tessa, daughter

Gabriel Lanza (married Mary Renata Anastasio)

Sebastian, son
Roland, son

Carlotta Lanza (married Sergio Giordano)

Thomaso, son
Cecilia, daughter

Amityville 2007
Lorelei

I was sleeping soundly when I was awakened by a knock on my balcony door. I laid in bed for a few minutes trying to gather my thoughts. Am I awake? Is this a dream or reality? It's reality, I finally decided. I pushed back my covers, got up and walked over to my balcony door. I peeked outside the sheer curtains. Adrian. He'd climbed the trellis at the corner of the house, hopped into the elm tree across from it and followed its branches to my balcony railing. He had a bunch of wildflowers he'd just picked from the field across from the Inn in his hand. Daisies and brown-eyed Susans. When I opened the door, he took me into his arms, picked me up and twirled me around.

"Good morning, beautiful," he said, and I smiled.

"Hi." He sat me back down and presented the flowers to me. "For me?"

"Yes. Do you like them?"

"I love them," I said.

He leaned over and softly kissed my lips. Bluebell got up off the bed and stretched herself, arching her back and swishing her tail. She walked over to the edge of it to greet my prince – because one day we were going to ride off together on a white horse toward the setting sun. Just me and him.

"Good morning, Bluebell," he said as he rubbed her head.

She began to purr loudly, and he picked her up. She looked up to him and nuzzled her face against his chin. Kisses. I think she felt the same way about him as I did. We loved him too much. At least that's what Papa said.

He sat Bluebell back down onto the bed and turned to me. It was Sunday morning. Mamma and Papa had gone to mass, but I had played sick. Adrian slowly unbuttoned the front of my white, cotton gown and kissed my collarbone, pushed the sleeves back over my shoulders. My hands found his waist and I pulled his shirttail out of his pants while he loosened his tie. He was supposed to be at church, too.

Adrian and I made love every day. Sometimes more than once. He said he never stopped wanting me. I told him I felt the same way. It wasn't very often we got to make love in my bed or in his, but they were my favorite places, because afterward we could curl up under the covers together and fall asleep. Sometimes, if we had time, we'd wake up and fall in love all over again. Bluebell hopped down off the bed and meandered across the room. She jumped up onto my dresser and sat down. She began washing her face, but she kept one eye on us as we kissed.

"She's watching us," I told Adrian as I looked over his shoulder. He turned momentarily.

"You think?"

"Uh-huh."

I felt his mouth on my neck and I unbuttoned his pants, let them slide over his hips and down his legs. He stepped out of them and pushed me back onto the bed, crawling over me as he did. He tugged at the bottom of my gown. I lifted my hips and he pulled it up my legs. I felt his lips between my breasts, and I arched my back toward him.

"Mmm…"

I unbuttoned Adrian's shirt and he finagled his way out of it. Within a few minutes we were completely naked under the pink ruffled comforter of my white canopy bed. He took my hands in his, wove our fingers together over my head.

"I love you," he said as he pushed inside of me.

"Mmm…"

Our lovemaking is gentle. It is always warm and comforting. He treats me as if I am a delicate flower. His kisses taste like honey. Being with him this way brings tears to my eyes. I am overcome with emotion. So many sensations course through my body, most of them I don't even understand. I wonder if all love is this way, or if it is just ours.

Adrian propped his elbows on the bed beside me, but he didn't let go of my hands. I couldn't even imagine making love to anyone except him. I pushed his hair back over his shoulders and he lowered his face into the crevice of my neck. I could feel him breathing there, an intake of breath and a slow exhale as the anticipation grew. I breathed with him. We breathed together. I felt his lips graze against my ear. He drew in his breath once more and when he lifted his head to look at me, I smiled. I closed my eyes and he kissed my eyelids. He let go of my hands, ran his fingers across my shoulders and down my arms. I shivered. No one else had this. No one had what we had. No one our age had even imagined it yet. No one our age knew this kind of love existed. It was passion and adoration, a gentle but fierce need. A tender devotion.

A soft but relentless rain began outside my balcony door. The sheer curtains blew in the wind and a fine mist floated across Adrian's bare back and settled on my upper arms. I couldn't tell if his damp shoulders were a result of the rain, or the desire he had for me.

"Lora," he mumbled into my hair.

"I know," I managed.

I slipped my arms under his, my hands grasp his shoulder blades. I felt his muscles tighten against my palms. I felt the essence of him strengthen inside me and my heart beat faster. Waves of expectation coursed through me, and then, paradise redefined. I held onto him and he pressed his lips against my temple. I always had to remind him to breathe.

Lightning lit up the now darkened sky. I closed my eyes as a crash of thunder echoed around my room. Boom. Boom. Boom. A reverberation that matched our emotions. A dreamlike consciousness that ended in a mirrored gasp. I held tightly onto Adrian's shoulders and he kissed my forehead. Another low rumble of thunder as the storm passed over us and the rain subsided. A ray of sunlight peeked through the passing clouds and Adrian smiled again. He had the most beautiful smile.

"I love you," I said before he could.

"I love you more," he answered.

A thousand wishes bestowed. A burning desire fulfilled.

My knight in shining armor. The princess he saved.

Eternal. Endless. Everlasting love.

Bliss.

I believed then that moments like those would grace the rest of my life. I didn't believe I'd ever have to search for happiness because I'd already found it. I had everything I'd ever dreamed of. This boy I loved hopelessly, loved me hopelessly in return.

He would get his music scholarship and wherever he went to school I'd go, too. We'd get an apartment and once we graduated college, we'd get married. We'd do it before we returned to Amityville to live at the Inn with Nana, so *The Empire* couldn't dictate our future. We'd have a little boy first, then a little girl. But things didn't turn out that way. *The Empire* did dictate our future. A lot sooner than we could have ever imagined.

I prayed fate would bring Adrian back to me. I petitioned God. I begged Papa. I cried to Mamma. I found comfort in Nonna's assurance that Adrian was okay, even though she told me he was heartbroken, too.

A month or so later when those dreams were only a distant memory, I discovered I was carrying Adrian's child and by Empire authority forced to marry a man I didn't love. Gianni Vallario. Papa said Gianni loved me. I knew this wasn't true because if it had been true Gianni wouldn't have treated me like a possession. He would've treated me like Adrian treated me - a princess. He would've put me before himself because that's what love does. All I was to Gianni was a maid, a cook, and a guarantee he could have sex any time he wanted. What I wanted never mattered.

The first time I held mine and Adrian's baby in my arms I experienced a kind of love that transcended any preconceived notion I might have had about motherhood. I would do anything for this little boy, I thought. He was the second love of my life but only because his father was my first. I might not have had Adrian anymore, but I had his son. Throughout the first few years of Stef's life that knowledge was the only thing that kept me sane. Of course, what Mamma had done in secret gave me peace. A kind of peace I would have never found any other way.

"You might be Lorelei Vallario," she whispered to me at my bedside after Stef was born. "But my grandson will not be subjected to Empire sovereignty." She squeezed my fingers in hers. "This child will know his true father. I told you and Adrian to trust me, didn't I?" I nodded. "I'm not sure Adrian understood what that meant at the time but he will one day. Okay?" I nodded again. "Let me see this little prince he gave you."

She handed me two pieces of paper from her pocket then took her grandson into her arms. She kissed his tiny head. This was not only a mother's love; it was the tenacious determination of an Empire wife making sure justice trumped a cold dynasty rule. I looked down to the papers she'd given me.

STATE OF NEW YORK
DIVISION OF VITAL STATISTICS

This is to certify that a birth certificate has been filed for
Stefan Antonio Vallario (Male)
on May 20, 2008 *at* Oceanside, New York
Maiden Name of Mother: Lorelei Roslyn Anastasio *Age of Mother:* 16
Father: Gianni Jerome Vallario *Age of Father:* 21

And then the other paper:

NEW YORK STATE DEPARTMENT OF HEALTH
VITAL RECORDS SECTION
APPLICATION FOR CORRECTION OF CERTIFICATE OF BIRTH

RE: Infant – Stefan Antonio Vallario
Date of Birth – May 20, 2008 *Place of birth* – Oceanside, NY
Father's Name: Adrian Cristiano Bennett *Age of Father: 17*
Mother's Name: Lorelei Roslyn Anastasio *Age of Mother: 16*

EXPLAIN REASON FOR ERROR OR OMISSION:
Father recorded at birth is not biological father. Documentary evidence submitted herewith in support of this application included. (see attach.)

TO BE COMPLETED BY THE APPLICANT:
Under penalties of perjury, I hereby affirm that the statements made herein are true and correct to the best of my knowledge.

SIGNATURE OF APPLICANT (MATERNAL):
Roslyn Elene Benedetti Anastasio
RELATIONSHIP TO INFANT: grandmother
SIGNATURE OF APPLICANT (PATERNAL):
Mary Elizabeth Montenari
RELATIONSHIP TO INFANT: *****

TO BE COMPLETED BY REGISTRAR OF VITAL STATISTICS:
The above information has been added to the local record of birth on file in this office.

SIGNATURE OF REGISTRAR: *Mary Elizabeth Montenari*
DISTRICT NO: 49335768

"Thank you," I said quietly and smiled.

"You're welcome, Angel." She smiled, too. "We'll talk about the details later."

"Okay."

Gianni walked into the room and I quickly hid the papers under my covers.

"How's my Angel?" he asked as he kissed my forehead, and then to my mother as he looked over to Stef, "Isn't he gorgeous?

"I think he looks like his mother," Mamma teased and she winked at me.

"You might be right," Gianni admitted.

"I'm always right," Mamma said. Gianni chuckled.

"I know better than to argue with Roslyn Anastasio."

"You do," she stated.

"I think everyone in *The Empire* knows not to argue with Roslyn Anastasio," he stated. Mamma smiled.

Mamma's reputation preceded her. No one argued with her. My friends from school used to always tell me they were afraid of her, but my mother didn't have a mean bone in her body. She just didn't take crap off anyone. I'm pretty sure my Papa was included. Even so, she knew her place as an Empire wife and she portrayed her part flawlessly.

"You guys need anything?" Gianni asked. "I think I'm going down to the cafeteria and get something to eat."

"I'm good," I managed.

"Me, too," Mamma said, and Stef began to fret a little. She bounced him in her arms.

"Let me have him," I said as I reached for my son and she gave him back to me.

As soon as she did, he stopped fussing and snuggled into me. I unbuttoned my gown and he turned toward me. He opened his little mouth like a baby bird searching for sustenance. Nonna told me that all babies should be nursed, that it increased their immunity and gave them essential vitamins they couldn't get any other way.

"Here you go," I encouraged him. He latched onto me and began to suck contentedly.

"See?" Gianni said as he stuffed his hands into his pockets. He backed toward the door. "He might look like his mother, but he got his desires from his Pop." He pointed to me. "I know I gotta share, though."

"Stop it," I said, and he laughed.

As soon as Gianni was gone, I reached under my covers and pulled out the pieces of paper Mamma had given to me just moments ago. I handed them back to her. Papa walked into the room to see his grandson and I panicked, but Mamma casually put the application for correction behind her back and handed the birth certificate to him.

"Feels good to see the Vallario name on there," she said to him as he draped his arm around her shoulders. He pulled her into him and kissed her temple.

"It does," he said.

He walked over to my bedside and gazed at my son. Adrian's son. The tiny baby the love of my life and I had created together.

"You've got a beautiful Mamma, little man," he said. "Grow up and make Nonno proud."

He offered his finger to Stef and Stef instinctively wrapped his tiny hand around it. I glanced over to Mamma who was still holding the application for correction behind her, but when Papa leaned over to kiss my forehead, I watched her quickly stuff the truth back into her pocket.

"You saw my bones being formed as I took shape in my mother's body...All the days planned for me were written in your book before I was one day old."

Psalm 139: 15-16

Woodlawn – Present Day
Lilah

"You have no idea what you're doing," Isabel said as I sat on the toilet.

I was holding the plastic stick from the pregnancy test between my legs and she was sitting on the edge of the tub across from me.

"I should slap you," I said. "Of course, I don't know what I'm doing. I remember to take my birth control pills."

"Really?" she said. "Are you sitting on the toilet with a pregnancy test between your legs right now? Because I'm not."

"I hate you, Isabel." She laughed and I did, too, even though it should not have been funny. "I can't pee."

"This should help," she said as she reached over and turned on the faucet. I waited a moment.

"Nope." She turned on the hot water.

"Give me your hand," she said.

"I feel like I'm at summer camp," I told her but I started to pee.

"Ha!" she said. I jerked my hand back.

"What if I miss?" I asked as I looked between my legs.

"You're not going to miss," she assured me. I finished and pulled the test stick back out and looked at it. Isabel reached for the cap on the sink.

"Well, give it to me," she ordered. "Don't just sit there staring at it." She took it from me and reattached the cap. I sat on the toilet looking at her for a minute. I didn't even wipe.

"We should not be doing this," I said. "We are too old for this."

"Maybe you are," she said. "Not me." I stared at her. "Oh, come on, Lilah, age is just a number."

"Right," I said. "If age is just a number then why did I find a gray hair on my head this morning?"

"Wait until you see a gray hair down there," she told me as she pointed between her legs.

"I don't have any hair down there," I reminded her.

"Do you think I should start shaving all of mine off, too?" she asked. I shrugged.

"Well, if you don't want to see gray hair down there then that would be the answer."

"I love it when you give me advice about personal hygiene."

"You're welcome."

"You could dye your hair blonder like mine," she suggested.

"Just because I can't see it doesn't mean it isn't there."

"Three minutes," she announced.

"Oh god, Isabel." I leaned over with my head in my hands. "What if I am?"

"Then you are," she said. She laid her hand on my leg.

"What will Adrian say?" I asked as I looked up to her. She shrugged.

"I have no idea."

"Oh my god, Isabel! You're supposed to make me feel better!" I slapped at her hand and she retracted it. "You're supposed to say something like, 'Oh Lilah, I'm sure he'll be thrilled. He's probably been secretly wanting this all along.'"

"I'm not that kind of friend," she said. "I'm not going to tell you something that might not be true. He might freak the hell out and say something like, 'Are you serious, Lilah? Are you fucking kidding me right now? I thought you said you were on birth control?'"

"He doesn't say the word 'fuck,'" I reminded her.

"I can see him standing there with his hands low on his hips," she continued, ignoring me. "You know the way he stands when he's really agitated?" I just stared at her and she held up her hands. "I'm just saying."

"You are the worst friend *ever*," I said as I wiped myself.

"Three minutes," she reminded me.

"What?" I said as I pulled up my jeans. "It hasn't been three minutes."

"It has. Aha! I knew it! Pink line."

"What the hell does that mean?"

"It means you're pregnant."

"Give me the stupid thing." I jerked the test stick out of her hand and gazed at it. "That is not what that means, you moron. That means the test is working." She looked over my shoulder as the second pink line began to emerge. She pointed to it and I watched it turn from light pink to dark orchid.

"I think that means you're pregnant," she said quietly.

"Holy cow," I said. "It can't be right." Isabel took me by the shoulders as I turned to her. "How did this happen??"

"Basic sex education," she said. "You have sex. You make a baby."

"I wasn't trying to make a baby!" I said. "I just wanted to have a good orgasm!! I take my pills every day."

"Lilah, honey," Isabel said. "I got pregnant with all three of my boys by taking my pills…"

"I know that!!" I said pulling away from her.

"Well, don't be mad," she told me. I opened the bathroom door. "It'll be fine."

"It will be fine??" I asked as I turned around. I walked over to her dresser and looked in the mirror above it.

"Yes," she consoled. She came over and stood behind me.

"It will be fine," I said to my reflection. "It will be fine. Oh my god…" I turned around to face her.

"What??"

"How old am I?"

"You're thirty-eight."

"I can't have a baby!" I told her. "I'm too old to have a baby! Doctors tell you all the time not to have babies this late in life."

"What the hell kind of doctor have you ever heard say that???" Isabel asked as she put her hands lightly on my upper arms. "Maybe back in the thirties. Not now. Good grief, Lilah. Your own mother was forty-seven when she had you."

"I'll be almost fifty when this baby is ten!!" I exclaimed. "Adrian will be…." I stopped and counted on my fingers then looked back up to Isabel. "Almost forty. Holy shit."

"Why is this bad??" she asked. "I am seriously failing to understand why this is so bad. "A baby is a miracle."

"Yeah," I said as I walked away from her. "A baby is a miracle, alright. Shit."

"Well, let's go have a drink," Isabel said. "Process this new information."

"I can't drink!" I exclaimed. "I'm pregnant!"

"Oh god!" She brought her hand to her chest. "Who will I have happy hour with for the next nine months???"

"I'm gonna slap you!"

"Come on," she said as she grabbed my hand. "You can have a wine cooler."

"That's still alcohol," I reminded her.

"No, it's not," she said. "It's the equivalent of eating grapes."

"Ha." I followed her down the hall. "You think you're so funny."

We walked into the kitchen and I sat down at the counter bar, closed my eyes, and put my head in my hands while Isabel made herself a drink. She turned from the refrigerator as I looked up and handed me a wine cooler. I took it and she tapped her glass up against it.

"Cheers!" she said. "To having a baby with your sex-on-a-stick boyfriend."

"You're twisted," I said and shook my head.

"I made you laugh," she said and pointed at me.

"It's not every day you walk through the foyer of your house and see a pregnancy test stick laying on the hall table," Isaac said as he walked around the corner and into the kitchen. He held it up. "Who's pregnant?"

Isabel and I both pointed to each other then she leaned over the counter and slapped my hand.

"No," she said to Isaac. "Not me."

"Isabel," I said. "Don't lie to your offspring. Tell him the truth."

"Are you pregnant for real, Mom?" Isaac asked.

"No," Isabel said as she turned from the counter. "I am not pregnant."

"Are you pregnant?" Isaac asked, pointing at me. I said nothing. "Holy shit."

"Isaac," I said, jumping up off the bar stool and walking over to him. I took him by his shoulders. "If you tell anyone this, I will shave off your eyebrows tonight while you're sleeping."

"I won't tell anyone," he said, laughing. He wrapped his arms around me and picked me up, turned me around. The fact that he was strong enough to pick me up and turn me around blew my mind. When did mine and Isabel's kids get this big??

"This is amazing," he said.

"This is not amazing," I said as he sat me back down. "I'm too old for this."

"Jeez, Lilah. No, you're not."

"See?" Isabel said. "I told you."

"Does Adrian know?" Isaac asked as I walked back over to the bar and sat down.

"It's not his," Isabel said.

I picked up an orange out of the bowl on her counter and threw it at her. I missed but only because she ducked out of the way. It hit the door of the refrigerator and fell to the floor. Isaac chuckled.

"No," I said. "He doesn't know so don't say anything to him. I've got to figure out how to tell him."

"Be naked," Isabel suggested. "That always works."

"Congratulations," Isaac said to me. He walked over and kissed my cheek then took my wine cooler out of my hand. "I think it's awesome but this wine cooler is now mine." He turned and walked out of the kitchen. Isabel laughed.

"The wisdom of Isaac Lund," she said.

"Nine months," he called out over his shoulder.

"You suck, Isaac!" I called in return. He poked his head back around the doorframe.

"You know," he said. "This is so amazing I'm going to take it upon myself to buy you a Slurpee every day at Happy Hour for the next nine months."

"You're so thoughtful," I said.

"Who's pregnant?" Matt asked as he walked around the corner behind Isaac.

"Lilah," Isaac told him. He looked to me.

"Is it Adrian's?" he asked. I picked up another orange and threw it at him. He caught it then held up his hands.

"What?!?" he exclaimed. "I think given your and Mom's history, that is a legitimate question." I looked over to Isabel and she shrugged.

"He's not wrong," she said to me.

Sometimes hearing the truth from our kids is enlightening. This time it wasn't only enlightening. This time it was frightening. Not because of my pregnancy. Just because the accuracy of Matt's statement made me sick to my stomach. Somehow, ever since I met Adrian, I had developed a conscience.

McCain

I walked down the center aisle of the auditorium. The acoustics of the room made the music bounce off the walls. Figuring out that Vonnie's mother was not just some random Lilah but *my* Lilah wasn't hard. Reasoning Vonnie was in the talent show was even easier. I knew if Vonnie was playing her drums her mother would be in the audience somewhere. I hadn't seen Lilah in twenty years but I knew when I did, I would recognize her immediately.

I was about halfway down the aisle when I spotted her. It was dark so no one noticed me. Lilah was just as beautiful as she was back then but now, she glowed. She was happy. It reminded me of the first night I met her. Before the drugs. Before I lost control. I watched her. She was surrounded by friends and family and holding a little girl in her arms I wished was mine.

I didn't think I'd need my gun. I wasn't planning on using it but I'd loaded it anyway. My grandfather used to tell me never to load my gun unless I intended on shooting it. This was the first time I'd ever not heeded his advice. Even though he had passed years ago I could still hear his words in my mind in times like these. He used to tell me taking control of a room wasn't about anything except respect. I had succeeded in gaining respect many times over the course of my life with no violence involved. Tonight was different though, because Lilah was having an affair with the man who put my son behind bars. I reached around behind me to make sure the gun was still there. It had warmed to the same temperature as my skin and become a part of me. I started walking again.

The auditorium was packed with teenagers dancing and screaming at the stage. Vonnie played her drums. She wasn't only beautiful. She was charismatic. She could have anyone in the palm of her hand in minutes. She didn't have Lilah's blonde hair but she did have her green eyes. Lilah once told me less than two percent of people have green eyes. Hers were bright green with flecks of gold in them. Vonnie's were blue green but they were still beautiful. She had Lilah's high cheekbones and Lilah's figure. She also had Lilah's attitude.

I had to laugh the first night I met Vonnie. She told me I needed to shave because I'd be much more handsome if I did then she started talking about how her mom was having an affair with a guy that went to her school. It didn't necessarily seem like she thought it was wrong just a little crazy given her Mom's age. I knew right then Vonnie would betray Bret because Lilah had betrayed me. I should have warned Bret about her that night but within minutes Vonnie had me entranced. She was smart. Too smart for Bret.

No one noticed me as I walked down the aisle. I noticed then that Adrian was playing the keyboard and that was a little unexpected. I wasn't sure if he'd seen me. I wondered if everyone else knew what I did, that "Tristan" wasn't Tristan at all. When I got to the second row from the front, he locked eyes with me. The music slowed and Vonnie stopped playing her drums. I listened as Adrian played a solo. The piano echoed across the auditorium. Every girl in the room screamed his name.

"Tristan!!"

I looked up to him once more and he slowly but deliberately lifted the back of his shirt just high enough for me to see the holster sticking into the back of his jeans. I pushed past the people in the second row and made my way to the opposite end where Lilah was standing. I knew Adrian was watching me but what did he know? He didn't know my history with Lilah. He didn't know anything about me and Lilah at all. Before I got to her the music stopped and Adrian yelled into his microphone.

"Everyone!! Get down!! Now!!"

People started falling to the floor around me. It was instant chaos. Adrian sidestepped the keyboard and jumped off the edge of the stage into the audience. He hopped over two empty chairs mid-way down and reached for me. People scattered in every direction and I lost sight of Lilah. Adrian grabbed me around my neck from behind, slipped his hand into the back of my jeans and took my gun. He pulled me back further into him then shoved his knee into the back of my legs and took me down to the floor with him. Within minutes he was on top of me and Tina was beside him.

"I need back-up at the high school," I heard Tina say into her radio. "Possible volatile drug-related incident."

Adrian held my neck in his hand, my cheek against the sticky floor. Before I could speak, he'd dug his knee into my back and pulled my hands behind me. He handcuffed me and got up grabbing my arm in the process and jerking me to a standing position.

"Get up!" he said disgustedly.

I saw cops in black ballistic vests coming through the side doors from every angle, some with DEA written across their backs, others with POLICE, all with semi-automatic rifles. They began directing the crowd out of the emergency exit doors. It seemed no one around here took any chances with any kind of misconduct which was totally Adrian's fault, not mine. I guess my presence and the possibility of the unknown alarmed him. In a matter of minutes, he had apprehended me and handed me off to another guy. He hopped up onto the stage. The auditorium fell silent immediately. He leaned over on his knees for a moment to catch his breath then stood back up.

"As you can all see I am a little out of breath," he said into the microphone. He put his hands low on his hips then ran one of them through his hair. "But, hey, all is good. There has been a minor security breach. But there's no reason to be alarmed."

Apparently, I was the minor security breach. *Minor.*

"Tristan!!!" some unknown girl yelled. He pointed to her.

"Yeah, baby…. I got you."

Son of a bitch.

"I love you," she yelled. He held up his hands, smiled and nodded in her direction. Not a reciprocation but a humble acknowledgement. Arrogant bastard.

"I can assure you guys everything is under control. Let the officers escort you outside for a moment. This is only a precautionary measure so there is no reason to be frightened."

Vonnie walked up behind him. I'm not sure where she came from but Adrian wrapped his arm around her waist as the man I had come to know as Base dragged me toward the exit. Vonnie looked to me as she grabbed the microphone from the middle of the stage. She screamed into it before Adrian could stop her.

"Fuck you!" she yelled at me. "You motherfucking son of a bitch."

"Hey!" I heard Adrian say as he grabbed it away from her. He smiled and shook his head as he pulled her tighter into him. "Cool it, Von."

Von? Was that his pet name for her? I was going to beat his ass the next time I saw him. Who did he think he was? Her father? Whatever part he played in her life, 'Von' didn't seem to think his reproach was funny, but everyone else in the auditorium did including Lilah. She glanced over to me. This woman who used to be mine. I loved her. She was the first woman I'd ever loved but I didn't know how to show it to her then. I'd treated her like she was a possession. Like she belonged to me. Like I owned her.

A lot of men try to own their women but it only works if the woman wants to be owned. You need to be careful with women because they all have a different line and if you cross it there's no going back. If that woman you adore doesn't want to be owned, they'll do what Lilah did to me.

They'll leave.

—

"What kind of weapon are we talking about?" Tina asked Adrian as we stood outside the auditorium.

"It's just an everyday pistol," he said to her. "Nothing major."

What the hell is an everyday pistol?

"You recorded any of the charges yet?" Tina asked.

"You ought to charge him with attempted murder," Base told Adrian.

"What the hell, man?" I asked him. "You know good and…"

"Shut-up," Base yelled at me. "If I want you to talk, I'll let you know. Otherwise, shut your pie-hole." Adrian laughed.

"Pie-hole?" he asked Base.

"You making fun of me, Schoolboy?" Base countered.

"Nope," Adrian answered. He turned to Tina. "I'm gonna charge him with brandishing a firearm, possession and malicious intent."

"You can't charge me with malicious intent!" I yelled. "You fucking bastard. I didn't hurt anyone."

"Shut-up!" Base told me as he jerked my arm. "You gon tell me your intentions were pure and innocent??"

"I…"

"You might want to stop talking," Adrian told me. "Not a smart choice without a lawyer."

"You never read me my rights," I told him, and Base threw me up against the wall beside him.

"What'd I tell you?" he said.

"Well, then," Adrian said. "Let's get that formality out of the way." He walked over to me and leaned up against the wall beside me. I looked down. "You have the right to remain silent," he said. "If you give up your right to remain silent, anything you say can and will be held against you in a court of law. You have a right to an attorney. If you desire an attorney and cannot afford one, an attorney will be obtained for you before police questioning. Do you understand?"

"Yeah."

"Let's go."

Base let go of me and Adrian grabbed my arm and led me to a police car sitting in the parking lot.

"Get in the car," Adrian said as he put his hand on my head. He let me go and shut the door behind me. He leaned into the open window. "I'll see you at the station," he said.

"I can't wait," I retorted.

"Me either," he said and walked away.

Isabel

I had never seen Adrian in action. I am fully aware of what he does for a living but it never really resonated with me until I saw him jump off the stage that night. Within minutes he had prevented a possible tragedy and brought an entire high school audience under control. I didn't know of any teacher or staff member in the entire school who was capable of either one. It was quite impressive. My only negative response to the whole situation, after realizing the people I loved most were safe, was that I didn't know where Isaac had gone. I looked around and grabbed Matt's arm from behind.

"What?" he asked, turning around

"Where's your brother?"

"Which one?"

"Isaac, you idiot. Abe is standing right next to you!"

"Well, gosh Mom. You don't have to call me names."

"Where is he?" I asked.

"How would I know??"

We followed the crowd through the side door closest to us. I wanted to make all the children hold hands but I quickly reminded myself that while they still needed my protection, they were pretty capable on their own. When we got outside, I gathered everyone around me next to the magnolia tree at the corner of the building.

"Where is Isaac?" I asked all of them.

Everyone shrugged. I was going to strangle him the next time I saw him. He might have been bigger than me but it didn't mean I still couldn't wrangle him into a corner. But that wouldn't be necessary. Isaac was the only child of mine who responded more favorably to verbal reprimands. I usually had to beat Matt and Abe with the wooden spoon first.

Tom's mother was the one who told me how effective 'the spoon' was with errant children and how I should carry one with me wherever I went just in case my little angels decided to be devils instead. I didn't heed her advice because I didn't want to be arrested but I did beat Matt one day in the grocery store parking lot with my flip flop. It didn't have the same effect as the spoon.

"When was the last time you saw Isaac?" I asked Abe.

"This morning before we left the house," he said. I turned to Ben.

"When was the last time you saw him?" I asked.

"Not since last night when he was at the house," he said.

"Damn it," I said as I pulled my phone out of my back pocket.

I scrolled through my favorites list and touched my finger to Isaac's name. He better answer. It rang five times, then voicemail. 'You've reached Isaac Lund. Please leave your name, number and a brief message and I will return your call as soon as possible.'

"This is your mother," I said. "If you don't call me within the next fifteen minutes, I am filing a missing person's report."

"I don't know why you still tell your kids that," Lilah said as she bounced Maria on her hip. "They know you don't mean it."

"No, they don't," I said as I scrunched up my face. "They know it's a possibility." Lilah rolled her eyes and I touched my hand to her arm. "Hey, look."

Over on the side of C building was Adrian and two other officers. Adrian was the only one not in uniform but despite that you could see by his demeanor he was in an official capacity. They had all surrounded a man and we watched as Adrian led him out to the parking lot.

"This is so crazy," Ben said to me.

"What is?" I asked.

"Adrian putting somebody in a police car," he said. "I feel like we're playing cops and robbers or something."

"He doesn't look like he's messing around," I told him.

"No," he said. "Not at all."

"Your hero," Michael said to Lilah.

"Shut up, Michael," Ben told him.

Adrian shut the police car door and headed toward us. Lilah leaned closer to me.

"Here," she said. "Take Maria. She weighs a ton." I reached for Maria and she took me around my neck. I kissed her cheek.

"You are getting entirely too heavy to be carried, little girl," I said to her. She laughed.

"Hey, baby," Adrian said. Lilah wrapped her arms around him and he held her against him. "You okay?"

"Yeah," she answered.

"I'm good, too," I spoke up. "In case you were wondering."

"I'm never worried about you, Isabel," he said as he pulled away from Lilah. "In an emergency situation such as this you're my most trusted civilian."

"That's funny," Matt said. I slapped Matt on the back of his head.

"Thank you, Adrian," I said. "You're my most trusted DEA agent."

"You're the only DEA agent she knows," Lilah added.

"Shut up, Lilah," I said. "I was trying to make him feel good."

"Thanks," Adrian said and laughed. "I needed to feel good, for sure." He leaned over and kissed Lilah. "I gotta get out of here, baby. But I'll see you in a little bit, okay?"

"Okay," she answered.

"Why does that man look familiar to me?" Lilah asked me as Adrian walked back over to the police car. We watched as Adrian talked to him. I wished to God I knew what he was saying.

"I don't know," I told her. I leaned closer to her and whispered into her ear. "I'm sure it's someone you slept with at some point." She rolled her eyes and shook her head.

"Or you," she said. She narrowed her eyes as she looked toward Adrian.

"What is it?" I asked.

Vonnie came out of the auditorium doors with Hunter. He had his arm wrapped around her shoulders and he pulled her into him and kissed her cheek. You could tell she'd been crying because she had dark mascara circles underneath her eyes.

"You okay?" Ben asked her.

"Of course, I'm okay," she said. "Do I look like I'm not okay?"

"Kind of," he answered. "Do you need a hug?" She smiled.

"Kind of."

"Well, damn, Hunter," Ben said. "Give her a hug."

I looked over to Lilah and she smiled. We had just talked earlier in the day about how happy it made us when our children showed genuine love and concern for one another. Lilah leaned over to me.

"Holy cow," she said. "I know who that man is."

"Who?" I asked excitedly, amazed she'd figured it out.

"It's McCain," she said quietly.

We watched as Adrian patted the top of the police car and it took off.

"Oh, my Lord," I said as I narrowed my eyes like she had. "You're right."

"I know," she said as she turned to me. "What the hell is he doing here?" I raised my eyebrows.

"Well, if he's come for you, he's about twenty years too late."

"That's not funny," she said.

"I didn't mean it to be funny. Just factual."

"This is totally freaking me out," she said and I could see the fear on her face.

"Don't worry," I told her.

"You," she said, turning to me once more. "The one who always tells me to expect the worst is telling me not to worry??"

"Adrian has it under control," I told her. "Clearly, you can see that."

It amazed me how in tune Adrian was with Lilah. Most days I felt a bit of relief I didn't have to be so vigilant about her welfare. Other days it made me mad she depended on someone other than me. I realized this was stupid and petty so I tried to banish the thought from my mind every time I had it.

"Do you think it's possible Adrian already knows about me and McCain??" Lilah asked me.

"I don't know," I said. "But if he doesn't, he's about to find out."

"You think McCain will tell him?"

I leaned my head to the side and grimaced.

"He will, won't he?" she asked.

This question required an answer but not one Lilah wanted to hear. Despite that fact this wasn't a time to hold back the truth.

"Yeah," I told her as I laid my hand on her arm. "I'm pretty sure he will."

Amityville – Present Day
Tiffany

I tried to catch my breath but the anticipation was mind-numbing. Isaac ran his hands over my body, his fingers grazing my ribcage, his lips on my shoulder. I wrapped my arms around his neck and he lifted me off the bed toward him. *Lips on You* by Maroon 5 played softly in the background from the speaker he had hooked up on the other side of my bedroom. Isaac Lund. The master of seduction.

"You're shaking," he said, and he kissed me softly. "You okay?"

"Yeah," I said. "I just…I guess I just missed you."

"Just breathe," he said as he laid me back down onto the bed. "You're so tense."

He brought his hands around and massaged my shoulders then moved down my arms to my hands. My body blazed with an intense warmth. Not a full-fledged fire but inevitably headed in that direction. He ran his thumbs up and down the inside of my wrists and I shivered again. I'd never had a guy touch me the way Isaac touched me.

"I'm going to take my time with you," he said.

I didn't know his plan but it seemed like keeping me in suspense gave him great pleasure. I could feel every inch of my body vibrating. It was an unrelenting expectation. A forcible want. Excitement.

Anticipation. Uncertainty. My impatience was palpable. I reached my hand down and unbuttoned his jeans. The zipper slid down on its own.

"How did that fit in there before?" I asked teasingly as I touched him.

"I don't know," he said, sucking in his breath. "But it's not going back in there. I can tell you that much." I smiled against his kiss.

Every man in America should be required to take a class on how to pleasure a woman before getting their man card. I am pretty sure Isaac could teach it.

"Who taught you how to do this?" I breathed and he chuckled. He quickly moved over me and I pushed his jeans down over his hips. His phone rang.

"It'll go to voicemail," he said breathlessly.

"Turn it off," I ordered. "Now."

"I can't," he said. "It's on the dresser. Mmm…you feel so good."

The ringtone he had for Isabel echoed across the room.

"This is the woman who struggled through hours of childbirth to bring you into this world, and if you don't answer, she will keep calling until you do. It's probably not an emergency but she'll act like it is. Your Mom. Your Mom. Your Mom."

"It's been too long," Isaac breathed. "I can't do it."

He drew in his breath and pressed himself into me. To think Isaac had abstained from sex ever since I'd been gone blew my mind. Maybe he did truly love me. His body tensed and he squeezed his lips together, grabbed my hand. It was one of the deepest connections I've ever experienced with anyone. I imagined our souls meeting, falling in love, and dancing together. I wrapped my legs tightly around his hips.

"Mmm…" he hummed into my ear. His phone rang again.

"This is the woman who struggled through hours of childbirth to bring you into this world, and if you don't answer, she will keep calling until you do…"

"Don't think about it," I whispered in his ear.

He looked into my eyes as the phone continued ringing. I took his face into my hands and pulled it down to mine. I opened my mouth and placed it against his. I ran my tongue across his bottom lip and it pushed him over the edge. He kissed me gently afterward and his phone rang again.

"She'll keep calling until you answer," I told him as he laid his head against my chest once more. I ran my hands across his back.

"Yep," he breathed. "Over and over and over."

He jumped up and went over to the dresser. I felt the result of our lovemaking seep onto the sheets beneath me. We didn't use condoms anymore. We'd talked about it. I had a birth control implant in my arm and, let's face it, sex just doesn't feel as good with a condom. I'd made Isaac go to the clinic, though. He wasn't happy about it but everyone knows Isaac is not exactly a choirboy. I watched him now as he stood naked in front of the mirror above my dresser. His body. OMG.

"Hello?" he answered as I wrapped my comforter closer around me. "Holy shit, Mom." I listened but I could only hear his side of the conversation. "Do you know what I'm doing right now?? No?" He hesitated. "Well, guess."

I could not believe Isaac was being this open with his mother. The relationship Isabel had with her children was mind-boggling some-times. They told one another *everything*.

"Yes," he said. "I'm glad you figured out that I'm not home." Hesitation. "I'm in Amityville with Tiffany." Another hesitation. "No, I am not fucking with you." He walked back over to the bed and slipped under the covers next to me, drew me into him. "Tiffany and I just had the most amazing sex ever."

I was going to kill him.

"Wanna talk to her?" he asked.

"No!!!" I mouthed as I waved my hands in front of me. "No!!" But it was too late. He handed me the phone. "No!!" I mouthed again.

"Just talk to her," he said. "It's not as bad as you think. Mom is cool."

"Hi, Isabel," I said reluctantly. I couldn't tell if my face was heated into a blush or devoid of color altogether.

"Are you on the pill?" she asked me.

There is no shame in Isabel. Not even a little bit.

"No," I answered.

"Please tell me you use some kind of birth control."

"Yes."

"Oh good," she said. "Because I'm not ready for a grandchild yet. And you both better get your asses down here to Virginia within the next twenty-four hours or I'm coming up there. Do you want me to come up there?"

"No, Ma'am."

"See you then," she said.

Click. Isaac laughed, and I punched him in the ribs.

"That was not funny," I said to him, but I was laughing, too.

"My mom loves you," he told me.

"She didn't sound like she loved me," I said.

"She does," he assured me. "The conversation would have been punctuated by a lot more profanity if she didn't."

"You know," I said. "Under any other circumstance I would think you were joking, but because I know your mother, I know you are not."

"I am not," he said as he leaned over and kissed me. His phone rang again. 'This is the woman who struggled through hours of child-birth to bring you into...' I handed it back to him. "What now?!!" he asked as an answer. He hesitated as he listened to her. "Jeez, Mom. Tiff and I are kind of, you know, having a moment." Hesitation. "You know, like the afterglow?? *But you keep calling me.* What?" Another hesitation. "Hold on." He handed me the phone. I widened my eyes and he motioned for me to just take it.

"Hello?" I said.

"Leave Isaac's truck up there," Isabel told me. "Take it over to the Inn or something but leave it there."

"Why?" I asked.

"Because he's not going to be needing it for a long time."

Click.

Woodlawn

McCain

I had one phone call when I got to jail. That's one of the first questions they ask you before they put you in a cell. I've never really had anyone to call so most of the time I always passed on that offer. Every now and then I would call my aunt but she lived in Kansas so there wasn't anything she could do for me. She was my favorite aunt, though, and she always talked to me and made me feel somewhat better. But she had died two years ago and ever since then every time I went to jail, I had no one to call at all. But today I knew who I was going to call. Fuck Adrian Bennett. The deputy took off my handcuffs as soon as we walked through the locked doors.

"You get one phone call," he said.

"I need a phonebook," I told him. He stared at me for a moment then yelled at the girl behind the intake desk.

"Hey, Kara!" She looked up. "You got a phonebook over there?"

She didn't answer him but she plopped it on top of the counter. He walked over and snatched it then handed it to me.

"Make it quick," he told me. "You got eight minutes."

I always wondered why they gave you eight minutes. I mean, granted, eight minutes is better than no minutes but why eight? Why couldn't they give you ten? What was the significance of eight? Probably the same significance they had for making you get up at four-thirty in the morning for breakfast. I looked at the cover of the phonebook. Woodlawn and surrounding areas. I flipped to the back and thumbed through the pages. I was hoping there was only one person who had this last name. If there wasn't, I was the third duck in the pond.

My Mimi used to say that all the time. I think she made it up but she once told me if there are a pair of ducks and another one flies in; they will kill it. I never truly believed her until I watched it unfold on several occasions. Apparently, ducks are rather territorial. And I wasn't the third duck in the pond. There was only one Trenton in the phonebook so it had to be Lilah. I picked up the phone and dialed her number. A guy answered the phone. Her husband? Probably.

"Trenton residence."

"Hi…um…could I speak to Lilah?"

"Uh, she's not here right now. Can I take a message? Or I can give you her cell phone number if you'd like."

Holy shit. Jackpot.

"That would be awesome," I said. "Let me get something to write it down."

"Sure."

I called to the deputy standing at the desk.

"Hey! You got a piece of paper and a pen?"

"What do I look like?" he asked. "A stationary store?"

Kara, the girl behind the desk, handed him a piece of paper and a pen.

"Don't be a jackass Ralph," she told him. "Give him the damn paper." Ralph handed it to me.

"Thanks." I went back to the phone. "Sorry about that. I'm ready." He rattled off the number and I wrote it down.

"Thanks, man. I really appreciate it."

"Yep."

I hung up the phone, tore off the sheet of paper and stuck it in my pocket. Ralph the deputy grabbed my arm.

"Let's go."

I laid the pad of paper and pen on the desk.

"Thanks," I told Kara.

"Sure thing, babe," she said to me and winked.

Adrian

"Tell me why you're here, McCain," I said as I shut the interrogation door. "Because the last time I talked to you I told you I didn't want to see you in Woodlawn again. Ever."

"Fuck you," he said.

"Did you come to save Bret from himself? Because I think we both know that is a fruitless effort."

"You think I don't have a fucking brain of my own?" he asked.

"I think your brain has deceived you," I answered as I propped my hands on my hips.

"What the hell does that mean?"

"You know Luther is in custody now, right?" He said nothing and I walked around the table. "You know what he told me?"

"Don't give me a bunch of shit," McCain said. "I know your game." I smiled and nodded.

"Sure, you do. Luther told me who you're working for."

"Luther is full of shit," he said.

"Angel Ramirez. That name sound familiar to you?" I asked. McCain looked down then slammed his handcuffed hands on the table.

"Man, I don't know nothing 'bout Angel," he said. I walked back around the table.

"That's not what Luther said."

"I told you. Luther is full of shit."

"Luther is taking time off his sentence because he's talking," I told him. "You wanna talk to me and do the same thing or you wanna spend the rest of your life being somebody's bitch?"

McCain jumped up out of his chair and flipped the table over. Apparently, this was a favorite trick of his. I didn't move. There was a knock on the door.

"Yeah?"

"Surprise!" Jenny opened the door and came inside. I shook my head and smiled.

"You just couldn't help yourself, could you?" I asked her. She smiled and turned to McCain.

"Mitchell McCain," she said as she held her cup of coffee in her hand. "I've heard some interesting things about you. The last one was that you've moved up the chain of command."

"Fuck you," he said.

"I don't think that's going to help you at all," she retorted.

"You want me to talk?" McCain yelled. "You fucking want me to talk???" Jenny looked at me and I raised my eyebrows, looked away. "You bring Lilah in here and I'll talk."

My mind raced. I had been certain he was at the talent show because of Vonnie. But Lilah? Why? What connection could he possibly have with Lilah?

"Who's Lilah?" I asked as Jenny looked to me in disbelief.

"You know who she is," he said. "I saw you with her at the school."

"Let me talk to him," Jenny told me and I walked toward the door.

"Yep."

"I'm not bringing Lilah in here," Jenny said as she leaned toward McCain. I opened the door. "You talk to me or you ain't talking at all. You got it?"

"You alright?" Tina asked as I shut the door behind me. I turned to her.

"Yeah," I said. I ran my hands through my hair. "How does he know Lilah?"

"I don't know," she said. "Maybe he just knows Lilah is Vonnie's mom."

"But why would he say to bring her in here?" I asked as I scratched the back of my neck. "What could he possibly have to say to her?"

"You know," Tina said. "It's possible he's just bullshitting you. I mean, it wouldn't be hard to find out who your significant other is and we already know he's met Vonnie. Did you ask her anything about him?"

"No," I said. "It's clear she's met him before after her little display of affection at school."

"You call that affection?" Tina asked.

"Irony," I said. "I just don't want Vonnie to freak out over it. That's all."

"She didn't seem to be freaked out at the school," Tina told me.

"She's a good pretender," I said. "She was terrified when we first brought her home from the hospital because she didn't know where Luther was and she was afraid he would come after her." I walked over to the water cooler and filled a cup with water.

"Did you remind her she lived with an armed man who isn't afraid to shoot his gun?" Tina asked.

"I did," I said and smiled. "But it took a while for her to calm down. She knew I could take care of her. She was just afraid of what might happen that required me to take care of her. She slept in our room for a week once she came home."

"What was that like??" Tina asked. She punched me in the ribs. "You and Lilah in bed for a whole week with supervision."

"There were a few afternoon delights," I admitted and laughed. "I will tell you that."

Jenny came out of the interrogation room. She stood in front of me.

"Adrian," she said. "McCain knows Lilah."

"Personally?" I asked as I looked over to Tina.

"Personally," Jenny confirmed. "Apparently they lived together when she was in college."

"Are you sure that's the truth?" I asked.

"He has a picture of her in his wallet," she said.

"A recent picture??" Tina asked.

"No," Jenny said. "An old picture of her back then." I sat my water cup down on the table behind me and went into the interrogation room. "Adrian!!" Jenny called.

I slammed the door behind me. I walked over to McCain and yanked him up out of his chair by his shirt, threw him up against the wall. Jenny had taken off his handcuffs. Probably in an effort to get him to talk more. An empty promise but usually effective in most cases.

"You listen to me, you piece of shit," I said as I stepped backward. "You stay the hell away from Lilah. You don't call her, you don't text her, you don't write to her, and you sure as hell don't come anywhere near our house. Do you understand me?" He smiled and I grabbed his chin, pushed him back up against the wall again.

"What are you afraid of, Mr. Bennett??" he asked. "Think she might change her mind about you?"

"Change her mind about me?" I asked as I gestured to myself. "Yeah, that's what I think. Because you have so much more to offer her than I do."

"You'd be surprised what I have to offer her," he said. "It'd probably only take once. You know what they say about drug addicts. They are always just a thread away from coming back."

I grabbed him by his shirt with one hand and punched him in the face with the other. Blood poured from his nose. Jenny and Tina rushed through the door. Jenny grabbed me under my arms and pulled me backward. Tina grabbed McCain.

"Stop it," Jenny said to me and McCain laughed, wiped the back of his hand across his nose. I stepped back away from him.

"Let's go," Tina told McCain. "You're done."

Jenny was still holding me by my arm. I tried to control my breathing but I was so angry it was difficult.

"Come on," Jenny said. "Chill. Okay?"

"I bet her pussy still tastes the same," McCain called over his shoulder.

I pulled away from Jenny and ran toward him. I grabbed him by the neck and slammed him into the wall behind him. I held him there with my hand. Tina stood in shock as I addressed him.

"I will forcibly break every bone in your fucking body if I ever hear you say anything like that again. I don't give a rat's ass about anything except how satisfying it will be to beat the hell out of you. And don't think for one minute I won't do it because I can hardly wait. It's like a fucking party invitation for me, you got it?" He said nothing. "And you know what else I'm going to do??"

"Adrian," Jenny said from behind me. "Let him go." I turned to her but I didn't let go of McCain.

"I'm going to let him go," I said turning back to him. "I am going to make sure you go to the shittiest, most vile prison I can find on this side of the Mississippi. They will tear you another asshole with their dicks."

"Adrian!!" Jenny shouted and I put McCain down, let go of his shirt.

"I'm not playing with you, you sick bastard," I yelled at him.

"Adrian," Jenny said as she grabbed my arm. "Let's go." We walked in the opposite direction. "I hope I never have to see anything like that happen again. Because I can tell you right now that if I do, you will be put on administrative leave." I said nothing. "Indefinitely. Are you catching my vibe?"

"Yeah," I said as I rubbed my hand across my mouth. "I'm catching your vibe."

"I want you to go home," she said. "And take a cold shower."

"A cold shower?" I said. I turned to her. "You think that's what I need??"

"I think you need to chill out, is what I think," she said. "Order a pizza, take it home and watch some old CSI episodes with Lilah."

"Funny," I said as she walked me to the front door.

"Pay attention to how many times they beat up their suspects," she said as she took my jacket off the back of a chair and handed it to me.

"I've seen them beat up suspects before," I said, defending myself.

"Not like that," she informed me. "You don't issue threats about what you have the power to do as an officer of the Drug Enforcement Administration of the Department of Justice of the United States of America."

"Right," I said as I put on my jacket. I zipped the front. "You gonna be here tomorrow?"

"I'm going to be here until I can get Terrence down here to finish up this case," she said. "You are officially dismissed." I took a step backward.

"Are you kidding me right now?"

"No," she said as she waved to me. "Good night, Adrian."

Amityville

Tiffany

"Tiffany!" Isaac called. "I don't know how you think we're going to fit all this stuff into your car." I leaned over the balcony outside my apartment.

"Your mother told me to leave your truck here," I told him. "And that's exactly what we're doing." He turned around to face me.

"I don't know why you're listening to her," he said. "She was just kidding."

"She didn't sound like she was kidding. And I am not about to get on Isabel's bad side from the beginning." I turned to go back inside.

I heard him grumble, but he must have figured out a way to make everything fit because a few minutes later I heard him slam the back door of my SUV shut. My phone rang and I searched the kitchen for it. I finally spotted it sitting on the stove with a tape measure and a box of instant macaroni and cheese. Just for the record I do not eat instant macaroni and cheese. Isaac does which I find extraordinarily weird since Isabel has such an obsession with nutritional values.

"Hello," I answered.

"Hey girlie girl," Vonnie said. "I hear you're on your way to where all roads lead."

"Yeah," I said and laughed. "Woodlawn: the center of the Universe."

"It is," she told me. "What time are you going to get here??" I looked at my watch.

"Well, if it were up to me, we would have left three hours ago but Isaac is having a meltdown about his truck."

"I know," she said. "Ben told me Isabel said he had to leave it there. Something about you guys having the most amazing sex ever?"

"How does Ben know that?!?" I asked.

"I think he was standing nearby when Isabel called Isaac," she said.

"I cannot believe Isaac told Isabel that," I said. "What the hell is wrong with him?"

"I don't know," Vonnie said. "Those guys tell their mom everything."

"Probably because they're afraid not to."

"True statement," Vonnie agreed. "She's not even my mother and *I'm* afraid not to tell her everything."

"Well," I said. "She says I have to stay with you guys because she doesn't want Isaac and me sleeping in the same bed."

"Does this not sound odd to you?" Vonnie asked.

"They are so weird," I said. I picked up a granola bar off the counter and ripped the wrapper off it. "I mean I love Isabel and Lilah but they are strict about the weirdest things and then other stuff most moms would be fanatical over they just don't care."

"I know," Vonnie agreed. "Mom fusses at me constantly about leaving empty glasses in the living room but if she came home and I was throwing a wild party she'd be fine with it. Anyhow, Mom wanted me to call and ask if you were okay staying in my room with me. I have an extra bed in here."

"Tiffany!" Isaac called from the front door.

"What?!" I yelled as I put my hand over the phone.

"We need snacks for the road!" He came to the kitchen doorway. "Are we going to have a snack basket??"

"What the hell is a snack basket?" I asked and I heard Vonnie laugh.

"The snack basket," she said. "That's what Isabel always takes on road trips. It's the only time she lets the guys eat snack food. Well, she knows they eat stuff like that at our house but *she* only allows them to have it when they're on vacation." I walked over to Isaac and kissed him quickly.

"We will make a snack basket, babe," I told him. "We'll stop at the Petro Shop on the way out of town."

"But I wanted some of your sugar cookies," he whined. I picked up a plastic container and handed it to him.

"Voila!"

"You're amazing," he said, and we kissed again.

"Oh wait," Vonnie said. "I'm going to put flannel sheets on the other bed in my room for you. Do you want roses or pandas?"

"Definitely pandas," I said and smiled. "I'm so excited! Did I tell you I have about three weeks of vacation I've never used so I'm cashing in?"

"No!" Vonnie said excitedly. "Oh, yay! I thought you could only stay for the weekend! I'm so excited!! But who's going to take care of the dolphins while you're gone?"

"Oh, I asked Nelson to do it," I said. "He loves them almost as much as I do."

"Awesome," she said. "So, I'll see you later tonight?"

"Yep!"

"Love you, Tiff. Muah!"

"Muah!"

I clicked off the phone and stood staring at Isaac. He held a bag of pretzel sticks in his hand and a can of Mountain Dew sat on the counter beside him.

"You're drinking awfully early," I said.

"Well shit, Tiffany, it's already noon." He looked at his watch. "And I can't have beer because you're going to make me drive."

"I am," I confirmed.

"Come here," he said holding out his hand. I walked toward him and he pulled me into him. "Has anyone told you how beautiful you are today?"

"No," I said and smiled. He kissed me.

"The car is packed, the keys are in the mailbox, and this apartment is no longer yours," he said.

"I'm depressed," I said and pouted.

"Why?" he asked. "You're moving into the Inn when you come back and that is one cool address."

"It's bittersweet, though," I confessed and looked down.

"Nana," he said as he entwined his fingers in mine.

"Yeah."

"I wish I could have met her," he told me.

"Me, too."

"What do you think she would have thought about us?" he asked.

"What do you mean?"

"I mean, you know, you being…" he hesitated.

"Beautiful?" I asked and smiled.

"Yeah…" he hesitated again.

"And you being…" I started. "Okay, I've never asked you this because I feel like it's a touchy subject."

"You mean having a white mom and a black dad?"

"Yeah," I said. "I hate it that I have to ask you that question. I mean it doesn't matter one way or the other and I think…"

"Hey," he said, laying his hand against my cheek. "Mom says mixed, Dad says bi-racial. It doesn't matter to me. Nothing offends me and if you had my Mom and Dad for parents, nothing would offend you either."

"I can only imagine," I said. "I want to meet your Dad and to answer your earlier question, Nana would have loved you. She used to say we're all the same on the inside. The outside is just a wrapper."

"Cool," he said as he leaned back against the counter and pulled me into him. I held up my granola bar and he took a bite.

"I don't think I've ever told you this but when Adrian and I first started school people used to make fun of us because of our obvious non-Caucasian heritage. Nana went down to the school and pitched holy hell. She told them if we ever came home again and told her someone made fun of us, she would pull us out of school and talk to the village council."

"What's the village council?"

"Oh, it's the people who control whatever goes on in Amityville. We went to a private school and Nana told them if we were going to be bullied because of our race then the school didn't deserve the village grant and she would make sure they didn't get it anymore."

"Wow," Isaac said. "Nana didn't mess around."

"No," I said. "Not at all. So, I don't think your heritage would have mattered in any way, shape or form."

"She sounds like an amazing woman, Tiff. I'm so sorry you lost her." I teared up. I didn't want to but the tears came anyway. Isaac wiped them away. "Hey. Look at me." I looked up to him. "You have an amazing family in Woodlawn that loves you very much."

"You think?" I asked.

"I know," he said and smiled. "We all consider you and Adrian family and I'm not just saying that to make you feel better. We truly do."

"Thank you," I said.

"We should get going," he told me. "Otherwise we're going to push getting there for dinner."

"Okay," I said and backed up. I wiped the remainder of tears from my cheeks.

"I did something, Tiff," he said as he tucked a piece of my hair behind my ear. "And I hope it's going to make you happy."

"Oh, no," I said. "What is it?"

"Well, let me rephrase that. It *will* make you happy."

"You got me a puppy??"

"No," he said and laughed. "I didn't know you wanted a puppy."

"I don't really," I said. "But if someone gave me one, I'd keep it."

"I'll keep that in mind." He chuckled. "You know I decided to take a year off and start school next fall, right?"

"Yeah," I said. "To your mother's dismay."

"Well, I applied to Adelphi and I got in." He smiled, one of the biggest smiles I'd ever seen.

"Here?" I asked pointing down.

"Yeah."

"Why?"

"You, goofy. I can't go somewhere and not be close to you."

"Are you screwing with me right now?"

"No," he said. "I am not screwing with you right now."

"What are you going to study?"

"Mom keeps asking me that and I haven't given her an answer because she'll drive me crazy about it but I'm going to start out with my basic classes and see where it takes me. I'm thinking I want to do pre-law." I widened my eyes.

"Are you serious?"

"Uh-huh." I wrapped my arms around his neck and he picked me up.

"I am so excited!"

"Me, too," he said. "I just have to find an apartment up here." I stared at him.

"Are you joking?"

"No," he said. "I have to live somewhere and you just gave up your apartment."

"You can live at the Inn," I told him. "There are twenty-four bedrooms in that monstrosity of a house. I'm pretty sure we can find one you'll like."

"Are you kidding?"

"About what?"

"The twenty-four bedrooms??"

"No," I said and smiled. "It was a country inn, remember? There are twelve bedrooms on the family side and twelve on the guests' side."

"Holy shit."

"On the bay," I told him. "Like sand in our back yard."

"Holy shit," he said again. "Will you show it to me before we leave?"

"Well, we have to take your truck over there."

"Oh, right. I forgot about that."

"We can't go in, though. It's locked and Adrian is the only one who has an actual key right now. I mean, I can get in, but the police will come."

"Why??"

"It's a long story for another time," I told him.

"Okay. Do you think it will be okay with Adrian for me to live there?"

"I doubt he's going to care one way or the other. You guys are like best friends."

"We were like best friends before he found out I was sleeping with his sister."

"You're still his friend," I assured him. "Come on, let's go see my brother."

"You tell him everything, don't you?" Isaac asked.

"Pretty much," I answered. "But I will tell you this…" I held up my pointer finger. "…I do not tell Adrian about my sex life." Isaac chucked. "Like you and your mother."

"Good to know," he said and kissed me.

"But if you keep telling your mom shit like you did yesterday, I *will* tell Adrian about our sex life."

"I don't need to tell Mom most of the time," Isaac said. "She just knows."

"What is she? Psychic or something?"

"No," he said. "She's just very, very smart."

"Holy shit," Isaac said when he got out of his truck at the Inn. He walked toward me. "This place is amazing."

"It's home," I told him as he got closer to me.

"It looks like the castle at Disney World." I laughed.

"Cinderella's castle?"

"Yeah," he said. He wrapped his arm around me and we leaned against my car.

"Can I take a picture?" he asked me.

"Sure," I said. "If you want."

"Mom is going to flip her lid when she sees this."

He pulled his phone out of his pocket and focused the camera on the Inn. That's when I saw Henry and Roberta coming around from the side yard to investigate our presence. When Henry saw Isaac, he took off at a full trot toward us.

"Get in the car!!" I shouted to Isaac. I opened the car door and shoved him inside.

"What?? Why??" I slammed the door and walked around to my side.

"Henry!" I chastised. "Must you always be so ornery?" He squawked at me and I pointed back to the Inn. "Take Roberta home right now!" He stared at me for a moment then turned and walked back across the yard. Roberta followed him and I got into the car.

"What the hell was that?" Isaac asked.

"That," I said. "Was Henry the peacock."

"That was a peacock?? It looked like an ostrich."

"Ostriches are much bigger than that," I said as I started the car. "And don't think I'm driving just because I'm in the driver's seat. As soon as we get through the gate, we're switching sides."

"That bird looked dangerous," Isaac commented.

"He's not dangerous," I said as I drove toward the gate. "He's just protective of the people he loves."

"Adrian told me he comes after him every time he pulls in the driveway. That doesn't sound like love or protection to me. That sounds like assault." I laughed and stopped at the gate.

"He'll get used to you," I told him. "It just takes time. And, anyhow, Adrian and Henry have a troubled past."

"I'm not even going to ask what that means," Isaac said.

I got out of the car and walked toward the gate. Isaac got out behind me and walked over to it as I twisted the key in the lock.

"This place is like one of those old castles you see on a cliff in England. Remember Manderley?"

"You mean the house in *Rebecca*?"

"That's the one."

"Holy cow, Isaac. It's not that big."

"It's close."

"Well, don't jinx it. That house burned to the ground." I turned to him. "How do you know about *Rebecca*?"

"It's a classic book," he said. "I had to read it in my advanced literature class."

"Ah…" I opened the driver's side door. "You're driving."

"I'm very well aware of that."

"Thank you, honey." I leaned over and kissed him and he grabbed me around the waist.

"You are my princess," he told me. "Most people say that as a term of affection. You know?"

"Uh-huh."

"You actually are a princess."

"Growing up in a house that looks like a castle does not make me a princess."

"It does. Don't argue with me." I smiled and wrapped my arms around his neck. Henry stood at the gate, squawking.

"I don't have a good feeling about that bird," he said when we got back inside the car.

"Why not?" I asked.

"Because he is not going to like me if he's that protective over you."

"Don't be silly," I said. "Just let him chase you a few times and he'll get it out of his system."

"That sounds like fun," Isaac commented. "I cannot believe some of the things I'm willing to do for you."

"Aw." I ran my hand over his hair. "You love me."

"I do," he said and smiled. He looked over to me. "You just don't realize how much yet."

Woodlawn

Adrian

It had taken a while for everyone to get used to mine and Lilah's relationship being 'okay.' Knowing about it and us being one, big, happy family wasn't as easy as we made it appear. Being eighteen and then suddenly twenty-seven was not an easy pill for Ben and Isaac to swallow. They weren't angry but it was hard for them to see me as an adult after I had successfully convinced them and everyone else, I was a high school senior.

There weren't very many days when someone didn't call me Tristan at least once. Even Lilah calls me Tristan sometimes. Mostly when we are making love. I told her I didn't care what she called me if I could keep sleeping in her bed. We usually went to bed early when I was in Woodlawn because it gave us the privacy we craved, but tonight we'd decided to watch a movie in the living room. I put the DVD Lilah had picked out in the DVD player while she made popcorn then we settled on the sofa together. We mostly watched movies she liked simply because I didn't care. I just wanted to be close to her. I picked up the popcorn bowl and put my feet on the table.

"Don't put your feet on the table," she chastised.

"I took my shoes off, so I could put my feet on the table. I hardly think my socked feet are going to scratch the coffee table."

"I never let the kids put their feet on the tables whether they have on shoes or not."

"Well, I'm not one of the kids." She slapped my arm and I raised my eyebrows. "I'm just saying."

"Did I ever tell you when I first met you, I thought you smelled like chocolate chip cookies?"

"You said cookies," I said and smiled. "I didn't know it was chocolate chip cookies. Do I still smell like chocolate chip cookies?" She leaned over and sniffed my neck.

"Yeah," she told me. "Kind of. More like vanilla now."

"It's probably because of my hair." I leaned closer to her and she ran her fingers through it, pulling it away from my head and letting it fall back down onto my shoulders. "Did you just have an epiphany?" I asked and laughed. She twirled a piece of my hair around her finger.

"Is it your shampoo?"

"Actually, it's Tiffany's shampoo," I admitted. "She got me hooked on it one summer when I was having an obsession with my hair."

This was not the full truth. The full truth was that Tiffany and I were separated the last year of foster care, going to live in two different places with two different families. We were devastated and it traumatized both of us. It was the first time we'd ever truly been apart so when my foster mom took me to the store to buy toiletries, I asked her to buy me the same shampoo Tiffany used. Vanilla Coconut. It's a little hard to admit but it comforted me then and still comforts me today.

"Where is it?" Lilah asked.

"What do you mean 'where is it?' It's in the shower."

"Why have I never seen it?"

"Because you have so much crap in there you can barely move around," I said. "That's why." She took my hand and kissed the back of it. I settled down further into the sofa, crossed one leg over the other.

"What do I smell like?" she asked me.

"I don't know," I said as I wrapped my arm around her. "My fantasy."

"Oh, ha ha."

"No, you smell like roses. You always smell like roses."

"That's a cop-out," she said.

"No, it isn't. I swear." I leaned over and kissed her cheek. "And musk. It's a sexy scent. All the girls now wear stuff that smells like candy."

"Like your hair," she said and giggled.

Someone punched the code into the front door and Isabel walked into the living room from the foyer with a plastic grocery bag in her hand. I looked over to Lilah. She shrugged. I had given up on this situation in Lilah's life. Isabel had never called before I lived here. Asking her to call now seemed rude. Plus, her boys were always doing something away from home, and she hated being alone. How do you say no to that?? She plopped down in the chair next to mine and reached for some of the popcorn in my bowl. I pulled it away from her.

"Get your own popcorn."

"You're mean," she said, and she got up with her bag. "I'm going to make us some cocktails. How the hell can we watch a movie without a drink?"

"Did someone say popcorn?" Ben asked as he came down the stairs.

"Get your own," I called over my shoulder.

Maria was following him, and she came over and jumped up into my lap. I'm not sure what I'd done to deserve Maria's affection, but she loved me, and I loved it that she loved me.

"You smell like candy," she said, and Lilah laughed. I just shook my head.

Isabel came out of the kitchen with a tray of purple cocktails and handed one to each of us. I held mine up.

"Cheers," I said. Isabel and Lilah just stared at me.

"What?" I asked before I took a sip.

"You can't just say 'cheers,'" Lilah explained. "You have to toast to something."

"To not watching *Titanic* AGAIN," Ben interrupted. Lilac gave him the evil eye and he held up his hands. "Just saying."

"To us…" I started.

"…getting into the hot tub together again," Isabel finished.

"Good Lord," Lilah said.

"What?" Isabel asked. "That was fun. When can we do it again?"

"The next time we all get trashed and there's a hot tub," I said. "Cheers." We all bumped our glasses together.

"Ya'll are sick," Ben called from across the room.

"Wow," I said after I'd taken a sip of my drink. "That burned going down. What the hell is that?" Ben laughed.

"It's straight grape vodka with just a hint of grenadine and some Hypnotiq," Isabel explained. "I'm calling it Purple Carpet."

"I don't have any grape vodka," Lilah said. "Or Hypnotiq."

"Which is why I brought it with me," Isabel answered.

"Why are you calling it Purple Carpet?" I asked.

"Because it's purple and if you drink too many, you'll be laying on the carpet."

"Perfect," I said. "After a day like I had today that's exactly what I need."

"Oh, baby," Lilah said as she rubbed her hand over my shoulders. "I'll give you a massage later tonight, help you release some of this tension."

"That sounds awesome," I said. I leaned over and kissed her softly.

"Not an image I want to have in my mind," Ben declared from across the room.

"You should give your drink to Ben," Isabel told Lilah.

"I should," she said and smiled. I looked at her suspiciously and Isabel took Lilah's drink out of her hand and gave it to Ben.

"Wow," he said. "Thanks."

Vonnie came out of the kitchen with a huge bowl of popcorn. Apparently, she had come down the back stairs without any of us noticing. I wondered if she'd heard our conversation about having a threesome again. Jeez, I lost more credibility with these people every day, but it didn't seem to matter. This was life with Lilah and Isabel. No judgements. No unnecessary 'rules.' I'm not sure Nana would have agreed with the threesome part, but she would have agreed with the no judgement part.

"Let's watch a movie, guys," Vonnie said. I motioned to the television.

"We *are* watching a movie." She scrunched up her face then smiled and plopped down on the club chair across from me and Isabel.

"*Titanic,*" Ben told her.

"Are you serious?" she asked. "How many times have we watched this?"

"Your mother likes this movie," I said defending Lilah.

"Be quiet!" Maria said. "Ya'll are talking over the movie!!"

"It hasn't even started yet," Vonnie told her.

"Yes, it has!" Maria said pointing to the television. "There's Rose!"

A knock at the front door.

"Are we expecting company?" Lilah asked.

"I invited Hunter over," Vonnie informed us. She went to the door and ushered him inside. He grabbed her around the waist and kissed her, softly at first, then deeper.

"Hey!" Ben shouted. "That's enough!"

Vonnie turned around and stuck her tongue out at him, then led Hunter into the living room.

"Hi everyone," Hunter said as Vonnie pulled him over to the club chair. He sat down and pulled her into his lap.

"Nope," Ben said. "That chair is big enough for both of you. She doesn't need to sit in your lap."

"Oh my god, Ben," Vonnie said. "Shut up."

I sat there for a moment taking all this in. Within the next fifteen minutes everyone had come into the living room. Vonnie and Hunter in the club chair. Abe on the floor in the beanbag chair. Ben stretched out across the loveseat until Michael came in and shoved his feet off and sat down beside him.

"Hey, man," Michael said to Hunter.

"Hey," he said in return.

"See?" Vonnie said to Ben. "Can you not be nice like Michael?"

"I'm not being nice," Michael said. "I just have manners. I don't have to like him to acknowledge he's here." Vonnie flipped him the bird.

"Where's Matt?" Isabel asked Abe. He shrugged.

"I think he had a date."

"With who?" she asked.

"I don't know. Some girl named Eden."

"Eden Wilson?" Vonnie asked.

"I think so," he answered.

"Aw...I'm so glad. She's had a crush on him forever," Vonnie said.

"Well, hopefully, it goes well," Abe replied.

Ben reached over to Vonnie and grabbed some of her popcorn. She slapped his hand. Someone punched in the code for the front door, and Matt came into the living room with a girl who I could only assume was Eden. He grabbed her hand and walked over to us.

"This is Eden," Matt said. "Eden, this is, well, everyone."

"Hi," she said quietly.

"Hi," we all said in unison. If you hadn't known any better, you'd think we rehearsed it.

"Come sit by us," Vonnie said to Eden. "We can all fit."

She hopped up and sat back down in Hunter's lap then looked over to Ben and stuck out her tongue. He narrowed his eyes at her. Eden sat down beside them. Matt threw his hands up in the air.

"What about me?"

"You're on your own, buddy," Ben said, and he and Abe laughed.

"Is it family movie night?" Matt asked. "Because I have this awesome new movie to suggest."

"It was supposed to be Lilah and Adrian night," I interjected.

"If you two want to be alone you should go upstairs," Vonnie said. "This is a room for everyone. That's why it's called a..." She raised her hands in quotation marks. "... 'family' room."

"Our family," Maria said as she looked up to me.

"Yeah, honey," I answered as I squeezed her tight. She giggled and I kissed her cheek. "Our family."

Lilah looked over to me and smiled. It was the first time anyone had ever insinuated I was a part of this family. I wasn't sure what had happened to make me a part of it, but it felt amazing. I only wish Tiffany could have been there with us that night, though, because I wanted her to feel it, too.

It was nearly midnight when Lilah and I closed our bedroom door. I always forgot how long *Titanic* was until we watched it again. There was a cool breeze that night and I wanted to open the French doors out onto Lilah's balcony. However, my desire was momentarily sidetracked when I discovered at some point (it looked like more than once) someone had painted them shut. I wish I knew who because I'd still be sending them hate mail.

"I'm going to open these."

"You can't," she explained. "They're painted shut."

"No shit. Why in the hell would someone do this?" I asked as I inspected them.

"We never used them," she explained. "The balcony looks out over the street. Whoever designed it wasn't thinking it through very well."

"So? It's a balcony. You can still sit on it and enjoy the night air."

"1906. They had no air-conditioning. We have air-conditioning."

"I'm going to open them," I told her. I leaned up against one of the doors with my shoulder and pushed a little, but they didn't budge.

"Adrian," she warned.

"Guess I need to exert a little more force." I stepped back.

"Don't do it, Adrian," Lilah begged as she stood by in her nightgown. "The balcony isn't that big and you're going to go through and fly over the railing."

"No. I promise you. I'm not."

"Well, you're gonna knock your shoulder out of joint."

"Do I look like I'm sixty?" I asked turning to her.

I grabbed ahold of the doorknob and slammed my shoulder into the doors. It did kind of hurt but they popped open. I had to catch myself for a moment, though, so I didn't stumble into the railing and over the side, just like Lilah had said.

"Voila!" I said when they opened. She shook her head and walked through the bathroom doorway.

"Good for you," she called over her shoulder. I followed her.

"That's all I get?" I asked. She sat down at her vanity and began brushing her hair.

I stripped off my t-shirt and unbuttoned my jeans, hopped on one foot as I stepped out of them. I always took a shower before bed. Lilah stopped brushing her hair and turned to me, watched me undress. She lowered her eyes and smiled.

"You have paint chips in your hair," she said as she turned back around to her mirror.

"I know," I called from behind the glass shower door.

Lilah and I had sex almost every night. I'm not complaining. I'm only saying she has a much higher sex drive than I do. There was never a moment when I didn't want to be close to her, but it didn't always have to be sex for me. It also didn't have to be with the lights on. Ambiance was no longer a thing for me, either. I could make love to Lilah on top of the washing machine and it would not take away from the overall experience. She crawled into bed and cuddled close to me. I wrapped my arm around her. She had this thing about the hair under my arms. She said it was dark and sexy and always smelled clean. I told her it was called deodorant. Now, she laid her head against me and inhaled.

"You're such a weirdo," I said and laughed.

She smacked me on my chest. I leaned over and kissed the top of her head and she looked up to me, allowing me to kiss her lips gently. I turned and she pulled me over on top of her.

"I just want you."

"You do?" I asked. I put my leg between hers. "Really? Are you sure?"

"You know I'm sure," she said and smiled.

I kissed her neck and ran my hands down her ribcage. Goosebumps erupted over her skin. We had a routine, but it never ceased to be exciting. I slid down the bed and slipped my hands under the small of her back. She arched her body against me, and I grabbed ahold of her hips and held her still in my hands. Afterward I moved up her body slowly and nestled my face into her neck. I wasn't in the mood for wild, passionate sex so I moved against her slowly. This wasn't my usual repertoire.

"How was that, baby?" I asked. She ran her hand over my hair and pulled out the hair band. When she did, my hair fell softly onto her shoulders.

"What is going on?" she asked as she ran her fingers through it.

"What do you mean?"

"Why are you being so tender with me?"

"Do you not like tender?" I asked and smiled.

"Well, yeah. I like tender, but you're usually not this tender. You're acting like I'm a porcelain doll."

"Aren't you?" I asked and chuckled.

"Seriously. What is going on?"

"I just want to feel close to you," I explained. I kissed her chin.

"You *are* close to me," she said. "You're inside of me. How much closer can you get?"

"I didn't mean physically."

"Ah…Like soul to soul?"

"Something like that," I admitted. "I want to tell you about a dream I had last night."

"Yeah? What kind of dream?" she asked. "A bad dream?"

"No. Nothing like that."

I moved off her and laid onto my side, propped my head in my hand. We did that on a regular basis. Sometimes we both had an epiphany. Sometimes, neither one of us did. I ran my fingers down her breastbone.

"I dreamed you were going to have a baby." She looked at me strangely.

"Was it yours?" she asked and smiled.

"Funny," I said. "Of course, it was mine."

"Well, that's good."

Mary Angela always said you dream about what you're thinking of most, and generally if the dream isn't a warning, it's a wish. I'd been thinking about the decision Lorelei and I'd made, and I didn't regret that decision but maybe subconsciously I wanted it to be Lilah instead. That would have been the wish. Maybe it was a warning, too. I needed to make a spreadsheet. Things I can tell Lilah. Things I cannot tell Lilah. Things I should tell Lilah. Things I should not tell Lilah. Things that will make me lose Lilah.

She tucked a piece of my hair behind my ear. She always played with my hair at night while we laid in bed. It's going to sound completely weird and maybe even a little Freudian to admit this, but it made me remember the nights when Mama used to brush my hair before she put me to bed. She'd run her fingers through it and tell me how lucky I was to have such thick, silky hair. Sometimes she'd even kiss my cheek. Those were my favorite nights with her.

"I have a confession to make," I said.

"What's that?"

"I think I kind of liked it," I admitted.

"Oh, yeah?" She smiled then laughed.

"Is it funny?" I asked.

"Kind of."

I was a little surprised at her reaction.

"You can't tell me you've never thought about that," I said.

"Okay," she said as she turned toward me. "I have a confession to make, too."

"Really?" I asked and smiled. "Did you have that dream, too? Are we intuitively connected?"

"No and, apparently, yes."

"Explain yourself, woman!" I teased as I kissed her neck.

"I'm pregnant."

I drew in my breath and fell back against my pillow. I looked up to her, ran my hands through my hair. It was a nervous habit I'd tried to quit many times but never successfully.

"Are you kidding?" I asked.

"No," she said and shook her head.

"We're going to have a baby?" I asked as I pointed to my chest. I motioned back and forth between us. "Me and you?"

"Yeah," she said as she leaned toward me. She kissed me softly. "We are." I wrapped my arms around her and pulled her into me, nuzzled my face into her neck.

"This is amazing," I said into her hair.

"Is it?" she asked as she pulled away from me a bit.

"Yes!"

"I wasn't sure how you'd react," she said. "Isabel told me you might be upset."

"Isabel is crazy if she thinks that," I said as I slid further down into the bed. "Why would she tell you that?"

"I guess she just wanted to prepare me for the worst," Lilah said, laying her head on my chest.

"She is the master of doom and gloom," I said. I ran my fingers across Lilah's bare back, and she drew circles on my chest.

"No, she's not," Lilah protested. "She just likes me to see every angle of every situation, to prepare myself, so I won't be disappointed."

I turned on my side toward her and laid my hand on her stomach.

"There's a baby in here," I said as I kissed her forehead.

"Yeah," she said and smiled. "There is."

"I can't wait to have a baby with you," I told her. "You just made me very happy."

"Wait until you're an actual father," she told me. "The first time you hold your baby in your arms. It's amazing. The love you feel for your children is indescribable. You would do anything, even something you never dreamed of doing before, just because your child needed you to do it."

I ducked my face into her neck and kissed her collarbone. I wanted to say, 'I know,' but I couldn't.

Tiffany

"Welcome home!" Lilah said as I came through her front door. She hugged me. Home. She'd said *home*. "I'm so glad you're back!" she told me.

"Me, too," I said as I sat my bag down in the foyer. "Although I'm grieving my apartment already."

"Oh, it will be fine," she said taking my hand. "Change is good."

"I hope you're right," I said and smiled.

"Tiff!" Ben called as he came down the stairs. He walked over and picked me up, turned me around in a circle.

"Hey!" Isaac shouted. "She's mine." Ben held onto my waist as he sat me down.

"You look good," he said. I kissed Ben's cheek.

"You, too. Where is my brother??"

"Tiffany!" Vonnie said as she came into the living room. She ran over and hugged me. "I missed you, girl!"

"I missed you, too, Hon."

"Well," Lilah said. "We are having a feast tonight!"

"I hope it's not on my account."

"It's totally on your account," Adrian said as he walked in from the kitchen.

He picked me up and twirled me around like Ben had. Over the years I've had people tell me the closeness Adrian and I share is unusual for brothers and sisters. Sometimes when we go places together, we hold hands but only because that's what we've been doing since we were little kids. It's hard to break a habit you've had since childhood. Adrian kissed my forehead as he sat me down.

"Okay," Isaac said coming between us. "That's it."

"I'm her brother, you freak," Adrian said and punched Isaac in the arm.

"It is dinnertime," Lilah announced. "And Adrian and I have some news to share."

Adrian walked over and put his arm around her and kissed her temple.

"Where's Isabel?" I asked.

"Did I hear my name?" she said as she walked through the back door. I couldn't help but wonder if I was getting ready to get a lecture.

"The life of the party just arrived," Matt said sullenly.

"Don't pay any attention to him," Abe said. "He's just mad because Mom grounded him."

"I love it," Isabel said as she walked over and took my hands. I looked over to Isaac. He shrugged. "I couldn't ask for a better girl for Isaac. I just hope you can make him behave."

"Is that possible?" Adrian asked.

"Your sister," Isaac said, looking over to him. "She's reformed me."

"Ha," Adrian said. "I'll believe it when I see it, but you better not get on her bad side because her bad side is my bad side."

"Stop it," Lilah said to Adrian as she grabbed his hand. "Be nice."

Adrian laughed but he wasn't kidding. There had been a few times over the years when Adrian used his DEA status as a calling card. Or his gun. Both worked well. It was not uncommon for Adrian to stop by my apartment to "visit" before I went on a date. He said it was just to hang out and eat my food, but he was always wearing his DEA POLICE t-shirt or he would take his gun out of its holster and lay it on the coffee table in front of him. He never said a word to anyone, but if looks could talk he would've been saying something like, 'Hurt her and I will find you. No matter where you are.'

"Tiffany!!" Maria said as she arrived on the scene. She held out her arms and I picked her up.

"Hi, sweetheart!" I said and kissed her cheek. "Are you glad to see me??"

"You smell good," she said.

"I do?" I asked.

"Like marshmallows!" Everyone laughed.

"Why thank you," I said. "I love marshmallows!"

"Me, too!" she exclaimed.

"Come here, Maria," Adrian said as he took her from me.

"Guess what, Tiffany??" Maria asked excitedly.

"What, honey?"

"Mommy and Adrian are going to have a baby!" I looked over to Adrian and he smiled. Lilah smiled and bowed her head.

"Was I not supposed to tell?" Maria asked Adrian.

"No," he said and kissed her cheek. "But it's okay."

"I'm going to be an aunt?" I asked, gesturing to myself.

"You are," Adrian said.

"Was this planned?"

"That's kind of a rude question," Adrian said, chastising me.

"No, it's not," I told him. "It's not like we're all strangers."

"It was not planned," Lilah said as she looked to Adrian and then back to me. "But we are very excited."

"It's a love child," Isabel added.

"Isabel is obsessed with the phrase 'love child,' Lilah explained.

"What is a love child, Mommy?" Maria asked.

"Yeah," Vonnie said. "What's a love child?"

"It's a baby you didn't plan," Adrian answered, probably to keep Isabel from saying something inappropriate.

"What does that mean, Mommy?" Maria asked Lilah.

"It's when you have sex for fun and end up with a baby," Isabel said before Lilah could answer Maria.

"Holy cow, Isabel," Adrian said. "She's six."

"What's sex?" Maria asked.

"Go ahead, Mom," Isaac said. "Tell her what sex is."

Everyone stood still, in complete silence.

"Yeah, Mom," Matt said. "Tell Maria what sex is."

"No, don't," Adrian added but, of course, Isabel ignored him.

"You know," Isabel told us. "You guys have sticks up your asses. You shouldn't pretend sex doesn't exist. How else do you explain babies? The stork? An egg on a fencepost? Immaculate conception?" She looked over to Ben. "Your mother and I made sure all of you knew the proper terms for your sexual organs."

"Here we go," Ben said. Isabel pointed to Abe.

"What do you call what's in your pants?"

"Why me??" he exclaimed. Isabel motioned with her hand for him to answer. "My penis."

"Right." She turned to Vonnie. "Vonnie…"

"My vagina," she said before Isabel could finish.

"I have a gina!!" Maria said excitedly, and Adrian's face turned crimson. Maria looked to her mother. "Don't I, Mommy?"

"You do," Lilah confirmed.

"So, what's sex?" Maria asked.

"Sex education at its best," Isaac added

"Sex is how two people make a baby," Isabel explained.

"Why?" Maria asked.

"Because that is how God designed us to procreate."

"What is prokrete?"

"Have babies," Ben said.

"I cannot believe we are having this conversation," I told Isaac.

"Welcome to our family," he said.

"Does this have to be a family conversation?" Adrian asked. Lilah sighed.

"Maria needs to know this is not an embarrassing subject," Isabel said. "Sex is a wonderful thing." Lilah chuckled.

"I didn't know what sex was until I was fourteen," Adrian added.

"That is such a lie," I said, and he raised his eyebrows.

"When two people want to have a baby, they have sex," Isabel said to Maria.

"How?" Maria asked. Isabel pointed to Lilah.

"Oh no," Lilah said. "You started this. You finish it." Isabel closed one of her hands.

"Sex is when a man puts his penis…" She put her finger from her other hand into it.

"Holy shit," Matt said as he covered his eyes. Isabel looked over to him.

"You probably need a refresher course yourself. So, listen and learn."

"The man puts his penis inside the woman's vagina and plants a seed," Isabel explained to Maria.

"Why can't he plant the seed with his hands?" Maria asked.

"Because his hands don't have the seed."

"I need a beer," Ben said.

"I think we should continue this conversation at another time," Adrian suggested. "Because it is getting out of hand."

"Ha," Ben said. "Out of hand."

"Is this for real?" Vonnie asked. "Are you really having a baby, Mom?"

"Yes," Lilah said quietly. "I'm really having a baby." Vonnie ran over and gave Lilah a hug then turned to Adrian.

"I have to admit," she said. "This feels really weird."

"Sorry," Adrian said and looked down.

"It's cool," Vonnie said. "But can I call you Dad??" Adrian smiled and shook his head.

"Whatever floats your boat," he said and grinned.

"I'm just kidding," she said. "Come here, Maria. Let's go fix drinks for everyone!" We all followed Vonnie and Maria into the kitchen.

"Everyone," Lilah said. "Isabel's buttermilk biscuits are on the table along with all the condiments and your utensils. Grab a plate. All the food is on the buffet."

"This is amazing," I said to Lilah as I hugged her. "Thank you so much."

"You're welcome."

"And I just want to say that you and Adrian, well, having a baby, I think it's wonderful. I've never seen him so happy."

"I'm pretty happy, too," she said and bowed her head. "He makes me very happy."

"I can tell," I admitted.

"Hey," Isabel said as she walked up to us. "I told Lilah they should name the baby after me. Don't you think that's a good idea?" I smiled and looked over to Lilah.

"We're going to announce names at dinner."

"You are??" Isabel asked. "How do I not know about this??"

"Because Adrian and I decided we weren't going to tell anyone until tonight," Lilah said.

"Me," Isabel said. "Me. You've never kept a secret from me in your life."

"It's not a secret," Lilah said, and I smiled. "It's a surprise and you're going to ruin it if you don't stop talking. Go get a plate. Chill out."

"Fine," Isabel said as she walked away.

"Hey!" Lilah called to her.

"What?"

"I love you."

"Uh-huh."

I walked over to Isaac and the buffet. I had never seen so much food in my life.

"Wow," I said. "I've never seen this much food. Ever."

"Well." He shrugged. "This is par for the course for us. A lot of people. A lot of food."

"Okay," I said. "But you're going to have to tell me what all of this is because the only thing I recognize is the ham and the fried chicken."

"Southern cooking," he said and took my hand. He squeezed it. "It's the best food ever."

We stood at the end of the buffet as Isaac pointed out every individual dish.

"So, Mom and Isabel compete when they're cooking," he said. "I don't know why. They've been doing it since the beginning of time."

"Like a real competition??" I asked.

"No. Just for fun."

"Oh."

"I'm not even sure who makes what anymore…"

"Oh, hey! Everyone!" Isabel shouted with her hand in the air. "Someone…" she looked to Isaac. "Asked me to make my Almost as Good as Sex Pie…."

"Did you really?" Isaac asked with a huge grin on his face.

"I did," Isabel told him. "I know it's been forever, but this is a special occasion!"

"Almost as good as sex?" I asked.

"According to Mom the original recipe was called Better Than Sex, but she insists it's definitely not, but it's *almost* as good as sex."

"So typical of your mother."

"Yep." He pointed down the table. "That's corn pudding."

"Never heard of it," I said.

"That is squash casserole."

"Eeww," I said. "Squash? Seriously?"

"It's good," he said. "Trust me."

"Lilah's deviled eggs."

"Oh yum. "I've had those before, and they are amazing."

"I know, right?" He pointed to the next dish. "That's Lilah's macaroni and cheese. It's heavenly. Those are black-eyed peas and the dish beside it is stewed tomatoes. They go together."

"Eeww," I said again. Isaac laughed.

"Mashed potatoes, of course, and gravy – from the chicken."

"Uh, broccoli casserole, maple pecan sweet potatoes, coleslaw, potato salad, kale – which I eat with the deviled eggs…"

"Not even going to ask what Kale is," I muttered.

"It's a Southern thing," he said. "Oh wow, I hope Lilah made her hummingbird cake."

"Does it have hummingbirds in it?" I asked and grinned.

"Uh, no."

"Not to be rude," I said, "But why does the kale have chunks of ham in it?"

"Because Mom cooks it with a hambone."

"Okaay. I hope your Mom is planning on teaching me how to make some of this stuff because all I know how to make are sugar cookies, coconut rice and Palak paneer."

"I like your Palak paneer," he said as he leaned over and kissed my cheek.

"Thanks."

"Okay, everyone!" Isabel called. "If everyone has fixed their plate let's get to the table so we can say the blessing." I looked over to Isaac.

"We always say the blessing," he explained. "We're in the Bible Belt."

"Nana always said the blessing, too," I told him as we fixed our plates. Soon after we all sat down at the table and Isaac reached for my hand on one side and Vonnie reached for the other on the other side.

"We hold hands for prayer," she informed me, and we all bowed our heads.

It was quiet. A rare thing at Lilah's house. After a moment Ben looked up.

"Who is saying the blessing?" he asked.

"Oh," Isabel said, looking over to Lilah. "I thought you were."

"I can," she said. "Okay. Dear God, thank you for this day and for our family. Thank you for us all coming together tonight to celebrate Tiffany…" Isaac squeezed my hand. "…coming home." He squeezed it again. "And for the new, sweet little life who will soon be a part of us. Thank you for this food and bless it to the nourishment of our bodies. In Jesus name, I pray. Amen."

"Amen," everyone said.

"Let's eat!" Ben said. "Pass the chicken."

"Well, Isabel said after we'd finished dinner and started dessert. "Let's here the names for the precious, sweet life that's coming in about…" she hesitated and looked to Lilah. "…how many months?"

"We're not sure," Lilah said. "I'll find out when I go to the doctor next week."

"Okay," Isabel said. "So, whenever. Spill the names so we can all tell you why we don't like them." Adrian looked over to me.

"Always drama with Isabel," he said.

"I heard that!" she called to him across the table. "Stand up!"

"Do I have to stand up??" Adrian asked.

"Yes." Adrian stood.

"This feels weird," he said, and he grabbed Lilah's hand. "Don't make me do this alone." She stood up beside him.

"You do the girl and I'll do the boy," she told him.

"Are we gonna find out what it is?" Matt asked as he stuffed a forkful of pie into his mouth. "Because I don't know if I can take the suspense."

"Don't talk with your mouth full," Isabel chastised.

"Probably not," Lilah said as she looked up to Adrian. "I think we're going to let it be a surprise."

"Damn it," Michael said.

"Shut up, Michael," Vonnie told him. "I want to hear the girl's name first."

"Ha," Lilah said as she punched Adrian in the ribs. "You go first."

"We thought long and hard about the middle name," he told us. "I think it's a little over the top and completely unnecessary, but Lilah insisted. The girl will be named after my Nana, Sicily." He looked to Isabel. "And you." Isabel brought her hand to her chest.

"Me??? Why me??"

"Would you rather us not?" Adrian asked.

"You're the best thing that ever happened to me," Lilah said. "You deserve recognition."

"Aw…"

"It wasn't my idea," Adrian said. "I wanted it to be Gladys."

"Eeww…" Vonnie said.

"I'm just joking," he said. "It will be Sicily Isabella Bennett." Isabel put her hands over her face and leaned over on her elbows on the table.

"Gosh, Mom," Isaac said. "Get ahold of yourself." Adrian chuckled.

"Okay, okay," Lilah said. "I picked the boy's first name." She looked up to Adrian. "Which will be Cristiano.'"

"I love that name," Vonnie said.

"Me, too!" Maria added "We can call him Crissy!"

"That's a doll baby," Vonnie told her.

"I'm still calling him Crissy," she said, incensed.

"Adrian picked the middle name," Lilah told us.

"You tell them," he said to her.

"Nope. You picked it. You tell them."

"I feel like this name is going to suck," Isaac said. Then to Adrian, "I'm just kidding, dude."

"It's Xander," Adrian said. "Cristiano Xander."

Everyone was silent. We all looked at one another.

"What?" I asked. "Of all the wonderful names we have in our family and you pick Xander?? Where the hell did that come from??"

"I like it," he told me. "What's wrong with it?"

"I don't think I can even say that name," Vonnie said. Maria put her hand on Vonnie's arm.

"It's Zander," Maria told her. "It starts with a Z. Right, Adrian?"

"Actually, it starts with an X," Adrian said. "But it sounds like a Z." He pointed at her. "You are so smart!" Maria beamed.

"Not to be a Debbie downer," Isabel said. "But why don't you just spell it with a Z then?"

"Because I like it with an X," Adrian told her.

"I'm just going to call him Android," she replied.

"Come on, guys," Lilah said. "Adrian likes that name. I think it's cool."

"Mom," Ben said as he looked to Lilah. "Not to be a Donald downer but no one at school is going to know how to pronounce it if you spell it with an X. He'll suffer his whole life. Name him Bob or Bill or something."

"No!!" Adrian and Lilah said at the same time.

"Okay, guys," Adrian told everyone. "I will ponder this. In the meantime, write your suggestions down on a piece of paper and I'll consider them."

"I'm going to write down Xander!!" Maria said excitedly. "I love you, Adrian, and I think it is a pretty name!"

"Why, thank you, Maria," he said. "You are my favorite child."

"I thought I was your favorite child," Vonnie said as she cut a piece of the Hummingbird cake.

"Lord," Lilah said as she sat down. Adrian sat down beside her.

"I was shot down," he told her.

"Honey, if it is a boy, you can name him anything you want. It's our baby, not theirs."

"It takes a village," Isabel said.

"Well, this village sucks," Adrian said, and we all laughed together.

I was sitting on Lilah's front porch a little after midnight when Adrian came out of the front door.

"What's up, Buttercup?" he asked as he plopped down on the sofa beside me. I raised my eyebrows.

"What did you just say?" I asked and smiled. He bumped his shoulder into mine.

"I said, what's up, Buttercup?" He laughed.

"Are you drunk?" I asked him.

"No," he said. "Just happy."

"I'm glad," I said taking his hand in mine. "You really are, aren't you?"

"Uh-huh." He propped his feet up on the wicker table in front of us, slid down further into the cushion. "Bet you never thought my assignment would turn into this, did you?"

"No," I said and smiled.

"Better than Savannah, Georgia?" he asked.

"Oh, yeah."

"This is like family," he said. "You know? I mean, I keep asking myself what we did to deserve this."

"I know," I said. "Me, too. Where's Lilah?"

"She went to bed. Pregnancy wears you out, apparently."

"Anyone else up?"

"I don't think so."

"Isaac told me he applied at Adelphi for next fall. I told him he could live at the Inn with us."

"What am I going to do about that?" Adrian asked.

"Why? You don't want him to??"

"No, I don't care about that. I just, well, everybody's here and we're there."

"I know," I said as I pulled at a string on my jeans. "I don't think this hole over my knee is supposed to be this big." I ran my finger underneath the stitching. "And now you and Lilah are having a baby." I turned to him. "What will you do? Stay here?"

"I can't be here all the time," he told me. "The thought did cross my mind to move everyone up there but somehow that seems a little unrealistic." He ran his hand through his hair. "Don't you think?"

"Probably," I said and nodded. "It would be so cool for everyone to be at the Inn, though, wouldn't it?"

"Yep."

"Oh, my god," I said as I raised the arm of his t-shirt.

"What??"

"You got another tattoo." He smiled and brought his finger to his lips.

"Sshh…"

"Why? Does no one know?"

"No one knows."

"Not even Lilah?" I asked.

"Not yet."

"It's really red," I told him. "Did you put antibiotic ointment on it?"

"Yes, Nana," he said, and I slapped his leg. "It's red because I just did it this morning."

"Read it," he said as he put his feet down and sat forward.

He pulled his shirt sleeve up over his shoulder and I examined his new artwork. A shadowed cross with decorative curls, some light, some dark, and through the middle of the cross: FAIRY TALE.

"Well, that kind of sums up our life, doesn't it?" I asked.

"Especially now," he said. "Because I feel like we're living one." He stood up. "Want a beer? Wine? Something?"

"Remember when we were little how we used to sneak out into the courtyard after bedtime and drink chocolate milk?"

"Yeah," he said. "I remember."

"How about chocolate milk?" I asked. He pointed at me.

"You got it!"

I propped my feet up on the table in front of me then pulled my knees into my chest and rested my chin there. I'd ask Adrian what he was going to do about his circumstances, but what was I going to do about mine? We had just inherited the Inn and there was so much work to do. I had so many responsibilities at work with my new study, which would only intensify by the time Isaac arrived for school. Now Lilah was going to have my brother's baby. I had a family. It was surreal.

"So," Adrian said as he came back out onto the porch and handed me my chocolate milk. "Jenny took me off this case."

"What case?"

"Here."

"I thought everything here was over."

"Well," he admitted. He took a sip of his milk. "So, did I. But we kind of had a security breach at the talent show."

"What do you mean?" I asked.

"Not too long ago, Jenny told me I couldn't come back here because Bret's father was here looking for me."

"Oh," I said, surprisingly. "That's not good. Where is he now?"

"He's in jail."

"Oh, well, good."

"Not exactly."

"It's not good he's in jail??" I asked, confused.

"Oh, no," he said. "It's good he's in jail. It's not good he knows Lilah."

"He knows Lilah??? How?"

"Jenny is here."

"In Woodlawn?"

"Yeah," he told me. "She's taking over the case until Terrence can get down here because I kind of went off the deep end on this guy."

"Where's Stef?"

"He's with Sharla."

"Terrence's Sharla?" I asked, surprised.

"Yeah," he confirmed. "She thinks he's Jenny's nephew."

"Oh, the tangled webs we weave."

"You said it, not me." He handed me his phone. "Play it."

"What is this?" I asked as I sat my milk down on the table beside me. I took his phone from him.

"That's the hidden camera at the station…." He said as I began watching it. "…and me…and McCain. Jenny sent it to me and told me if anything like it ever happened again, I would no longer have a parking spot." I looked over to him and he shrugged. I looked back to his phone and watched in silence.

"Holy shit," Adrian. "What the hell is wrong with you??"

"You didn't hear the first part," he said. "What he said to me."

"This is Bret's father?"

"Yes."

"Apple doesn't fall far from the tree, eh?"

"Oh, no," he said and raised his eyebrows.

"What did he say to you?" I asked.

"Nope," he said and shook his head.

"Tell me," I insisted.

"No."

"Adrian, you better tell me now," I said. He took a deep breath.

"He told me he bet Lilah's pussy still tasted the same."

"Oh, my Lord," I said as I brought my hand to my mouth. "He really said that?"

"Yep."

"I'm surprised you didn't pull out your gun and shoot him right there on the spot," I said.

"I thought about it."

"Jeez, Adrian." I looked over to him. "I totally get it, but you gotta learn to control yourself a little better."

"That has never happened to me before," he said. "Ever. In six years, I have never had anyone piss me off the way he did. Never. And I've worked with a lot of less-than-thou individuals."

"Well, you've never had anyone talk about the woman you love."

"No."

"Was he involved with Lilah at some point?"

"He claims in college," Adrian said.

"Do you believe him?" I asked as I gave him back his phone.

"Jenny said he had a picture of Lilah in his wallet."

"What??" I said, turning to him. "Why?"

"I don't know," he said and shrugged.

"A current picture??"

"No."

"This isn't good, Adrian."

"No," he said. "But it's out of my control now. Jenny dismissed me from the case."

"Can you blame her?"

"I know," he said shoving his phone back into his pocket. "I get it. I know what I did." He looked down. "I know I'm too emotionally involved."

"Does Jenny know Lilah is pregnant?" I asked.

"No. But I'll tell her. It's not a secret."

"Maybe it should be," I said.

"Well, we just told everyone," he said. "So, it's a little late for that."

"No," I said, laying my hand on his arm. "It needs to stay in *our* family for now. If this man…. who claims he knows Lilah…or whatever he claims…finds out she's expecting your child, well, I can't imagine after what's happened between you and him, he would react in a favorable way." Adrian took a deep breath.

"You think Lilah might be in danger?" he asked.

"How can you not?" I asked. "I mean, he had her picture, Adrian."

"Lilah is always safe with me," he said. "I would never let anyone hurt her. Ever. You know that."

"Of course, I know that," I said. "I'm not doubting your capability to take care of her, but I think it goes a little further than that. We're not talking about two high school boys fighting over who gets the prom queen."

"Memories," he said thoughtfully.

"Don't even go there," I said because I knew he was thinking about Lorelei. "Granted, McCain isn't *The Empire,* but I think you're fooling yourself if you think he's not as dangerous."

"Oh, come on, Tiff. Be realistic."

"I am being realistic," I said as I brought my hand to my chest.

"So, what are you suggesting?" he asked.

"I'm suggesting you don't let Lilah out of your sight." He turned to me.

"Do you know how impossible that is right now?? I can't take her to Amityville for so many reasons."

"Well, you can't be here all the time either," I said. "So, you need to find someone you trust who is."

"Hey," Ben said as he poked his head out the kitchen door. "There you are."

"There he is," I said to Adrian.

And he knew exactly what I meant.

"Hey," Vonnie said as she walked into her bedroom.

"Where have you been??" I asked teasingly as I laid my book in my lap.

She threw her bag onto the foot of her bed and flopped down on her pillow. She pulled it out from underneath her head and put it over her face.

"What?" I asked and laughed. She spoke but it was unintelligible. "What?" I asked again and she pulled the pillow off her face and sat up. She put her hands over her face.

"Hunter," she said.

"Is he cute?" I asked.

"Oh my god," she said as she fell back onto her pillow again. "He's dreamy."

"Dreamy, huh?"

"And he's the best kisser."

"When do I get to meet Mr. Dreamy?" I asked.

I pulled the comforter up on my bed and leaned back against the headboard. She got up and came over, sat down in front of me. She pulled her legs up and crossed them underneath one another.

"You're know you're like the closest thing to a sister I've ever had, right? I mean I have Maria, but she's six." I smiled.

"I feel the same way," I said as I reached out and touched her arm. "Tell me about him."

"Oh my gosh, Tiff, he's so incredibly hot."

"Where did you meet him?"

"At a party," she told me. "He doesn't go to my school. He goes to some private school in Richmond, but he invited me to go to lunch, so we did, and that's when I found out he had a band and needed a drummer."

"Sounds like a match made in heaven," I told her.

"I'm surprised Adrian hasn't told you about him."

"Well, contrary to popular belief, he doesn't tell me *everything*. Although, I must tell you this, because now that everything is out in the open it feels wrong not to."

"What is out in the open?" Vonnie asked, concerned.

"Lilah and Adrian."

"Oh."

"I knew, Vonnie. I knew the whole time and I couldn't tell you."

"It's okay," she said as she looked down and then back up to me. "That whole..." She moved her hand around in the air. "...situation was fucked up."

"Yeah," I said. "But you and Adrian are okay, right?"

"Oh yeah, definitely, even though he shot me." We laughed together. "Have you ever been shot?"

"No," I said. "Of course not."

"It hurts so bad. I felt like I was on fire and I didn't know why. I didn't know getting shot felt like that." I didn't know what to say to that information, so I said nothing. "Anyhow," she said. "I figured you knew about Mom and Tristan." She stopped and shook her head. "I can't believe I just called him that."

"It's funny," I told her and laughed. "He's used to it. He expects it."

"That's good to know," Vonnie said and smiled.

"Listen, I know Adrian put forth this image here in Woodlawn, like he was the coolest, most popular kid..."

"Well," Vonnie said. "He was."

"Yeah," I agreed. "He's a good actor. He made it look like he didn't care about anything and that is true to some extent but Adrian, well, he's very conservative." Vonnie narrowed her eyes at me. "Do you know what I mean?"

"I'm not sure."

"Adrian is not a drinker, a druggie, a guy who sleeps with older married women…that's about as far from who Adrian truly is as you can get." She smiled.

"Yeah, I'm kind of getting that now."

"He loves your mom," I said. She looked down again.

"I know."

"It still bothers him that he broke up your parents' marriage," I told her.

"He didn't," she said shaking her head. "Mom has always…uh… you know."

"Fooled around?" I asked.

"Yeah," she said. "I think Daddy finally just got tired of it. I think he always thought she'd turn it around at some point and come back to him."

"That's sad," I said.

"Yeah."

"I'm sorry, Vonnie."

"It's over," she said. "It's in the past and I've let it go." She smiled. "That's what therapy will do for you." I reached out and pulled her into me, gave her a hug. "I heard you and Isaac last night," she confessed as I let her go. "Was he in here?"

"Holy shit, Vonnie," I said.

"Was he?" she asked again.

"Yes," I admitted as I looked upward.

"Did you really think I wouldn't know? Oh my god. Did you do it in my bedroom???"

Now, I put my hands over my face.

"Eeww…gross…I can't believe you did that to me!!! Jesus, Tiff."

"We were trying to be quiet," I said and laughed.

"You and Isaac were having sex in this bed…" She jumped up and pointed to it. "…while I was in here!!! What the hell is wrong with you guys???"

I put my arms over my head then pulled the comforter up over me.

"I'm sorry," I said from under the comforter. I peeked out. "He is, like, the sexiest guy I've ever known, and I can't even put into words how amazing he is in bed." She flopped down on her bed, put her arm over her forehead. "I'm sorry," I said again. "I have to get used to the fact that you're like my boyfriend's sister."

"It's not a big deal," she said as she turned to me. "People tell me stuff about him all the time. You can't imagine the things I've heard over the years."

"Like what?" This, I was curious to hear.

"Oh, just that he's good in bed. My friends used to want to talk about his penis with me. I was like, 'Nope! No way!'" She held up her hand. 'Just stop now.'"

"Wow."

"They used to try to get me to hook them up with him," she said. "I always told them they were on their own. I am not about to get involved in Isaac's love life, but I can tell you one thing."

"What's that?"

"You must mean something to him. He goes through girls like I go through underwear. So, if he still wants to be with you and no one else, well, that's just unusual for him. I love him, but he's a player."

"He told me he loves me," I confided.

"Get out!" she said, and she jumped up out of her bed and came over to me, flopped down on mine. "No, he didn't."

"He did. I swear."

"Holy, baby Jesus. I'm going to write this down. Maybe I'll take out a billboard." She spread her hands out in front of her. "I'm gonna put fluffy clouds and glitter on it and it's going to say, 'No more fantasy land. Isaac Lund is off the market.'"

"Funny," I said and laughed.

I loved that about Vonnie. She was funny, smart, charismatic, and well, a little bit of a bad girl. Okay, a lot of a bad girl, but we were always laughing about something. She had a lot of Lilah in her, but unlike Lilah, she could put you in your place in a minute. Like Isabel. Having both on your side at once was like owning an expensive insurance policy. She reached over and hugged me.

"I love it!" she exclaimed. "You guys being together is awesome." She pulled back. "Wait. You do love him, too, right?"

"Yes," I said. "Very much." She smiled.

"I am so happy!" she said.

"Me, too! You have no idea! I mean, I fell in love with him a long time ago."

"I think he fell in love with you, too," Vonnie told me. "He just didn't know what it was." We laughed together.

"Tell me about this Hunter guy but…" I said holding up my finger. "Tell me he's a good guy. No more sketchy boyfriends." She bowed her head.

"I know," she said quietly then looked up. "That was so hard, Tiff." I nodded, and we were quiet for a moment. "There was a part of me who loved Bret, you know?"

"I do."

"He was bad to me, but sometimes he was good," she explained. "I kind of felt sorry for him sometimes."

"Why?"

"I just don't think he ever had anyone really love him, you know?"

"Yeah."

"I'm not sure what happened with him and his dad, but his mom kicked him out, and he had nowhere to go."

"But he had his own apartment," I said. "Didn't he?"

"It was Luther's."

"Who is Luther?"

"He was Bret's supplier."

"Ah…"

"Anyhow, it's over."

"Just to be clear," I said. "And I totally get that you felt sorry for him, but he was more bad than good. Maybe it wasn't his fault he turned out that way, but he was still *that way*. He was bad news, Vonnie, and apparently, a loose cannon."

"Okay, Isabel," she said. "I get it." I smiled.

"Did you ever find out what happened to him?" I asked.

"Well, he didn't die," she said.

"That's good."

"Maybe," she admitted, and I widened my eyes.

"Vonnie!!"

"What?? You're the one who just said he was bad."

"Well, yeah. But not like he deserved to die!"

"He did," she affirmed. "I'm not going to tell you why, but he did."

"Jeez, Vonnie."

"I'm just saying, but yeah, he got out on bond and went to live with his mom until the hearing, somewhere down South. Far away from me. I'm fairly certain Adrian had something to do with it."

"Oh yeah," I agreed. "I'm sure. Adrian is very protective over you."

"A good person to have on your side," she said and smiled.

"Don't think he'll get you out of anything if you ever get arrested again," I told her. "I mean, I know what happened with Bret but I can tell you now it was your 'get out of jail' free card. Adrian will bring the hammer down if he thinks you're doing something you shouldn't be."

"Not me," she said and batted her eyelashes at me. "Not sweet, little Vonnie."

"Uh-huh. I know what happened between you two before."

"What???" Vonnie asked innocently.

"Before you knew about him and your Mom and you tried to get in his pants," I said. She brought her hands to her face and put it over her eyes. I laughed.

"Oh, wow," she said. "Did he tell you about that?"

"Yeah," I admitted. "He thought it was funny."

"Oh my god," she said. "I am *so* embarrassed. I had kind of forgotten about it. Thanks for the reminder, Tiff." I laughed again, reached out and rubbed my hand up and down her arm.

"It's all good," I assured her.

"Okay," she said. "Can I admit something to you I've never told *anyone*?"

"Sure."

"You promise you won't tell Adrian? Or Mom?"

"Uh…" I looked upward.

"It's not bad…or illegal…just embarrassing. But I need to verbalize it. My therapist told me saying it out loud was important and I'm afraid if I tell her she'll lock me up somewhere."

"Oh my," I said. "What is it?"

"Adrian and I kissed," she said and her face flooded red.

"I know," I said and smiled.

"No," she said. "I mean, we really kissed. Like French kissed."

"I know," I said.

"Oh my god, I hate him so much!!!" she exclaimed. "He was just playing his part, wasn't he??"

I laughed. In fact, I couldn't stop laughing.

"Oh yeah."

Isabel

Lilah and I were sitting at my kitchen table for happy hour, although she wasn't drinking, and I wasn't just casually drinking. I was on my fourth glass of this new French wine Lilah had bought at some wine shop in downtown Woodlawn. It made me wonder why I ever bought wine at the grocery store when the wine there was so much better and on occasion, cheaper. Then I remembered why. I would have to parallel park. Drinking this much at once was highly unusual for me. I tried to be a responsible drinker most of the time. Okay, some of the time. Okay, never. But this whole McCain situation was making me fidgety. It was making Lilah fidgety, too.

"Adrian told me he knows who McCain is," Lilah said. I sat up straighter in my chair.

"And?"

"And he doesn't know much else. Only that we were together in college."

"Does he know about…" I lowered my voice to a whisper. "…Ben?"

"No," she assured me. "And I'd like to keep it that way for the time being."

"Agreed."

"He told me Jenny took him off the case because it was becoming too personal."

"Well, that's a good thing," I said. "Don't you think?"

"Definitely," she agreed. "He got a new tattoo."

"Is it your name on his private parts??" She waved her hand at me and smiled.

"No. You're such a pervert."

"Eh…what is it??"

"It's a cross that says Fairy Tale down the middle."

"Woo," I said. I sat forward in my chair. "Tell me he got it on his ass."

"Oh my god, Isabel. What is wrong with you?? No. It's on his arm." She patted her upper arm. "Right here."

"Isaac and Tiffany were in bed together when I called the other day," I told her.

"Doesn't surprise me. The boy Tom's mother calls an angel."

"God, if she only knew," I said. "I wonder how many girls he's slept with?" Ben and Isaac came through the sliding glass doors from the patio. "Speak of the devil." Lilah smiled.

"Man, it's a little chilly out there," Ben said as he walked over to me. He slipped his fingers into the back of my shirt onto my bare neck.

"You little shit," I said as I jumped up. "I'm gonna beat the hell out of you!!"

"You gotta catch me first," he said teasingly as he leaned forward and stuck his hand against my neck again. He quickly backed away. I ran down the hall after him and grabbed him by the back of his jacket. I swatted him on the back of his head, and he laughed.

"Hey, Mom?" he said walking back toward the kitchen.

"Yes, sweetie?"

"This guy, Terrence, he said he works with Adrian??"

"Okay."

"He just called the house. He said he tried to call your cell phone, but you didn't answer."

"She never answers calls if she doesn't know who it is," I said.

"Neither do I," Isaac chimed in.

"Anyhow, he said Adrian had asked him to come over and talk to you?"

"About what?"

"He said he was taking over the case here." Lilah and I exchanged glances.

"Everybody out," I said. "Clear the room."

"What?" Isaac said. "Why?"

"I need to talk to Lilah," I said. "This is important." Ben and Isaac just stared at me. "Go!!" I pointed to the sliding doors.

"Mom!" Ben said.

"Yeah?"

"I told the Terrence guy to call you again and I would tell you to answer. His number is 631 something."

"Okay. Thanks, honey."

"Wait," I said. "Where are the two of you going?"

"You told us to leave," Ben said.

"Well, I know. But where are you going??"

"Play pool at Lilah's," Isaac told me.

"Okay…love you…"

"No drinking!!" Lilah called after them.

"It's a school night," I added.

"Aw, come on," Ben said as he turned toward us.

"No!!" Lilah and I said at the same time as they walked out the door.

"They'll be trashed by the time you get home," I said.

"Probably," Lilah agreed. "Remember when they both got arrested for drunk in public??"

"When Ben peed on the railway tracks in the middle of Center Street?" I asked and she nodded. "Good times."

"You probably shouldn't have beaten my child with the wooden spoon at the police station," she told me. "I'm not saying he didn't deserve it."

"Yeah," I agreed. "But Roy will ignore any and every law known to man if he thinks I'll give him a blow job."

"Have you ever actually given him one?" Lilah asked.

"Eeww…" I said. "No. Gross."

"Yet telling him you will works every time."

"It's Roy!" I pointed out.

"Well, yeah."

"When Tom and I got married his mother gave me the wooden spoon and told me she knew white people didn't beat their kids, but I better beat her grandchildren when they did something wrong, or she would do it herself."

"She's a riot," Lilah said.

"She loves *you*," I told her. "Not so much me."

"She does, too, love you. At least she used to until you cheated on Tom." I picked up a fake bunch of grapes out of the basket on the table and threw them at her. She reached up to catch them and they fell into her lap.

"Shut up," I said.

We were quiet. Lilah gazed out of the kitchen doors. Her moods changed like the phases of the moon, yet she consistently wondered where Vonnie got it from.

"What are you thinking?" I asked her. She held up her hand.

"I'm thinking Adrian will want this ring back once he figures out the rest of my story with McCain."

"Oh, stop it," I said as I flopped back into my chair. "You know how much Adrian loves you."

"A heroin addict and a DEA officer," she said. "What a combo."

"Stop it," I said again. "You are not a heroin addict."

"I'm in recession," she admitted.

"When was the last time you did heroin?" I asked her. "Or any drug, for that matter??" She shrugged.

"Well, I drug myself to sleep every night."

"Well, so do I!! Who doesn't???" I asked and Lilah widened her eyes.

"Most people."

"I think you are totally wrong," I told her. "I think a lot more people drug themselves to sleep than you think. I mean, think about this world we live in. Watching the news these days has the same effect on me as the *Insidious* movies."

"Oh, ha."

"Come on, Lilah. Adrian loves you more than life. He may not care. I mean, that was a long time ago. You're not even the same person anymore." She didn't comment. "Are you?"

"No."

"You know he wants that baby with you," I told her. "That's not going to change just because you were a heroin addict twenty years ago."

"Yeah," she said absentmindedly. She looked up to me. "Should I tell him about that?"

"Yes. Definitely."

"What if he asks why I haven't told him before?"

"Tell him the truth," I suggested.

"What's the truth?"

"That you were ashamed and afraid to tell him but now…" I hesitated. "…all this stuff happening…you wanted to tell him yourself before someone else did. Say you're sorry you didn't tell him before."

"And you think that will work?" she asked.

"Give him a blowjob afterward," I said and laughed. She rolled her eyes. "Like, actually do it. Don't play cat and mouse like me and Roy."

"Good grief, Isabel."

"Don't blowjobs always work??" I asked.

"They do," she agreed.

"And men wonder why we're smarter than them," I said. "We live by our heads and our hearts and…"

"…they live by their dicks," she finished. We laughed.

"Yep."

"Hi," I said when I opened Lilah's front door the following afternoon. In front of me was an extraordinarily handsome black man. Almost as handsome as Tom, although I doubt we could make angel babies like Tom and I did.

"Hi," he said. "You're not Lilah."

"No," I said and smiled. I'm Isabel." I extended my hand and he took it. "Please, come in. We've been expecting you." I ushered him through the door. "Although I wasn't quite expecting you to be so gorgeous."

"Thank you," he said and smiled.

"Are you single?" I asked him as I looked for a ring.

"Yes," he said. "But soon to be married."

"Damn it," I said, and he chuckled. Lilah walked into the living room.

"This…" I said to her as I motioned my hand toward him. "…is Terrence, who is much better looking than I ever expected him to be."

"You have to ignore her," Lilah said as she walked toward Terrence. She extended her hand and he took it. "Isabel is…"

"Horny," I said. Lilah shook her head back and forth and Terrence laughed. "I'm trying to get back together with my ex-husband," I explained. "So, I am trying to refrain from having sex with other people. It's been a difficult endeavor."

"Please come in," Lilah said. "Sit down. May I get you something to drink? Tea, Juice, Kool-Aid…"

"Alcohol," Isabel added.

"Would you stop it?" Lilah chastised me. "He's already told you he's engaged so the possibility of you getting him into bed is non-existent." Terrence laughed.

"You two crack me up," he said. "But then Adrian did tell me to expect this. Iced tea would be great. Thank you."

"Isabel," Lilah said. "Go get this man some tea. I'm not leaving you alone with him."

"Fine," I said, a little incensed.

I walked into the kitchen and to the refrigerator, took out the tea. I wondered what kind of questions Terrence would ask Lilah regarding this case. I wondered even more what answers she'd give him. Certainly, she wouldn't tell him everything. I carried the tea back into the living room and handed it to Terrence.

"Thank you," he said as he took it. He took a swallow. "There's nothing like Southern sweet tea."

"Adrian tells me it's not tea," Lilah said. "He calls it syrup."

"It is very tasty," Terrence commented. He sat his tea down on a coaster on the side table and reached for the case file beside him. "Do you mind if I ask you a few questions?"

"No," Lilah said. "I expected you would."

"Okay then," he said as he looked up to me. "Are you staying?"

"Yes," Lilah and I answered together. Terrence chuckled.

"Alright," he said. He opened the file. "I'm not sure how much you know about all this. I'm not sure what Adrian has told you and Jenny didn't want us to collaborate until I talked to you first."

"How come?" I asked.

"Well, she never really gives a reason for anything," he said and smiled. "But I'm guessing it's because she doesn't want me to get any preconceived notions about the case. She's all about facts and opinions."

"And she's afraid Adrian will give you his," I said.

"More like the way Adrian would present the facts," he replied. "Because when you're personally involved in a case, facts tend to be overshadowed by opinions even when you don't intend them to be."

"He's smart, too," I said to Lilah. She rolled her eyes again.

"So, let's get started," he said as he took a pen from the inside of his jacket. "I might not be able to write as fast as you talk but we'll see what happens." He smiled. "I'd like to start with some basic questions."

"Okay," Lilah said.

"This Mitchell McCain," he said. "You know him?"

"Yes," she said.

"Do you want to elaborate?" Lilah looked over to me

"Want a drink?" I asked her.

"Three," she answered. Terrence chuckled.

"Forgive me," he said. "But I can't help but wonder how Adrian responds to the two of you?"

"He ignores us most of the time," Lilah said. "Just shakes his head and walks away."

"Sounds like him," he concluded.

"You really want a drink?' I asked Lilah.

"A glass of wine?" she answered.

"You got it."

A glass of wine every now and then when you're pregnant never hurt anyone and that information came from my doctor. Although, she probably told me that because she didn't think I could go cold turkey. Wrong. I can. Blame it on my curious nature, or my chemistry degree, or both, but I love creating cocktails. Every now and then my drinks turn out not so good, but neither Lilah nor I believe you should waste alcohol, so we usually just keep mixing stuff together until it tastes right.

"Sauvignon Blanc or Pinot Grigio?" I called around the corner. "That's what's open."

"I don't care," she called back.

I didn't want to miss any of this interview, so I grabbed two glasses and the Pinot Grigio out of the wine fridge. I went back into the living room and sat the glasses down on the coffee table.

"…and well, he would come into the bar and he always flirted with me," Lilah said. "I wasn't exactly a model student so I kind of got kicked out of my dorm and he offered to let me live with him."

"He was involved in drugs back then as well?" Terrence asked.

"Yeah."

"Did the two of you do drugs together?"

"Yeah." Lilah looked down.

"Hey," Terrence said. "There's no judgment here. Okay?"

"Yeah."

"What kind of drugs did you do?"

"You name it," she said. "I've probably done it at least once."

"How interesting you ended up with a DEA agent," Terrence said and smiled.

"I know, right?" I commented. They both looked over to me and I held up my hands. "Sorry."

"I no longer do drugs," Lilah said as she looked over to me. "Unlike some people I know."

"Just wait until you have children," I told Terrence.

"Children make you do drugs?" he asked me. I could see the smile behind his question even though he wasn't showing it.

"And a million other things you never thought you'd do," I answered. "And every now and then it turns out to be something illegal."

"Do you want to stay for dinner?" Lilah asked, changing the subject. Probably to keep me from being arrested.

"I'd love to," Terrence said. "Thank you for asking. I'm sure there are some nice restaurants around here, but I don't know about any of them yet." Lilah smiled.

"I'm sure Adrian would love for you to stay," she said, and he smiled in return. I couldn't tell if it was agreement or surprise.

"What was Mr. McCain's connection with the drug community back then? Do you know?"

"I know he had a lot of…" She held up her hands in quotations. "…friends. They were always in the bar with him."

"Did you know any of them personally?"

"A few."

"Would you be comfortable giving me names?"

"Sure," she said. "If I can remember." She put her fingers to her temples. "Angel something."

"Ramirez?" Terrence asked.

"Yes," Lilah confirmed. "Another guy, Luther."

"Luther Brown?"

"Yes," Lilah said. "It seems you already know."

"Some of them," he confirmed. "I just wondered how far back he went with these people."

"A long way," Lilah said.

"Yeah. Did you know then where McCain's drug supply came from?"

"No," Lilah said. "He would leave sometimes and not come back for days, but he never told me where he was going. Most of the time he didn't even tell me he was going."

"Out of town?"

"Pretty sure, yes. But I don't know where."

"It's okay," Terrence said. "This is an investigation. Every little bit helps. What kind of drugs did McCain sell? Do you know?"

"Pretty much anything you wanted," Lilah told him. "Mainly heroin, though."

"Is that what you did?"

"Mostly," Lilah admitted. "I guess you know how expensive that habit can be."

"I do," Terrence said. "Did being with McCain pay for your drug habit?"

I took a deep breath. I didn't know how long it had been since Lilah had said these things out loud and I wondered what kind of toll it would take on her. She looked down again.

"Yes."

"So, he used your addiction against you."

"Yeah," she said. "I guess."

"What happened between the two of you?" Terrence asked.

"What do you mean?"

"Why did you go your separate ways?"

"I...well...I decided I couldn't do it anymore," she said. "I... just...I..."

She put her hands over her face, and I wanted to go over and sit beside her and hold her hand, but I wasn't sure if it was appropriate in this situation or if she would even want me to. Sometimes Lilah was affectionate with the people she loved. Other times, she didn't want to be touched.

"I..." she continued. "I called Isabel." She glanced over to me. "And she came and got me and took me back to her apartment and helped me through my withdrawal. She helped me get back on my feet." Terrence looked over to me.

"I think now I might understand your friendship a little better," he said and smiled. I nodded.

"I always thought McCain would come after me, but he never did," Lilah said.

It was then I thought about Ben. Would Lilah tell Terrence that McCain was Ben's father?

"Do you think it was because he couldn't find you?" Terrence asked.

"No," Lilah said. "He could've found me. He could find anyone."

"Do you think he's here in Woodlawn because of you or his son?" Terrence asked.

She doesn't have a choice, I thought. Terrence already knew about Ben. I saw the horror on Lilah's face. This time I got up and walked over to her and sat down on the arm of her chair. I put my arm around her shoulders, and she began to cry so I rubbed her back.

"Does Adrian know?" she managed.

"I'm not sure," Terrence said. "I think he probably has the same questions but like I told you we haven't collaborated yet."

Lilah looked up to me as if to ask permission. I shrugged and shook my head. I couldn't tell her what to do. I didn't know what to tell her. I didn't know what was best. Did we acknowledge it? I think it was the first time I hadn't been able to give Lilah an answer. It was the first time I didn't know the answer because I always knew the answer. I knew it because even though Lilah knew it, too, she wouldn't acknowledge it. Even to herself. She once told me it was how she stayed sane.

"Ben doesn't know," she finally said.

"I'm sorry," Terrence said. "Who is Ben?"

Lilah looked up to me again and I shook my head. She got up.

"I'm sorry," she said. "I have to excuse myself for a moment."

"Lilah?" I called after her. She waved her hand behind her.

"I'm fine," she said. "Talk to Terrence." I looked back to Terrence. It suddenly dawned on me what question needed to be asked.

"What is McCain's son's name?" I asked.

"Oh," Terrence said. "I'm sorry. I thought you knew." I just stared at him. "He's Bret's father."

It was the first time in my life I'd ever felt faint. I slid down into the chair where Lilah had been sitting, leaned over on my knees and rubbed my temples with my fingers.

"Are you okay?" Terrence asked me.

"Yeah," I said. "Yeah, I'm good."

Dear God, I prayed. Tell me what to do. Like, right now. Tell me now. And, by the way, thank you for taking Lilah out of this room.

"Isabel," Terrence called. "Sit up. Look at me. I need to know you're okay." I sat up.

"I'm okay."

"What is it?" he asked. "What are you not telling me?"

"She doesn't know," I told him.

"She doesn't know what?" he asked me.

"She doesn't know McCain is Bret's father," I said quietly. "Neither did I, in fact, until now."

"Are you telling me McCain has another son?" he asked. I stared at him again.

"You're good at your job," I commented.

"I like to think so," he said. "Who?"

"I can't tell you," I said.

"Why not?"

"Because no one knows," I whispered.

"Who's no one?" he asked. "Because I know you don't really mean no one. Obviously, you know and I'm thinking Lilah does also so saying no one knows is not factual."

"You're not as handsome as you were when you got here," I commented. He smiled.

"I need you to tell me the truth, Isabel," he said.

Ben came down the stairs into the living room. I wondered if it was God answering my prayer or the devil just fucking with me.

"Hi," he said as he walked over to Terrence. He extended his hand. "You must be Terrence. Adrian talks about you all the time."

"That's scary," Terrence said as he took Ben's hand.

"It's all good," Ben said and smiled.

"You are?" Terrence asked.

"Oh, sorry," Ben replied. "I'm Ben. Lilah's son."

Terrence looked over to me and I warned him with my eyes. He looked back to Ben.

"Good to meet you, man," he said. "Adrian talks about you, too."

"Also, scary," Ben said and laughed.

Lilah came back into the living room.

"What's scary?" she asked, and I could tell she was terrified to hear the answer.

She was afraid Terrence had figured it out. She was afraid Ben knew, too. Not what you think, I thought. If there was such a thing as telepathy, I wished for it. She looked to me and I shook my head slightly so no one else would notice. I watched the relief flood over her face as she realized that no, Ben did not know. But Terrence knew and I would have to tell Lilah Terrence knew. I had no choice because if I didn't tell her he undoubtedly would. The scariest part was I had no way of knowing when that would be.

Whenever there is bad news to be delivered to Lilah, I am always the messenger. I am the messenger because I know how to handle Lilah. I know what you can and can't say to her. I know how to break devastating news without devastating her. No one has ever understood the relationship Lilah and I have but it's based on us understanding one another in ways no one else ever could. Not Eric. Not Tom. Not even

Adrian. So, my first point of action was to make sure Terrence did not tell Lilah or Adrian what he knew. Lilah needed to tell Adrian about Ben but there was a lot of work to be done between us before she'd be able to do it. For the time being, we could keep our secret. Except now one other person knew. It always happens that way. One person knows, then two, then three. Then it's not a secret anymore.

It's just a lie.

McCain

There is a specific time for everything when you are in jail. Breakfast: 4:30 a.m.; Commons Room: 9:30 a.m. – 10:30 a.m.; Lunch: 11:30 a.m.; Recreation: 1:30 p.m. – 2:30 p.m.; Dinner: 5:30 p.m.; Phone calls: anywhere between 7:30 p.m. – 10:00 p.m.; Lights out: 11:00 p.m.

I guess it goes without saying that the phone call time used to be the most dreaded part of my day because I had no one to call. But not this time because I was going to call Lilah.

"Hello?" she said. Her voice. Her voice was like the voice of an angel.

"Hi," I said.

"Who is this?" she asked. And not in a friendly way.

"It's McCain."

Silence. Nothing. No surprised response. No mad response. No response at all. But she didn't hang up.

"Are you there?" I said after a bit.

"Yes."

"Can we talk for a minute? I really want to talk to you."

"You only have eight minutes," she told me. I chuckled.

"How do you know that?"

"Because Vonnie was in jail this past summer and that's what she told me."

"Well, she's right."

"I know."

"How are you doing?"

"Is that really your first question?" she asked. "Hold on. I need to go outside on the porch."

So, she did want to talk to me. Otherwise she would have hung up by now.

"I almost didn't answer," she said. "But you know how they come on the line and say it's from the department of corrections and ask if I will accept the charges?"

"Did they say my name?"

"No. I just thought it might be one of mine or Isabel's kids." I chuckled again. "It's not funny. That is not out of the question. They do the craziest things all the time so you never truly know with them."

"It's good to hear your voice." Silence. "I mean, it's just been so long and I wasn't sure whether you would talk to me or hang up on me." Silence.

"What happened after I left, McCain?" she asked.

"I waited around for a week or so hoping you would come back but then I talked to Leslie and he told me about his talk with you at the bar."

"The talk where he told me to look at myself in the mirror?"

"Yeah. After he told me that I knew why you had left and I knew you weren't coming back."

"I'm sorry," she said. "I just couldn't live that way anymore."

"I get it. Truthfully, I do."

"Did you look for me?" she asked.

Silence. On my part this time. I took a deep breath and let it back out.

"I wanted to," I said. "But I thought if I did, you'd just tell me you didn't want me anymore. I didn't want to hear that come out of your mouth. I mean, if I didn't hear then I could always have the hope that maybe Leslie was wrong."

"I'm sorry."

"Don't be sorry. I understand." Silence, then, "I did look for you a few years later but I guess by then you'd gotten married and had a different name."

"Yeah."

"Are you happy?" I asked. "You looked happy at the talent show."

"Yeah."

I thought about asking her about Adrian at this point but I didn't. It wouldn't have been in my favor anyway because she'd probably tell him and then I'd be in a bigger mess than I already was.

"You have three minutes remaining," the computer-generated operator said.

"You have three minutes remaining," Lilah repeated and I could tell by her voice she was smiling.

"Do you think we could talk again some other time? I mean, would it be okay if I call you again?"

"Yeah," she said. "Just hang up if someone else answers, though."

"Isn't this your cell phone number?" I asked.

"Yeah but I'm always leaving my phone laying around and sometimes one of the kids or Eric will answer it for me. Well, Eric used to answer it for me."

"Eric is your husband?"

"He was."

"Oh, you got a divorce?" I asked.

"Yeah."

If I hadn't already been in Woodlawn and already knew she was with Adrian I would've taken that as good news but I could tell she and Adrian were in love. I could tell by watching them together at the talent show.

"I'm sorry." I said.

"Well, you know. Things happen."

"Yeah." Silence. Then, "So, my time is probably almost up."

"Yeah."

"But I'll talk to…"

"You have zero time remaining…"

Click.

Vonnie

"Hey!" I told Hunter as we laid on the sofa together. "Quit it!!" He nuzzled his face into my neck, but he took his hand away from where it had been.

"Come on, Von."

"Don't call me that!!"

"You let Adrian call you that," he reminded me.

"Only because I like him more than you," I teased. I slid my leg up between his and he kissed my warm lips.

"Oh yeah?"

"Oh yeah," I repeated.

"You've kind of got me in a delicate situation right now."

"Do I?"

"Uh-huh." He kissed my collarbone. "But I'm paying attention."

"You should keep paying attention," I told him. He looked up to me.

"You'll give in eventually," he said.

"You think?" I asked. "Because at this point, the only reason I have for holding out is knowing how badly you want it."

"So, you can keep the upper hand."

"You bet," I said and laughed.

He unbuttoned my shirt down to my navel and kissed just below my breasts. I rested my hands on the back of his neck. I was taking a chance by being on the sofa with him in the living room but taking him up to my room was out of the question so I had to work with what I had. He unbuttoned the top button of my jeans.

"What did I tell you?" I asked. I smacked at his hand. "I can't do that here."

"Where can you do it?" I pushed him off me and stood up, buttoned my jeans.

"Want a wine cooler?" I asked.

"Sure," he said as he sat up.

He rearranged himself as he watched me walk into the kitchen. When I opened the refrigerator, Ben walked through the back door. He took one look at me with my unbuttoned shirt and walked directly into the living room. He picked Hunter up off the sofa by his collar and punched him in the face before I even had a chance to intervene.

"Ben!!" I yelled as I ran into the living room behind him. "Stop it!"

"You better stay the hell off my sister, man. What the fuck??"

"She..." Hunter started. He wiped his bloody nose.

"She what?" Ben shouted. "She started it. Is that what you were going to say?"

"No..."

Ben turned to me.

"Get your ass upstairs," he said as he pointed to me.

"You're not my parent!!" I yelled at him.

"You better get up those fucking stairs right now before I put Mr. Romance in the hospital."

"You're not telling me what to do," I said, and he grabbed me by my arm.

"I'm not kidding, Vonnie."

"What are you going to do?" I asked. "Beat him up just because he likes your little sister? Huh?"

"Hey man," Hunter said to Ben as he tucked his shirt into his jeans. "No hard feelings. I understand how you feel. I have a little sister, too."

"Do you?" Ben asked as he stepped toward him. "Is she at home fucking her boyfriend on the sofa right now?"

I could immediately see the anger on Hunter's face. He grabbed Ben by the front of his t-shirt and pushed him to the floor. Before I knew it, they were in a full-blown fist fight.

"Hey!!" Adrian yelled as he came down the steps. "Stop it!! Now!!"

Mom came down behind him. When I looked up to her, she motioned for me to button my shirt. Adrian came over and pulled Ben off Hunter. Hunter jumped up and tried to grab Ben again. Adrian stepped between them, holding both at arm's length by the front of their shirts.

"What the hell is wrong with you guys?" he asked.

"You better tell this motherfucker to keep his hands off my sister," Ben said.

"I love your sister!" Hunter yelled.

He loved me??

"You just want to get in her fucking pants," Ben yelled back.

It amazed me Adrian hadn't said anything else at this point. He just stood between them to keep them from killing one another.

"You have no clue what you're talking about," Hunter said as he wiped the blood from his nose. "I respect your sister."

"The hell you do," Ben countered.

Adrian looked back and forth between them.

"You want to counter?" he asked Hunter.

"Well, fuck yeah, I do," Hunter said. He looked to Ben. "Just because you fuck everything with pants on doesn't mean every guy does. You have no respect for girls at all!"

Ben struggled to get away from Adrian, but Adrian held him in place.

"This is a verbal confrontation," Adrian said to Ben. "Keep your hands to yourself. And let's stop with the 'f' word and have a more civilized conversation."

Mom and I looked at each other. She smiled, happily acknowledging her trust in Adrian. I smiled, too. He was one of the best things that had happened to our family in a long time.

"Closing words?" Adrian asked Ben.

"Stay the hell away from my sister," Ben told Hunter.

"And you?" Adrian asked Hunter.

"Stay the hell out of my business."

"My sister is MY business," Ben retorted.

Adrian looked to Hunter.

"He's not wrong," Adrian said, and Ben smiled. Then he turned to Ben. "But you need to understand that Hunter is not about hurting your sister. I believe he genuinely cares for Vonnie, so you need to chill out."

"Why the fuck…"

"Not the 'f' word," Adrian interrupted. "Use another word."

"Why do I need to chill with my own sister?" Ben asked. "She's my responsibility."

"No, I'm not," I said as I brought my hands to my chest. "Since when am I your responsibility??"

"Since Dad left," he said to me and Mom sucked in her breath, brought her hands to her face.

"Why don't you let Vonnie be your Mom's responsibility?" Adrian asked. "It's not in your job description."

Hunter looked to me and I shook my head, looked down.

"Hey," Hunter said to Ben and Ben looked up to him. "I get it."

Ben just stared at him. Adrian let go of their shirts.

"I've never really had a Dad," Hunter continued. "So, I know how you feel about Vonnie." Ben still only stared at him. "Man, I care about your sister. I'm not gonna hurt her. I promise."

"Rebuttal?" Adrian inquired of Ben.

"Yeah," Ben said. "Okay."

Mom walked down the steps from the landing where she'd been standing. She went over to Ben and opened her arms.

"Thank you," she said to him, and he wrapped his arms around her. If I hadn't known any better, I might have thought Ben was becoming a little softer around the edges.

"Thank you??" Hunter said unbelievingly as he held up his hands. "He was about to beat the shit out of me."

Ben pulled away from Mom and pointed at Hunter.

"Don't forget that," he said. "Because I still can."

"So, can I," Adrian said as he looked to Ben. "Don't forget that."

"Right," Ben said.

"Shake hands," Adrian told them both.

"Fuck, no," Ben said.

"Ben," Mom added. "Do it."

"Why??" Ben asked her.

"Because it is more than obvious Hunter cares about your sister. Give him the benefit of the doubt unless he proves you wrong."

Michael walked through the front door looking like he'd just come out of a wind tunnel. His shirt was buttoned crooked and the corner of it stuck out of the zipper of his jeans. Sparkly pink lip gloss coated his lips.

"Well, someone had a good night," Ben said. "Did you finally get in Chantal's pants?"

I could tell Hunter was trying not to laugh. So was I. And Adrian. And Mom.

"What??" Michael said. "Why is whatever going on here suddenly about me?"

"Because apparently your luck is much better than mine," Hunter commented.

"No joke," Ben added and laughed. Michael grinned.

"Both of you can suck it," he said and laughed.

Adrian looked over to Mom and winked. "Since everyone else is getting lucky tonight, wanna go upstairs with me and…you know?"

"I would love to," she answered as she held out her hand.

"Gross," Michael said.

"I love this family," Hunter told me, and Ben laughed.

Adrian

A couple of days later while I sat at what Jenny said was my temporary desk at the station in Richmond, I pondered Tiffany's advice. Karen had emailed me all the documents I needed from my current case in Amityville and despite the need to exercise my critical thinking skills I couldn't get past Lilah's involvement with McCain.

She knew I knew about their relationship in college because I'd told her and she'd confirmed it but she hadn't offered me any other information in return and I hadn't asked. Maybe I should have asked but I can sense Lilah's moods and as soon as I brought up McCain's name her eyes had darkened. It wasn't fear. It was uncertainty laced with, as odd as it might sound, arrogance. There were things that happened with her and McCain she didn't want me to know. But why wouldn't she want to tell me? What if she knew things about McCain no one else did? What if those things would affect the outcome of the case?

The thought crossed my mind that McCain had placed Bret here to seduce Vonnie and in the process get to Lilah. Was he that clever and strong-willed? Would he go to the extreme of placing his son in a dangerous situation to get to the woman he claimed to love? Did he hold a grudge against Lilah for leaving him? Had he been looking for her all this time? Certainly, he'd found her a long time ago and just recently decided to contact her. But why? Was he mentally unstable or just determined?

Tiffany told me I should talk to Lilah again. Not to find out what she knew but to find out if she was even aware of what was going on. I didn't want to scare her but I did want to prepare her for whatever might happen. Isabel would have my head. She was the one who always said not to upset Lilah. Well, Lilah was a grown woman and while I was all for protecting her, I also thought her being unaware might just be more dangerous. Maybe I shouldn't only talk to Lilah. Maybe I should talk to Isabel, too. Talking to Jenny about all these possibilities was inevitable as well.

Now I found myself in a situation where I had two cases, not just one, but two cases that were personal to me. Despite Jenny dismissing me from the Woodlawn case I wasn't entirely dismissed because I knew things no one else did. I thought about how wonderful it would be to put McCain, Bret, Luther and Gianni all in one cell and practice my shooting skills. Terrence once asked me if I could kill someone and get away with it, would I? My answer then was, of course not, and I meant it. But now my answer had changed. I could think of several people I'd like to kill and if Nana had been around for me to confess that to, she would have assured me I was going to hell. Nana's words were always soft and comforting, like an old favorite blanket. But if she thought your soul was in danger they could become as sharp as a knife. She held nothing back if she felt you weren't right with God.

I remember the time she sat me down and talked to me about forgiveness. She used the two criminals on the crosses beside Jesus as an example. I was a smart kid and Nana said I was almost always too logical but I didn't want someone to tell me what to believe. I wanted someone to tell me why I should believe it. I asked her why Jesus would want to forgive a criminal who'd spent his entire life hurting and deceiving other people. I asked her how it was fair he got to go to heaven at the last minute after all he'd done. She told me Jesus forgave him as an example to us about how we should always forgive the people who hurt us. No matter what they do. A sin is a sin, she'd said. But forgiveness is also forgiveness. There are no degrees of either one. She'd told me justice was paid by the Lord, not by people here on earth. I thought about that now. I remember asking her back in high school after Gianni beat me up if she thought he would ever get the justice he deserved and she nodded enthusiastically.

"Of course, he will."

"Well, I'd like to give it to him myself," I told her.

"Oh, my sweet boy," she'd said. "Do you want to forfeit your right to heaven by doing something now the Lord will do Himself in His own time?"

That was a loaded question.

"When will He do it?" I'd ask. "Because I want to be there." She'd laughed.

I was still waiting and I still wanted to be there. Then I had a horrible thought. I thought now I was in a position where I could kill Gianni and get away with it. But Nana's words instantly flooded my heart and I regretted that thought.

"Dear God," I prayed silently. "Please forgive me for thinking what I just did." Jenny touched me on my shoulder and I jumped.

"Whatcha dreaming about, lover boy?"

"Jeez, Jenny," I said. "You scared me to death."

"I just got off the phone with Lorelei." I leaned back in my chair and ran my hands through my hair. Just what I needed. More complications to my already sordid life.

"And?"

"You need to get back to Amityville." She laid her hand on my shoulder. "Gianni is in the City."

"New York City?" I asked. Jenny nodded.

"Yes, and I don't think I have to tell you Lorelei is terrified."

"She called you?"

"Yeah. I've already put out an APB on Gianni because I didn't want to waste any time but this is your case and you need to be up there to deal with it."

"Why didn't she call me?"

"I don't know."

"What is it?" she asked as she stood up. I took a deep breath and ran my hand over my mouth. I searched my pockets for my phone. Shit. I'd left it in my car.

"I have a few things I have to deal with before I can go."

"Such as?"

"Can I talk to you in private?"

"Of course," she said. "Come on." I followed her down the long corridor to the opposite end of the building and into the glass cubicle she was using for an office.

"What's up?" she said as she sat down at her desk. I sat down in front of her and leaned forward with my elbows on my knees but I didn't say anything for a minute.

"I'm worried about Lilah," I finally said as I looked up to her. "I don't know anything about her involvement with McCain."

"Have you asked her?" Jenny inquired.

"No," I told her as I sat back in my chair. "I mean, I told her I knew about her relationship with him in college and she confirmed it but I don't want to freak her out and I get the feeling that whatever happened between them back then freaks her out. I don't think I have to tell you I'm worried about leaving her here without me."

"Adrian," Jenny said. "I've been thinking about something I know you are going to hate."

"What?"

"Just hear me out, okay?"

"Alright."

"I've been wondering whether you need to just take a little time off…" I started to speak and she held up her hand. "Wait. Just listen for a minute. Okay?"

"Okay."

"You are amazing at what you do and I don't give compliments very often. You know that."

"Yeah."

"So, when I say you're amazing at what you do it means you're amazing at what you do."

"Thanks," I said and smiled.

"You work hard, you always close your cases, you put everything into your work. You have from day one. I don't want you to think I fail to recognize these things."

"Yeah."

"But I think it might be in your best interest to take a little break."

"Maybe," I said. I crossed my ankle over my knee.

"When was the last time you took a vacation?"

"What's vacation?" I asked and chuckled.

"See?" she said. "That's what I mean."

"Okay." I leaned forward on my knees again and looked to the floor.

"Terrence and I have everything covered here," Jenny told me. "Look at me." I looked up. "I know what you're thinking."

"You always claim to know what I'm thinking," I said.

"You're thinking about Lorelei."

"Yep."

"Go to Amityville," Jenny instructed.

"I thought you wanted me to take a vacation," I said and smiled.

"After this."

"Yeah." I laughed. "That's what I thought."

"Don't tell Lorelei everything."

"Come on, Jenny. You know me better than that."

"Give her as much information as you feel is safe," she said. "You know what is confidential and what is critical and what you can safely acknowledge."

"Yeah." I looked down again.

"Comfort her." I looked up and grinned. "Not like that." I chuckled. "And tell her you've had some things arise down here you need to deal with…." She hesitated. "That is not a lie. That is the truth. Do not tell her anything about Lilah and McCain."

"Well, good grief, Jenny, I'm not stupid."

"Just making sure we're on the same page."

"We are."

"Good."

"Hey, look, Jenny. I was thinking about how to approach McCain – before all this happened."

"You mean before you caused me an immense amount of grief and possible backlash?" I looked down.

"Yeah. I'm sorry about that."

"You gotta control your emotions, Adrian. You always have before but this is too personal which is why you need to be out of it."

"I know but I wanna talk to McCain one more time."

"No."

"Come on, Jenny. I know how to work him. I know what he cares about."

I also knew what I cared about: Lilah. If Jenny would let me talk to him, I could solve my own problem of leaving Lilah alone and close this case all at once.

"Adrian, asking me to put you in a room with him again is like asking me to turn in my resignation."

"I promise you, Jenny. It won't be like that. Let me redeem myself."

"Redeem yourself??" she asked and raised her eyebrows.

"Just let me talk to him. Please."

"I get the feeling this means a lot to you."

"Yeah," I said and nodded. She fell back in her chair.

"Damn it," she said as she brought her hands to her head then ran them through her hair. She pointed at me. "You fuck this up and both of us will be looking for another job. You got me?"

"Yes."

"I am only doing this because…"

"I'm amazing at what I do," I said and grinned.

"Give you one compliment and this is what happens," she said. I shrugged. "I'm not sending you in there by yourself. If I let you do it you must agree to having two other officers in there with you. No one on one."

"Okay."

"When do you want to do this?"

"Your call," I said.

"Alright." She stood up from her desk. "Let me think about it. You know what you want to say?"

"Not really," I admitted. "You know I'm better talking to people on the spur of the moment."

"You freak me out when you say shit like that," Jenny said. She smiled. "But I love you for it. I'll get Base and Tina to go in there with you."

"Oh, come on, Jenny." I stood up. "Not Base."

"Why not?"

"Because he's an asshole," I said. I followed her down the hallway.

"That's exactly why I want him. Just because you're going to be nice doesn't mean McCain will be and I'm not having the two of you in a fist fight again over a piece of ass."

"Jeez, Jenny. Can you please not refer to Lilah as a piece of ass?"

"Well, as far as I'm concerned with you and McCain that's exactly what she is." I scratched the back of my neck. "No offense."

"Okay."

"Work it all up," she said as she turned around to face me. "Get things moving. I'm going to the hotel bar for happy hour." I looked at my watch.

"At 3:30?"

"Who's the boss?" she asked. "Me or you?"

"You," I said. "Definitely you."

I turned the corner and walked toward the front office. There was always paperwork. Before anything else, paperwork.

"Hey Smarty Pants!" Jenny called from around the corner. I turned and she held up the coffee cup she was holding in her hand. "Here's to hoping you can win over McCain." She paused. "I'll tell you what… you get anything pertinent out of him…and I mean, major…we'll talk about a raise."

Lilah safe *and* a pay raise. I didn't think there could ever be a better incentive than that. I grinned and pointed to her.

"Done."

Lilah

"You know," Isabel said. "It really sucks I have to do happy hour all by myself now. It makes me feel like an alcoholic. You know they say when you drink alone…." She poured vodka into her glass. "…it's a sign you're an alcoholic."

"I'm with you in mind and spirit," I told her. "Just not body."

"We used to drink wine when we were pregnant before," she said. "And you had a glass of wine when Terrence interviewed you. I don't see what the big deal is…I mean, I'm not suggesting we do frozen shots of tequila."

"That would be good, though," I agreed.

"Yes," she said and took a sip of her drink. "Yes, it would."

"Isabel," I said tucking my foot up underneath of me. "I'm almost forty. I'm freaking out over the fact I'm pregnant at this age."

"Women have babies at our age every day, Lilah."

"I wasn't even trying to get pregnant," I told her. "And I just, I don't know, I feel like it's an omen or something."

"You getting pregnant without trying to get pregnant is an omen??" She took another sip of her drink.

"Yeah, I mean. I had to try for my babies. I wasn't like you."

"I hear ya."

"Remember I wanted another baby after Vonnie was born and it took me nearly ten years until I got pregnant with Maria. Do you not find that weird??? That now, suddenly, I'm not trying and not only that, I was trying to prevent it, and this is when I get pregnant. Is that not strange to you?"

"Maybe manly man has extra powerful spermatozoa," she commented.

"What did you just call him??" I asked and laughed. She grinned.

"Manly man."

"Oh, Isabel…"

"Well, he is," she said.

"Hey, hey, hey," someone said as they came through Isabel's front door. "I come bearing gifts." Tiffany came around the corner.

"What have you been up to??" Isabel asked. "You look like the cat that just swallowed the canary."

"I bought something for Lilah," she said. She handed me a blue shopping bag. Robin's egg blue. Tiffany blue.

"You are so sweet," I told her as I stood up. I hugged her. "Thank you, Tiff. What in the world is it??" I sat back down in my chair and untied the ribbon that attached the two handles together and pulled away the tissue paper. Inside was a big, blue Tiffany box.

"Well," Tiffany said. "I saw something you and Adrian's baby needs to have. I was going to give it to you when we had a baby shower but I'm not so good at waiting so here it is now." I laughed and pulled the box out of the bag. "Louis Tiffany has a very special place in our family," she explained. "Fairy Tale is full of Tiffany chandeliers, lamps, dishes, everything you could ever imagine. Nana was obsessed with Tiffany."

"An expensive obsession," Isabel commented.

"Well, yes," Tiffany said. "But she earned it."

"Is that why your mother named you Tiffany?" Isabel asked. "Because of Nana's love of Tiffany things?"

Tiffany stiffened. Her breath quickened. Her mother. Adrian's mother. The woman who had abused the man I loved. He hadn't told me much about her other than what I'd read in Nana's journal but he'd told me enough to know she wouldn't have done anything for anyone except herself.

"No," Tiffany answered as she looked down. She looked back up to Isabel as if she had remembered something she hadn't thought about in a long time. Suddenly Tiffany wasn't the Tiffany I knew anymore. She was a protector. Someone's confidant to a dangerous secret. I watched her.

"She…" Tiffany hesitated. "My mother was a complicated woman. Let's just leave it at that for now but it wasn't because of Nana."

"May I open this?" I asked trying to change the subject.

"Yes," she said. "Wait! You know I'm going to be the aunt who spoils this baby completely rotten, right?"

"I can only assume," I said. "Since you're giving it Tiffany before it's even born."

"Nothing but the best for the Bennett's," she said and smiled.

I untied the wide white ribbon from around the box and took off the top. Isabel peered over my shoulder. Inside was an almost 12" inch teddy bear with Tiffany blue paws and a Return to Tiffany Love tag. It was the softest teddy bear I'd ever held in my hands. I looked at the tag. Mohair. Whose child has a mohair teddy bear??? Mine and Adrian's child. That's who.

"Oh my gosh, Tiff," I said. "Why did you do this?"

"Because I can," she said.

Isaac walked into the living room with a Slurpee.

"You did it, didn't you?" he asked.

"I did," she admitted as he walked over and handed me the Slurpee. "It's nice to know someone can afford a Tiffany teddy bear." Tiffany smacked at him. "I can only afford a Slurpee but I have a question."

"What is it?" I asked him and laughed.

"Do you love me less because I'm poor??"

"Oh, stop it," I said. I stood up and hugged him. "You know how much I love you."

"Lilah saved me from a herd of wild antelopes once," he told Tiffany.

"It wasn't antelopes," Isabel said, rolling her eyes. "It was goats and we were at the petting zoo at Maymont Park. You exaggerate everything."

"They came after me," Isaac said. "Right? Lilah, you remember?"

"I do." I looked to Isabel. "And they did come after him." She walked over to the bar to fix herself another drink.

"They came after him because he had his pockets full of corn," she said. "I told him not to fill his pockets with corn but he didn't listen so he got what he deserved. It's not like they were killer goats. They were babies."

"They weren't babies," Isaac said. "They were bigger than me."

"Of course, they were bigger than you," Isabel countered. "You were four."

"Aw," Tiffany said to Isaac as she looked over to him. "That's so sweet."

"It wasn't sweet," he said. "They tried to eat my clothes off!" We all laughed.

"And what did you learn?" Isabel asked him as she came back and sat down in her chair.

"Not to put corn in my pockets when I'm around goats," he said and smiled.

"Yep," she said. "You're welcome. Life lesson."

"I love this," I told Tiffany as I held out the teddy bear. I hugged her. "Thank you."

"You're welcome," she said. "Once we find out whether it's a boy or a girl, we can pick out a baby ring."

"Since when do babies wear rings?" Isaac asked as he turned to her.

"Not all the time," she said. "Only for formal photographs."

Isabel looked over to me and I shrugged. We took our kids to Walmart for pictures. Occasionally we got one where someone wasn't crying.

"Remember the year Ben smacked the Easter Bunny in the face?" Isaac asked and laughed.

"With his lollipop," I clarified.

"That was hilarious," Isabel said and laughed with him. "Shut down the photo booth for an hour."

"We should do that again," Isaac said. "When was the last time we all had a picture taken together?"

"Great idea," Isabel said as she pointed to him. "We should take one soon since everyone has gotten so much older."

"Nana had a photographer who always came to the Inn to take family pictures," Tiffany explained. "I don't think we ever went to see the Easter Bunny."

"What??" Isaac asked. "You were deprived of the Easter Bunny?" Tiffany smiled.

"I don't think we were deprived," she said. "Nana always said Easter was about the resurrection."

"That's when Jesus went to heaven, right?" Isaac asked.

"You know what the resurrection is," Isabel said. "Don't make me look like a complete heathen."

"What about Santa Claus?" he asked Tiffany. "Did you go see Santa Claus?"

"Father Christmas," she told him.

"Who is Father Christmas?" I asked. She shrugged.

"He used to come to the Inn every year for Nana's Christmas parties and take pictures with the guests."

"So, you didn't go see Santa Claus?" Isaac asked.

"What difference does it make?" she asked. "Gosh. You act like Christmas is just all about the presents."

"It's not?"

"I'm gonna smack you," Isabel told him and he laughed.

"I'm just kidding, Mom." He looked over to Tiffany. "Do you have plans tonight?"

"Uh…" She looked upward. "No."

"Why do the two of you act like you're not together?" Isabel asked.

"It's not me!" Tiffany said. "But I think Isaac is still getting used to the fact he only has one girlfriend." She laughed as she looked over to him and shook his head.

"You should stay with us tonight," he said.

"No," Isabel said. "She can keep staying at Lilah's like we agreed. And you better not be thinking about wandering around in the middle of the night."

"What makes you think anything like that would happen?" Isaac asked. He brought his hand to his chest. "Tiff and I are just friends."

"Right," I said. "I've never known you to be just friends with *any* girl."

"Wow," he said. "Thanks, Lilah."

"Friends with benefits," Tiffany said and smiled. Isaac motioned back and forth between them.

"Is that what we are?" he asked her and grinned.

"Is that what you want us to be?" she asked him.

"How about we do the friend part now and I'll take you out to dinner," he said.

"No benefits later," Isabel said shaking her finger at them. Tiffany smiled at Isaac.

"He should only be so lucky," she said.

Isabel was fifteen when she lost her virginity. It didn't happen for me until after I turned sixteen but Isabel is always ahead of the curve when it comes to sex. She told me the first time she had sex it felt like fireworks going off inside her which was a lie. I have never over the course of the last twenty-two years ever had sex when it felt like fireworks were going off inside of me. It feels good but not like fireworks.

Isabel later confessed she'd lied about the fireworks thing. When I ask her what it really felt like she told me if felt like a combination of good menstrual cramps (I didn't know there was such a thing) and peeing after you've had to hold it for a long time. She said my toes might involuntarily curl, but when she warned me I might pee myself, I got scared. It wasn't until much later in our sex lives we realized it wasn't pee. It was what Isabel calls a female ejaculation.

I never had that experience with a man until I was with Adrian but when it happened, I didn't remember what Isabel had told me and I did indeed think I had peed. I was mortified until Adrian assured me it was not pee. He seemed rather proud he could make me do it and

I remember wondering how on earth a high school boy would know about female ejaculation. I didn't ask him, of course. Because like I've said before – I don't ask questions that I don't necessarily want to know the answers to.

Isabel and I agree you're never going to have mind-blowing sex with someone the first time you make love with them. It might be exciting, sensual or satisfying or maybe it's all three but not mind-blowing. Not the first time. Good sex takes time with the same person over and over. Technically I guess you could be having sex with more than one person over and over and it could be mind-blowing but I think mind-blowing sex requires a soul connection and you can't have a soul connection with more than one man at a time. Trust me, I've tried.

When I have sex with Adrian it feels like an electrical current is coursing through my body. It's a spark that turns into a flame and gradually sweeps its way up my body. A lot of women claim the best sex comes when a man knows how to use what he's got. Adrian knows how to use what he's got and what he's got is, well, mind-blowing.

It was a while before I had an orgasm with Adrian simply because it's all about trust for me. I can pretend to have a good orgasm if I think a man's self-confidence is dependent upon it but I never have to pretend with Adrian. I know his self-esteem is not based on whether he can make me orgasm. Nowadays when we have sex it's impossible for me not to have one. And, yes, sometimes it does feel like good menstrual cramps and peeing after you've been holding it for a long time.

"What are we going to do when you're too fat for me to get on top?" he asked that night as I slipped under the covers beside him. I rubbed my hand over his bare chest. Sex with Adrian was never sex. It was making love. *Every single time.* I cuddled against him and he put his arm around me.

"When I am that pregnant and I emphasize pregnant, not fat…" He chuckled. "…I will get on top." He raised his eyebrows.

"I like that idea."

"Or you can get behind me," I suggested.

"I like that idea even better."

"Of course, you do."

"What do you think the baby thinks when we have sex?"

"Are you serious?" I asked looking up to him.

"Yeah," he said. "I want to know. I mean, is it like a tsunami? Does it hold its breath until it's over?"

"Adrian." He grabbed me and pulled me over on top of him, kissed my lips softly.

"I love you, Lilah," he said as he ran his fingers across my cheek. I laid down on his chest. "How does this work?"

"What?" I asked.

"Can I make love to you like I always do?"

"Uh…" I rose up to look at him. "What are you referring to?" He blushed. "Are you blushing??" I asked and laughed. He lowered his eyes. "You seriously *are* blushing, aren't you?" He smiled.

"Well, I've never actually said it out loud before."

"Goodness," I replied. "Are you sure you're twenty-seven?" He flipped me over. Just like he always did, when I least expected it and started unbuttoning my camisole.

"You know," he said. "I think we should just get rid of this altogether. Raise up."

"Adrian…"

All I got back from him was, "Mmm…"

"Shit," I breathed. It was a little louder than it should have been.

"Hey," he said as he moved down my body. "You know we aren't alone in this house. Vonnie and my sister, *my sister...*" he emphasized. "...are on the other side of that wall."

"Mmm-hmm." He kissed my stomach.

Adrian has the most beautiful lips. Soft, full, cherry red. Against his dark skin it is hypnotizing. I pulled his hair behind his neck because it was tickling my thighs.

"Just do it," I begged. "Come on, Tristan."

I felt him laugh against me. He thought it was funny I still called him Tristan sometimes. I'm glad he thought it was funny because it happened a lot more than I wanted to admit. Sometimes certain things he says or does isn't Adrian at all. They are Tristan. Adrian wouldn't do them but Tristan does. Like when he pinned me up against the outside of the house and had his way with me. And then there is that little part of me that senses what it felt like to think he was eighteen. It felt good to think a boy his age would still find me so attractive and it felt a little naughty. Okay, a lot naughty. The only person I would admit this to is Isabel but being naughty feels good. It's like you have a secret about something so amazing and you want to tell the whole world but you can't.

"I'm so close," I managed.

When you're with a man this way you most often wait impatiently because you have no idea whether he will be able to please you. I can remember lying in bed – or wherever I was – wondering if once I got there (sometimes it took longer than others) he would do it the right way. Most often my orgasms were met with disappointment. That's what happens when you masturbate on a regular basis. Men are sub-standard. But with Adrian there are no levels of concentration. There is only unadulterated bliss. Like now.

It's the dipping of a plane in a wind tunnel. The coolness of the Caribbean water surrounding my heated body. It's the thunder that surprises me out of nowhere. The warmth from the fire when I'm cold. The coolness in my throat from a menthol cigarette. A feather bed when I'm tired. The mirage when I'm thirsty. The dawn when the night has lasted way too long. I struggled for breath. He came back up my body and pressed his mouth onto mine.

"Mmm," I hummed against his lips.

"Was that good, baby?" he asked as he pushed himself inside of me. He moved against me slowly.

"You taste like flowers," I whispered as I ran my hands through his hair. He chuckled.

"I taste like you," he murmured.

"You do?"

"I have a confession to make," he said as he looked into my eyes.

I never knew when he looked at me this intently whether he was about to render good news or be seriously sarcastic, which happened a lot more often than you would think. Adrian is a serious guy but he also has a hilarious sense of humor.

"What's that?" I asked against his lips.

"Sometimes," he said sincerely. "When I'm missing you, I go into the bathroom and just pull out one of your feminine wipes and lick it." I slapped his arm.

"You're sick!!"

"What?" he asked. "Am I not supposed to do that? Is that weird?" I leaned up and kissed him and he smiled. "No, seriously. Is it weird??"

"Would you stop it?" I asked and laughed.

Me and Adrian. Full blown conversations during sex. I loved him so. He started to move against me again.

"Is it my turn?" he asked.

"Oh yeah," I said.

"Did you enjoy that?" he whispered.

"Uh...yeah..."

"Okay, good," he said. "Because this isn't going to take very long."

"Oh?"

"Like now..." he managed. He always locked our fingers together when it was about to happen for him so I knew he meant it. He held his breath as he pressed himself into me.

"Wow," I said afterward. "Have intercourse much?"

"The way you move," he said breathlessly. "It's just...holy cow..."

"Yeah?"

"Did you?" he asked. "I can never tell." I widened my eyes.

"You didn't give me enough time!!" He rolled off me and propped his head in his hand.

"I think it's about you being pregnant," he said.

"What's about me being pregnant?"

"The high. I mean, I think it subconsciously turns me on."

"You're weird," I concluded.

"We already know that," he said. "I lick feminine wipes in an attempt to not miss my girlfriend." He smiled, leaned over and kissed my neck then hopped up to take his after-sex shower. I grabbed my phone off the bedside table and texted Tiffany momentarily forgetting she was in the room next to me.

> *Me: How was dinner with Isaac?*
> *Tiffany: Good.*
> *Me: That's it?? Good??*
> *Tiffany: LOL. I don't kiss and tell.*

Me: *Ha! Have you talked to Adrian?*

Tiffany: *No. But I just heard him....and you.*

Me: *Holy cow.*

Tiffany: *LOL*

Me: *We should have a big breakfast in the AM. Surprise him.*

Tiffany: *Okay. For what?*

Me: *Just to say I love you. He'll be going back to Amityville soon.*

Tiffany: *When??*

Me: *He said in a few days.*

Tiffany: *Want me to help you?*

Me: *Wanna fry bacon?*

Tiffany: ☺ *Sure.*

Then I texted Isabel.

Me: *Come over in the AM for breakfast.*

Isabel: *Ugh. It's Sunday. I want to stay in bed and drink mimosas plus I need to grade chemistry tests.*

Me: *You better get your ass over here. I'll help you grade the tests later. We're going to surprise Adrian.*

Isabel: *With what?*

Me: *He's leaving in a few days. Don't you want to tell him bye?*

Isabel: *I just saw him today.*

Me: *Did you tell him bye?*

Isabel: *Ugh. Okay.*

Me: *What did Isaac say about his date with Tiff?*

Isabel: *He didn't come in here.*

Me: *He always comes in your room to tell you about his dates.*

Isabel: *I know.*

Me: *Then why didn't he??*

Isabel: Probably because he did what I told him not to do. I can always tell.

Me: What would that be?

Isabel:?????? Duh.

Me: Good Lord. I didn't hear them.

Isabel: Ugh. I'll see you in the morning. What time?

Me: Five.

Isabel: What??? Why???

Me: I'm just kidding. Eight. I love you.

Isabel: Love you, too. Although sometimes I wonder why.

Me: Is there an emoji for sticking out your tongue?

Isabel: You need to take a computer class.

Me: They don't teach you emojis in a computer class, you dingbat.

Isabel: Go to hell, Lilah. Want me to bring something in the AM?

Me: Just yourself.

Isabel: ☺

Then I texted Tiffany again.

Me: I heard you.

Tiffany: You're sick.

Me: LOL. Tell Isaac I heard him, too.

Tiffany: Did you really?

Me: No. But I just talked to Isabel.

Tiffany: She's like the Gestapo.

Me: Hahaha. Yep.

Adrian walked back into our bedroom. Completely naked.

The End.

Adrian

"Hey," Jenny said when I answered the phone.

"Hey, what's up? You back in New York?"

"Yeah," she said. "Where are you?"

"I'm still in Virginia."

"Why?" she asked.

"Because I need to talk to McCain??"

"Oh, right," she said. "Out of sight, out of mind. Let me know how it goes because…"

"…my raise is dependent upon it."

"Yeah, and I hate to do this to ya," she said. "But we've got a huge bust here day after tomorrow not to mention Lorelei has called me fifty times asking when you're coming back."

"I know. She called me, too."

"Did you comfort her?" Jenny asked and chuckled.

"Ha. If I show up for the bust will I get a bigger raise?"

"Doubtful. You're good but you're not that good."

"Well, I'm going to show you how good I am when I talk to McCain tomorrow."

"You're awfully confident," Jenny said.

"I'm always confident. You have to be confident going into certain situations if you want them to go your way."

"I like that attitude," she said.

"I know. By the way, did you also know I am in the process of having a delicious breakfast with all the people I love the most right now?"

Lilah walked through the kitchen and I grabbed her by her waist and pulled her into me, kissed her forehead.

"I can't do this without you, Adrian. You've been working these guys and I just got a tip from an anonymous caller."

"Gotta love an anonymous caller. Are you talking about Carlos and his boys?"

"Yep."

"Damn. Okay."

"You wanna fly back? I'll pay."

"No," I said. "I am not going to be in Amityville without a car. The last time I was in Amityville without a car I had to walk to work."

"That was a total fluke," she said. "I would have given you a car if Randy hadn't wrecked it."

"You could have rented me a car," I told her.

"Not in the budget."

"Of course not," I said. "To prevent history from repeating itself I will drive."

"Alright," she said. "Thanks, Adrian.

"Yep."

Click.

"You have to go back to Amityville now, don't you?" Lilah asked as I laid my phone on the counter. I wrapped both of my arms around her.

"Yeah, baby. I'm sorry."

"When will you be back?"

"Uh…I'm not sure right now. As soon as I can."

"I guess I just have to accept that answer," she said. "Don't I?"

"Pretty much," I said as I kissed her forehead again. "Give me a real kiss." She looked up to me and I leaned down, touched my lips to hers.

"Hey!" Isabel said as she walked by with her plate. "No PDA in front of the children!"

"Or me," Ben said.

Isabel walked back over and pulled on the sleeve of my t-shirt.

"Let me see this new sexy tattoo you got," she said. I pulled my sleeve up over my shoulder.

"Meet your approval?" I asked. She examined it then ran her finger over it.

"Why is it puffed up like this?" she asked. I looked down to it.

"Because it's still a little swollen. It'll go down." She looked up to me.

"Did you bleed?"

"Well, yeah," I said. "A little bit."

"I want to get a tattoo," she said. "Will you go with me?"

"If you want."

"Make me an appointment," she said as she walked away.

"She doesn't mean it," Lilah said.

"I know," I said.

"Let's go to bed early tonight," Lilah whispered as she leaned into my chest.

"Because you're tired?" I asked. I ran my hand over her hair. "Or are you inferring something else?"

"I know you will find this hard to believe," she said. "But I am actually tired every night these days."

"Must be that growing baby inside of you." She lifted her head and smiled. I put my hand on her stomach. She put hers over mine.

"I'm worried," she said.

"About what?" I asked. I leaned back against the counter and pulled her into me. She stood in between my legs and I took her hands in mine, entwined them together.

"I don't know. I just…well…" She looked down. "I feel like I'm too old for this."

"You are not too old for this," I told her. "Definitely not."

"Are you excited?" she asked me.

"Excited??" I widened my eyes. "Are you kidding? Am I excited? I'm ecstatic!" She smiled. "Nana would love it if she knew our girl's name was going to be after her."

"I love it more that my name is in it," Isabel called from the table.

"This is a private conversation," I called back to Isabel teasingly.

Naming a baby isn't a simple endeavor. It's a major decision because your child must live with it for the rest of her life. I don't think I would've named Stef, Stefan. But that was Lora's choice and she had every right to make it. I'm sure it would have had to be a family name regardless. It always does with *The Empire*. After the family conversation with everyone about our boy's name Lilah and I decided to change it to Alexander, which is her father's name, and just call him Xander. We agreed it would simplify the pronunciation if we did it that way. And it would thrill Lilah's father. I kind of liked the way it sounded, too. Cristiano Alexander Bennett.

"Do you want a boy or a girl?" Lilah asked.

"I want whatever we get," I said.

"I want a girl," Vonnie said.

"We never have any privacy," I commented.

"You're in the kitchen," she pointed out as she scrunched up her nose.

"Why do you want a girl?" I asked Vonnie.

"Because I think she'll be cute," she said and walked away.

"Come on, Adrian," Lilah prodded me. "You must have a preference. What is it?"

"Gosh," I said. "I don't know. I'm gonna fall in love either way."

"I want a little girl, too," she said and smiled.

"Really?" I asked, surprised. "How come?"

"Because I want her to look just like you."

"You just want a little Indian girl," I said.

"Yes," she said. "I do. My children are all…"

"One hundred percent American."

"Well, yeah. Although I think our ancestors were English and French."

"How many centuries ago?" I teased. She slapped my chest.

"I want a little girl with your eyes, especially your lashes, and your dark hair."

"Yeah?"

"Has anyone ever told you that you should've been a girl?"

"My entire life," I admitted and I leaned down and kissed her again.

"Tell me you'll be back by the weekend," she said.

"This is the weekend," I told her smartly.

"Next weekend," she clarified.

"Okay," I said. I kissed her once more. "I'll be back by next weekend."

"You promise?""

"I promise."

I pulled her into me even closer and wrapped my arms around her. I inhaled her roses and musk. Lorelei was right. Lilah was my circle and I was her tranquility. She tells me when she's upset all she needs is my arms around her to make things better. She once asked me how I could be so cool, calm and collected at the tender age of eighteen. I'd laughed and shrugged. It was true I was cool, calm and collected. I am usually able to convey that quality to most anybody. Maybe it was my training in Quantico – the ability to remain calm under any circumstance but I reasoned it had more to do with my mother.

I learned early in life how to suppress my emotions because I didn't want Mama to know I knew she loved me less. She showed me affection but it wasn't always sincere and I knew the difference. The weirdest part about it all was I could read Mama's emotions better than anyone. I loved my Mama. She only loved me occasionally. When my Mama was herself, she was the best Mama ever but she was rarely that Mama. At least, not to me.

What I feared most with Lilah was us having a baby who inherited my spiritual abilities. Up until the night when Dada told me he could see them, too, I was terrified. I never wanted any child of mine to feel what I felt back then. Lora had assured me Stef didn't possess our gift. It made me wonder why Tiffany didn't have it either. Were Lorelei and I chosen? And by who?

Despite all these questions I felt there was plenty of time to figure out all the answers but life is always deceptive that way. There is always a haze, a fog, an indistinct miasma. It's when you feel comfortable enough to let down your defenses that it takes over, creating shadows and obscurities, making you question the Fairy Tale life you think you're living.

Later that morning after breakfast I pulled Ben aside.

"Hey," I said as I walked over to the coffee pot. I watched him pour himself a cup. "You know that stuff is gonna kill you one day."

"Gotta die of something," he said and smiled. "Might as well be this." He took a cautious sip.

"Can we talk for a minute on the porch?"

"Sure." He followed me out the back door and we sat on the wicker furniture across from one another. I leaned forward with my elbows on my knees.

"You know I have to go back to Amityville," I told him.

"Yeah." He watched me a moment. "I get the feeling that isn't what you want."

"It's not," I said. "I wish I didn't have to leave at all."

"Because of Mom," he concluded.

"Yeah. I'm a little concerned about her being here without me."

"Why?"

"This is the part in our conversation where I need to preface the following content. What I'm about to tell you relates to my case here and is highly confidential."

"The case with Vonnie?" he asked as he pointed to the floor.

"Yes."

"Did Bret get bailed out?"

"Well, yeah, but I've taken care of that situation. He's gone to Florida to live with his mother. It was a condition I put in as a bail requirement."

"Oh, well, that's good."

"Yeah," I agreed. "But the man at the talent show?"

"The one you attacked? That was awesome, by the way."

"Thanks," I said and smiled. "Are you ready for this?"

"Sure."

"That man was Bret's father," I told him. Ben's eyes widened and he sat his coffee down on the wicker table between us.

"Wait," he said. "Come again?"

"His name is Mitchell McCain. He came to Woodlawn to create havoc or better, get to me. At least that is what Jenny and I originally thought."

"Jenny?"

"She's my boss."

"Oh, right." He picked up his coffee cup.

"Then I thought McCain came here to get to Vonnie," I explained.

"Does she know this?"

"No, and I don't want her to," I said. "It will totally freak her out and he can't get to her. He's in jail for now."

"For now?" he asked. I shrugged.

"I'm not in control of the system. I wish I was but I'm not. Ben, this next piece of information is highly classified information. If Jenny knew I was telling you I'd probably lose my job. You must assure me this is only going to be between you and me."

"Yeah, yeah," he said. "Okay."

"Just to be clear, this is not a secret like the relationship I had with your mother this past summer. This information could be a life or death situation."

"You can trust me, Adrian," Ben assured me.

"McCain isn't here to get to Vonnie," I said. "He's here to get to your mother." The color drained from Ben's face.

"Because of you??"

"No. I mean, obviously, he's not thrilled about the relationship I have with your mom. It's related to it but not directly. Apparently, McCain and your mother had a romantic relationship in college."

"What?" Ben asked leaning forward. "Bret's father and Mom had a relationship??" I nodded. "How do you know this?" I took a deep breath.

"When I took McCain back to the station after the talent show Jenny showed up. When she interrogated him, he pulled a picture of your Mom out of his wallet and told us if we would bring Lilah into the station, he would talk to us."

"Please don't do that," Ben said. "I'm not sure what that would do to Mom."

"Don't worry," I said shaking my head. "That will never happen."

"Okay, good. Where did he get the picture?"

"I'm not sure but it's not a current photograph. It's from back then when they were in school."

"That was twenty years ago," Ben pointed out. "Why would he want to have anything to do with her now??"

"Well, I don't think he knew where Lilah was for sure but when he got to know Vonnie through Bret he figured it out."

"Shit."

"Yeah. Vonnie must have mentioned your mom in some capacity and McCain realized who she was."

"This can't be good," Ben said. "I mean, I know you said he's in jail but what if he gets out?"

"That's my exact thought, too. But I'm not in control of whether he's granted bail or not. I can recommend he doesn't get it, which I will do, but that doesn't mean it will happen."

"I know you said he had a romantic relationship with Mom," he said. "But do you know the extent of that relationship? I mean, did they go out on a few dates or have a real relationship?"

"They lived together." Ben widened his eyes again.

"My mother," he said motioning over his shoulder. "Lived with Bret's father?" I looked down.

"Yeah."

"Does she know he's here?"

"Yes," I said. "She is aware he is here. She recognized him at the talent show."

"That must have freaked her out."

"It did but she has no idea he's Bret's father." I pressed my lips together. "I'm going to have to tell her."

"Let Isabel do it," he said and smiled.

"Trust me, I've thought about it. It will probably be a joint effort between us."

"What does he want Mom for?" Ben asked. "Is it to hurt her? Or does he still love her?"

"It's not to hurt her but I don't believe he is mentally stable and there is no way to predict what a mentally unstable person might do. He may do something he doesn't consider detrimental to Lilah."

"Such as?" I took another deep breath.

"Well, God forbid, but I think the worst-case scenario would involve some kind of hostage situation."

"Are you fucking kidding me??" Ben practically yelled.

"Hey," I said. "I said worst-case scenario. It doesn't mean I think that's what will happen. In fact, I think it is highly unlikely but as I also said, what mentally unstable people will or won't do is nearly impossible to foresee. Your mom needs twenty-four-hour care. I don't want her to ever be alone and I need you to help me make that happen."

"Have you talked to Isabel about any of this?" he asked.

"No," I admitted. "Not yet."

"Well, honestly, it would make *me* feel better if you did. At least then if I'm not around Isabel will be. Between the two of us we can make sure Mom is never by herself."

"Do you want to talk to Isabel or would you rather me do it before I leave?" I asked.

"I can do it," he said. "Isabel is easy to talk to, especially when it involves Mom."

"I would not ask you to do this if I was going to be here all the time but I'm not. I hate it but I have another case now and I'm going to be going back and forth between Amityville and here on a regular basis. I wish I had a choice but I don't. I'm trusting you with this, Ben. And, for the love of God, please do not repeat what happened with Vonnie and Hunter the other night no matter what happens."

"I can't promise you that," Ben told me.

"Prove to me you're an adult and not a kid with anger issues."

"Yeah. Okay," he said as he lifted his hand for a fist bump. Not an entirely appropriate action for the situation at hand but fitting for the kind of friendship I had with Ben. I bumped my fist against his.

"There is nothing on this earth more important to me than your mother and her well-being. I love her with all my heart. If anything ever happened to her, I would never be able to forgive myself."

"Or me," Ben said and smiled.

"Well, yeah. That, too."

"I won't let you down," Ben promised me.

"Thank you."

"You know," Ben said. "I've never really had any enemies in my life."

"Well, I was one of them not too long ago." He smiled and shook his head.

"Nah, it wasn't that bad. I just wanted to beat the hell out of you."

"In order to protect your mom," I concluded and looked down. "Which makes you the perfect person for what I've asked you to do."

"Yeah."

"No enemies, for real?" I asked.

"Nah...I have a bad temper but not really. I can tell you one thing, though."

"What's that?"

"This Mitchell McCain?" he said. "You've told me more than enough about him. He might just be the first enemy I've ever had."

McCain

When you're in jail you have to pay for everything. A fee for being here every day. I know. That's fucking crazy. I mean, they put me here and now I gotta pay for it like it's a damn hotel. The food sucks and anything from the snack bar is outrageous. A little pack of peanut butter and crackers is three dollars. I hate the government. They're always taking your money for something you shouldn't be responsible for in the first place.

I never filed taxes until I was twenty-one then Leslie told me eventually the government was gonna catch up with me. So, ideally, that meant I had to get a job. I mean, you can't put drug dealer on your tax return as your primary occupation. I didn't have time for a job so I worked out a plan with a friend of mine who owned a laundromat. After that, I filtered my money through him. We used to laugh about it all the time. Laundering your money through a laundromat. You couldn't get any more original than that.

Calling Lilah was always my most favorite time of day. We'd talked two other times since I first called her. Because I have no money, she pays for our phone calls. I can make the initial call but it makes her pay before they'll let me talk to her. She has to punch in her credit card number to continue the call. After that they interrupt your conversation – probably every eight minutes - and tell you that you have to pay more money to continue. We never talk very long because she can't get away from everyone else for an extended period of time. She makes the initial payment and then she'll make one more. So, I'm guessing we talk for about fifteen minutes before they cut us off.

"Hey," she said when I answered. "Are you there?"

"Yeah. God, I hate that damn automated system. I mean, sometimes I'm just standing here waiting for it and everyone else is yelling for me to get off the phone so they can have their turn."

"Did you tell them to fuck off?" she asked and laughed.

"You know me so well."

"Well, not anymore."

"I haven't changed that much," I said.

"How's the drug business these days?"

"I'm getting old, Lilah."

"Aren't we all?"

"I know, right?"

"Can I ask you a personal question?" she asked.

"You can ask me anything."

"Will you tell me the truth?"

"Of course."

"You promise?"

"I promise," I assured her.

"Did you ever meet Vonnie?" I sighed

"Yes. She's beautiful. She looks like you."

"Did you sell her drugs?"

"No. Never."

"You promise?"

"I promise."

"Where did she get them from?"

"That I cannot tell you."

"Why not?" she asked. "You told me you'd tell me the truth."

"I will. I just can't answer that question."

"Why?"

"Because they record everything on these calls."

"And what?"

"And I don't want to incriminate anyone. They already know I have them. But I have no way of knowing if they know who else does and even if they weren't recording it, I still wouldn't tell you."

"Why not?"

"Because that's how you get yourself killed, Lilah."

"You're an asshole," she said.

"Why? Because I don't want to die?"

"You should tell Adrian then. I know you talk to him. He would probably help you if you did."

"Fuck no. I'm not talking to that son of a bitch. You have no idea the stuff he's said to me since I got arrested."

"Was it anything you didn't deserve?"

"Fuck yeah."

"I find that hard to believe," she said.

"Why? Because he's Mr. Perfect??"

"I'm trying to help you, you asshole."

"You have one minute left," the automated voice said. "Please make a deposit for an additional eight minutes."

Silence.

"Lilah?"

Nothing. This time she didn't pay. She just hung up.

Fuck.

Vonnie

It was almost two o'clock in the morning when I heard a tap on my bedroom window. I looked over to Tiffany's bed. She was gone. Typical. She was probably at Isabel's in Isaac's bed with him. Godspeed to them both if Isabel figured it out. I got up, pulled my curtain back and peered outside. Hunter. I opened the window.

"How the hell did you get up here?" I asked.

"Trellis," he answered as he came inside. "Damn, this house is old."

"I told you. 1906."

"It's amazing," he said.

"Where is your car?" I asked him.

"Parked at the catholic church down the street. I figured they were the only people who wouldn't automatically tow it if they couldn't find the driver." He laughed.

"You're insane."

He stood at the foot of my bed just watching me. He said he loved me which felt amazing and scary at the same time but only because I was pretty sure I loved him, too.

"Is that a graveyard on the side of the house?" he asked as he grabbed his shirt from behind him and pulled it over his head.

I never told anyone about our graveyard mostly because I thought I heard voices when I went out there and I was not entertaining that at all. Grandma Loretta said it was of the devil.

"Yeah," I said. "Who cares."

"We could do a séance," he said. He started to unbutton his jeans.

"What are you doing?" I asked.

"I'm going to sleep with you tonight," he told me. "I'm cold."

"That is not the reason," I said and rolled my eyes. I walked over to him. Our bodies came together and he placed his hands on my waist. He kissed me softly then leaned closer to my ear.

"Wanna Hulu and screw?" he asked. I slapped his chest and laughed.

"It's Hulu and hang, you weirdo." I pulled back the comforter on my bed. He came up behind me and moved my hair off my neck, kissed the back of it.

"How about Amazon Prime and sixty-nine??" he asked. I turned around.

"How about Amazon Prime and dine?"

"I'm broke," he said. "Sixty-nine is free." I burst out laughing.

"If you think it's free, you're sadly mistaken."

"You're going to make me pay for love?" he asked facetiously.

"Yes."

I got in bed and he crawled under the covers with me. I ducked my head into the crevice of his arm as he pulled me closer to him.

"Sixty-nine now and dine later??" he whispered.

"No!" I said and laughed again. I ran my hand down his chest to his happy trail.

Hunter has the sexiest body I've ever known. He's all muscle. He body-builds and is always going to bodybuilding competitions. The only concern I have about this is that he and Ben workout at the same gym and one day they are going to run into one another and both get kicked out for trying to kill one another. Because Ben is not a forgive and forget person when it come to me and boys.

Hunter's eyes aren't brown. They are, gosh, all different colors. Sometimes they are dark gray, sometimes they have a greenish tint, sometimes gold. I love that about him. His hair is blonde with strands of caramel brown. He smells like cinnamon and cedar. Like Christmas. He tastes like strawberries. When I told him this, he admitted it was his little sister's lip balm. He told me not to tell anyone because he stole it from her. I told him I would put it in my 'I do not remember' file. When he asked me what that was, I told him it was things I didn't remember. That was when he told me I was the craziest person he knew. I took it as a compliment. Now, he pulled at my underwear.

"Chill out," I said. "Are you here because of me or my vagina?" He grinned.

"I love it that you say vagina," he said as he kissed my neck.

"Isn't that what it is?" I asked.

"Well, yeah," he said, and I could feel him hard against me. "But not many people refer to it that way."

"Not many people refer to it at all," I told him. He ran his fingers down my side from my armpit to my waist. I shivered.

"Stop," I said and giggled.

"What?"

"You're going to get me in trouble."

"Why?"

"Because," I said. "You're here and we can't have sex. Someone will hear us."

"I can be quiet," he said and smiled.

"What if I can't?" I teased. I raised my knee up between his legs like I always did. It drove him crazy. He lowered his face to my chest and kissed my breastbone, my chin, my lips.

"I can gag you if you want," he told me.

"Uh…no," I said. I reached down and grabbed him and he sucked in his breath.

"Easy now," he said as I pushed his boxers down. He tugged at my underwear again and I slapped his hand.

"Nope."

"You're driving me crazy," he breathed. "Are you gonna make me beg??"

"Yeah."

"Please, please, please…"

"You're so pitiful," I said and pouted.

"Totally."

I slid my underwear over my hips and he grabbed them and pulled them down the rest of the way. When his stomach touched mine, a bubbly feeling coursed through my veins. I thought about how I held my breath when I went underwater and whether it would be effective in this situation. Maybe.

His pressed his lips to mine softly and I slipped my tongue into his mouth. He ground his hips into mine. He grabbed my hands and pushed me back up against the headboard of my bed. I let out a deep breath as he pushed inside of me. I sucked in air and held it but not for long. I bit my lip and felt my heart pounding in my chest. He must have felt it, too.

"You okay?" he asked.

"Yeah, yeah."

I didn't want to tell him this was only the fourth time I'd ever had sex. Lots of people thought Bret and I had this crazy sexual relationship but we really didn't. I don't remember the first time we did it because I was so drunk. At least I think I was drunk but I might have been roofied. I was hungover and upset the next morning but Bret assured me everything was fine. I have no idea if he used a condom and I asked him but he said he was drunk, too, and he didn't remember. I was a nervous wreck until I had my period two weeks later. Hunter's hair tickled the side of my face and I brought my hand around to push it behind his ear. It wasn't as long as Adrian's but one side came down to his chin. Sometimes when we were making out and he was on top of me it went into my mouth. I brought my legs up and wrapped them around his waist.

"Yeah," Hunter said. "Like that."

He kissed me again. This time he kept kissing me and it intensified the moment. I'd read in my Cosmo magazine that your lips can be a trigger for a good orgasm. I hadn't had one yet but so far, so good.

"Mmm…" I hummed.

This feeling started inside of me. It was like when water on the stove begins to simmer. It starts out as a slow effervesce but ends in a full-blown boil. That bubbly feeling again. I closed my eyes and raised my hips to meet his.

"It's so fucking hot in here," I said as I shoved the covers off us.

"I know," Hunter managed.

The air from the ceiling fan above us circled the room and a cool breeze floated across our bodies. Beneath it, heat again. An intense warmth moved from my forehead down to my toes. Hunter ran his hands down my arms and held onto my fingers. I squeezed his tightly. The heat that had moved down my body to my toes came back up and across my hips. I felt a line of perspiration run down between my breasts. Hunter's body slid over mine.

"Can I?" he asked.

"Yeah."

Bret asked me this the second time we had sex but I had no idea what he was talking about. This time I knew what was getting ready to happen and it wasn't just happening for Hunter. It was happening for me, too. Did this always happen when you were in love? Hunter ground his hips into mine and I tried to hold my breath. I could feel him as he pushed himself further inside of me. It was sort of painful but a good pain. Is there such a thing?? A shiver went down my spine. It was one of the most incredible feelings I've ever had. I couldn't have stayed still if my life depended upon it. An echo reverberated from one side of my room to the other. It was a moment before I realized it was me. My heart thumped inside my chest and I closed my eyes tightly.

"Shit," Hunter said as he tried to catch his breath.

A heaviness moved across my body almost instantly, easily coaxing me into the afterglow. I had never experienced that before either. I'd read about it but it had never happened to me. I leaned up and kissed Hunter. Sweat beaded above his lip.

"Mmm," I said. "You're salty."

"Am I?" he asked as he laid his head on my shoulder. I ran my fingers through his hair.

A knock on my bedroom door. I kicked Hunter's leg and he jumped up and grabbed the covers at the bottom of the bed, pulled them up over us. I pulled the sheet up under my chin and shoved Hunter further down the bed underneath my comforter. Enter Maria.

"I can hear you," she said simply. "And I know you're naked."

"Mari…."

"I'm just warning you," she said. "Mommy will hear."

I was speechless. Hunter laughed.

"Hi Hunter," Maria said. Hunter poked his head out from under the covers.

"Hello, Maria."

"You should be glad it was me and not Ben," Maria told him. "Because he would beat your ass."

"You're right."

"It's called a warning," Maria said and she shut the door.

"She is a piece of work," Hunter said to me.

"I know," I said and laughed. "You can't hide anything from Maria."

Adrian

I walked into the interrogation room with Tina in front of me and Base behind me.

Base was one of the scariest creatures the DEA owned. He was about 6'5" and probably weighed close to three hundred pounds. On his lower left arm, he donned a Grim Reaper tattoo. He said it was to let 'them' know he didn't take any prisoners. If you saw him in a dark alley, you'd tuck your tail and run the other way but he was a teddy bear. And that was just the way he liked it. We all knew Base wouldn't hurt a fly unless he had to and then, well, if you didn't know Jesus as your Lord and Savior you better be asking him into your heart.

"I ain't talking to that mother fucker," McCain said when he saw me.

"I think he might be able to help you," Tina said as she sat down at the table. She locked her fingers together in front of her. She was a badass, too, but you'd never know it to look at her. She was tiny but she was all muscle and she knew how to fight.

"Fuck him," he said but I was silent.

Base walked around the table behind McCain and grabbed the back of his t-shirt in his hand, nearly pulled him up out of his seat.

"You gon talk to him," he said. "I don't like the son of a bitch, either. But you gon talk to him."

"Wow, Base," I said. "Thanks."

"Anytime," he said.

I sat down at the table beside Tina. She glanced over to me. If you didn't know any better, you'd think she was planning my death.

"I'm gon stand right here behind you, Mr. McCain," Base said. "Cause we ain't having a repeat of what happened before." Base looked to me. "We ain't having a repeat of what happened before. Are we, Adrian?"

"Nope," I said. "I come in peace." McCain sat back in his chair and stared at me.

"You still a pussy," McCain said to me. He narrowed his eyes.

"Hey," Base said as he grabbed McCain's t-shirt again. "Shut the fuck up. Schoolboy trying to help you, man."

Base had been calling me that ever since I came to Woodlawn. Unfortunately, a lot of the other officers had picked it up, too. Tina laughed. It was always a game until it was time to dance.

"He's right," I said. "I do want to help you."

"The hell you do," McCain said.

"I was totally out of line before," I admitted to him. "But you know, we can work together."

"Sure, we can."

"You know how?" I asked him. No answer. "We have one thing in common." No answer.

"Can't wait to hear this," Base commented and I raised my eyebrows at him. He smiled.

"Lilah," I said. McCain looked up to me in surprise. I had his attention. "I love her. I'd do anything for that woman. You love her, too, don't you?"

I was taking a chance by asking this question and Tina knew it. Now, she raised her head to heaven.

"Lord," she said. "Bless us all." Base chuckled.

"Do you love her, McCain?" I asked him.

"I don't have to answer your stupid questions." I took a deep breath.

"You know, I'm not sure what you know," I said as I leaned forward on my elbows. "I'm not sure what Bret's told you. You know Vonnie is Lilah's daughter? I know you know that, don't you?" No answer. "She's beautiful, isn't she?" I waited. "You think Vonnie's beautiful?"

"She looks like her Mama," he said quietly. He looked down to the table.

"Yeah, she does." I watched him. "You know girls like her, they get caught up in this drug scene. They don't even know what they're getting themselves into. You know that?"

"Yeah."

"You know you can help me take those people off the streets. That's the opportunity I'm giving you. Helping Lilah. Helping Vonnie. You wanna work with me? We can work together – take time off your sentence."

"I don't know."

"Why don't you know?" I asked. "I know you love them. Don't you?"

"Yeah, man, but I ain't no snitch."

"What if I told you I'll take care of you?"

"How the fuck you gonna take care of me?"

"You'd be surprised," I said. "I need an informant. You wanna do that for me?"

"Damn," Base said under his breath.

Silence. Then McCain said, "I don't know man. What's in it for me?

"I already told you. Take time off your sentence."

"I don't wanna go to jail," he told me.

"I don't blame you," I said. "I wouldn't either."

"How do I know you're telling me the truth?" he asked.

"You know I can't draw up an agreement with you. We just have to trust each other. You help me, I help you. You know what I'm saying?"

"What am I looking at?" he asked.

"Without helping me?"

"Yeah."

"Six or seven years??" I guessed. "Maybe more. But that at least."

"And what if I do?"

"Be an informant?" I asked.

"Yeah."

"I don't know," I said. "We have to talk to the DA but I guarantee it'll be a lot less.

"A helluva lot less," Base added as he punched McCain in the back.

"Man, I don't want to go to jail at all."

"I know you're not the pin. It isn't Angel either. Who is?" He shook his head, put it in his hands.

"Here we go," Tina said.

"I don't know him, man."

"You know who he is, though," I said. "Don't you?"

"I don't know his name."

This is when the moment comes to take a leap of faith because when they're telling you they don't know something it means they do.

"Alright. Let's do this. You wanna make a call for me?"

"I don't know."

"He'll never know," I assured him. "I'll cuff you just like I do him. Afterward he'll be in the system for a long time."

"There's a web, man," McCain said. I motioned to myself.

"You think I don't know that?" He looked down. "You think you could make a call? Make it happen tonight?"

"I don't know. I don't know about tonight."

"But you'll call him...place an order?" I asked. He slammed his hand down onto the table.

"Hey," Base said as he grabbed his shirt again. "Chill out."

"Damn it..." McCain said.

"Do it for Lilah," I said because a little extra incentive never hurt anyone. "Would you do it for Lilah? Because I'm gonna make sure she knows what you did and how you're helping me. You want me to tell her you're helping me, helping me get guys off the street who do things to hurt her and her daughter?"

"Yeah, yeah." He brought his hands to his face, took a deep breath.

"How long you been doing this?" I asked him. He sniffed, wiped his nose with his hand.

"I don't know, man. Too long."

"You can make it right," I told him.

"Alright."

"See, I'm not about throwing the book at you just for fun. I'm trying to make a difference. You can be that difference. You know that, right?"

"Yeah."

"I'm gonna make arrangements for you to make that call," I said. "You wanna do it now?"

"I ain't got no phone, man."

"Tina," I said. "Go get his phone." She stood up.

"You got it."

"When Tina comes back, I'm gonna let you call him...or her... whoever it is...you don't have to tell me any names or give me any numbers. You understand?"

"Yeah." He wiped his hand over his mouth. Tina came back with his phone in a plastic bag. I unzipped it and took the phone out, turned it on.

"It's still got a charge," I said as I handed it to him.

He took it, put in his passcode, and lit up the screen. I watched him scroll through his contact list. There were no names, only numbers.

"You want me to do it now?" he asked.

"Yeah."

"You promised you'd help me," he said. "You still gon help me? 'Cause I ain't doing this shit for free, man. I get myself killed."

"I gotcha," I said. "You have my word."

"You want me to put it on speaker phone?" he asked me.

"Nope," I said. "I trust you." He looked at me then like he couldn't believe what I'd just said. "You trust me? You believe me when I say I'm gonna help you?"

"Yeah, man...I don't know why...I'm fucked."

"No," I said. "You're not...make the call." He took a deep breath and hit his contact button.

"It's ringing," he said as he tapped his fingers on the table nervously. "He might not be there, man."

I knew that was a lie. They are always there. Because if they aren't, they lose business.

"Hey," he said into the phone. "I'm down, man."

Tina looked to me and I looked back. Base nodded at me.

"Naw, man. I gotta have it before then…. tonight…I don't know…Give me a time. Uh-huh. Westside? That little store on the corner? Yeah."

I looked to Base and he nodded again. He had the number because he was standing behind McCain and in a flash before McCain even put the phone to this ear his eyes had scanned the phone. His memory was like a steel trap.

"Get the red SUV," I told him.

"Yep," he said as he walked out of the interrogation room.

I wrote red SUV on a piece of paper and handed it to McCain. There was no way anyone was meeting him without knowing his vehicle.

"You going?" I whispered as I leaned over to Tina.

"Hell, no, I ain't going," she whispered back. I laughed.

"I can do 9:30," McCain said. "Don't bring no kids with you this time." He hesitated. "Shit, man. Ain't they got a Mama? A red SUV… Yep. See ya."

"Is he bringing his kids with him?" I asked McCain when he hung up.

"I'on know, man…I told him not to."

"Jesus," I said as I stood up. "Tina, I hate to do this to you, hon, but I'm gonna need you to go. If this trash bag shows up with his kids, you're gonna have to take 'em."

"Damnit, Adrian," she said. "Every time I work with you, I end up doing this shit." She got up and walked out the door.

"You love me," I called after her.

"Nope," she said over her shoulder. "I don't. I could be home cooking fried chicken right now and watching Jeopardy." I laughed.

"You ready?" I said to McCain.

"Can you take these handcuffs off me?" he asked.

"I'll take them off when you get in the car." He stood up and I stood in front of him.

"You know what we're doing, right?"

"Yeah."

"You take off in our vehicle nobody will ever help you again. That's when you get the whole enchilada. You feeling me?"

"Yeah, man. I got it."

"We're gonna be behind you, far enough back. You probably won't even see us. I'll have three other vehicles surrounding that block. If we can take him with you there, we'll take you first but it ain't gon be pretty."

"Alright."

"If he tries to take off after the transaction before we get there, you take off, too. Go to the 7-11 on Grace. Wait to hear from us there."

"He got dogs."

"Dogs?" I asked. "Dogs and kids??"

"Them kids, he protecting them."

"With the dogs?" I asked.

"Yeah, man."

"What kind of dogs? Have you seen them?"

"Yeah. He got pit bulls."

"In the car??" I asked unbelievingly.

"Yeah."

"Shit." I leaned out the door of the interrogation room. "Terrence??"

"Yep?" he said as he came around the corner.

"We got kids, possibly dogs…God only knows what else. I need three vehicles around Pine and Myrtle Streets. We're meeting at the Stopover on the corner. McCain, you stay with Terrence." I turned to

Tina who had just returned wearing her ballistic vest. "Can you get him hooked up with the car?"

"Yep," she said. "You got it."

I ran down the hall to the equipment room, grabbed my ballistic vest and holsters. When I got to the armory, Base had already opened it up.

"I got a present for you, man," he said as I pulled my polo shirt over my head. A mint green polo was not a good shirt for a drug bust.

"What?" I asked.

"I was thinking 'bout that mint green polo you got on, had to be a gift from the lady, right?"

"What is your point, Base?" I asked as I took my guns. I signed the discharge papers and he handed me a long sleeve black t-shirt.

"It's so you." He laughed. I held it up in front of me. On the back in big, capital letters, DEA.

"What is so me?" I asked. "This is just our regular shirts."

"Turn it over."

I turned the shirt around, looked at the front. In block letters, 'I'm not your everyday Popo." I laughed. 'I'm the mother f*cking D.E.A.'

"Base, you're a piece of work," I said as I pulled it over my head. I put on my vest and snapped the sides. "You went to all that trouble just for me?"

"I love you, man," he said as he slapped my shoulder. "Give it to your girl after tonight. She can wear it to bed."

"I'm sure she'll love that," I said.

"Tonight's the night," he told me as he pulled on his vest.

"We hope," I said as I headed back down the hall.

"Hey, Adrian?" he called after me.

"Yeah?"

"Good job, man. You did good."

"It ain't shit yet," I said. "Once this goes down, it'll be shit."
Base chuckled.

"I'm backing ya up," he said. "You son of a bitch."

"Life would not be worth living without you, Base," I said to him
as he caught up with me.

"I didn't know you felt that way," he told me. "That's sweet." I
laughed.

The adrenaline was pumping. This was one of my favorite parts of
the job. It was also one of the scariest parts of my job. Because every
time I went into one of these situations I never knew if I'd come back
out alive. Tina met us at the back door.

"Time to tango," she said. "Let's do it."

"We ain't going to KFC after this," I told her.

———

"Get out of the car slowly," I yelled as I pointed my gun at the
suspect. "We have you surrounded."

"He gon run," Base said. "I can just feel it."

"He ain't going far."

"You gon chase him?" he asked.

"If I have to," I told him.

"I got ya back if you do."

"Get out of the car or I will l pull you out of it," I shouted to the
suspect again. The man got of his car and stood on the other side of the
door. "Put your hands up in the air."

"Do it," Base yelled when he didn't. "Or I'm coming over there. Don't make me come over there." He held up his hands.

"Shut the door," I yelled. "Get up against the car." Surprisingly, he did what I told him. I could hear a baby crying but no dogs.

"Man, don't shoot me. My kids in here."

I walked toward him. Base went over to the other side of the car and opened the back door where the kids were. When I got to the man, I pushed him up against the car and spread his feet apart with one of my own. He couldn't have been more than twenty. Here he was making a living selling drugs and he probably wasn't even old enough to drink. I stuffed my gun back in the holster and pulled his hands behind his back, handcuffed him.

"Tina," I yelled over my shoulder as I began to search him. "Kids."

"Man, don't take my kids."

"I hate to be the bearer of bad news," I said. "But you don't get to keep your kids when you get busted. They got a Mama?"

"Yeah."

"Where is she?" I asked as I turned him around, put my hands low on my hips.

"I don't know, man. She passed out at the house."

"She's passed out at the house," I repeated. "Did you hear that, Tina?"

"Yep," she called back. "Come on, baby," she said to one of the kids. "Miss. Tina gonna take care of you but don't worry you'll see your daddy soon. I promise."

Both children, one about 3, the other not old enough to walk, willingly went with Tina. They both looked like they'd just crawled out of a dumpster.

"McCain," the man called over his shoulder as I led him to the waiting police car. "This is shit, man."

"You set me up," McCain said as Terrence led him to another car.

"The fuck I did."

"Hey Base," I yelled. "Get the car registration." He peered at me over the top of the car.

"You think I'm a novice or something?" he asked.

"Where you taking my kids, man?"

"We'll talk about that at the station," I said. "Alright?"

"Yeah."

"Get in the car."

"That was a lot easier than I thought," I told Base after I had deposited the man in the car.

"Me, too. Thought for sure he was gonna run."

"The kids," I said. "He didn't want to leave the kids."

"Yeah."

"Alright," I said as I punched him in the arm. "You taking me back to the station?"

"How else you gon get there? Take a cab?"

"Hey Terrence," I called and he walked toward me. "You going to check out the house?" I handed him the registration card Base had taken out of the suspect's vehicle. "Find out where it is and we'll scope it out tomorrow. See what our options are."

"Yep," he said.

"I'm going home when I get back to the station," I told Base. "Let everyone else handle the mess we made."

"Sounds good to me," he said. "You can give your Ms. that t-shirt."

"Yeah." We walked toward his vehicle. "Sweat and all."

"Women like that shit. Take it off when you get home and throw it at her."

"Base, I don't need pointers on how to get lucky. I get lucky almost every night."

He shoved me with his hand and I sidestepped to keep from falling on the pavement.

"You think you cool?" he asked and laughed. "Don't ya, boy?"

"I know I'm cool," I said and laughed with him.

Amityville

Adrian

Being back in Amityville after being in Woodlawn is always a major transition for me. It shouldn't be but when you have two women and two different cases in two different places, well, I don't think I need to explain it any further. Throw in a twin sister who knows everything, a son who wants to know everything, and a boss who demands everything and you've got plenty of potential for complete mind disintegration, ruin, decay, total annihilation of any good brain cells you may already have in your possession.

I feel like Lorelei knows more than Lilah and that troubles me because I want Lilah to know everything, too. I seriously need a spreadsheet for all this shit. Tiffany tells me one day my brain is going to explode if I don't write it all down somewhere but as soon as I take it all out of my brain and put it into a computer or onto a piece of paper is when someone else finds it. So, no. People have no idea how much case information I keep in my head for that very reason.

My days in Amityville are always hectic simply because I try to limit them to only a few days at a time. Jenny understands this and tries her best to accommodate me. I poked my head into her office before I went to my desk.

"Hey."

"Welcome to New York," she said as I walked in and sat down.

"Aw, thanks."

"Good job last night," she said. I brought my hand to my chest.

"Did you just give me a compliment?"

"McCain is freaking out," she told me.

"Why?"

"Because he's in jail," she told me. "Duh."

"He's been in and out of jail his entire life."

"Yeah," she said. "But he's doubting your promises."

"Oh. Well, I'll go talk to him when I'm back in Woodlawn. I talked to the DA this morning."

She gave me the thumbs up sign.

"Awesome," she said. "What's up?"

"I need clearance to get into Riverside Correctional."

"You're on vacation," she joked.

"Right."

"Let me guess. You wanna talk to Gianni's old cellmate, Lenny Walker."

"Yes," I affirmed, pointing at her. "You can read my mind. I'm gonna see what I can get out of him. I think he might know a lot more than I do."

"Likely," she said. "Offer him something if you want but make sure it's not anything prohibited." I rolled my eyes.

"Like I've never done this before."

"Up his parole hearing," she suggested. "I'm sure he'll do something between now and then to screw it up anyway so it won't matter."

"Great minds think alike," I said and she smiled.

"Let me know how it turns out."

"Sure."

"I sense you've been talking to your Amityville wife?" she said as she looked up to me. "Is this a fact or just my overactive imagination?"

"Quit it, Jenny."

"Oh, good grief, Adrian. Go to Riverside then spend some quality time with Lorelei."

"Funny," I said. "I'm gonna catch up with Karen then I'll head that way."

"I'll call you if I need you."

That was Jenny's dismissal.

"Okay. Thanks," I said as I walked out of her office.

"Oh hey," she called and I poked my head back around the door-frame. "Call me after you talk to Lenny."

"Right."

"Thanks, Adrian."

"Yep."

—

I just gotten back from my meeting with Karen when Jenny appeared behind me. She seemed distressed. Jenny is rarely distressed so when she is you know something serious is going on.

"Hey," I said as I looked up to her. "You look distressed." I smiled. "Are you distressed?"

"Where have you been?"

"I told you I needed to go upstairs to go over some stuff with Karen," I explained. "Why? What's up?"

"Rita has a little girl downstairs."

"What?" I asked. "What do you mean she has a little girl?"

"They did a drug bust this morning at the Sunset Apartments."

"This morning?" I asked. "Why this morning?"

"It's a long story but I need you to come talk to this little girl," she said. "No one can understand anything she's saying."

"Okay," I said as I stood up.

"I'm not sure if she understands what we're saying to her but we can't understand anything she's saying to us," Jenny explained as we walked down the hall together. "I think she might be speaking French. At least, that's what it sounds like."

We took the stairs down to the intake room because it's faster than the elevator. When I walked into the room I sucked in my breath. This little girl. She was about the same age as Maria and Serena and she was terrified. She had on a dark pink flowered dress and clear jelly sandals. There was dirt on her legs and arms, a smudge of it on her face. It didn't look like her hair had been combed in days. I squatted down in front of her.

"Parlez vous anglaise?" (*Do you speak English?*) I asked her. She smiled but not because she understood me. I think it was because she realized I might be able to understand her.

"No ho sé," she said. I looked over my shoulder to Jenny.

"Not French."

"Spanish?"

"No," I said. "It sort of sounds like Italian. Hold up. Let me see something."

"Parlez vous Italien?" (*Do you speak Italian?*) I asked her in French.

"Sense italià," she said.

"Espanol?" (*Spanish?*)

"No ho sé," she said for the second time. I looked up to Jenny.

"I think that means 'I don't know.' I think before she said, 'No Italian.'"

"So, if it's not French and it's not Spanish and it's not Italian," Jenny said. "What the hell is it?"

"It might be Catalan," I said. "Let me ask her in French and see what she says. She might be able to correlate the two languages."

"Okay," Jenny said as she stuffed her hands into her pockets.

"Parlez vous Catalan?" She smiled. A big smile. I was right.

"Sí," she said.

"It's Catalan," I verified.

"What the hell is Catalan?" Jenny asked.

"It's a language they speak in Barcelona, other places in Spain. I don't know. It's part French, part Italian, part Spanish. She is picking out certain words from my French she understands." I looked back to the little girl.

"Quel est votre nom?" (*What is your name?*) I asked in French. She smiled again.

"Estela."

"That's her name," I told Jenny.

"Vous appelez Estela? Je mappelle Adrian." (*Your name is Estela? My name is Adrian.*)

"Sí."

"Je connais quelqu'un qui parle le Catalan," I said. "Voulez-vous luti parler?"

"Sí," the little girl said excitedly.

"What did you just say?" Jenny asked.

"I said, I know someone who speaks Catalan. Would you like to talk to her?"

"Who do you know that speaks Catalan??" Jenny asked.

"Lorelei," I said as I looked over my shoulder to Jenny.

"I thought she spoke Italian, Sicilian, whatever the hell that language is *The Empire* speaks."

"She does but she also speaks Catalan," I said standing up. I looked down to the little girl. "Je reviendrai. D'accord?"

"No," Estela said and she jumped up out of her chair and grabbed ahold of my legs.

"What did you say?" Jenny asked me once more.

"I told her I would be right back," I explained. "But I'm not sure she understood that. I think her saying no means she doesn't understand."

"Well, it seems as if she doesn't want you to go anywhere," Jenny said and smiled.

I was going to take a chance. I take too many chances but when you're in my line of work sometimes taking a chance is your only option. I reached down to Estela and took her hand in mind.

"Tu veux que je te retinene?" (*Do you want me to hold you?*) I asked her.

"No," she said but she raised her hands for me to pick her up so I did.

"What?" Jenny asked.

"I asked her if she wanted me to hold her," I said as Estela laid her head on my shoulder.

"But she said no," Jenny said.

"I know. I think that was just coincidental." I laid my hand on Estela's back. "Will you call Lorelei for me? Ask her to come over here?"

"Yeah," Jenny said. "Sure."

"I was going to do it but I think I've got another job right now." I smiled and patted Estela's back.

"Why don't you bring her upstairs to the conference room," Jenny suggested. "It's not as sterile up there." We started walking toward the stairs, me carrying Estela. "I talked to CPS and told them about the language barrier. I need to call them back and tell them we figured it out."

"Call Lorelei first," I told Jenny. "Ask her to bring an outfit of Serena's over here. They're the same size."

"You got it."

I took Estela into the conference room and sat her down on the sofa. I sat beside her. We had many items in the conference room for children because sometimes it took a while for CPS to get here. I imagined currently they were looking for a translator before they came over here but I had already found one.

"Voulez-vous coloriez?" (*Would you like to color?*) I asked Estela.

She didn't understand me so I got up and got the crayons and coloring book. She smiled as I laid them on the table and motioned for her to climb up into the chair. She was filthy. I could tell by the way she smelled it had been quite a while since she'd had a bath. CPS would take care of all that but at least if Lora brought some clean clothes Estela would have something to wear after they bathed her. We sat at the conference room table and colored. About twenty minutes later Lora poked her head through the door. I could tell by the look on her face she was upset over how Estela looked.

"I know," I said knowingly. Lora sat her bag down on the sofa and took off her coat. She walked around the table and squatted down in the floor in front of Estela.

"What's her name?" she asked me.

"Estela."

"Estela? Hola, em dic Lorelei."

Estela didn't only smile. Her entire disposition changed.

"You're going to have to tell me what you're saying," I told Lora.

"I just told her my name." She looked back to Estela.

"No tingueu por. Tindrem cura de vosaltres. Bé?" Lorelei looked to me. "Don't be afraid. We are going to take care of you. Okay?" I nodded and so did Estela.

Jenny came and leaned up against the doorframe.

"How's it going?" she asked. I gave her the thumbs up sign. "Good. CPS can't be here until six tonight." I looked at my watch.

"That's seven hours from now," I said unbelievingly. "Why? That's ridiculous." Jenny shrugged.

"They're busy, I guess."

"That is insane," I said. "This little girl can't sit here for seven hours."

"Estela?" Lorelei said to her. "Quants anys tens?"

"Cinc," Estela said. Jenny looked to me and I shrugged.

"She's five," Lora said.

"La meva filla, Serena, també té cinc anys. Voleu conèixer-la?" Lorelei asked Estela. Estela smiled.

"Sí," she said. Lorelei turned to me and Jenny.

"I told her I have a daughter the same age as her and asked her if she wanted to meet her."

"And?" Jenny asked.

"She said yes."

"Can you bring your daughter over here?" Jenny asked. Lorelei stood up.

"I can but I think seven hours is a bit much," Lora said. She looked at her watch. "I can take her to my house, get her cleaned up and let her and Serena play until CPS can come get her." She looked to me. "I mean, if that's okay with you." I motioned to Jenny.

"Yeah," Jenny said. "If you're willing to do that."

"I don't mind," Lora said. "Serena is restless today. I'm not sure why. This will give her something to do."

"Okay," Jenny said. "Sure." Lora squatted back down in front of Estela.

"Estela, voldria anar a casa meva per una estona amb la meva filla? Hi ha moltes joguines que puc veure una pel·lícula. Si?"

"Sí," Estela said and smiled. Lorelei turned to me.

"I just asked if she wanted to go to my house for a little while and play with Serena. She said yes."

"Well, let's do it," Jenny said. "Adrian, you want to go with Lorelei to take Estela over there?"

"Sure."

"Voleu venir amb mi?" Lora asked as she reached for Estela's hand.

"Sí," Estela said.

"Well, let's go," I told Lorelei. "Let's do it."

"Sure," Lora said, then to Estela. "Estàs preparat?"

"Sí," Estela said. "Puc menjar alguna cosa a casa teva?"

"Per descomptat, què us agradaria?" Lora asked. Estela smiled and shrugged. "Aposto a que t'agrada el caneló. Voleu?"

"Sí!" Estela said excitedly. Lorelei looked to me.

"She asked me if she could eat at my house so I told her yes then I asked her if she liked cannelloni and she said yes. She's excited."

"*I'm* excited," I said as I brought my hands to my chest. "I like cannelloni, too. Can I have cannelloni?"

"Good grief, Adrian," Lorelei said. She looked to Estela. "És una ximpleria." Estela laughed. "Vol saber si també pot tenir canelons." Estela laughed again.

"Are ya'll talking about me?" I asked.

"Ya'll?" Jenny said to me and laughed. "You haven't even been in the South that long."

"I told Estela you were silly," Lora said as we got to the front door. "She agrees with me."

"Twenty minutes and you've already convinced her you're smarter than me," I said.

"Well, I am," Lorelei said and smiled.

"Alright, guys," Jenny said. "*Ya'll* have fun." I pointed to Jenny.

"You're funny."

"I'll let you know when I hear anything else from CPS," she said as she headed back inside. "Thank you, Lorelei. I really appreciate this."

"Not a problem," Lora said. "You know if you ever need a translator I'm just right down the street."

"I didn't realize you spoke anything other than Italian," Jenny said. "Or I probably would've called you before now."

"I'm happy to help however I can," Lora said.

"Thanks, Lorelei."

"Sure."

We walked out to the parking lot, me carrying Estela once again. I put her in the backseat of Lora's car and when I stood back up, she leaned over the roof toward me.

"Hey," she said.

"What?"

"She has lice," Lorelei said. I didn't understand her.

"What?" I asked. Lorelei scratched her head.

"Lice."

"Are you kidding?" I asked widening my eyes.

"Nope."

"Well, shit, what do we do?" I asked.

"It's not a big deal," she said. "I can get rid of them. I just wanted you to know so when we get to the house, we can take her straight into the bathroom before she encounters anything else."

"Holy shit, Lora. What about your car?"

"Oh, I can fumigate it after we get back to the house."

"Why are you being so cool about this?" I asked. "This is disgusting."

"It's really not," she said. "The kids get it every year at school. Who do you think all the parents come to when they can't get rid of it themselves??"

"If I have lice, I am going to be so mad," I said and Lora laughed.

"It's not funny."

"Get in the car," she said. "Stop being a baby."

I slid into the passenger side and she got in and closed her door.

"Hem d'anar a banyar-nos i rentar-nos els cabells i després tinc un bonic vestit que podeu portar. Bé?"

"Sí," Estela said. "Tens més d'un?"

"Sí. Podeu triar el que vulgueu. Bé?"

"What the heck are ya'll saying?" I asked Lora as she pulled out onto the road.

"I just told her we were going to take a bath when we got home before we did anything else. And I told her I had a pretty dress she could put on. She asked if I had more than one."

"This is sad," I told Lorelei.

"I know," she said. "She's so beautiful. You think she's Spanish?"

"She must be," I said. "If her first language is Catalan."

"Estela?" Lora asked as she looked in the rearview mirror. "Has estat a Barcelona?"

"La meva mare viu a Barcelona," Estela said.

"Her mother lives in Barcelona," Lorelei said.

"Who does she live with now? Ask her."

"Estela, amb qui viu ara?"

"El meu oncle, Alexandre."

"She lives with her Uncle Alexandre," Lorelei told me.

"Who probably also has lice," I said and we both laughed.

"Watch this," Lora said. She pressed her phone icon on her steering wheel.

"Palazzo Cremisi, Renaldo speaking."

"Hey," Lora said.

"Hello, Miss."

"Everything there okay?"

"Of course," Renaldo said.

"I have news," Lora said.

"That means unfortunate news," Renaldo said dryly. "Yes?"

"Yes," Lora said. "The little girl? She has lice."

"Oh my," Renaldo said.

"And we're on our way there now," Lora informed him.

"Shall I get the ethanol for the tincture?" he asked.

"Yes, please. We'll have to boil all the clothes and the car has to be fumigated. Also, Adrian may have lice as well." Renaldo laughed. I think it's the first time I've ever heard him laugh.

"I'm sorry, Miss," he said.

"Renaldo," I said. "I am in this car and I heard you laughing. It's not funny."

"Oh, but it is, Sir. You must have a sense of humor when it comes to these unfortunate incidents. How else shall we endure our time here on earth?" Lora looked over to me and smiled.

"This is why I love him," she said. "We'll be there in about ten minutes, Renaldo."

"Very well," he said. "See you in a bit. Adrian, would you be willing to do me a favor?"

"After you laughed at me," I said. "I don't know."

"Oh, don't be a hooligan," Renaldo said. "Strip off all your clothes on the porch. Don't bring your lice into the house." Lora burst out laughing.

"I hate both of you," I said.

"You look ridiculous," Lorelei said to me.

Evidentally the only effective way to get rid of lice is with tea tree oil and dish detergent. One killed the lice, the other killed the eggs. Don't ask me which one did what. As soon as we walked through the door, me in my boxers and Estela in her underwear, the process had begun. Renaldo whisked Estela away to the downstairs bathroom. Lorelei sat me down in a kitchen chair with a squirt bottle in her hand.

She shook it up with her finger over the tip, like you would a mixed drink. Serena stood by and giggled. I pointed my finger at her.

"You, little girl," I said. "Are going to get it when this is over." That only made her giggle more. I laughed with her. "How do you know for certain I have them?" I asked Lora.

"Estela is covered in them, infested in the worst way," she explained. "She was laying on your shoulder with her hair in yours. What do you think??"

"I hate my job," I said and she smiled.

"No, you don't."

"I do."

"Lean over on your knees, put your hair over your head." She started putting the tea tree oil mixture into the roots of my hair, massaging it in with her fingers.

"Serena, honey," she said. "Mix up another bottle for Mamma. You know how much?"

"Yes, Ma'am," Serena said. "You have too much hair, Adrian."

"I do," I agreed.

Lorelei continued running the tip of the bottle across my scalp. I could feel the liquid seeping into my hair and running down across my forehead.

"Towel??" I asked as I held out my hand and Lorelei handed me one. I brought it to my forehead. "How long does this procedure take?"

"Well," Lora said. "I only have to do the roots and then massage it into the rest of your hair but then we'll need to wrap it in a towel on top of your head for a few hours."

"What???" I asked, astonished. "A few hours??"

"Yes," she said. "It takes a while to kill them and we don't want to take any chances of them figuring out an escape route." She laughed.

"Did I mention how much I hate my job right now??"

"You should probably call anybody who had direct contact with Estela. They probably need to be treated, too."

"Jesus," I said as Lorelei continued massaging my scalp. "Serena, will you give me my phone on the table?"

"Yes, Sir," she said and she handed it to me.

"This is starting to burn," I told Lora.

"It'll burn a little," she confirmed. "Tea tree oil is a strong natural remedy. You never want to use any essential oils by themselves but especially the tea tree oil."

"Hey," I said when Jenny answered the phone. "You need to tell any of the guys who had direct contact with Estela to get treated for lice. Lorelei said they are extremely intelligent." Lora rolled her eyes.

"Extremely intelligent?" Jenny asked and chuckled.

"Yeah," I said. "She's treating me with a tea tree oil tincture but my understanding is they can escape if you aren't careful."

"You're so crazy," Lora said. She wrapped a towel around my head and twisted it on my forehead, helped me sit back up without losing it.

"Is that what I tell the guys?" Jenny asked. "Tea tree oil?" I looked over to Lorelei and raised my eyebrows.

"Put her on speaker phone," Lorelei said so I hit the speaker on my phone.

"Talk to Lorelei," I told Jenny.

"I use my tea tree tincture," Lorelei said. "It's $28 but they can use tea tree oil and dish detergent. If that doesn't work, tell them to call me."

"Great way to do business, " Jenny commented.

"I'll have to mix up another batch if they want it," Lora said. "So, let me know ahead of time."

"You have to massage it into your scalp," I added. "And you have to keep it wrapped in a towel for a few hours."

"Are you now an official on lice treatments?" Jenny asked and laughed.

"Yes."

"Awesome," she said. "Everything else there going okay?"

"Yep," I confirmed. "Renaldo is treating Estela."

"Great. Thank you, Lorelei, for your help."

"Sure."

"Let me know when you hear from CPS," I said.

"Will do."

At six o'clock that night we still hadn't heard from Child Protective Services so Jenny called them only to have them say it would be closer to nine before they arrived. Apparently, they'd had an earlier incident with a family of five children. They were having a hard time placing them. No one wanted to take all of them together yet they were terrified to be apart. I told Lorelei I thought I had a difficult and stressful job but I didn't envy the social workers with CPS. Here you have these precious children and no where to take them. I'm not sure I could have dealt with it emotionally. I am especially sensitive when it comes to kids, so I asked Lorelei an impossible favor I thought with certainty would be denied. Not a magical favor. An everyday favor. Although I'm sure a magical favor wouldn't have been denied either.

"Okay," she said without even thinking it over. She was cutting up vegetables for a Sicilian stir-fry called la caponata. I didn't even know there was such a thing as a Sicilian stir-fry. "Technically, it isn't Sicilian stir-fry," she said. "That's just what I call it."

"So, it's cool with you for Estela to stay here until CPS has a placement for her?" I asked as I leaned up against the counter beside her.

"Have you seen her and Serena together?" she asked as she looked over to me. "They're having a blast together."

"That's good," I said as I peered around the corner. "I feel sorry for Estela. Poor little girl."

"It seems they aren't having any problems understanding one another despite the language barrier."

"Kids are amazing," I offered.

"I know, right? We can learn a lot from them," she said as she dumped all the vegetables she'd cut up into the pan on the stove. She looked to me once more.

"It'll take about twenty minutes," she said. "It seems to me someone needs a shampoo." I motioned to myself.

"You don't like my slicked back James Dean hair?" I asked. She put her hands on her hips.

"I'm not feeling it," she said and smiled. She put a chair in front of the kitchen sink and I sat down and leaned my head back against the rim of it. "Lift," she said as she placed a towel under my neck. "Better?"

"Mmm-hmm."

She ran her hands through my hair and started wetting it down with the sprayer weaving her fingers in and out as she did. I know women get their hair shampooed by someone every time they get their hair done but guys don't. I can't remember anyone ever shampooing my hair except Nana when I was little. Lorelei shampooing it now felt incredible.

"Sorry," she said. "This isn't Vanilla Coconut."

"I don't care what it is," I admitted. "It feels like heaven. Of course, it doesn't hurt that your boobs are in my face."

"You're such a pervert," she said and laughed. She rubbed her fingers into my scalp a little longer then rinsed the shampoo out and did it again, running her fingers to the ends of my hair.

"What is this?" I asked. "It smells herb-ally."

"It's a rosemary and mint cleansing hair conditioner I make."

"Ah..."

"Most shampoos dry out your hair horribly," she explained. "So, I concocted a cleansing conditoner. It's good to leave on for a few minutes but I'm massasging it in to get rid of the tea tree oil." She rinsed my hair again and squeezed my hair together, helped me sit up as she wrapped another towel around my head.

"Feel better?" she asked.

"Incredibly better," I said as I towel dried my hair.

She leaned over to me. It was like that night on the beach. Instinct. Impulse. Natural reaction. Whatever you want to call it but our faces came together. It wasn't Lorelei. It was me. Totally me. I put my hand on her cheek, leaned forward, and kissed her lips softly.

"Thank you," I said quietly. She stared into my eyes and I held her gaze.

"You're welcome," she said and smiled.

Later that evening after I had helped Lora put Serena and Estela to bed, I walked back downstairs to get a bottle of water. CPS still hadn't found a placement for Estela and Lora had a headache so I suggested she take a hot bath. I told her I'd stay with the girls for a while until she was done. Once I'd put her to bed I'd leave and go back over to the Inn. Tiffany kept telling me I needed to stop feeling obligated to Lorelei for these kinds of things and that it wasn't my responsibility to be Lora's back-up plan when things didn't go her way but Tiffany didn't understand the relationship I had with Lorelei. Despite our earlier kiss we were just friends. At least that's what I believed. I wasn't so sure what Lorelei believed.

I opened the refrigerator and pulled out a bottle of water then leaned up against the counter. Lorelei's datebook. Did I dare look through it? I couldn't stop myself. It wasn't just a calendar. It was a daily schedule, a list of clients with their addresses and phone numbers, some of Serena's school papers, a list of what she'd titled as 'Things I want but will probably never get.' Number one: A husband. I had to laugh. It was also a diary of sorts. In the back there was a sleeve with various papers inside, one of which was a page out of a magazine. I pulled it out and unfolded it. It was an advertisement for a Paloma Picasso ring and at the top she'd written, 'Maybe one day.' I slipped it into my pocket.

She had probably thought I'd forgotten about her birthday with everything else that had been going on but I hadn't forgotten about it at all. Now I knew what I would give her. I closed her datebook. She would be so surprised. I pulled out my phone and typed the jewelry designer into my browser. It was the first ring that popped up and it was beautiful. I clicked on her size and put it on hold until I could get into the City.

Happy Birthday, Lorelei Anastasio.

The next morning, I drove into the City to Riverside Correctional. I despised all the crap I had to go through to get inside. I presented my DEA credentials to the officer at the front desk. I didn't recognize her.

"Sign this," she said without even acknowledging me. She handed me back my card. I signed the guest entrance list. "Driver's license," she said.

"Which one?" I asked and smiled. She didn't smile in return.

"Whichever one you want to give me," she said sullenly. "Do you have an alias?"

"I have about twelve aliases," I said. "Is Kiara here?"

"Kiara!!" she yelled behind her. "Some DEA guy here for you."

Kiara poked her head through the intake window behind the front desk.

"Adrian!" she said excitedly. "What up, boo?"

She came to the door behind the desk and buzzed herself through it. She proceeded to come down the few steps that separated the front office from the lobby.

"Lord," she said as she hugged me. She smelled like the tropics. You know that suntan lotion with the pineapple on the front of the bottle? That one. "When did I last see you?" she asked.

"Not sure," I answered.

"Oh, come on, boy, you aren't happy to see me??"

"Well, of course, I'm happy to see you. I ask for you, didn't I?"

"You so sexy," she said as she punched my arm.

"Thanks."

"You know I told Calvin I would leave him for you."

"Oh?"

"We're getting married next week!" she told me.

"If you don't leave with me today??"

"You haven't lost your sense of humor, I see."

"I try."

"Who are you here for?"

"Lenny Walker."

"Damn. That son of a bitch."

"Yep."

"Well, come on back."

I followed her down the hall and she buzzed me through the door leading to the prisoner quarters. She led me into the visiting room, handed me a sign in sheet, which I signed, then gave me an entry card.

"I'll put him in three," she said as she headed back out the door.

"Okay, thanks Kiara." She blew me a kiss.

"You're welcome, boo."

Lenny Walker was afraid of me. I saw it in his eyes as soon as he walked through the door. He didn't want me to know he was afraid, though, so he played it cool.

"Heard you know a friend of mine," I told him.

"Who?" he asked.

"Gianni Vallario. You friends with him?"

"He ain't my friend," he said as I sat down at the table in front of him.

"No?"

"No."

I tapped the entry card Kiara had given me on the table as I leaned back in my chair.

"He ever beat you up?" I asked him. Lenny narrowed his eyes at me but didn't say anything, so I went on. "He beat me up once. He ever tell you about that?"

"You's got a cigarette?" he asked me.

I always had cigarettes when I went into prisons even though I didn't smoke them because everyone wanted one. I reached inside my coat pocket and pulled one out, handed it to him.

"Thanks, man." I held out my lighter.

"Yep."

"He beat you up?" he asked. He didn't ask this out of concern. He asked because he thought it would get me off track.

"Yep," I said. "He did. In high school."

"Man, you guys go back a ways, huh?"

"Yep." He took a drag off his cigarette.

"He know what you doing now?" Lenny asked.

"Oh yeah," I said and smiled.

"You know his wife," he said. It wasn't a question so I didn't answer it. "Man, she a dangerous woman."

"Oh, yeah?" I asked. "Why is that?"

"She a sorceress." I laughed. I probably shouldn't have. "It ain't funny, man. That woman crazy."

"Is that what Gianni told you?"

I crossed one foot over the other, tapped my entry card on the table again. It seemed like a thoughtless action but it drove most people in Lenny's position crazy. Kind of like when I had to listen to *The Real Slim Shady* at two decibels higher than an air horn. I could tell he wanted to reach over and grab it out of my hand.

"He never tell you," Lenny said. "But he afraid of her, too."

"Who?" I asked.

"Gianni."

"Gianni is afraid of his wife?" I asked, surprised.

I didn't say Lorelei's name because I didn't want Lenny to know I knew her that well. I also didn't want him to know she was no longer Gianni's wife. Then I wondered if Gianni knew she was no longer his wife. He did. He just didn't want anyone else to know.

"Yeah, man. She cast spells on him."

"You don't believe that, do you?" I asked Lenny.

"That shit is real, man."

"What kind of spell did she cast on him?" I asked curiously.

"You didn't comes here to talk to me about her spells," he said and grinned at me. "You comes here to talk to me about where he is."

"I don't think you know where he is, do you Lenny?"

"No, Sir. I don't."

"Aw, come on, Lenny, don't call me Sir...you know I ain't old enough for that yet."

"I know," he said and laughed. "I bet I's older than you."

"You think?" I asked and smiled.

"How old is you?" he asked.

"You want the truth?"

"I wouldn't ask ya if I didn't want the truth."

"I'm twenty-seven."

"You gots a wife?" he asked. He took a puff off his cigarette and I watched the smoke trail from his nostrils.

"No," I said. "I ain't got time for a wife."

"You playing the field, ain't ya?" He grinned. He only had a few teeth that I could tell.

"Always," I said.

"Gianni thinks you's sleeping with his wife," he told me. I raised my eyebrows and nodded.

"That doesn't surprise me," I said.

"He don't like you, not one bit."

"I didn't think so."

"Why you after him?" he asked.

"I think that's kind of obvious," I stated.

"Naw, I mean I know he gone and all but is that the only reason??"

"Who's asking the questions, Lenny?" I asked and smiled. "Me or you?"

"I just curious," he said and laughed. I tapped the card on the table again.

"Do you know where he is?" I asked.

"No."

"Lenny," I said as I leaned forward on the table. "I may not be friends with Gianni but I can be friends with you. You understand that, right?"

"Yes, Sir."

"Do you know where he is right now?" Lenny looked down.

"Naw."

"Lenny," I said. "Look at me. Do you know where Gianni Vallario is?"

"No," he said. "That's the truth. I swear it." I leaned back in my chair again.

"Okay," I said. "I believe you." I didn't.

We were silent for a moment except for the card. I kept tapping the card.

"Tell me something about Gianni I don't know."

"What's in it for me?" he asked.

"When's your next parole hearing?" I asked him.

"In the Spring."

"How does January sound to you?" I asked.

"He's looking for his kid," Lenny told me.

"Gianni is looking for his kid?" I asked.

"Yeah."

"How old is his kid?"

"I don't know, man. He a kid."

"He?"

"Yeah."

"His son isn't with his wife?" I asked.

"Naw, man. She crazy, I told you."

"Right."

"He ain't on Long Island," Lenny said.

"Gianni or his kid?"

"Gianni," he said. "I don't know nothing 'bout his kid."

"Where is he then?"

"You got another cigarette?" he asked.

"I got a pack of cigarettes if you tell me where Gianni is," I told him.

He looked away from me, stared at the wall beside him. I didn't say anything and he finally looked back to me.

"He ain't here," he said.

"Where's here?" I asked.

"Here," he said. "He ain't in New York."

"Is he in Jersey?"

"He left the country, man."

This was shocking news for me but I didn't show it.

"You know where he went?" I asked.

I didn't expect an answer. I didn't need an answer. I knew where Gianni Vallario had gone. He'd gone where all *The Empire* goes when things get tough. He'd gone to Sicily.

"He went to Italy, man."

The following night before the bust I went to Palazzo Cremisi. I needed two things before I did a bust. Good food and reassurance I would come back out alive. Lorelei could give me both.

"Thanks for cooking for me," I said.

"Yep."

"Are you mad?" I asked. She turned from the stove.

"No."

"You sound mad," I said. "I know when you're mad." She rolled her eyes.

"I'm not mad," she reiterated. "I'm just…. I don't know what I am."

"Frustrated? Impatient? Bewildered?" I asked. She smiled.

"Aggravated."

"Because of Gianni…" I hesitated. "…and me."

"Because of everything. The fertility treatments, fucking Gianni, everything."

"Where are the girls?" I asked as I sat down at the kitchen table. "I was kind of looking forward to seeing them."

Lorelei walked over to the bottom of the stairs.

"Girls!" she called up the stairs. She looked back over to me as Serena and Estela came running down the stairs. "Ask and you shall receive." They stopped at the bottom and looked over to me.

"Hi Adrian," Serena said. She reminded me so much of Maria. Smarter than she should have been.

"Hello, Miss. Serena. Hello Estela."

"Hello," Estela said in return.

"I'm teaching her English!" Serena said.

"That's awesome," I said as I looked over to Lorelei. She smiled. Serena leaned over to Estela and whispered in her ear and I looked to Lorelei again. She shrugged.

"Thank you," Estela said. I sat amazed.

"Tell him the rest, Estela," Serena ordered.

"Per ajudar-me," Estela said.

"In English!" Serena said excitedly. Estela looked over to her and to Lorelei.

"Està bé," Lora said. "Pots dir-li. Ell t'estima. Recordes?" Estela looked to me and then back to Lorelei. "Està bé," Lorelei said again.

"For..." Estela started.

"Help..." Serena interuppted.

"Serena Michele!" Lora chastised. "Let Estela do it." To Estela, "Endavant, Estela."

"Helping me," Estela finished.

"You are very welcome," I said.

As soon as I did she ran to me and gave me a hug. It almost brought tears to my eyes. This was one of the reasons I did what I did. Little girls like Estela made risking your life every day worth it.

"Mamma is taking us to buy clothes tomorrow," Serena said excitedly.

"That's awesome," I said.

"Serena," Lorelei said. "Go see if Renaldo wants dinner. Tell him I'm making pasta *con le sarde.*"

"Okay," Serena said. She grabbed Estela's hand as they headed toward the back door.

"I'm making this pasta con le sarde for you," Lorelei said to me as the girls went out onto the porch. "That should tell you how much I love you."

"I haven't had any of that since Nonna," I said as I leaned back in my chair.

"Yeah," she said. "She used to make it all the time. It was Nonno's favorite dish."

"Well, I wasn't going to mention your house smells like fish," I said jokingly.

She swatted me with the dishtowel she was holding and I stood up. I took a fifty dollar bill out of my pants pocket and walked over behind Lorelei. I stuck it in the back pocket of her jeans.

"What are doing?" she asked as she turned around and reached behind her. She pulled the money out of her pocket. "What is this for?"

"The girls," I said. "Clothes."

"Do you know how many clothes Serena has??"

"Estela."

"I know," she said as she held the money in her hand. She folded it up. "Serena has enough for both of them but I just thought Estela needed some of her own."

"Well, now you don't have to go to Walmart."

"Ha," she said.

"Take them to the mall."

"Thank you, Adrian."

"I just don't think everything you do should be on your Papa's credit card. He doesn't need to know you have another child to feed."

"You're right."

"I know," I said. "Wine?"

"I put a good bottle of chianti in the cooler."

I retrieved it and she handed me a corkscrew and two glasses. I opened the bottle and laid the cork on the table, poured both of us a glass.

"Thanks," she said as she took it.

I took a sip of mine and sat back down at the table. She went to the refrigerator and pulled out a plate of multi-colored grapes. She was the only person I knew who bought every kind of grape the grocery had in stock at the same time. She sat the plate of grapes in front of me.

"Well, I have good news that will probably help soothe your mind," I said.

"What is it?"

"Gianni isn't in New York."

"How do you know that?"

"Because I talked to Lenny Walker yesterday."

"Who the hell is Lenny Walker?" she asked.

"He was Gianni's cellmate at Riverside," I told her. "And, by the way, he thinks you're a witch."

"Lots of people think I'm a witch," she said. "What's new?"

"He told me Gianni thinks you cast a spell on him."

"I wish I could cast a spell on Gianni," she said. "But I can guarantee you it wouldn't be white magic."

"Aw, come on, Lora. You don't do black magic." She stared at me.

"I don't, but I can," she assured me as she leaned back against the counter. "Nonna used to tell me to never use black magic. She said it wasn't about karma. It was about whose side we were on. I didn't want to ask Nonna whose side we were on, so I asked Nana."

"Let me guess," I said. "We're on God's side." Lora smiled.

"Yeah, but back then her answer perplexed me. I never imagined God..." she motioned around herself. "...could have anything to do what everyone around here calls magic."

"Nana and Nonna," I said. "Two extraordinary women."

"I miss them," Lora said.

"Me, too," I confessed. "You know Nana always told me to make sure I chose the straight and narrow path, that few would find it."

"Nonna used to tell me it was our responsibility to create that path,"

"That sounds like Nonna." I paused. "Gianni has left the country."

"He's gone to Sicily," Lorelei guessed. "Hasn't he?"

"Yes."

"Are you positive?" she asked. "You're sure this Lenny guy didn't just tell you that to get you off track?"

"Do you think I'm that naïve?" I asked. "Airline records. Thursday at four forty-five."

"You're not just telling me that, are you?" I picked up a grape and popped it into my mouth.

"I would never lie to you about that." She turned from the stove.

"Will you always be honest with me about it?"

"About Gianni?"

"Yeah."

"Yes, I will."

"You promise?" she asked.

"Yes. I promise," I assured her. "What else is going on? Because I know it's something."

"I only have one treatment left."

"Why only one?" I asked.

"Because I don't have money to do any more."

"You didn't have money before," I said and laughed. "You just had a credit card."

"You know what I mean," she said. She picked up a grape off the plate and sat down in my lap. "I can't put it on my card again. Papa will kill me."

"You know, this is where I fail to understand what that card is for exactly, because it's obviously not for your electric bill."

"Papa and I had a huge argument before I came here and I told him I didn't need his money."

"Oh…." I bounced her on my leg and she draped her arm across the back of my shoulders. "That was a bad call on your part."

"Tell me about it."

"So, Tony pays for you to have a fatherless child but not your electric bill." She stood up.

"He'd pay the electric bill…it's just…"

"You're too proud." She smiled.

"You know me so well."

"Yep."

"What time is your thing?"

"The bust?" I asked. She nodded. "We don't have a specific time but we're meeting at nine."

"It sounds scary doing it in the dark," she said.

"What happened to 'Everything will be fine, Adrian?' She scratched her head then bounced her hair on her shoulders. "I need 'Everything will be fine, Adrian.'"

"Everything will be fine, Adrian," she said as she got up and walked over to the stove.

"Really?" I asked. "We light it up. As soon as we get in the house the spotlights come on. It'll be like broad daylight."

She came back over and sat a plate of freshly fried arancini in front of me.

"Did you make these just for me?"

"Leftover risotto," she answered dryly.

"Wow," I said as I picked one up. "I love you, too." I stood up and popped it into my mouth. "Ah...hot, hot, hot." I sucked air into my mouth.

"Well, they just came out of the fryer," Lora said. "You should have let them cool first."

"I'm going out to the car to get my things while you finish up," I told her as I continued to suck air into my mouth.

"What things?" she asked.

"All my stuff for the bust."

"Such as??"

"Clothes...." She pointed at me.

"Don't screw with me, Adrian. Don't you bring any guns into this house." I raised my t-shirt.

"Like this one??" I asked and smiled.

"I mean the Glock," she said. "It freaks the Spirits out." I walked over to the back door.

"It can't possibly be because they're afraid they'll die."

"Oh, ha ha."

"I don't have any other guns than this one right now. They're at the station and I have to sign them out anyway. You think I just drive around with M4 223's in my car?"

"I don't even know what a M4 223 is."

"It's a semi-automatic rifle," I told her. "For precarious situations."

"Is tonight a precarious situation?" she asked and smiled.

"Every night I do this is a precarious situation," I said. "This is one of the things I've been working on for quite a while." I opened the door. "Done a shitload of surveillance. Gonna find out who's who in the zoo."

"You truly are crazy," she said. "You know that?"

I laughed and walked out the door. When I came back in, she had the pasta *con le sarde* ready and we sat down and ate together. The girls didn't like pasta con le sarde so they were eating the arancini with tomato sauce. Jenny was right. As much as I didn't want to admit it, Lorelei *was* my Amityville wife. I was used to being taken care of when I was in Amityville by Nana. I didn't plan on Lorelei being the one to take over that chore. It had just kind of happened that way. After dinner I took a quick shower and reappeared in the kitchen.

"Are you going shirtless?" Lora asked as she turned from the sink. I dug through my bag on the kitchen table.

"It's a little chilly for that, don't you think?" I pulled a green long sleeve t-shirt over my head, then my dark blue DEA short-sleeve one. Lorelei watched me.

"Do you guys have bullet-proof vests?"

"Yes."

I dug through my bag for my socks and sat down in a kitchen chair. I pulled my jeans up, put them on and hooked my ankle holster around my leg.

"Not messing around tonight, huh?" Lora asked.

"Nope," I said. "Task force with the state police. Forty-five officers, three houses on the same block. Unknown number of suspects. I've bought from this guy five times, a little more each time. He's got my money. Enough to get a search warrant."

"What do you mean he's got your money?"

"I photocopy the money I buy with before I buy so I can match up the serial numbers when I get the stash from the money house. If I can match up the serial numbers with my copies, I've got a conviction." I pulled on my boots and began to lace them.

"You're so smart," she said. I shook my head.

"Nah, just commonsense."

"That is more than commonsense," she told me. "That is being smart." I smiled and stood up.

"Maybe." I grabbed my bag and threw it over my shoulder then walked over to her.

"Please be careful," she said as she grabbed my t-shirt in her hand. She pulled me toward her.

"Okay. I will." I laid my hand lightly on her waist and kissed her cheek. "Thanks for dinner."

"You promise to be careful?"

"Yep," I assured her. "Watch the eleven o'clock news," I said as I walked out onto the back porch.

"Will you be on it?" she called after me.

"Never," I called back.

"Big dogs on this operation, huh?" I heard one of the suspects say to the other as they sat on the porch steps of the house we'd just ransacked.

"U.S.D.E.A, Nigga. Ain't no regular Popo," the other one said. "They gonna take Carlos down."

"Wait until they tell my P.O. about this."

"Hey," I said as I walked up to them. "We don't find any drugs or money in this house, you're clear. It's not a big deal." I put my gun back into my holster. "I'll talk to your P.O. You'll be alright."

"Thanks, man."

"Yep."

I walked over to Jenny.

"What up, dog?" she asked.

"Dog," I said. "Ha ha. That damn thing near bit my arm off."

"Gotta love Rottweilers."

"I don't get it," I said. "You know, one of my uncles had a Rottweiler. Two of them. They were the sweetest dogs." I motioned to the house. "How do they get like this?"

"They make 'em mean," she said. "Life or death."

"Jeez."

I looked up, saw the girlfriend coming out of the house with the baby. She walked over to me and Jenny.

"Thank you," she said to us but before we could say anything in return she walked away.

"There's your reason for why we do what we do," Jenny said. "That little boy."

"Pretty much the only reason you need, isn't it?" I asked.

"Hey, Adrian!" Warren called from the porch.

"Yep?"

"We're clear."

My radio went off.

"Hey Adrian…got the stockpile at this house…looks like we got 'em."

"Whatcha got?" I radioed back.

"Four guns, thirty pounds of pot, kilo of coke."

"Damn," I said to Jenny. "We're at the wrong house."

"Seems that way," she said.

"I'll be over there in a little bit," I radioed back.

"Yep."

"But no money," I said to Jenny as I walked away from her toward the suspects. She shrugged.

"Can't have it all," she said and smiled.

"You hear that?" I asked them. "Stand up."

"Yeah, man."

"That means you're at the *right* house," I said as I took off their handcuffs.

"Hell, yeah," one of them said. I pointed to him.

"I'll catch up with you next time, though," I said as I smiled and walked away.

"You dreamin', man," he called after me, and we laughed together.

A television reporter who had crossed the crime scene tape walked up to me with his microphone.

"Sir, Sir, can you tell us what's going on?"

I stared at him and Jenny chuckled because she knew what was about to happen.

"Turn off the camera," I said as I held up my hand.

"Sir?"

"Now!!" I said forcefully.

"But, Sir…" he called as he followed me. I stopped and turned to him.

"Do you not understand English?" I asked. He stared at me and I pointed to our van a block or so down the street. "This is a U.S.D.E.A. investigation. By law you are considered an accomplice if you are inside the investigation area and can be prosecuted to the fullest extent of the law. Are you in the investigation area?"

The cameraman took down his camera and the reporter pulled his microphone away from me.

"And you might want to reconsider showing that footage," I called over my shoulder as I walked away. "It's the only concrete evidence I have against you."

"I'm sure this will be on the news," Jenny said when I walked past her. "God knows what they'll report without any footage."

"Fake news," I said and grinned. "The American people are used to it."

Lorelei

It was close to midnight when I decided to take a bath. I hadn't been feeling well lately and I couldn't help but wonder if it had to do with my fertility treatments. I wasn't taking any drugs but, nonetheless, I knew it was messing with my hormones. It was almost as if my body knew what was going on but refused to cooperate. Maybe it didn't like the fact the proposed implantation was fake. Well, I would have preferred it to be real, too, but life doesn't always work that way. Sometimes, you must improvise. Ari asked me why I didn't come up with a potion to help me get pregnant. I told her if I could do that, I'd be richer than Bill Gates.

I closed my bathroom door and sunk down into the bubbly water. Most times when I took a hot bath, I poured myself a glass of champagne. Okay, honestly, it was usually more than a glass but I'd been limiting my alcohol intake since I'd started trying to get pregnant. I put in my earphones and listened to Whitney Houston sing. I thought about her death all the time. A lot more than I ever thought I would.

I laid my head back against the rim of the tub and closed my eyes. It was cold outside and my bathroom window had completely fogged over. The weatherman on one of our local channels said to expect freezing rain overnight so I'd put flannel sheets on the girls' beds. Palazzo Cremisi was beautiful and an historic site in Amityville but it was old and, consequently, cold. Serena and Estela begged me to light the fireplace in their room but that was a definite no-no overnight. I could have easily given Estela her own room but she would have been afraid in the dark in an unfamiliar house. She wanted to stay with Serena anyhow.

Maybe I lost track of time and I may have even fallen asleep for a little bit but when I opened my eyes Adrian was sitting in the red satin brocade chair in the corner with his ankle crossed over his knee . He'd always thought it was funny I had a chair in my bathroom but it was one of the only chairs left from the dining room set my great grand-mother had in her formal dining room. I used to call it the red room when I was little because everything in it was red.

"Holy shit," I said as I pulled my earphones out of my ears. "You scared the living daylights out of me. What the hell are you doing here??"

"I'm happy to see you, too," he said. "Also, you need to change the code on your back door. It's still the same numbers as when we were in high school."

"I know," I said. "I don't know how and I keep forgetting."

"What is the significance of those numbers?"

"You're a detective," I said. "You figure it out."

"Do I need to use my Batman decoder ring?" he asked. "Because I let Terrence borrow it and he hasn't given it back yet."

"Oh, ha ha." I held my breath and went under water, rinsed the conditioner out of my hair.

"I'll give you a hundred dollars if you can figure out the signifi-cance of that code by Christmas," I said when I surfaced.

"You don't have a hundred dollars," he said.

"I have a hundred-dollar gift card for Victoria's Secret." He laughed.

"What the hell am I going to do with a Victoria's Secret gift card??"

"Buy something sexy for Lilah."

"Right," he said. "Seriously though, you need to change the code."

"I just told you I don't know how."

"I'll fix it for you."

"Oh, Adrian," I said. "You're going to change it and then I won't remember what it is."

"I'll change it to something you'll remember."

"Like what?" I asked, aggravated with him.

"My birthday." I thought about that for a moment.

"Okay," I said. "That works. What are you doing here this late?" I asked him. "I thought you'd go back to the Inn."

"I like to surprise you," he said. "I mean, for all you know I could be dead right now."

"Well, can you not surprise me like this again because I nearly had a heart attack."

"I'm alive, by the way."

"Good for you."

"I have an issue, though, and I think you might be able to help me with it."

"Oh, no. What is it?"

"Why 'oh no?'" he asked and laughed.

"Because every time you say that to me, I end up getting myself into something I don't want to get into."

"Such as??" he asked.

He always did this to me. Whenever I tried to call him on something he always asked for a specific example. I have not once, ever in my life, been able to give him a specific example and he knows this.

"You know I can't give you a specific example right now."

"Because there are none," he told me. "Do you want a cat?"

"Hell, no. I don't want a cat. Why? What kind of cat?"

"See?" he said pointing to me. "If you weren't considering it you wouldn't have ask what kind." I rolled my eyes. "We found it in a box in the basement at the drug house."

"What kind???" I asked. He shrugged.

"I don't know. It's a cat."

"No," I said. "Absolutely not. I don't do cats. I'm not having a litter box in my house."

"I'll be right back."

"Adrian!!" I called as he walked out of the bathroom. He came back with the cutest, sweetest little kitten I've ever seen. Golden brown with black spots.

"Oh, my goodness," I said. I couldn't help myself.

"I don't think he's quite six weeks old yet," he said. "So, you'll have to feed him every few hours."

"With what??"

"You'll take him??" he asked excitedly.

"I didn't say that. I just asked what you feed him."

"You'd have to go to the pet store. They have milk for kittens who've been taken away from their mothers too soon."

"Adrian," I whined. "Oh my…jeez. Like I don't already have enough stuff going on."

"Serena and Estela will love him. Cats require no maintenance. They're laid back and low profile."

"Low profile?" I asked and laughed.

"Yeah," he said. "Cats do their own thing."

"Does he have a name?" He looked to the ceiling.

"Uh…" He looked back to me. "What's the cat's name in Aladdin??"

"The tiger?"

"Yes."

"Rajah?"

"That. That's his name."

"Let me see him," I said. I held out my hands.

"How about you get out of the tub first," he said. "He's fragile."

"Oh, my goodness."

I stood up and he handed me a towel. Being naked in front of Adrian after all this time didn't seem to be wrong and it certainly wasn't embarrassing. At least it wasn't for me. I wrapped the towel around myself and stuck the corner back inside of it, held out my hands.

"Give him to me." Adrian held him out and I took him into my hands. I held him up in front of me.

"Hi, little one," I said. I leaned forward and kissed its little nose.

"It's a match made in heaven," Adrian said.

"I'm going to kill you," I told him. "You did this on purpose. You brought this poor little thing in here because you knew I couldn't say no." He shrugged.

"Well, you *can*," he told me.

"What am I going to feed him tonight?"

"I don't know. That's your problem." I reached out and smacked him on his arm as I walked into my bedroom. He followed me.

"How's Lilah?" I asked as I sat Rajah down on my bed. He began meowing at once. "I forgot to ask you earlier."

"No, you didn't," he said. "You don't care about Lilah."

"I do," I said motioning to myself. "I like Lilah." He stuffed his hands down into his pockets.

"What do you like about her?" he said with a sly smile. He was being facetious and he knew I knew he was being facetious.

"That she puts up with you," I said.

"She's good," he said. "I told her about our kiss."

"What kiss?"

"After Nana's funeral."

"Oh, good grief, Adrian. That was over two months ago."

"I know but I still hadn't told her."

"You opened a closed door," I said.

"What does that mean??" he asked.

"Well, now, she's going to wonder if there is something going on between us."

"Is there?" he asked as he raised his eyebrows.

"It's not like she would have ever found out," I told him as I pulled underwear out of my drawer. I slipped them on underneath my towel then reached under my pillow for my nightgown. "It was just a simple kiss."

"One, it was not just a simple kiss. It was soul kissing."

"Soul kissing," I repeated as I unwrapped my towel. Adrian covered his eyes. "Who, besides your sexy foster mom, has ever called touching tongues soul kissing??" He shrugged.

I walked over to my dressing table and picked up a hairband then twisted it around my wet hair. It would put it into a million tangles but I would deal with that in the morning.

"You've told Lilah about our history?" I asked.

"Some of it."

"Uh-huh."

"What??" he asked. "What am I supposed to be telling her?"

"Have you told her about Stef?"

"I can't give out information about my cases," he said. "You know that as well as I do."

"You haven't told her about us trying to have a baby, either."

"I know," he said. He took a deep breath.

"Well, then, do it."

"It's not that simple."

"It's a conversation," I told him. "How hard can it be? You want me to do it??"

"Yeah," he said jokingly. "Let me give you her number."

I pulled the covers back on my bed and picked up Rajah. I held him close to me while I settled into bed. Adrian sat down beside me. He reached over and rubbed Rajah's little head.

"Your birthday was last week. You thought I'd forgotten. Didn't you?"

"Possibly," I said. "You've been kind of preoccupied with everything else going on."

"I told you I'd take you into the City and I was thinking I'd have to change those plans if I couldn't locate Gianni but I did so we can still go if you want."

"You don't have to do that," I said. "It's fine. Just get me a card."

"You were excited about going into the City."

"I wasn't going through fertility treatments then." I hesitated. "Nor did I own a cat."

"Renaldo will take care of the cat while you're gone," he told me. "You know he will."

"Probably."

"So, what's the issue with the treatments?" he asked.

"They're just messing with my hormones or something. I feel like I'm pregnant but I'm not. I'm tired all the time. I don't even know if I have enough energy to go into the City."

"What do you want to do, then?"

"I'd have to get Renaldo or Ari to keep Serena and probably Estela...and thanks to you, Rajah."

"Yeah," he agreed. "Is that an issue?"

"Well, I don't know," I said. "I'm not sure how long I'm going to have Estela. How long am I going to have Estela?"

"I don't know," he told me. "It's not looking good at this point."

"What do you mean, 'good?'"

"When Jenny told Child Protective Services you had Estela and you spoke Catalan, they kind of put Estela on the back burner."

"What does that mean?"

"It means you have Estela indefinitely."

"Were you planning on telling me this??" I asked, appalled. "Or did you just deem it unnecessary?"

"I thought you liked Estela."

"Well, I do, but I wasn't planning on having her for very long, and now I also have a cat." I looked down to Rajah and kissed his little head.

"Estela loves you," he told me. "She needs you."

"Damn it."

"Why damn it?" he asked.

"Because I love her, too." He laughed.

"I know," he said. I thought for a moment.

"What do you think of going to Angelic Manor?"

"In the Hamptons?"

"Yeah."

I could tell his mind was turning circles. I wasn't sure why. Maybe it was because the DEA wouldn't approve of one of their agents staying in an Empire compound.

"No one else is there?"

"Not at the moment," I told him.

"It'll be cold as a witch's tit up there," he said and laughed.

"Ha, ha."

"If that's where you want to go, we can."

"There's a couple of really nice restaurants nearby. You could take me for a birthday dinner and then we could make a fire in the big stone fireplace and watch an old movie."

"*Vicky Cristina Barcelona*?" he asked and smiled.

"That would be perfect."

"Okay," he said. "Make arrangements for the girls and Rajah. We'll go and I'll take you out for dinner but we can only stay for one night."

"Thank you, Adrian."

"Go to sleep," he said and kissed my forehead. "I'll let myself out."

"You spoil me," I told him when he got to my bedroom door.

"Someone has to do it now, don't they?" he asked and smiled. "And who knows what might happen to me if I don't." I shook my head in amusement.

"Like I would ever cast a spell on you," I said.

"Wouldn't be the first time," he told me as he shut my door.

Silly boy.

Most people consider talking to the dead, palmistry, tarot readings and apothecarists to be magic. They're not. Nonna used to tell me the kind of magic people *thought* we had — black magic - was of the devil but we do not practice that kind of magic. We are not magical beings with special powers. We are normal people who possess a very special gift. We believe sometimes, as Nonna used to say, God likes it when we help ourselves. Not outside of His power but within it.

Father McMery once told Nonna he considered God's creation to be God's magic and through God's power we could accomplish great things in our lives, things so great they were beyond human understanding. It's probably why we've been a part of Father McMery's congregation since the beginning of time. Of course, the fact he welcomes us and anyone else associated with *The Empire* into his church at all is considered sacrilegious to the general population but the general population tend to believe in perfectionism when it comes to parishioners which Father McMery says borders on hypocrisy. I needed to go back to church. I wonder what the villagers would say if I appeared on a Sunday morning or at evening prayers. I know what Father McMery would say, "Welcome, my child. It is so good to see you."

There are so many words in other languages the English language can't express. There are feelings, situations, understandings, even wishes and anticipations that have no words in the English language. None. Strangely enough, if you investigate it thoroughly, which I did in my college thesis you will learn there are many languages that do not have a word for the English word magic. In most languages the essence of the word magic is simply expressed as being a miraculous event.

Talking to the dead is a gift given by God. God gave me the ability to see and commune with the dead. Nonna assured me it is not something the devil would ever permit simply because it scares him. What might the dead tell me if the devil weren't in complete control of them? A lot of things he doesn't want me to know, that's what.

Palmistry is a learned talent. It isn't given or bestowed. It is simply another language, which is the original reason I became interested in languages to begin with. If you can read a book you can read a palmistry chart, and if you can read a palmistry chart then you can memorize it, and if you can memorize it then you can read palms. Not so magical after all. The same is true of tarot cards, mostly.

Tarot cards supposedly predict the future and are up to chance and coincidence. In all honesty I don't believe in tarot cards. I don't think they're harmful. I use them every day but I always tell my clients tarot cards are not predictable and they are certainly not dependable indications of what is going to happen in their lives. I can tell them what the tarot cards mean because I've memorized them just like I have the palmistry chart but I don't believe they possess any kind of magical power.

The main difference between the two is palmistry is mainly about the past and tarot cards focus on the future. The past is evident. The future is iffy at most and the reason the future is iffy is because we can change the future. In fact, we change the future every day. Every decision we make over the course of a day changes our future. This is why I don't believe in tarot cards. So, when people ask me to do a tarot card reading for them (like Ari) I tell them there are no guarantees and if they don't like the outcome then it's up to them to do something about it.

Then, of course, it comes down to spells and apothecary. Being an apothecarist is simple. It's being nature's pharmacist. If there's an ailment out there I probably have an antidote for it somewhere and if I don't, I'll either research and create it or reach out to other apothecarists for sage advice and treatment. Discovering the benefits of God's creation is, like being able to talk to the dead, a gift from Him. Anyone can do it but it takes a great deal of time, experimentation and patience. Not for me because I had Nonna but I think most apothecarists will tell you they also had a grandmother or wise elder who taught them about natural medicines as they grew up. It's hard to be an apothecarist if you haven't been around it since childhood. I'm not saying it's impossible because, like Adrian, I don't believe anything is impossible if you work at it hard enough, but it's difficult.

Spells, well. I guess spells are as close to magic as you can get and they are referenced as white magic and black magic. Basically, that means good and evil. White magic stems from goodness and wanting to bring good to humanity and into the world in general. I'm not sure where black magic stems from. I just know I don't practice it. I am sure I am capable of it, just like other people can cause harm in other ways, but I do not wish to inflict harm on anyone. I get mad but I do not get even. Karma takes care of those things for me.

I don't toy with Spirits. I respect them because I know for sure, if they want to, they can kill me. Ari freaked out the first time I told her this but then I reminded her people on earth can do that, too. My friendship with Ari has allowed me to understand Nonna and Nana's friendship a little better because up until I explained my abilities to Ari, she was just like everyone else. She believed everything she'd heard — that *The Empire* operates via witchcraft. We are not witches. We simply know a lot of things most people don't know.

I believe God provides us with the tools we need to overcome evil. I also believe the devil can intercept those tools. Nonna once told me evil can be disguised as good just as well as good can be disguised as evil. *The Empire's* only secret? We know the difference.

I found an old kennel in the cellar Mamma used to have for her little Pomeranian and nestled Rajah inside of it with a bunch of old towels. I had no idea what to feed him so I had to look it up online. Of course, every pet store within a hundred-mile radius was closed for the day so I had to make do with what I had until morning. I couldn't help but think during the night Rajah was good practice for the new baby I would have soon. Hopefully I would have a new baby soon.

A little research told me to give Rajah yogurt if I didn't have anything else but to get him on the formula as soon as possible. He licked the yogurt off my fingers and fell asleep each time afterward. I sat up and looked over to him now. He was sleeping peacefully so I laid back against my pillows. It was early and the sun was just beginning to rise. That was when I remembered my dream and a sudden sense of dread came over me.

Caris. Was it simply a harmless dream or was it a Spirit trying to talk to me? I had learned over the years Spirits can talk to you in many ways. They can write on mirrors, like Ana had with Adrian; they once used Serena's alphabet letters on my refrigerator door to convey what they needed; and once a Spirit even left a one-word message on my front sidewalk with tiny rocks: misery. They were in misery. That night I had a dream where that same Spirit pleaded with me to help them. But this dream. Was it a Spirit or simply a harmless nightmare?

Caris. Sometimes I could see visions in my head of what these Spirits looked like when they were here on earth. Other times they would manifest themselves in front of me but I didn't have as much power as Adrian did so that didn't happen very often. In this dream I saw Caris. She was walking across a pond on top of the water. She was wearing a long, crimson evening gown and she was barefoot. Her long, dark hair was piled on top of her head in a messy bun and her lips glistened with dark red lipstick. She beckoned to me with her finger, but I stood still. She was smiling and then, without warning, the water parted and she was sucked underneath. I watched her struggle but I still didn't move. I could hear her calling my name. Then she screamed something unintelligible. I tried to focus.

I have this one talent no one else does. At least I don't know of anyone else who possesses it. I can rewind. If I have a dream, I can rewind it. If I hear something and don't understand it, I can rewind it over and over in my mind until I figure it out or hear it the way it was intended. Now I rewound Caris' scream in my mind again and I shivered. It was the scream of a dying woman pleading for forgiveness but this wasn't forgiveness for her soul. This was forgiveness from someone here on earth. Whose forgiveness did she need? I closed my eyes and brought my fingers to my temples.

"Tell me Caris," I said aloud. "Tell me who you want to forgive you. I'll tell them. I'll make sure they know. Tell me. I can help you."

"No," I heard in my mind.

"I know you think I can't," I told her. "But I promise you, I can. I can make it better."

"Why would you want to help me?" she screamed inside my head.

"Because I can. I always help Spirits. That's my job."

Silence. I waited. Adrian once told me when working with children you had to have patience. Spirits were the same way. They didn't trust you unless you proved to them you were trustworthy. Suddenly it dawned on me what Caris needed to hear.

"Because I love your son," I told her. "That's why. I know he has our gift. He told me." It was the first time in my life I'd ever heard a Spirit speak audibly to me and it scared me and amazed me at the same time.

"Adrian," she said quietly. "Tell him he's a..." Her voice trailed off and I lost it. I couldn't hear her audibly anymore. I couldn't even hear her in my mind.

"Caris?? Are you still there? Talk to me. Please. What is he? What is Adrian??"

I waited. It does no good to plead with Spirits. They are on their own time and have their own agendas. There were no more words inside my head. I sat there patiently but Caris was gone. Maybe she would return but not today. No, not anytime soon. I nearly jumped out of my skin when I heard Rajah whimpering a few minutes later. I got up and unlocked his kennel, reached inside to take him into my arms. Serena and Estela burst through my bedroom door.

"Mamma! Mamma!" Serena called as she wrapped her little arms around my neck. She nearly knocked me over onto the floor. Estela came flying in behind her.

Serena had always risen early so it wasn't a surprise she was awake now.

"What? What is it, darling?" I asked as I wrapped my free arm around her waist.

"A kitten!!" she called.

"Un gatet," Estela said excitedly.

"Yes," I affirmed. "A kitten."

I handed Rajah to Serena and she took him from me and held him close to her. She kissed the top of his little head.

"I love kittens!!" she exclaimed.

"Be careful with him," I told her. "He's tiny."

"Is this my kitten??"

I hadn't thought of that yet but why not?

"Yes," I said. "You can thank Adrian the next time you see him."

"Adrian brought me a kitten???"

"He did," I told her. To Estela, "L'Adrian et va portar a tu i a Serena un gatet." (*Adrian brought you and Serena a kitten.*)

"M'encanten els gatets!" Estela said. (*I love kittens!*)

"No tots?" I said and she laughed. (*Don't we all?*)

"I love Adrian, Mamma," Serena said.

"I love Adrian, Mamma," Estela repeated.

I love Adrian. I used to write it on my notebooks, my mirror, with chalk on the sidewalk at school. Mr. and Mrs. Adrian Cristiano Bennett. That's what I dreamed of. Being Mrs. Adrian Cristiano Bennett. That's what I always wanted to be.

"Mamma!" Serena exclaimed. "He's purring!"

"Yes, darling," I said. "He is."

"I love Adrian so much!!" Serena exclaimed as she looked up to me. I smiled.

You're not the only one, I thought.

———

The next day I called Ari and asked her to come for dinner. I rarely had people for dinner. I love to cook and everyone always tells me I am a good cook but other than cooking for Adrian and Ari I rarely cook for other people.

"You don't want to go out?" Ari asked. "We could go to that little place on the water that has the really good-looking bartender. You know, Elias?"

"Yeah, but I sort of want a quiet dinner," I explained.

"Why?" she asked. "What's wrong?"

"I had a dream," I said.

"Oh, no."

"It wasn't bad. At least I don't think it was bad. Maybe. But I need to talk to you about it."

"Should I bring anything?" she asked.

"Like food?"

"Yeah."

"No," I said. "Just bring yourself. Any cravings?"

"Make something really good that doesn't require me or you to go to the grocery store."

"Hmm." I thought for a moment. "How about Pasta alla Norma?" Ari laughed.

"Okay, I'm fairly certain you are talking about some weird Sicilian pasta. At least I hope you are talking about some weird Sicilian pasta because my mother's cat's name is Norma."

"Must you be so witty all the time?" I asked.

"Eh, life is boring otherwise."

"Pasta alla Norma is macaroni with tomatoes, eggplant and ricotta."

"And fresh basil, I hope?"

"Always fresh basil."

"Sounds delicious! I'll see you around seven."

"Okay. Thanks, Ari."

"What are you thanking me for?" she asked. "You're the one doing the cooking."

"Moral support," I told her.

"Always," she said.

Making pasta alla Norma is a simple task as far as Sicilian dishes go, especially since I keep containers of frozen tomato sauce in my freezer year-round. I do a lot of meal preparation ahead of time for those days when I'm too mentally exhausted to think, and when you make yourself available to Spirits every day, that happens a lot more than you'd imagine.

Ever since Serena started school, I've insisted on taking and picking her up even though Renaldo told me he would be more than happy to do it for me. I didn't want the teachers and other parents to think I was an absent mother who depended on her butler to do everything for her. Just the fact I had a butler pissed off most people.

Honestly, I couldn't live without Renaldo. I didn't treat him like a butler because he'd been with our family for so long, he *was* family. Even so there were certain things he insisted upon, like not eating dinner with the family, even though the family was only me and Serena. Well, and now, Estela. I did convince him to have dinner with us the night of his birthday but he seemed uncomfortable throughout the entire meal so I never asked him again. I always fix him a plate from whatever I cook which pleases him immensely. To him that is me taking care of him and I like taking care of him. I love him.

Most days I schedule my consultations from ten to three. My appointment book is never booked with back to back clients so I usually have time during the day to attend to other needs. I had certain days for certain services. I did all my card readings on Mondays mainly because I dislike tarot cards and want to get it with over for the week but my family has been reading and interpreting tarot cards for eternity so, consequently, not reading them would be like getting rid of Nonna's favorite horsehair sofa. I enjoy reading palms, though, so I try to schedule them in between the tarot card readings if possible.

I work the apothecary on Tuesdays and Wednesdays which is basically like running a pharmacy with the only difference being I am the prescriber and the dispensary. I do Spiritual consultations on Thursdays and Fridays. Spiritual consultations are kind of like therapy. My clients tell me their problems, we talk about how to solve them and then, with their permission, I summon the Spirits for guidance.

Spirits are exactly like people here on earth. There are Spirits who want to help with anything they possibly can. There are Spirits who indicate they will help you and then not help you at all. Some Spirits will do things for me or other people out of the kindness of their hearts. Other Spirits want something in return. People's personalities do not change once they enter the Spirit world. If they were mean and hateful here on earth, they are also mean and hateful once they cross over.

A lot of people have asked me why these Spirits aren't either in heaven or hell. They are. Just because they roam the earth does not mean God hasn't judged them yet. Those in heaven are our guardian angels. They want to help us. Those in hell are demons and they want to cause us misery. Frequently, those demons will disguise themselves as angels. Knowing the difference is also part of my gift. Are there souls still roaming the earth? Of course. Nonna used to say they simply have unfinished business. I believe that unfinished business is God's way of giving them another chance. Not everyone agrees with that supposition. It is simply what *I* believe.

I have relationships with Spirits just like I have relationships with people. I know who to ask for what and who not to ask at all. I know who offers but never follows through and I know who has ill intentions. Obviously, there are new Spirits every single day as people here on earth cross over from one world to the other. There is no difference between getting to know a new Spirit and getting to know a new person.

A Spirit will never give you part of an answer to a question and then sit back with their arms crossed over their chests amused you can't figure it out. They will, however, give ideas for the answer. Small pieces of information that require you to figure it out on your own. Spirits don't give answers. They give clues. So, the ability to interpret those clues is paramount. I have been told by many people, outside of and within the Spirit community, that I have an extraordinary talent for interpretation and that is quite a compliment. I take pride in my abilities but I am not boastful about them.

It does no good to plead with Spirits. They will give you what they feel is safe for you to know. Can you imagine what life here on earth would be like if Spirits told us everything?? It would be complete chaos. Ari understands this. Not because she knows the Spirits but because she knows me and I talk to her *about* the Spirits. So, she has learned the personalities of certain Spirits through me. I talk to Ari about Spirits the same way I talk to her about people. I'm thinking eventually I'll be able to do that with Adrian once he fine tunes the relationships he has with the Spirits, but he has enough on his plate right now without having to worry about Spirits' personalities on top of it. Just dealing with the little girl he sees on a regular basis is overwhelming enough.

In truth, beginning your journey as a Medium couldn't be any easier than starting with a child. I think Adrian is very lucky to have had it happen that way because Adrian is the most logical person I have ever known. He can read between the lines easily otherwise he'd be completely unsuccessful as a detective.

He once told me facts and opinions are the difference between words and actions. Words can be facts but they are usually opinions. Actions are always facts. I'd never thought about it that way until he brought it to my attention. You can't argue with whether an action is a fact. Either you did it or you didn't. Adrian says you cannot have any kind of successful relationship with another person here on earth if you do not question the logicality of their actions. I believe that is also the case with Spirits.

Ari and Adrian are the only people who understand that concept. So, when I have questions about the Spirits or answers I don't understand Ari is the one who helps me decipher them. This is the reason I called her after my dream with Caris. I say 'with' because it is clear to me the dream involving Caris was a two-way dialogue. It wasn't just me watching something unfold in front of my eyes. It was me communing with the dead. It was a two-way conversation.

There was a reason Caris chose me. She had an agenda. Maybe it was a cry for help but that seemed improbable. Like I said, Spirits have the same personalities in the Spirit world as they had here on earth and everyone on Long Island knew what kind of person Caris Sutherland was. It wasn't someone who would ask for help. Caris needed something from me and Ari would be able to help me figure it out. I promised her I would help her so not helping her wasn't even an option. When you make a promise to a Spirit you must keep it, or you lose all credibility in the Spirit world.

"Layla girl!!"

I heard Ari come through the back door but Serena and Estela made it down the stairs before I did.

"Ari!!" Serena called as she ran toward her. Ari caught her and picked her up.

"How's my girl?" Ari asked. Serena wiggled in her arms and Ari reached down and tousled Estela's hair. "And how is my other little girl?" Estela looked up to her and smiled.

"Guess what I got??" Serena asked.

"What??" Ari asked excitedly. I came around the newel post and stood beside them.

"I got a kitten!!" Ari looked to me.

"Is she kidding?"

"No," I said and smiled. I touched Serena's arm. "Go get him."

She jumped out of Ari's arms and she and Estela ran up the back stairs to get Rajah out of his basket. Serena had insisted kennels were for dogs and Rajah needed a basket. I didn't disagree with her, so I helped her find one of Nonna's old fruit baskets in the cellar. Serena lined it with an old velour throw she found in her closet. Rajah seemed quite happy with his new bed.

"You have a cat??" Ari asked. "When did you get a cat? And why didn't you let me help you pick it out?? You know how much I adore cats."

"You don't even have a cat," I pointed out.

"Only because Roger tried to eat the last one I had."

"Yeah, that is unfortunate." We laughed. "But I didn't pick it out. Adrian brought it over here."

"Where in the world did Adrian get a cat??"

"Ari!!" Serena called as she came down the stairs carrying Rajah in her arms. "Look!!" Ari reached out and took him from Serena. She held him out in front of her then looked to me.

"This is a Savannah cat," she stated.

"What's a Savannah cat?"

"Do you know how big this little thing is going to get?" Ari asked.

"No."

"Big. Like a big cat."

"How big?" Ari held her hand down closer to the floor by her knee.

"Maybe bigger."

"Are you kidding me?" I asked, astonished. "What the hell kind of cat is that big??"

"Savannah cats," she said matter-of-factly. "Where did Adrian get it?" She held Rajah close to her and kissed his little head. "Oh, you're a sweet boy."

"Drug house," I told her. Ari's eyes widened.

"This cat came from a drug house?"

"Yeah," I affirmed. "Adrian told me they had two Rottweilers in a cage that we're turned over to the Humane Society and two kittens in a basket in the basement. Jenny took one and he took one.

"Why didn't they keep the Rottweilers?" Ari asked. "They're great dogs."

"He said he couldn't get near them," I told her. "If Adrian couldn't get near them, something was wrong. He said they'd been raised mean."

"That's sad," she said.

"Yeah, but this little kitten deserves a chance at a happy life. Don't you think??"

"Enjoy him while he's still little," she said and laughed.

"So, you say."

"Does he have a name?"

"Rajah," I answered. "Adrian named him."

"He's purring," Ari said holding him out again. She handed him back to Serena.

"Serena, darling," I said. "It's time for Rajah to eat. Do you want to give him his bottle?"

"Yes!!"

"Okay, go get his basket and I'll fix it for you."

"Like you don't have enough to think about these days," Ari said. "Just add a kitten who needs to be bottle-fed."

"It's not that bad," I said and smiled. "I don't mind."

"I didn't want to say this in front of the girls," Ari started. "But these cats are illegal in the state of New York."

"What???!!" I exclaimed. "Adrian gave me an illegal cat??" Ari raised her eyebrows and shrugged.

"I'm just sayin.'"

"I'm going to kill him."

"Hey," Ari said as she reached out to touch my arm. "Maybe he doesn't know."

"How could he not know??"

"I mean, I don't see him as being a cat type of person," Ari said thoughtfully.

"You know, you might be right," I said. "Because when I asked him what kind of cat it was, he said it was a cat. Like, it's a cat. All cats are the same."

"All cats are not the same," Ari said.

"I know."

"Remember Bluebell?"

"Oh, wow," I said. "Yeah. Aw, I miss her. She was the best cat."

"She was sweet. You need to talk to Adrian about this cat, though. I mean, maybe they aren't illegal anymore, but they used to be."

"What the hell am I going to do if it's illegal?"

"Adrian's a legal guru," Ari said. "Ask him. I'm sure if Rajah is illegal and you want to keep him Adrian will find some loophole because he can't say no to you."

"Right."

"I do have to tell you this, though," she said. "These cats are super protective over their owners." She looked down to Rajah. "He won't let anyone he doesn't know within fifty feet of you once he's grown."

"Wow," I said. "But, I mean, what can they do?"

"What do you mean?"

"What would they do to someone?" I asked. "You know, dogs bite. What do Savannah cats do?"

"This cat is like a domesticated wild cat," she said. She thought for a moment. "Let's put it this way. You remember the time Bluebell caught the rabbit and dragged it through the cat door without a head?" I laughed.

241

"Yeah."

"That."

"You lie," I said. She raised her eyebrows.

"You just wait and see how big he gets." She walked over to the stove. "Woo…Oregano Rolls. Thanks." She pulled one out of the pan and popped a piece in her mouth. "God, I love these things."

"I know."

"Say it."

"Say what?"

"What you call these," she said holding up the roll.

"They're Oregano Rolls," I said. "Just like you said."

"No, no," she said. "Say it in Italian." I laughed and she popped part of the roll into her mouth.

"Rotoli di oregano."

"I love to hear you talk in Italian," she said as she opened the refrigerator. "Say it in French."

"Ari," I groaned.

"Humor me!!" she said. She pulled out a bottle of wine I'd just retrieved from the cellar. "I'm about to help you solve a mystical puzzle. I hope you have more than one bottle of wine."

"Yeah. rouleaux d'origan. French. Happy?" She just stared at me, so I did what she wanted even though it was ridiculous.

"अजवायन रोल।"

"Hindi!" she said excitedly, and she motioned for me to go on. She popped open the bottle of wine.

"Rotllos d'orenga.

"Catalan!!"

"You got it. Oregano rullar." I grabbed two wine glasses and she poured both of us a glass.

"Swedish!"

"You're getting good at this," I said as I leaned up against the counter. I took a sip of my wine.

"Mamma!!" Serena said. "I'm ready."

"Shit," I said. "I forgot."

"Mamma!! That's a bad word!!"

"It is," I admitted. "I'm sorry, darling. I won't say it again."

I took the kitten formula out of the refrigerator and filled a coffee cup with water, stuck it in the microwave. Ari took plates down off the plate rack on the far wall and began to set the table. I pulled the cup out of the microwave and stuck the bottle with the formula inside of it.

"It'll take just a minute, okay?" I told her. "Here, give me Rajah. Go find out if Renaldo wants a plate."

"Okay!" she said as she handed me the cat.

She ran through the back door and down the porch steps with Estela following behind her. She was like Serena's shadow and Serena loved it. I looked through the kitchen window and watched them run down the path to the cottage. I always watched them until Renaldo answered the door. Amityville was a safe village for the most part, but you could never be too careful when it came to children.

"So, tell me about this dream," Ari said. She plopped down in a kitchen chair and I pulled the pasta alla Norma out of the oven. "Anybody I know?" I turned off the oven and leaned up against the counter, picked up my wine.

"Caris," I said quietly.

I'm not sure why I said it quietly. It just seemed like it should be a secret. It made perfect sense if you knew anything at all about Adrian's mother. She was the epitome of things you just didn't talk about.

"As in Adrian's mother?" Ari asked. She'd lowered her voice, too.

"Uh-huh."

"She's dead?"

"Apparently."

"Does Adrian know she's dead?"

"I don't think so. I mean, don't you think he would've told me if he did?" Ari shrugged.

"You would think. How did she die? Do you know?"

"Well, I watched her drown in my dream."

"Holy shit, Lay. That's horrible. I mean, even for Caris, that's horrible."

"I know."

"Mamma!" Serena called. "Renaldo said yes and wanted to know if we could watch Animal Kingdom with him." I bent over so I was eye to eye with her.

"Well, who's going to take care of Rajah if you go to Renaldo's?" She lowered her face and I picked up her chin with my finger.

"You may go to Renaldo's," I said.

"Yay!" Serena said. Ari stood up.

"I'll fix their plates."

"Thank you," I said. "Hey, Miss. Serena. Look at Mamma. You realize Rajah is your kitten, which means he is your responsibility, right?"

"Yes, Ma'am."

"So, what's next? What do you need to do before you go to Renaldo's?"

"Make sure someone is taking care of him?" she asked.

"Yes," I affirmed. She was so excited she knew the right answer.

"Will you take care of Rajah for me while I'm gone?" she asked me.

"Yes, I will. Thank you for asking."

"Yes, Ma'am."

"Can you carry this basket by yourself?" I asked her as Ari handed her the picnic basket.

"I put it all in plastic containers," Ari told me.

"Perfect."

Serena took the basket and Ari held open the screened door for her and Estela.

"Serena, darling?"

"Yes, Mamma?"

"Please ask Renaldo to bring you guys back up here after your show, okay? I don't want you two to walk back up the path by yourself in the dark."

"Mamma, it's not that far."

"Serena," I warned.

"Yes, Ma'am."

"Here," I said as I handed Rajah to Ari along with the bottle.

"Wow, thanks," she said, but she sat down at the table and began to feed him. "He's so eager."

"He's a kitten," I said. "All kittens are eager."

"I was thinking it was more because he was a male," she said, and I laughed.

"That, too."

I took the pasta and the rolls over to the table and sat down.

"Here's my first dilemma," I said. "I have to tell Adrian I talked to his mother. I don't have a choice."

"Why?"

"Wait," I said. "And when I tell him I talked to his mother the conveyance of that message is she's dead."

"Well, yeah."

"And I don't think he knows she's dead."

"Seems unlikely," Ari said. She pulled a napkin out of the napkin holder on the table and tucked it under Rajah's chin.

"Which means Tiffany doesn't know she's dead."

"Holy cow," Ari said because she knew just as well as I did Tiffany adored her mother. Neither of us ever understood why. "But, listen, you are not responsible for telling Tiffany. Let Adrian do it."

"I hate that."

"Why?? She's his sister. Not yours."

"It's just going to make her dislike me more than she already does."

"Why?" Ari asked. "It's not like you killed Caris. You're just the messenger."

"You're so blunt," I said. She shrugged.

"So, what did the wicked witch of Long Island have to say?" she asked as she looked down to Rajah. "Is he supposed to be eating this so fast?"

"Yeah, it's fine. So, I watched her drown. That was disturbing enough by itself. Then she was just screaming my name."

"You're giving me the heebie-jeebies," Ari said.

"Then she was screaming something else, and I had to keep rewinding it before I could finally understand it. She was yelling 'Forgive me.'"

"Very appropriate."

"And telling," I said. Ari shrugged again. "Apparently, she had a conscience."

"Probably because once she crossed over, she realized Hell wasn't going to be a cool place to live."

"Cool?"

"That was a play on words," she said and laughed. I shook my head in amusement.

"Anyhow, I asked her who she needed forgiveness from. Because, like you, I assumed she was referring to her soul in general."

"But she wasn't?" Ari asked.

"No."

"Predictable."

"I told her I could help her and I would tell whoever she needed forgiveness from what she said but she refused."

"Also, predictable."

"She asked me why I would want to help her."

"I'd like to know that, too."

"She's Adrian's mother!" I said. "It's not like she's a stranger." Ari rolled her eyes.

"Your heart needs to be a little harder. Why, no matter who she is, does a woman who caused misery to other people her entire life, deserve help from anyone?" Ari stood up and nestled Rajah into his blanket in the basket.

"It is my responsibility to help Spirits no matter who they are or what they've done," I said.

"Oh, right. You're the Mother Theresa of the Spirit World. I always forget about that part."

"Ari!"

"Oh Layla," she said as she leaned over me and squeezed my shoulders. "I'm just kidding. I love you." She walked back around the table and sat down in front of me. I laid a roll on her plate and she served both of us the pasta.

"I had to prove to her I truly wanted to help her," I told Ari. "Spirits like Caris think everyone has an ulterior motive because they do. I had to prove to her I didn't have one."

"So how did you do that?" she asked. She buttered her roll and popped a piece into her mouth.

"I told her I loved her son and I…" I hesitated. Ari didn't know. "Okay, I have to back up a little bit."

I sat for a moment watching Ari eat. I had to figure out how to tell her, and more importantly, why I hadn't already told her. I decided to just say it. After all, it was Ari. I watched her shove more pasta into her mouth.

"This is amazing," she said.

"Ari," I said. "Can you please not talk with food in your mouth?"

"Sorry," she mumbled. "It's just *so* good."

"Adrian can see the Spirits," I told her. She stopped chewing and stared at me. Her eyes searched mine, but I didn't say anything else. She chewed the rest of her pasta and swallowed it.

"How many?" she asked.

"All of them. If you can see one you can see them all. It's just up to them whether they want to present themselves."

"Why haven't you told me??"

"Because, well, honestly, I didn't think about it."

"You didn't think about it???" she asked unbelievably. "How can you not think about it?"

"It's not a big deal to me," I explained. "I mean, with Adrian it is, but not normally."

"He told you this?"

"Yeah."

"Has he always had this gift?"

"Yeah."

"And he's just now telling you?? You. Of all people not to tell."

"I know," I agreed. "He said it was because of Caris. He was afraid he'd end up like her. He was afraid if he talked about it, it would come to be."

"That makes sense although Adrian seems too smart for that logic. You'd think he'd worked his way through that by now."

"That kind of love runs deep," I said. "I know they had the relationship they had but he still loved her."

"Yeah." She stared off into the distance. "Damn. Who would've thought?" She looked back to me. "I mean, I've known Adrian forever and I can honestly tell you I did not see this coming. He's too fricking logical for this."

"There's nothing illogical about seeing a Spirit," I informed her. "When you see them, you see them. It isn't a guessing game. You know. There's no question about it."

"Okay," she said. "So, I'm digesting this new info. Move on with the rest of your story."

"So, I told that to Caris, too. I told her I loved Adrian and I knew he had our gift."

"Caris did not have a gift," Ari insisted.

"It would have been a gift," I asserted. "If she'd developed it the right way."

"True."

"I told Caris he told me about it and, apparently, that was what she needed to hear. Here's the creepy part."

"It gets worse?" Ari asked. "Because I've already got chill bumps."

"She spoke to me," I confessed.

"What did she say?"

"No, Ari. I mean, she *spoke* to me." Ari stared at me again. She turned her head to the side and bit her lip. She knew.

"Audibly?"

"Yeah."

"Did she manifest?"

"No," I said. "Just in the dream."

"But she spoke audibly to you after you woke up?"

"Yes. I moved from the dream into consciousness while we were talking."

"That's freaky as shit."

"I know," I agreed. "But listen. She said 'Tell him he's a ...'"

"A what?" Ari asked.

"I don't know," I admitted shaking my head. "She didn't finish the sentence. I asked her to tell me. I tried to rewind to see if I missed it somehow but there was nothing except, 'Tell him he's a ...'"

"Typical Caris. This is her way of having power over you," Ari informed me. "You realize this, do you not?"

"You think?"

"Oh, hell yeah. She's a manipulative woman. She knows what she's doing. I mean, you're the one who told me that. People don't change just because they cross over. They are still the same person. They're just a dead person."

"I..."

"She's using it as a tool," Ari said. She took a sip of her wine. "And you should just beware."

"You think?"

"It's a tactic. She knows you'll tell Adrian and she wants something from him."

"What could she possibly want that Adrian can give her?" Ari shrugged.

"I don't know." She pointed at me. "But I guarantee it's something."

"So, what consensus have we come to?" I asked.

"That you need to do some serious research before you do anything else, and for God's sake, don't tell Adrian anything yet. Petition the Spirits. Someone will tell you something."

"You think??"

"You have many connections," Ari reminded me. "You have many friends on the other side."

"True."

"So, this is a back-burner topic," she told me.

"For now," I said. "Because I don't have the option of doing nothing."

"I just think you should be very cautious. I mean, Caris is like the Delphine LaLaurie of Long Island."

"Don't say that," I warned Ari. "Delphine is a very dangerous Spirit and I do not want her here."

"You think she's gonna float up here from the French Quarter?" Ari asked and laughed.

"Shut up, Ari. I'm not kidding." Ari held up her hands.

"Okay, okay. I'm sorry. All I'm saying is there is more to this than a simple plea. Nothing with Caris Sutherland is ever simple. Lies.

Manipulation. Coercion. All just so she could get whatever it was she wanted at any given moment."

"Yeah."

"So, be careful."

"You think Caris will eventually finish her sentence?" I asked. "You think it could be a name?"

"Maybe."

"Because we both know Raymond was not his real dad."

"Yeah," I said. "You think it might be about that?"

"I think there are many avenues worth exploring," Ari said. "And not just ones in the Spirit world."

"Like here on earth?" I asked.

"Yeah."

"Who??"

"I think you should talk to one of your aunts," she suggested.

"What??" I asked, surprised. "Why would I talk to one of my aunts?"

"How old would Caris be now?" Ari asked.

"Uh…let's see. Adrian is twenty-seven. I think she was around twenty when she had him so late forties?"

"How old are your aunts?" Ari asked.

"Uh…. late forties," I said thoughtfully.

"Uh-huh."

"So, they were all around the same age as Caris back then."

"Yeah," Ari said. "They must have all gone to school together or at least run in the same circles. Don't ya think?"

"I don't think any of my aunts would have run in the same circle as Caris Sutherland."

"Well, no," Ari admitted. "But when you're that age circles intersect for many reasons."

"True."

"Which means there is a good possibility they have an idea of who Adrian's biological father might be."

"Damn," I said. "You are so much smarter than you look." She picked up an oregano roll and threw it at me. I caught it but barely.

"Seriously, though. Someone on this island knows who Adrian and Tiffany's father is."

"Yeah," I said thoughtfully. "I just have to find him."

Woodlawn

Isabel

"Hey, hey, hey," I said as I walked through Lilah's back door.

I'd brought a bottle of Moscato with me. I never drink Moscato but someone had given it to me as a gift and neither Lilah nor I ever waste wine.

"Holy shit, Lilah," I said when she turned from the sink. "You look exhausted."

"I am," she said. "But thanks for the reminder."

"Just keepin' it real."

"I think I'd like it if you'd keep it less real sometimes. Ya know?"

"Why?" I asked as I opened a kitchen drawer for the corkscrew. "You want me to let you go out looking like shit?? Best friends don't do that."

"But I'm not going anywhere."

"Well, if your plans change, put on some different clothes and some lipstick." She looked down at her clothes. She had on a pair of denim bib overalls she'd had since college and a pink polo shirt. Her hair was on top of her head in a messy bun.

"Thanks," she said sarcastically. "I always forget I'm not twenty-one anymore."

"God. Wouldn't it be great if we were twenty-one again?"

"No," she said as she turned on the dishwasher and leaned up against the counter behind her. "It would not."

"Why the hell not??" I asked. "Remember how sexy we were then??"

"Remember how we had two screaming toddlers??"

"Oh, no," I told her as I pointed to her. She laughed. "You had the screaming toddler. Isaac was an angel."

"Right."

I pulled the cork out of the Chianti and grabbed two glasses out of the corner cabinet. She wiped her hands on a dishtowel and we walked into the living room. There was a huge fire burning in the fireplace.

"Ben?" I inquired as I motioned to it.

"Of course," she said as she plopped down in her favorite chair. I poured her a glass of wine and handed it to her. "I can only have one glass."

"I know," I said. I poured some wine for myself and sat down across from her. Ben came flying down the stairs. He laid his hand on his mother's shoulder and kissed her cheek.

"I'm going to Isabel's to help Matt with his algebra."

"You are??" Isabel asked.

"Yeah," he said. "I'm good at math."

"He is," Lilah agreed.

"Awesome. Thanks."

"Yep."

I pulled a pack of cigarettes and lighter out of my pocket. I got up and walked over to the hearth.

"You are not smoking in here," Lilah chastised.

"I'm sitting right here," I told her. "The smoke will go up the chimney with the smoke from the fire."

"So, you say. I'll have to fumigate the living room after you leave." I took a puff off my cigarette and blew the smoke toward the fire.

"Kiss my ass, Lilah." She stuck out her tongue at me. "Did Ben decide what he wanted to do for school yet?" I asked.

"No," Lilah said. "He says he needs to take some time off from school and think about his future."

"Ha. He and Isaac must be in cahoots together because Isaac told me the same thing."

"I'm sure."

"In other words. He and Isaac need some time before college to goof off and do only God knows what," I concluded.

"Exactly," Lilah said and pointed to me.

"Isaac told me the other day he got accepted at Adelphi but he won't start until next year."

"Where is that?"

"Long Island," I told her. "He says he's moving up there."

"He is??" she asked. "When did that happen?"

"When he discovered what love is," I said. I motioned to myself. "I haven't even discovered what love is." Lilah laughed.

"I hope it is love for his sake and he doesn't discover later it's only infatuation."

"You and me both. He says he wants to move up there so he'll be closer to Tiffany."

"You mean live with Tiffany," Lilah said.

"Probably."

"Damn."

"I know, right?"

"How do you feel about that?" she asked. I shrugged.

"I just want him to be happy," I told her. "If Tiff makes him happy then he should be with her. I'll miss him, of course. He hasn't told Tom yet."

"Oh, boy."

"Leaving for college is one thing and Isaac could go to school in California if he wanted and it wouldn't bother Tom at all, but the fact he's picked a college on Long Island just so he can be with a girl is a different story."

"Did he apply to more than one school?"

"Yeah, and he got into all of them," I said. "That's what is going to blow Tom's mind. Isaac was dying to go to UVA. That's been where he wanted to go all along and he got in. Now he says he's not going because he's going to New York to be with Tiff."

"I don't see telling Tom this going well," Lilah said.

"Me, either."

"I told him he had to tell his father. Not me."

"Probably a wise decision on your part," Lilah said. I took a sip of my wine.

"You like this wine?" I asked her.

"Eh…it's okay. It's a little heavy for my taste."

"Me, too, but someone gave it to me and I can't let it go to waste."

"Who gave it to you?"

"One of the kid's parents," I told her.

"Now that is a cool parent."

"I know, right?" Silence. "We have to talk about McCain, Lilah," I said as I sat down.

"No, we don't."

"We do," I insisted.

"Why?"

"Has Adrian said anything about him to you at all?"

"Just about the relationship I had with him. He asked me if McCain was telling the truth."

"And you said?"

"I told him yes."

"And?"

"That's it."

"He didn't ask you anything else?"

"No."

"Why not?" I asked. "Do you not find that a little strange?"

"Because it's his work," she told me. "He doesn't talk to me about work very often."

"You know good and well McCain probably told him everything."

"Stop it," Lilah said.

"It's not going to go away just because we don't talk about it. We have to talk about it. Because there is more to this…" I pointed down. "… now that McCain is here. In Woodlawn. And you know what that is."

"Yeah."

"I told you from the very beginning you and Eric should have told Ben. We wouldn't be dealing with this right now if you had."

"I thought it was the right thing to do at the time. I know you didn't but it made Eric feel good."

"Fuck Eric," I said as I waved my cigarette around. "Who gives a shit about that? It should have never had anything to do with him at all. I think the whole adoption thing should've never happened if you want me to be honest."

"And what??" she asked. "He keeps McCain's name?? Uh, no."

"What did you just say??" She got up to get the bottle of wine off the buffet and poured me another glass.

"I said I didn't want him to keep McCain's name," Lilah told me.

"You gave Ben McCain's name??"

"Well, duh. He's his father."

"Who cares?" I said. "I thought you gave him your name."

"I did give him my name," she told me. "My maiden name is his middle name."

"How do I not know this??"

"I don't know. I thought you did."

"So, where is his birth certificate?" I asked.

"In the safe with everyone else's birth certificate."

"What name is on it?"

"Benjamin Winston McCain."

"Shit, Lilah," I said as I put my cigarette out on the hearth. I threw it into the fire. "You have to show that to Adrian. Now."

"Why?"

"Because he needs to know that," I told her. "Like yesterday."

"Well, it's not Ben's name now." I stared at her.

"It's his birth certificate," I reiterated as I stood up. "Like, what he needs for everything that matters and it's got McCain's name on it. How the hell did you get him into school?"

"I took the name change paperwork with me."

"And Ben never noticed that?"

"He was *five*," she pointed out.

"You tell Adrian as soon as he gets back," I told her. "And if you want me to, I'll come over here but you are telling him." I pointed at her. "This whole situation is out of control and it's not happening. You can sit back and let it happen if you want but I'm not. If you don't tell Adrian, I will. Are you understanding me?"

"Jeez, Isabel. It's not that big of a deal."

"It's not a big deal??" I asked. I walked toward her. "What planet are you living on? It's bad enough Terrence knows."

"Terrence knows??"

"Well, yeah, that's what this conversation was supposed to be about. Me telling you Terrence knows and how we need to deal with it."

"How does Terrence know?"

"Shit," I said bringing my hand to my forehead. I took another cigarette out of my pack and moved over to the hearth again. I had to have a cigarette before I told Lilah Bret was McCain's son.

"Holy cow, Isabel. You do not need another cigarette already."

"I do," I insisted. I lit it and inhaled, blew it back out and looked over to her.

I'd put the Bret/McCain issue in the back of my mind thinking I'd deal with it later. Probably exactly the way Lilah put Ben's birth certificate in the back of hers. All I had been thinking about was the fact Terrence knew not *how* Terrence knew.

"How does he know, Isabel??" Lilah practically yelled at me as she stood up.

"Because McCain has another son." She watched me.

"What the hell does that have to do with anything? I don't give a shit about whether he has other kids. Why would I care??"

"Because that's why he came here," I explained. "He came to Woodlawn to see his son."

"I thought he came to Woodlawn to see me," she said.

"Disappointed?" I asked.

"No," she said. "You're such a bitch sometimes. I just thought it was about me."

"It's not about you," I said. I inhaled and blew the smoke back out. "It's about his son."

"You are smoking in my living room!!" she told me.

"Who cares?" I asked as I waved my cigarette around. "I think you have much more to worry about right now other than the smoke from my cigarette."

"You don't even smoke in your own house," she yelled. "So, don't smoke in mine!"

"You want me to just tell you??" I asked. "Because after I do you won't care whether I'm smoking in your house. In fact, you'll probably want a cigarette yourself."

"What??" she asked. "Tell me!!"

"Bret is McCain's son."

She stared at me. Silence. I stared back at her.

"Like Vonnie's Bret??" she finally asked.

"Yes."

She leaned over and grabbed herself around the waist. I wasn't expecting it. I should've been expecting it because it was Lilah. I grabbed her arms.

"Hey," I said. "Lilah, honey. Come on. Stand up."

"I can't," she cried as she fell to her knees.

"You can," I told her. "Come on. Stand up."

I helped her stand but we just stood there. Neither one of us said anything. I am always silent with Lilah when she's upset because she needs time to think not listen to my opinion. Lilah is the type of person who doesn't want to hear your suggestions no matter how wise they might be. At least not at the time of the crisis. She has to sort through everything going through her mind before she can consider what is going through mine. She looked up to me.

"Do you know what that means??" she asked.

"It means a lot of things."

"No, I mean do you know the most important thing it means?" I took another puff of my cigarette and thought for a moment.

"That Bret and Ben are half-brothers?" I finally asked. She stared at me. "That's not that big of a deal, Lilah." She was still staring at me. "What???"

"Don't think about me and McCain," she said quietly. "Think about Bret."

"Oh, fuck," I said. "Holy shit."

"Yeah."

"Well, she's not really his sister," I pointed out. "I mean, they could step-siblings but they aren't truly related."

"That doesn't make it any better. That would be like Greg and Marcia dating."

"Who the hell are Greg and Marcia??" She widened her eyes at me.

"The Brady Bunch??" I laughed.

"Oh, good grief, Lilah. If you're going down that path it would be like Isaac and Vonnie dating."

"Not really."

"I'm just saying."

"I don't think she needs to know her brother and her ex-boyfriend are brothers."

"Probably not," I said and took another puff of my cigarette. I walked over to the fireplace and threw it into the fire. "But that means never telling Ben." She didn't say anything. "That's not a bad thing," I said. "Why does he need to know?"

"Where is Adrian?" she asked. "Is he here?"

This is a typical response from Lilah. She loses track of anything and everything going on that isn't directly related to whatever is currently happening.

"He's in Amityville," I told her. "Do you want me to call him?"

"No," she said as she pulled away from me. "I'm going to call him. Where's my phone?"

"Lilah," I said as I followed her. "I don't think you should talk to him about Ben over the phone." She turned toward me quickly.

"What makes you think I want to talk to him about Ben?" she asked.

"Uh…maybe because that's what we've been talking about?"

She stared at me. I hated when she did that because it meant her mind was turning circles and not necessarily in the right direction. She had devised a plan. Whether or not it was a good plan was yet to be known.

"I know what I'm going to do," she said quietly.

"Lilah," I said because suddenly it became clear to me. "I don't think that's a good idea."

"Why not?"

"Because he is a loose cannon."

"Not with me," she said.

"You haven't seen or talked to him in twenty years," I told her. "How do you know?"

"Remember how you told me Adrian worships the ground I walk on?" she asked me.

"Yeah."

"So does McCain," she said succinctly.

Lilah

Two days later Adrian arrived home. I hadn't talked to him about Ben yet but I'd promised Isabel I would. Now I watched him pace back and forth on the back porch with his phone to his ear. I lifted the window over the kitchen sink a crack so I could hear what he was saying. Isabel would have told me I was being paranoid but she always told me things like that then turned around and did the same thing herself.

"It's fine," he said. "Don't let things like that bother you. We both know how perceptive she is."

Who?

"I think it will be okay. They will be fine with Renaldo." He hesitated. "Okay, well then, Ari."

I took a deep breath. I didn't want to listen but I couldn't stop. I should've just walked away before I heard something I didn't want to hear.

"What did you buy?" he asked and laughed. "That's good. Does she like them?" He hesitated. "I'll bet." He had to be talking to Tiffany. He didn't talk to anyone else with such affection and joviality except me and her.

"Well, when do you want to do it?" he asked.

He leaned over the porch railing on his arms and looked out across the back yard toward the pond. He ran his hand through his hair. It was a nervous habit he had so maybe he wasn't as at ease with the conversation as I thought.

"You shouldn't worry about that," he said. "I'm sure Ari can handle it. Does she know Catalan?" He laughed.

What the hell was Catalan? If I hadn't known any better the thought would have crossed my mind that maybe he was talking to his mother. He laughed again.

"I know, right?" he said.

"What are you doing?" Vonnie said from behind me. I jumped and put my hand over my heart.

"Holy shit," I said. "You just scared the bejesus out of me."

"Well, what are you doing?" she asked as she looked over my shoulder and out the window. "Are you eavesdropping on Adrian's phone call??"

"Sshh!!" I said bringing my finger to my lips. "He'll hear you."

"Mama," she said and laughed. She pushed me out of the way. She leaned over the sink toward the window. "You're so funny."

"Why am I funny??" I asked. "He's talking to someone like he loves them."

"Well, I'm sure he loves other people besides just you."

"Who??"

"Mom," she said. She walked over to the refrigerator. She opened it and peered inside. "Stop obsessing over him. He's going to do whatever he's going to do."

"What does that mean??"

"You know Adrian as well as I do," she said. "He's a player."

"He is not a player," I said, defending him. She peeled the wrapper off the smoothie she was holding in her hand and leaned up against the counter. Adrian walked through the back door.

"You're a player, right?" Vonnie asked him.

"Uh…" I knew right away he was wondering what we'd heard. He laughed and ran his hand through his hair nervously. "Why are you asking me that?"

"I can just hear you talking out there," Vonnie said. She hadn't. "Sounds like you're talking to a forbidden lover. Were you?"

"Vonnie!" I chastised. "Stop it." She laughed and bumped her shoulder into Adrian's as she walked past him.

"Better get your act together, Romeo," she said. He took a deep breath and I watched him. He was silent for a moment.

"Wine?" I finally asked as I went to the wine fridge.

"Sure," he said.

"White good for you?" I pulled out a bottle of Pinot Grigio.

"Sure," he said again. I grabbed the corkscrew and began opening the wine. "Look." He ran his hand across the back of his neck. "I was talking to Lorelei."

I leaned back against the counter behind me. He walked toward me and took the bottle of wine out of my hand, sat it down beside us. He pushed himself into me. He put his hands on my neck and lowered his face to mine. We were centimeters apart. A tantric kiss and I melted. This was what he always did to me. I felt his lips on my ear and I shivered.

"I love you," he whispered. "More than I've ever loved anyone in my life. Do you believe me?"

Why did I get the feeling something was wrong?

"Yes," I whispered back.

"Truly?"

"Truly."

"Will you let me make love to you tonight?" he murmured.

"Yes." He pulled back and looked into my eyes.

"Lorelei is going away with a friend for a couple of days."

"A man??" I asked hopefully. He smiled.

"To the Hamptons. And she's worried about leaving her girls."

"Oh?" I said. "I didn't know she had any children."

"Yes," he said. "Serena. She's five, soon to be six, and Estela. She's five, too."

"Are they twins?"

"No. Estela is a foster child."

"She keeps foster children??" I asked in disbelief.

"Not usually," he said. "It's a long story but the little girl only speaks Catalan and Lorelei speaks Catalan, so she's keeping her until they can find someone else who speaks Catalan."

"And wants to be a foster parent," I added.

"Yes."

"That seems unlikely," I pointed out.

"I know."

"Does Lorelei know that?"

"Yeah and she's worried about going away and not taking them with her. She rarely leaves them but I was just telling her not to worry because they'd be fine with Renaldo for a few days, and she was telling me she was going to leave them with her best friend, Ari."

"Who's Renaldo?" I asked.

"Her butler."

I took in a deep breath. What?? She had a butler. Who has a butler anymore? Rich people, that's who.

"She has a butler??"

"Her family has a butler," he explained. "They gifted him to her."

"I don't even know what to say to that," I said. He chuckled.

"Long Island is another country," he explained.

"Ah…" He brought his hands up to my cheeks.

"Look at me," he said, so I did. "What did I tell you about Lorelei?"

"You said she was the love of your life," I said facetiously. He backed up from me.

"I don't believe I ever said that."

"You didn't," I said. "I'm just being petty and insecure." He leaned down and touched his nose to mine, our foreheads against one another.

"Lilah Anne Winston?"

"Yes?"

"Are you going to marry me?" he asked. I smiled.

"Yeah."

"Do you trust me?"

"Yeah."

"I can't tell you anything else about Lorelei right now."

"Why not?"

"Because she's involved in my current case."

"What??" I asked surprised. I did not know this.

"She's involved in my current case," he repeated.

"How?" I asked. "Why?"

He took me by my waist and led me over to the kitchen table with him. He sat down on the edge of it and pulled me in between his legs. He kissed my forehead.

"I will tell you one thing about this case," he said. "And then we can't talk about it anymore. You have to trust me. Okay?"

"Okay."

269

"This case runs deep through the livelihood of Long Island. A lot of people are going to be affected when this case comes to a close."

"Is it dangerous?"

"Everything I do is dangerous," he affirmed. "This case is underwritten."

"What does that mean?" I asked.

"It means there's going to be a lot of loss and damages I can't explain to you." I watched him. "There are people involved in this case I've known all my life. There will be casualties."

"Like deaths??" I asked. He shrugged.

"Most likely."

"And Lorelei is in the middle of all this?"

"Yes," he said. "So, I'm sure you understand how she needs my attention on a regular basis."

"I feel like I'm being snowed over right now," I said honestly. He took my hands in his.

"Let me tell you something," he said as he rubbed his thumbs across the back of my hands. "I guarantee if you met Lorelei somewhere and didn't know who she was you would love her."

"What makes you think that?" I asked.

He lowered his face to my neck and I shivered. I shivered whenever he was that close to me. He knew how to bring me to wherever he wanted me to be anytime he wanted me to be there.

"Because she's perfect," he whispered in my ear and I sucked in my breath. He kissed my neck. "Just…like…you."

"Oh, fuck no," Isabel said. "Where is he?"

"Isabel. It's fine."

"It is not fine," she told me. "Since when does a man tell the woman he loves another woman is perfect? What kind of crock of shit is that? Oh, my god. Where is he??" She paced back and forth across my living room. She was more upset over it than I was. She brought her hand to her forehead. I didn't answer. "Where the hell is he?" she asked for the third time.

"I think he went to the station in Richmond," I told her. "Chill out. Have one of these raspberry Jell-O shots I made for you."

"Did you have sex with him last night?" she asked.

"Well, yeah. We have sex almost every night."

"Well, if I were you, I'd be in my car right now driving my ass up to Amityville to meet this bitch."

"Isabel, you're blowing this way out of proportion." She pulled her phone out of her pocket and started typing. "What are you doing?"

"Wait a minute," she said as she continued typing. I handed her the Jell-O-shot and she took it from me, gulped it down, and went back to her phone. "How the hell can you be okay with this?" she asked as she shoved her phone into my face. It wasn't a picture. It was an advertisement.

Lorelei Anastasio, Spiritualist

Palmistry-Tarot

Apothecary-Favors

By appointment only

"Yeah," I said. "Adrian told me that's what she did. It's not a surprise."

"What the hell is a favor?"

"I don't know," I admitted. "I have no idea."

"Well, you better be asking lover boy what it means. Favors?? Is she serious?? Does she get paid for her favors??"

"I don't think that's what it means," I said.

I had no idea why I was defending Lorelei. Maybe because I believed Adrian. Isabel pulled her phone back out and typed something else into it, then presented it to me again.

"You know what that is?" she asked.

"An address??"

"It's her fucking address," she said. "Palazzo Cremisi. What the hell does that mean??"

"I don't know."

"I'm looking it up."

"Isabel," I said. "Would you stop it?? Holy cow."

"Palazzo Cremisi," she said. "An historic site in the village of Amityville…. has been owned by the Anastasio family since the 1800's…. Francesco and Mary Angela Anastasio…known for its waterside presence and the impact it presents to the community of this Long Island village."

"Okaay…" She held up her finger and continued to read.

"The Anastasio family has been a staple of Long Island for a century…" she read. "…known for their apothecary and their penchant for all-natural healings and favors." She looked up to me. "Once again, what is a favor??" I had to laugh.

"I don't know, Isabel."

"I'll bet Adrian gets favors for free. What do you think?"

"Stop it."

"We're going up there," she said.

"No, we're not," I said adamantly. "Absolutely not. I am not about to break the trust Adrian and I have with one another."

"So, you're going to let him shit on you while he has sex with this whore??"

"Isabel," I said. "Given the life I've lived I hardly feel like I have the right to pass judgement on the relationship he has with Lorelei. He's told me everything I need to know about her. She actually sounds like a nice person."

"You've lost your fucking mind," Isabel said as she headed toward the back door.

"Where are you going?" I asked.

"I'm going home to do some more research on this bitch."

"Lord."

"I'll have a power point presentation for you by morning."

"I have no doubt."

"You better be praying I don't find out something that pisses me off more than I already am."

"Okay." She pointed at me.

"And, when lover boy gets home tonight, tell him I said, fuck you."

McCain always called me between 7:30 and 10:00 at night. Originally, we tried to set a specific time so I could plan for it but when you're in jail you don't get to pick and choose. The last time I talked to him I hadn't paid for additional minutes because he pissed me off. Tonight was our night to talk though, and I'd already decided I'd accept the charges. At first, I wondered if would call me again after I called him an asshole but it was McCain and what I'd told Isabel about him worshiping the ground I walked on was true. He did worship the ground I walked on.

I waited and waited for him to call but he never did. I felt disappointment and a little sad. My heart sunk just a little bit especially since Adrian hadn't called me either. Isabel told me no man would tell a woman he loved that another woman was perfect but she had to be wrong. I knew Adrian loved me. I guess now I was just wondering if he loved me enough. Enough for what? Enough to not cheat on me with an old girlfriend who was probably much prettier than me? I sat in front of the fireplace and read for a while but I couldn't keep my mind on it so I turned on the television which I rarely did. Vonnie came down the stairs. She laughed.

"Mama!" she said.

"What?" I asked turning around.

"I cannot believe you are watching *Keeping up with the Kardashians.*"

"Is that what this is??" I asked. She came over and sat beside me on the sofa.

"Yeah." She bumped her shoulder into mine. "I'm proud of you."

"For what? Watching a bunch of conceited girls not living in the real world?"

"You're hilarious," she said. "Can I have a wine cooler? I'll watch with you."

I always treasured any time I got to spend with Vonnie. It didn't happen very often because she was always with either Hunter or Eden.

"Sure," I told her. She leaned over and kissed my cheek.

"Thanks."

When she came back, she plopped down on the sofa and put her feet on the coffee table in front of us. She leaned over and put her wine cooler under my nose

"Wanna smell it?" she asked. "I know you don't get to drink any-more." She laughed. I slapped her hand.

"You're awful!" I said and laughed, too.

"I'm just kidding, Mama. I love you."

"I love you, too, baby, but get your feet off the table."

"Ugh," she said but she took them down. "Where's Adrian?" I shrugged.

"I'm not sure."

"What do you mean you're not sure?"

"I'm not sure."

I wasn't about to tell Vonnie that earlier he'd told me another woman was perfect.

"Did you call him?" she asked. I held up my fingers.

"Three times."

"Where's your phone?"

I picked it up off the sofa and handed it to her and she unlocked it. She went to my call log. At first, I was worried she'd see the calls between me and McCain but then I realized that it never said who was calling. Just a number. She called Adrian.

"What are you doing?" I asked.

"Calling him."

"I told you I already called him. Three times."

"Well, now I'm calling him."

"Put it on speaker phone," I told her.

Adrian's voicemail.

"You've reached Adrian Bennett with the district four Drug Enforcement Agency of the Department of Justice. Please leave your number and message and I will return your call as soon as possible.

Please note that any messages will be recorded and used at our discretion. If this is an emergency please hang up and dial 911."

"Hey. It's Vonnie. Where are you?? Mom is having a nervous breakdown because you won't answer her."

"Vonnie!" I said trying to grab the phone out of her hand. "Stop it."

"You better have a good excuse when you finally talk to her because she is pissed."

Click.

"Vonnie!! I'm going to strangle you!!"

She laughed and handed me back my phone.

"I'm going upstairs," she said and kissed my cheek.

"I thought you were going to watch this show with me," I said.

"I was but I just thought of something I have to tell Eden."

"Fine," I said. "I love you, anyway."

"Love you, too," she said and she ran up the stairs.

Just in time. In fact, the timing couldn't have been any better. A text.

> *Hey. It's McCain. Sorry I didn't call tonight. This is my cell number. Call me when you can.*
>
> *Me: I have to admit I was a little disappointed.*
>
> *McCain: I thought you were mad at me.*
>
> *Me: I got over it.*
>
> *McCain: LOL. Will you call me tomorrow some time?*

"Lilah!" Adrian called as he came in the back door.

> *Me: I'll try.*
>
> *McCain: Okay*

I hopped up off the sofa and stuffed my phone into my back pocket. I walked into the kitchen. Adrian came over to me.

"Hi," he said.

"Hi."

"Are you mad?" he asked as he pushed my hair over my shoulders. He laid his hands on my waist and lowered his face to my neck.

"Should I be?" I asked. He kissed me there and chill bumps erupted on my skin.

"Uh…" He stepped back but held onto my hands.

"Maybe?" he asked.

"Why? What did you do?"

"I didn't call you back, that's what."

"I'm sure you had a good reason."

This wasn't how I felt at all. I was pissed but I'm good at hiding my anger until it boils over and seeps into my heart. That's when all hell breaks loose.

"What's a good reason?" he whispered.

"I can tell you what's not a good reason," I said quietly.

"Tell me," he said.

"You were with another woman."

"Never," he said, smiling.

"You were at a bar."

"Nope."

"One of your friends told you not to answer me because I'm a drama queen."

"Well, you are a drama queen," he said. "But no." He picked up my hand, kissed my fingers. Romeo.

"Did you think about what I told you yet?" I asked.

"About McCain knowing Ben is his?"

"Yeah."

"Yeah," he said. "But you haven't given me enough information to seriously consider it."

"What other information do you need?" I asked. "He's an asshole who took complete advantage of my drug addiction and tried to make me think he loved me."

I knew he loved me.

"I think he did love you," Adrian said.

"Yeah, right." I turned from him and walked over to the coffee pot. I pulled the pot from underneath of it and dumped the old coffee from the day into the sink.

"He's very passionate about you."

"That's funny," I said and laughed.

"Look, Lilah," he said as he leaned up against the counter. "I'm not telling you no…"

"Because you know better," I finished. He chuckled.

"Yeah. But seriously, I don't think you'll be dealing with the McCain you knew back then. Twenty years tends to change people. I don't think he's an exception. Maybe you could tell me what you're planning on saying to him. That would probably make me feel better." I put the coffee in the coffee maker and turned on the delay button.

"Is seven good for you?" I asked as I looked over to him.

"Yeah, sure." I programmed in seven.

"A.M.," he said and I noticed I'd programmed in P.M. instead. I wasn't thinking straight. I had too much on my mind. He kissed my cheek as I fixed it.

"I have something to show you," I said. "More information." I went into the dining room and he followed me. I took down the painting above the buffet. The safe.

"Wow," he said. "I didn't know that was there."

"That's the purpose of the painting," I said as I put in the combination.

I opened the door when it clicked and pulled out all my jewelry, the money I'd taken out of the bank when Eric told me the economy was going to crash (It didn't but I had never put it back.), and the manila envelopes rubber-banded together.

"Damn," he said when I sat the money on the buffet. "You planning on going underground?"

"Ha ha," I said.

I took the rubber band off the envelopes and took out the one with Ben's name on it. I untied the string and pulled out his birth certificate. I handed it to Adrian and he sat down on the edge of the dining room table. I watched him as he looked at it. He looked up to me.

"Who knows about this?" he asked. I motioned back and forth between us.

"Me, you, Eric, Isabel and now Terrence."

"Why does Terrence know?" he asked, widening his eyes. Then, "Oh."

"Yeah."

"Are you seriously planning on telling this to McCain?" he asked.

"I don't know."

"Well, don't tell him unless you tell Ben first."

"I don't think I'm going to tell Ben," I said. "Would that be bad?"

"No. Just make sure no one else tells him. *That* would be bad."

"How do you think he'll respond?" I asked.

"Ben or McCain?"

"Both."

"I think Ben would go off the deep end," Adrian said. "He'd calm down eventually but it wouldn't be good for a while. Look, I have something to tell you about that situation."

"What?" I asked, alarmed.

"I kind of asked Ben to watch over you when I was in Amityville because of McCain. He was off the chain at the time and I didn't know what he might be capable of."

"And?"

"I told him about McCain." My heart beat fast.

"What did you tell him about McCain?"

"I told him you were involved with him in college."

"What else?" I asked because I knew there was more.

"Okay," he said as he handed the birth certificate back to me. "Put this away before somebody comes in here." I put it back inside the envelope and closed it. I stuck all the envelopes back into the safe and Adrian handed me the money and my jewelry cases. I put everything inside and closed the door, twirled the lock. Adrian picked up the painting and replaced it on the wall.

"It's crooked," I said as I backed up. He moved it. "Okay, good."

We walked back into the kitchen together. Adrian went over to the corner cabinet and squatted down where I kept all the liquor. I used to hide it from the kids but it was a lost cause so I gave up.

"Should I drink vodka or gin?"

"You need a drink?" I asked. He smiled and looked over his shoulder. "Gin."

He came over to the counter and I took down two highball glass, filled them with ice. He poured the gin into his, left about three fingers from the top and added a little tonic

"Lime?" I asked.

"Please."

I didn't feel like cutting up a lime so I cheated with the lime juice I had in the fridge. I squirted it in his glass and he laughed. I put it back in the refrigerator door and pulled out the lemonade, poured myself a glass.

"Cheers," I said as I tapped my glass to his.

"Cheers," he said as he leaned back against the counter. He pulled me into him then leaned in and kissed me deeply.

"Mmm…I love a gin-laced kiss," I said.

"Especially since you're drinking lemonade," he told me.

"Tell me," I said. He took a deep breath.

"I almost feel like I should call Isabel about now."

"Is it that bad?" I asked. He didn't say anything at first.

Finally, "McCain is Bret's father."

"Oh," I said shrugging my shoulders. "I know that."

"How do you know that??"

"Because Terrence told Isabel and Isabel told me."

"Ah…so maybe I didn't need the drink after all."

"You can never not need a drink."

"True," he said and laughed again. "I'm sure you know after I told Ben about you and McCain, he wasn't happy with the situation."

"I'm sure."

"He told me he didn't think he'd ever had a true enemy in his life but after what I'd told him about McCain, he might be his first."

"Just one more reason not to tell Ben and I can't tell McCain if Ben feels that way."

"I don't think it's a good idea to tell McCain under any circumstances, if you want my honest opinion. Whether you tell Ben or not is up to you," Adrian said.

"What would it accomplish?" I asked.

"Is that a hypothetical question or do you want me to answer it?"

"I don't know."

"I can guarantee you Terrence knowing is not going to affect anything, ever. That is classified DEA information. We both know Isabel wouldn't dare a tell a soul. The only unknown factor here is Eric."

"Do you think Eric would tell him?" I asked.

"How would I know?" he asked and laughed. "He was your husband. Not mine."

"I don't think he would."

"Do you still want to talk to McCain about it?"

I looked down. Did I?

"I'm not sure."

"Why do you want to talk to him?" he asked. "Just to close an open door between the two of you?"

"Kind of."

"How about I invite him over for dinner."

"What???" I asked. "Are you crazy? What about Ben??"

"Life is boring, Lilah. McCain is harmless. At least, now he is. And he's been cooperating with me. He agreed to be an informant. He works with me every week."

"Are you kidding me?" I asked.

McCain working *against* the drug dealers? What could Adrian possibly have said for him to make a full 180-degree turn like that?

"No," Adrian said. "Not at all. He's trying to turn his life around and as far as I can tell he's sincere."

"Holy cow," was all I could manage.

"So? Are you against me asking him to dinner?"

"Uh...I don't know. Can I have Isabel here?"

"You can have whoever you want here," he said and laughed. "It's your house."

"It's *our* house," I told him as I leaned into him further. I kissed him softly.

"Is it?" he asked. He sat his drink down on the counter beside him and took my upper arms into his hands. "I love you." He looked deeply into my eyes. "And I know you love me, too."

"Make you feel good about yourself?" I asked and smiled.

"You have no idea," he said.

Isabel

Well, so much for the power point presentation on little Miss. Lorelei Anastasio because currently I was sidetracked with my own life. Tom had called and invited me to dinner. I felt like it was a sign. Either that or his mother had talked to him and told him what an idiot he was for not telling me how he felt. He wasn't an idiot. I was the idiot because I let this incredible and amazing man slip through my fingers.

When Tom and I first started dating in college we caused quite the scandal. We weren't just any mixed couple. We were the most beautiful Barbie doll girl on campus (I didn't make that up – people really called me that) and the least likely black guy she would ever give a second thought. He was the guy every black girl wanted to date and I was the white girl they all hated. What is it with black girls hating white girls who date black guys? Is it jealousy? Because I just don't get it. I mean, I couldn't give a rat's ass who dates whom.

My mother used to say in an ideal world we'd all be colorless. I never thought about it until I started dating Tom and then I couldn't help but wonder if she was on to something. Maybe a colorless world would be a peaceful world. But it wasn't just about color. It was about knowing love is love no matter who you give it to.

Tom always said I was the beauty and he was the brains. Lilah said it wasn't true because Tom had both. She said he looked like Shemar Moore with glasses. Maybe. Either way, we created the most beautiful, angelic babies ever known to man. They weren't babies anymore – or angelic - but we still loved them anyway.

I decided to wear something conservative which is highly unusual for me. Lilah always says you can either show your ass or your tits. Never both. I agree with her although I don't have great boobs like she does. Her boobs are literally like little pillows you can lay your head on at night to sleep.

I chose a simple black dress. It was form-fitting with a slit up one leg. I had the legs. Lilah had the boobs. It was cold outside so I put my distressed brown suede jacket over it. Lilah told me to never wear brown and black together but, damn, I looked good. I paired it with a pair of strappy black sandals. Not too high but high enough. Despite it being cold I did not wear pantyhose because it is impossible to get out of pantyhose gracefully.

I told Tom I would meet him at the restaurant. It seemed wrong for him to come to a door that used to belong to him and ask him to knock. We'd decided on a little steakhouse called Rhoda's in town. I hadn't been there in ages but it was cozy and quiet. It had a huge stone fireplace on one end of the main room where I hoped Tom and I would be seated. I already knew ahead of time Tom had made a reservation because Tom always makes reservations even if the restaurant doesn't require them. I walked inside and looked around for him. I didn't see him anywhere.

"May I help you?" the hostess asked.

"Um…yes. I'm looking for my husband."

I can't believe I just said that out loud, I thought. But I still considered Tom to be my husband. I wasn't sure if he still considered me to be his wife.

"What does he look like?" the hostess asked. "Maybe I can help you find him."

"It's okay," I said nodding toward the bar. "I see him."

I walked toward Tom and he turned to watch me from across the restaurant. He stood up when I got to him and took my hands as he kissed my cheek. Tom has always been unbending when it comes to rules and proper manners but then if I'd had a mother like Mama Etta I probably would be, too. Whenever our boys are around Mama Etta they behave differently. They are always respectful to their elders but when Mama Etta came to our house, they also became reverent. You had no choice to but to be reverent around Mama Etta because she ruled the roost, no matter whose house she was in.

"You look amazing," Tom said.

"Thanks," I said and smiled. I laid my hand on the lapel of his sweater. "You don't look so bad yourself."

Tom is the only man I know besides Adrian who can wear anything and make it look good. He had on a pair of black jeans with a blue denim shirt and a brown cardigan sweater over it. I couldn't wait to tell Lilah I wasn't the only one who thought it was okay to wear brown and black together. As I leaned into him his scent overwhelmed me. I used to bury my face into his neck after we made love and breathe it in. It's like that sweet smell you get from leaves in the fall. Being close to Tom always reminded me of the days when my sisters and I would rake huge piles of leaves from our yard and then jump into them.

"I feel like we're on a first date," he said as he pulled out the barstool for me. I sat down and he sat down beside me. "I thought maybe we'd have a drink before dinner. Is that okay with you?"

"Sure," I said. "I probably need it."

"Why?" he asked and chuckled as he looked over to me. "Are you nervous?"

"Kind of," I admitted.

"Me, too."

He reached over and put his hand over mine. We'd been divorced for almost two years now and he was still wearing his wedding band. It made me feel like shit. I decided to make light of the situation.

"I can't believe you still wear this," I said as I picked up his hand.

"Only on special occasions," he said and smiled.

"Is this a special occasion?" I asked.

"I think so."

"What can I get you two?" the bartender asked as he walked over.

"Bella?"

Tom had always called me Bella. The fact he did it now made me want to cry.

"Um…I think I'm going to do the bitter rose martini."

"Are you bitter?" the bartender asked me and smiled.

"Depends," I answered.

"On?" he asked.

"How badly you've screwed me over."

"I'll have a dirty martini," Tom said. "Don't listen to her. She's one of the most charming and delightful women you'll ever have the pleasure of meeting."

"I am??" I asked looking over to him.

"You are," he assured me. He looked to the bartender. "Tell me you have blue-cheese olives?"

"We do have blue-cheese olives," the bartender answered.

"That's great. Thank you." He turned to me. "So, tell me what you've been up to lately."

"You're not keeping tabs on me?" I asked and laughed.

"Not anymore."

It wasn't a slap in the face but it felt like it. I looked down. Change the subject, I thought. Something both of us are passionate about: our boys.

"Have you talked to Isaac lately?" I asked.

The bartender brought our drinks. Tom lifted his to me and I lifted mine.

"To our angelic children," he said.

"Yes," I agreed. "To our angelic children."

"You guys have kids??" the bartender asked and when we said nothing. "I'm sorry. I didn't mean to interrupt your conversation."

"Oh, it's okay," Tom said. "We have three boys. Nineteen, seventeen and fifteen."

"Wow," the bartender said. "You guys look like you're in your twenties."

Yeah. Right. He was a good bullshitter looking for a big tip. I wouldn't give him one but Tom was picking up the tab tonight and he always gave a twenty percent tip no matter what happened.

"Thanks," Tom said.

I had vowed to myself I wasn't going to be the one to tell Tom about Isaac's school choice but it seemed he was in an extraordinary good mood so I decided to go with it.

"Isaac has chosen his school," I told him.

"Yeah," he said. "I talked to him."

"He told you he's going to a school up in New York?"

"Yeah," Tom said. "It's not a bad school but he's choosing it for the wrong reason."

"I know."

"Tell me about this Tiffany girl," he said. I took a sip of my drink.

"Well, I think the first thing I should tell you is she's older than him."

"How much older?" Tom asked.

"She is Adrian's twin sister." Tom widened his eyes and sat back on his bar stool.

"Wow. I didn't know that," he said. "I didn't know Adrian had a sister."

"Well, you know about the whole situation with him. He brought his sister with him and they came in as high school students because of Adrian's undercover case. Isaac fell for her. You know how he is."

"Wears his emotions on his sleeve like his mother," Tom said.

"I don't wear my emotions on my sleeve," I said defending myself.

"Oh, really?" he asked. He sat back in his chair. "Who kidnapped my wife, Isabel, and issued a replacement?"

Well, there was the answer to my question. He did still think of me as his wife.

"Funny," I said. "Isaac had no idea how old Tiffany was when he met her. I'm not sure it would've made a difference anyway. He tells me he's in love."

"Has he ever told you before he's in love before?" Tom asked.

"You know Isaac," I said. "He's always been the player."

"Nice thing to say about your own son," Tom commented.

"Well, it's true. Isn't it?"

"Unfortunately," he said and chuckled. "Yes."

"He's off the market now according to him. He told me Tiffany made him into a different person and made him realize who he truly is."

"Who is he??" Tom asked and laughed. "Because ever since he turned fifteen, I've wondered if his body had been taken over by an alien."

"I know, right?"

"You wanna get a table?" he asked.

"Sure." He stood and laid some money on the bar. It was way too much.

"I don't need any change," he told the bartender.

"Thanks, man," the bartender said.

Tom put his hand on my lower back and led me into the dining room. His touch used to give me an energizing feeling, like I could conquer the world, but tonight it gave me a sinking feeling. The feeling that told me I was the one at fault. The feeling that told me this was my mess and I had to be the one to figure out how to clean it up. The host led us to table and we sat down. It was in front of the fireplace.

"How is Lilah?" Tom asked.

"She's so happy it makes me sick." He smiled.

I wasn't going to tell him about the current situation of this bitch on Long Island. Or the McCain situation. I'd save that for our second date.

"That's good. I'm happy for her."

"Yeah," I said. "Me, too. She deserves it."

"She does."

The waiter came and introduced himself.

"What can I get you two to drink this evening?" he asked. Tom glanced down to the wine list he was holding in his hand.

"We'll have a bottle of this white," he said as he pointed to it. "And also, an order of the mushrooms."

Tom didn't have to ask what I wanted to eat or drink because he already knew what I liked.

"Certainly," the waiter said. "I'll be right back with your wine."

"Thank you," Tom replied.

"Have you ever read the book of Esther?" I asked Tom after the waiter left our table.

"In the Bible?" he asked, surprised.

"Yeah."

"Um…I'm sure I have. Mama Etta made me read the Bible every night from the time I was six until I graduated high school." He unfolded his napkin and put it in his lap.

"So, you know what she did, right?"

"Seduced the king?"

"Yes."

"Is that what you're planning to do to me?"

"I hope so," I said and smiled. He shook his head and reached for my hand across the table.

"Isabel."

"I'm just kidding."

"No, you're not. That's what you do. Your mother should've named you Esther."

That stung. A little bit.

"Esther took a chance," I said.

"Are you reading the Bible??"

"No. Of course not." He laughed. "But Lilah is."

"Why?" he asked raising his eyebrows. "Not to be discouraging."

"Adrian told her he'd read the Bible so many times he could recite it backward so now she's testing him." Tom laughed.

"Typical Lilah."

"Yeah."

"Isabel," he said looking back up to me. "I don't want to give you the wrong idea with this dinner." I pressed my lips together. "We've been through a lot together." I nodded. "I loved what we had. I loved our family."

Past tense. Another sting.

"I want it back," I said. He looked at me from across the table, pulled his hand away.

"I'm not so sure I'm ready for that, Bella."

I thought then maybe I should change the subject again just because I didn't want to be rejected and I felt given his last comment rejection was inevitable. I deserved it. Of course, I deserved it.

"Well, changing the subject."

"From me and you?" he asked and smiled.

"Yes."

"Okay."

"I think we need to talk about this situation with Isaac and Tiffany a little more," I said.

The waiter brought our appetizer and wine and showed the bottle to Tom.

"Yes," he said after looking at it. He looked back to me. "What are your initial feelings on it?"

"I think he's nineteen."

The waiter poured his wine and he tasted it.

"Perfect," he said. Then to me, "He's going to go through a lot, you know."

"What do you mean?" I asked.

"It's exactly what happened to us, Bella. Unfortunately, the world hasn't changed much."

There was that thing about color again, sticking its ugly nose into everyone's business, where it didn't belong.

"Tiffany is very beautiful."

"I doubt that changes anything," he said bluntly. "You are very beautiful, too. It may even make it worse." He just redeemed himself.

"She's a marine biologist," I told him.

"Exactly how old are she and Adrian?"

"Thank you," I said to the waiter as he sat the wine on the table. "They're twenty-seven." Tom didn't seem concerned.

"And?"

"Well, I'm glad her age doesn't bother you. It bothers a lot of people."

"Like whom?"

"Just perception."

"Are you kidding me, Isabel? After everything we've been through and you're worried about what other people think?"

"I'm not worried about what other people think," I said. "I'm simply worried about Isaac having to deal with it."

"I think he can handle it. Let me see a picture of this girl. Do you have one?" I pulled out my phone and scrolled through my photos, handed it to him. He looked at it for a moment.

"Wow," he said. "Congratulations, Isaac."

"Yeah."

"Is he happy?"

"Very."

"What does Adrian think of this?" Tom asked.

"I'm not sure," I said.

"And Lilah?"

"She's counseling Isaac."

"That's scary," Tom said and laughed.

"I know, right??"

Our waiter reappeared.

"Are you ready to order your entrées?" he asked. Tom motioned to me.

"I'll have the lobster carbonara and a Caesar salad."

"I'll have the same," Tom added.

"Excellent," the waiter answered as he took our menus.

"You know Tiffany and Adrian have the Inn in Amityville," I told Tom. "Isaac wants to go up there and stay. Like, permanently."

"You know the main issue I have with this, Isabel."

"I know. The school."

"No," he said. "I told you. It's not a bad school but he's nineteen. We can't tell him no."

"Well, we can," I said and I took a sip of my wine.

"Yes, but it would create havoc. Unnecessary havoc."

"'I agree," I said catching his eye. "Tom?"

"Hmm?"

"The boys are all gone tonight."

"Where are they?"

"With your mother."

"Why don't I know this?" he asked. I shrugged.

"She asked them to come help her rake leaves and spend the night."

"She never fails to amaze me," he said and laughed. "The lawncare company told her they were charging her extra because of all the acorns and walnut trees. She told them to kiss her ass because she had three grandsons." I laughed.

"Sounds like Mama Etta," I said and laughed.

The waiter brought our salads and I picked up my fork. Tom once told me being left- handed was sexy. Lilah said the same thing about Adrian. I didn't get it but Tom was weird that way with me. He thought everything I did was sexy. At least, he used to. When the boys were little, he sat them down at the kitchen table and held a pencil in front of them to see if they'd reach for it with their left hand. All three of my boys are left-handed. I like to think it's because they inherited it but I doubt without Tom's encouragement it would have ended up that way. I looked up to him now.

"Tom?"

"Yes?"

"The boys are gone," I reminded him.

"Are you inviting me over?"

"Yes," I said. "Esther is inviting you over."

"Esther went to see the king. She didn't invite the king over."

"Is that so?"

"Uh-huh."

"Am I coming over?" I asked. He smiled.

"What's your objective?"

"Well, it's not to save my people."

He widened his eyes and laughed. I stood up and leaned over onto the table, kissed him full on the lips. He didn't stop me.

"I haven't tasted anything that sweet in two years," he said as I sat back down into my chair.

"It can be yours for a cheap price," I told him and smiled.

"It was mine," he said. Bam. "You gonna make me pay for it again?"

I stood behind Tom as he unlocked the door to his apartment. When he opened it the scent of bleach hit me in the face.

"Did you commit a murder earlier?" I asked as we went inside. He laughed.

"No. Mama Etta came over earlier today and did my laundry."

"Does she bleach everything in the apartment?"

He pulled his shirt out of his pants. I thought I might be getting lucky sooner than later but he showed me his t-shirt underneath. Burgundy with a huge bleach spot in the middle.

"You tell me."

"Why is Mama Etta doing your laundry?" I asked and laughed. "Did you forget how?"

"No," he said. "I don't have you."

I took off my coat and laid it across the back of the sofa. They were drawings everywhere and I walked over to his board. I flipped through them. Tom was one of the most talented architects I knew. Okay, he was the only architect I knew.

"Wow," I said. "You've been busy."

"I just got the contract for the new subdivision in Kenton."

"Seriously?" I asked as I put my hand on my hip. I flipped through the various house plans. "Wow. This is a really cool house."

"Which one?" he asked, walking over.

"This one," I said as I pointed to it. "Tell me this blank spot is where the pool will go."

"It's where the pool will go," he said as he put his hand on my waist. I flipped through the rest of drawings.

"Am I looking at all of this right? Are all these blank spaces for pools?"

"Yeah."

"Why do all the houses have pools?"

"Because I was brainstorming with the developer and he was talking about how when it comes to buying houses women are usually the ones in charge."

"Is that true?" I asked as I looked back to him.

"Maybe," he said and shrugged. "But I advised if that were the case every house should have a pool. I was being witty but he agreed with me."

"So, every house in this subdivision will have a pool??"

"Yes."

"That will drive up the purchase price, will it not?"

"Well, yeah," he agreed. "And the developer liked that idea."

"Because he benefits greatly."

"Well, putting in a lot of pools brings the individual pool price down." I turned to him. "You can contract one pool and pay out the ying-yang or you can offer a contract for a lot of pools and get a fairly large discounted price."

"You're so smart," I told him.

"Well, like I said, I was being witty. Not at all expecting my off-hand proposal to be accepted."

"But it was."

"Yes, and it's killing me. Hence, Mama Etta has been doing my laundry."

"Maybe you should accidentally run out of bleach," I said and laughed.

"Oh, she brings her own. I don't buy the right kind."

"Of course, she does," I said. I walked over to him and stood in front of him, laid my hand on his cheek.

"You can't tell me you've forgotten us," I said. He shook his head.

"No." He leaned in and kissed me softly and I wrapped my arms around him. He pulled back, his eyes searching mine.

"I want to trust you, Bella, but I can't go through what we went through again. Do you understand?"

"Yes," I said as I lowered my face. He raised my chin with his finger.

"Maybe we could take it step by step?"

"Like date again?" I asked.

"Something like that." I was silent. "Isabel, you were the love of my life."

"But I'm not anymore."

"I didn't say that. Remember when Isaac was born?" he asked and I pulled away from him.

"When you were still trying to decide whether you wanted to be a father?"

"Not fair."

"True," I said." "I'm sorry."

"You are an amazing mother to our boys," he said coming over to me. He laid his hands on my shoulders. "You always have been."

"Thank you."

"But not exactly wife material." I pulled away from him again. Another sting. Actually, that was full blown slap. From a close distance. I took a deep breath.

"Maybe I should go," I said backing away. He grabbed my hand.

"I don't want you to go, Bella. I'm just trying to be honest with you. How I feel is how I feel. Don't you want to know how I feel?"

"Not if you're going to tell me I'm not wife material after I took care of you for eighteen plus years."

"Did you?"

"Are you kidding?" I asked. I picked up my coat and walked into the foyer.

Now, I was angry.

"Isabel, I don't want you to be mad. We have to talk about these things if you want to move forward. Saying you don't want to hear what I have to say will get us nowhere even if it does hurt a little."

"Hurt a little? That hurt more than a little."

"And what you did to me hurt less?" he asked. I took another deep breath.

"So, we hurt each other."

"Uh…I don't think that should even be a comparison," he said. "A few true words verses a lot of bad behavior."

"Why don't you slap me in the face for real this time??" I asked as I opened the front door.

"You have to take responsibility for your actions, Isabel," he said. He put his hands in his trouser pockets. "Are you ready to do that?" I just stood there. "Shut the door."

"I fell in love with you the day I met you," I said as I closed the door.

"Did you not stay in love with me?"

"I did," I said. I looked down. "It just changed." He walked over to me, took my hands.

"How did it change?"

"We had the boys," I told him. He raised his eyebrows and let go of my hands, turned and walked back through the archway into the living room.

"So, we shouldn't have had children??" he asked. I followed him.

"That's not what I meant."

"What then?"

"It was hard when the boys were little," I said. He turned around. "You were working all the time. You don't have a clue what it was like to be at home with them twenty-four hours a day."

"Is that supposed to be an excuse for your behavior?"

"No." I ran my hand through my hair, tucked some of it behind my ear. "I guess I just kind of resented you for it."

"For supporting my family?" he asked unbelievingly.

"No," I said shaking my head. "It was more like I felt alone. I mean, I know I wasn't but…"

"You had Lilah," he said. "The two of you were together with all the kids every day."

"Not every day."

"Just about."

"Maybe I should have married *her*."

"Come here," he said. I just stared at him. "Please." He held out his hands and I walked toward him. "One step at a time. You can't expect any more than that from me, Bella." I looked down. "Do you think I should give you the benefit of the doubt?"

"I don't know," I said and shrugged. He took my face in my hands.

"I still love you," he admitted. "I will always love you but…"

"I love it when you say but…"

He pulled me into him and pressed his lips against mine, held me tightly against him.

"You know what Mama Etta told me?" he whispered into my ear. I rolled my eyes even though he couldn't see me.

"What?"

"She said you are a beautiful woman, that you are too beautiful."

"What is that supposed to mean?" I asked.

"That you have sex appeal and you know it," he said. "You use it but you don't need to because you have me. There isn't a man alive who wouldn't want to be with you."

"Physically, because obviously emotionally I'm a train wreck." He pulled back, ran his finger across my cheek.

"You kind of are," he said. My eyes started to water so I bit my lip.

"I'm working on it."

"I know," he said and smiled. "I believe you when you say that. I do."

"But?"

"Let me tell you something," he said and sighed. "You're hard on our boys, Bella. You're constantly telling them everything they can be, who they should be, and why they should be that way. Be hard on yourself. Tell yourself the same things. Remember when we were in school? Wait. Let me rephrase that. Remember when we were in school after you got pregnant with Isaac?"

"Yes," I acknowledged. "I was so pissed at you."

"Why?" I turned away from him.

"Because you obviously didn't want what I wanted," I told him. "We were getting ready to have a baby and you were in Rio partying your ass off."

"And I regret that but it is not my point."

"Of course, it's not." I started to walk away.

"Bella, listen to me!" he said as he grabbed my arm.

"What??"

"You made something of yourself," he said. "You worked, you studied, you raised a little boy. You did all those things and you were amazing at all of them." I looked down. "Look at me." I looked up to him. "You graduated with honors. You still have all of that inside you. Apply it to us. Work on us the way you used to work on everything else. Dedicate yourself to *us*." Tears popped out onto my cheeks and I wiped the corner of my eyes with my fingers. "Show me you can do it."

"You know what I want?"

"What?" he asked. "Tell me what you want. *Please* tell me what you want."

"I want what Adrian and Lilah have," I told him. Suddenly, he seemed angry, and he turned and walked away from me. "What??" I asked. "Is there something wrong with that?"

"Yes!" he exclaimed. "Yes. There is something majorly wrong with that."

"What could possibly be wrong with wanting what they have??"

"Because we had that, Isabel!" He was yelling at me now. "We had that!!" I bowed my head. "Did we not have that??" I nodded.

"I guess."

"You guess???" He ran his hands over his head and back again, exhaled. "That is exactly what we had. Jesus Christ, Isabel. You said you wanted it then – when I was 'in Rio partying my ass off.' You said you wanted it repeatedly so I married you. I gave you that love."

"I hope it wasn't just because *I* wanted it," I said. "I hope you wanted it, too."

"Of course, I did. I wouldn't have married you if I hadn't wanted it, too."

"So?"

"You said you wanted a family so I gave you one."

"A little closer together than I wanted," I said and smiled.

"You said our house wasn't big enough. I gave you a bigger one. You said you wanted a house with a pool so I gave you one of those. You said you wanted a Range Rover. I bought you one for your birthday. You said you wanted a Tiffany key. I went out and bought you one. I have given you *everything.*"

"And I appreciate all of those things. But they are things."

"Our boys are not a thing."

"That is not what I meant," I said. "I wanted your heart, Tom."

"You've had my heart for twenty years!!" he shouted.

"Have I??" I asked. "Because it seems like your career has always had your heart."

"Are you kidding me right now??"

"I don't know," I said as I ran my hands over my face and up into my hair.

"You don't know?? Look at me!"

"I am looking at you!" I shouted.

"You have my heart," he said quietly. "I know sometimes it didn't seem like it with all my work responsibilities but you have always had my heart, Bella. I hate it I love you so much. My life would so much easier if I didn't." I didn't say anything. "Tell me something."

"What is that?" I asked as I wrapped my arms around myself. It was almost a whisper but he heard me.

"You know you have my heart," he said. "At least, I hope you know. Do you?"

"Yes," I said quietly as I looked down. "I'm sorry."

"Don't be sorry, Bella," he said. He walked over to me and took my hands in his once more. "Look at me." I looked up to him. "Tell me when I'm going to get *your* heart. Tell me when I am good enough to be the only one."

"You are," I said.

"No, I'm not."

"You are."

"Bella, I saw you last week at that restaurant at the lake. What is it?"

"Lakeview?"

"Yeah, that one. With another man."

"We're divorced," I contested. "And it was dinner, for God's sake."

"You didn't sleep with him?" he asked. I wanted to lie but I couldn't. I had made up my mind I was never going to lie to Tom again. I pressed my lips together but I didn't answer. "Bella?"

"It wasn't anything serious," I said. "It was just…"

"For fun?"

"Tom…"

"Either you love me or you want to have fun with other men," he told me. "Which is it??"

"I…"

"You can't have both."

"It didn't mean anything," I said as he escorted me to the door.

He sighed and picked up my coat. He held it up for me. I slid my arms into the sleeves and he pulled it up over my shoulders. He opened the front door and I stepped out onto the porch.

"When you've made up your mind about what you want," he said. "When you think you can give me your whole heart, not part of it. All of it. Let me know."

"Tom, I…"

"Just let me know," he repeated as he shut the door.

I stood on the porch for a moment contemplating what he'd said. My whole heart. None of those other men got my whole heart. None of those men got any of my heart at all. The only person I felt comfortable giving my whole heart to was Tom. I always thought what was in your heart automatically presented itself to the people you loved but if your actions don't mirror your words those words mean nothing.

Over the years having man after man tell me how beautiful I was felt good. It felt amazing. Men had become an addiction to me just like alcohol becomes an addiction to an alcoholic. I didn't have to wonder whether those men loved me. Of course, they didn't love me. They didn't want the real me. They just wanted what I could give them. With other men I didn't have to care.

Tom was the first man who made me accountable for my actions. At first it made me angry but then I realized he only did it because he cared about me. The one thing I didn't want to do he'd done first. He got to see the real me because I began to care for him, too. And he loved the real me. Now all I had to do was figure out how to love myself.

I walked into Lilah's kitchen with a bottle of vodka in one hand and the glass I was drinking out of in the other. It was happy hour and despite my evening with Tom it was going to be happy. It was going to be so fucking happy I wouldn't be able to stand it.

"What are you doing with that??" Lilah asked as I sat it on the counter.

"I want to get trashed," I told her.

"Why??"

"Tom called me last night."

"Oh?"

"We went to dinner," I said.

"What??" she asked as she reached for my hand. I let her take it. "Why didn't you tell me?"

"It was kind of spontaneous."

"Well, tell me what happened," she said excitedly.

"Can you fix me a drink first?"

"You've already had a drink, it seems."

"Well, make me another one."

"What do you want?" she asked. Lilah never questioned my drinking habits. Probably because I never questioned hers.

"I'm brain dead." I leaned up against the counter. "Just make up something."

"Hmm," she said as she went to the refrigerator. "How about a classic orange crush? I have some freshly squeezed orange juice."

"Why?" I asked.

"Because I bought a box of oranges from the FFA at school and Vonnie needed something to do."

"I should have done that," I said. "I'm a teacher. I should support the FFA."

"Well, I did it for you," Lilah consoled.

"Thanks, hon. You're always saving me."

"I don't think buying oranges from the FFA is saving you, but okay. You're welcome."

"Don't use as much orange juice as you usually do," I instructed. "Substitute the two amounts."

"What does that mean??" she asked as she turned from the refrigerator.

"It's usually twice as much orange juice as vodka. Make it twice as much vodka instead."

"Oh," she said. "Ha-ha. Tell me about your dinner with Tom."

"First," I said. "Did you talk to Adrian about Miss. Magic?"

"Isabel."

"What??" I asked as Lilah filled her blender with ice. "I want to know what Adrian has to say about her."

"He never has much of anything to say about her," I told her. "I mean, he told me what she did for a living when I asked. He said she was nice. That we'd probably like each other. You know."

"Uh-huh."

"What is that supposed to mean?" she asked. She added the orange juice and the vodka.

"Nothing," I said. "Never mind."

"Nope," Lilah chastised. She turned from the counter "I'm not fixing your drink until you tell me what you're thinking."

I took a deep breath. I didn't want to tell Lilah things that weren't true and I had no way of knowing without doing a little research what was going on with Adrian and this little whore. But my intuition told me someone wasn't telling the truth.

"Let me do my power point presentation," I said and smiled. "I need more info."

"Well, what are you thinking?" Lilah asked.

"I don't know. I just feel like something is going on he's not telling you."

"Well, there's a lot he's not telling me. He can't give me information about his cases. You know that."

"Something other than work," I said.

"Like what??"

"I don't know. I told you. Let me research."

"Alright," she conceded. She turned the blender on and I watched her concoction swirl against the glass. "Tell me about your date with Tom."

"My date with Tom made me feel like shit."

"Why did it make you feel like shit?" she asked. "Did he bring up the pictures with Chris again??"

"No. I think he's past that."

"Well, that's good."

"Where the hell is Chris?" I asked. "Where did that motherfucker go?" Lilah laughed.

"His grandma made him move out."

"His grandma??" I asked.

"He was living with his grandma," Lilah told me. "You know. His wife kicked him out after she found out about you, and he had nowhere else to go."

"So, he moved in with his grandma??"

"Yeah."

"Well, why did his grandma kick him out?" I asked. She shrugged.

"I have no idea but Mrs. Jenkins told me at the grocery store it was because he had too many sleepovers."

"She said sleepovers??" I asked and laughed.

"It's Mrs. Jenkins," I reminded her.

"That's hilarious," I said, laughing. "I needed a good laugh."

"You're welcome," Lilah said as she poured her orange concoction into a glass." She handed it to me.

"Cheers," I said as I held up my glass. "To having sleepovers. God, I need a sleepover."

"You just had a sleepover with that dude you went out to dinner with last week," she said as we sat down at the kitchen table.

"He didn't have a clue what he was doing," I admitted. "It doesn't matter. My sleepover days need to be over."

"Ah, is that why you want to get trashed?? Because Tom told you that you couldn't have any more sleepovers?"

"Yeah, but I need a sleepover," I told her. "Amongst many other things in my twisted life."

"Why is your life twisted?" Lilah asked.

"Because I want to be with Tom but I can't have sleepovers…" I hesitated. "…like Chris, if I want to be with Tom."

"Not to be discouraging but I have to side with Tom on this one. I mean, I love sleepovers, too, but if I had a choice between a sleepover and Adrian, I'd consistently choose Adrian. If you feel like you must make a choice then you probably aren't ready to be with Tom."

"Wow, thanks."

"Well, who do you wanna have a sleepover with?" Lilah asked. "Anyone in particular?"

"Anyone except my vibrator," I told her. "I'm out of batteries." Lilah laughed.

"Holy cow, Isabel," she said as she kept laughing.

"What?" I asked. "It's not funny." Vonnie waltzed into the room and came over to give me a hug.

"I have extra batteries," she said with a slight smile on her face.

"Veronica Lauren!" Lilah chastised. Vonnie laughed.

"Well, I do." Then to me, "I'm sorry about what happened with you and Tom at dinner."

"How do you know about what happened between Isabel and Tom at dinner?" Lilah asked.

"A friend of Isaac's works there," she explained. "He told Isaac, Isaac told Ben and Ben told me."

"Nothing happened at the restaurant," I said. "What did he tell Isaac?"

"I have no idea," Vonnie said and shrugged. "But I think Isaac was kind of expecting you not to come home and you did."

"Good Lord," Lilah said.

"I'm moving," I told Vonnie. "Will you help me pack?"

"No," she said and laughed. "I'll be back at eight, Mom."

"Okay, honey."

"How are things going with her and her new boyfriend?" I asked once she'd left. "What's his name?"

"Hunter," Lilah informed me. "He's a good kid, I think."

"No drugs?" I asked.

"Pot," she said. "But after the cocaine thing that's not really a drug to me."

"It's never been a drug to me," I said and laughed. "Gotta pick your battles."

"Cocaine is a battle," Lilah said.

"For sure," I agreed.

"Tom told me he still loves me but he doesn't think I love him."

"Why would he think that?"

"Uh…shall I name all of them??"

"*Can* you name all of them??" she asked and smiled. "I know I can't."

"Remember when we used to take dick pics of the guys we slept with?"

"And compare them to each other," she said.

"Whatever happened to those pictures?" I asked. "We had them in that gold box. The one that had your Mom's stationary in it. Remember we took the stationary out and stole the box?"

"Yeah, but what did we do with it??"

"It's probably in your basement somewhere with all those boxes you never unpacked."

"We should find it," she said. "Before someone else does."

"Why waste our time?" I asked. "I'm sure one of the kids will find it eventually."

"You better think of a good explanation when they do," she told me.

"Who can we blame it on?" I asked tapping my fingers on the table.

"I don't think we can blame it on anyone," Lilah said. "Anyone who finds them will know it's ours."

"What the hell makes you think that?" I asked. "How is finding a box full of dick pics directly related to us? I mean, they could be any-body's dicks."

"Half of them will be white," she said. "The other half of them will be black."

"Ah," I said. "Well, yeah. There's that. I hope sleeping with a black guy is still on your bucket list."

"Maybe Adrian will let me sleep with Terrence," she said as an answer.

"Hell no," I said. "If anybody sleeps with Terrence, it's gonna be me."

"He's getting married," Lilah pointed out sadly. "So, probably not a good idea. For either of us."

"When has that ever mattered??" I asked.

"We can't do that to Sharla," she said. "She seems like she'd be such a sweet person."

"How do you know anything about Sharla?"

"Adrian told me she kept Jenny's nephew while Jenny was here."

"Does Jenny's nephew live with her all the time?"

"I think so."

"Why?"

"Who knows, but still, you have to be a nice person to agree to keep someone's kid indefinitely."

"True," I said. "Damn, I hate it when I have a conscience."

"It sucks," she agreed.

"Woo," I said. "We could do it *with* her."

"Fire up the hot tub," Lilah said and we laughed. "Me, you, Adrian, Terrence, Sharla...we can invite Tom."

"Tom says we need to date again," I said soberly.

"That's a date," Lilah said and I laughed.

"What's a date?" Adrian asked as he came through the back door. He leaned over and kissed Lilah's cheek. "Hey, baby."

I was still pissed with him for telling Lilah Lorelei was perfect but I decided not to show it. I would rake him over the coals later when I had enough proof to blow him out of the water.

"The hot tub," I explained.

"Ah…memories," Adrian said.

"It was fun, right?" I asked.

"I can't remember most of it," he said. "But I think so."

"I remember *all* of it," Lilah said.

"Don't be a party pooper," Adrian told her as he squeezed her shoulder.

"Yeah, Lilah," I said. "Don't be a party pooper. Let Adrian be a bad boy every now and then."

"I heard you had a date with Tom," Adrian said to me.

"How does everyone know about this??" I asked. "It just happened last night."

"Local police station news."

"Good grief," I said.

"And I'm supposed to be finding out if you're still single," he said as he retrieved a glass from the cabinet. He proceeded to make himself a drink. "A few of the guys want to go out with you."

"All at once?" Lilah asked.

"No," Adrian said and laughed.

"Well, there's your sleepover," Lilah told me.

"Funny," I said. "Honestly, even if Tom weren't in the equation, I think I'd be too depressed for a sleepover. I don't think I could do it right now without thinking about Tom."

"There's nothing wrong with that," Lilah informed me. "I used to pretend I was with other men all the time when I was having sex with Eric."

"Wrong," Adrian said. He walked over to me as he sat his drink on the table. "That is so wrong. Stand up, Isabel."

"Why?"

"Just do it," he said so I stood up. "You just need a hug."

"I do?" I asked as he took me into his arms.

Adrian picked me up and I looked over his shoulder to Lilah. She smiled. He sat me back down on the floor and before I knew what was happening, he had tipped me backward in his arms. He put his mouth over mine.

"Mmm…" was all I could manage.

"Good grief, Adrian," I heard Lilah say.

He kept kissing me and I felt his tongue inside my mouth. I gave in and kissed him back. Damn, it was good. I heard Lilah laughing. Now you know that's a good friend, when her man comes in and makes out with you in their kitchen and she thinks it's funny. Adrian stood me back up and wiped his hand over his mouth.

"That was a little sloppy, Isabel," he said. "You may want to work on that if you want to get back together with Tom."

And just like that, he'd charmed his way back into my good graces.

"Will you help me?" I asked innocently as I brought the back of my hand of my forehead. "I feel faint."

"Lord," Lilah said.

"I'm expensive," Adrian said as he picked up his drink and walked toward the living room. He turned and winked at me. "But maybe Lilah will lend you some money."

Richmond

McCain

I was sitting on my front porch smoking when Adrian pulled up in front of my house. The DEA was paying me to be an informant and my sentence had been suspended with time served. All thanks to Adrian. I rented half of a duplex downtown. It was a bad neighborhood but I had a bad neighborhood reputation so I fit in perfectly.

"Hey," Adrian said as he climbed the steps to the porch. He bumped knuckles with me. "Thanks for your help with the 2nd Street bust."

"Yep."

"May I sit?" he asked.

"Knock yourself out," I told him as I waved my hand outward. "I'm not sure about that sofa, though. It was here when I moved in." I took a hit off my cigarette. "Everybody in this neighborhood probably done had sex on it."

"Nice," he said. "Maybe I should sit in this chair instead."

"Good call."

He sat down and leaned forward on his knees. I liked Adrian. It was hard not to like him. We hadn't had a very good start but things had been working out pretty decent for me lately. I felt better about my life now than I had in a long time. I also had this hot chick named Desiree who lived next door. So far, she'd only given me one cup of sugar.

"What you been up to?" Adrian asked.

"Living the dream," I said as I leaned back in my chair. I stretched my feet out in front of me.

"Oh yeah?" he asked and laughed. "I'll take a wild guess and say it has something to do with her." He nodded in Desiree's direction as she came out of her front door. I laughed.

"That would be a good guess," I told him and laughed, too.

Adrian stood up as Desiree came up the steps of my porch. He was such a gentleman. No wonder Lilah fell so hard for him.

"Hi," she said to Adrian.

He looked her up and down. Even a gentleman couldn't help but take her in. She's like a tall glass of cold water on a hot, summer day. Her skin glowed a light brown and she smiled with pink, glossy lips. She had on a pair of denim cut-offs with hot pink crystal beads down the sides. In between each crystal was a riveted hole. It was easy to see she wasn't wearing any underwear. My grandfather used to call it riding dirty. I laughed.

"What's so funny?" she asked as she looked to me. Adrian smiled. I didn't even have to tell him why.

"Nothing, honey," I told her as I took a drag off my cigarette. "Whatcha up to?"

"I'm going to work but I was thinking when I got home tonight maybe you'd want another cup of sugar. I gotta pay my rent tomorrow." Adrian laughed again and I looked over to him and smiled.

"You got it," I said and exhaled.

"And you," Desiree said as she walked over closer to Adrian. He was about six inches taller than her and she reached up and twirled a piece of his hair around her fingernail. They were hot pink just like the crystals on her denim shorts. "...look delicious," she finished. "You want a cup of sugar?"

"She's expensive," I told Adrian.

"We can negotiate," she said to him as she took his hand in hers. "You wanna negotiate with me?"

"Sure," he said and chuckled.

Of course, he said sure. He wouldn't be here when she got back.

"I'm looking forward to it," she said. Then she looked over to me. "Can I give a cup of sugar to Mr. Dark and Dreamy here?"

"What are you asking me for?" I asked as I took a drag off my cigarette. "It's your sugar." Adrian laughed, and Desiree pointed at me.

"You my favorite boy."

"I know," I said and smiled. She walked back down the steps in her five-inch gold stilettos.

"Damn," Adrian said when she'd disappeared. "I hope you have something good for me to smoke because I might be going into cardiac arrest."

"Yep." I leaned back and pulled the tin I kept my stash in from between the cushions of my chair. I handed it to him.

"Paper's in there if you wanna roll it," he said. "Or I got a pipe in the house."

"Man," he said as he opened the tin. "I haven't rolled anything in years."

"Like riding a bike," I told him.

"You're a bad influence on me," he said as he laid the paper down on the table in front of him. He filled it and rolled it tightly, licked the edge, secured it together. He held between his lips. "Light?" I handed him my lighter and he cupped his hand around his cigarette. He inhaled and held it for a minute.

"I got a proposition for you," he said as he exhaled. He handed the lighter back to me and I slipped it into my pocket.

"What's that?"

"You might need to get out your good clothes," he said and smiled.

"Why? Did somebody die?" I asked. He chuckled.

"Nope. I just thought you'd want to be wearing something nice when you see Lilah."

My heart stopped beating for a minute but then it jolted itself back into existence and pounded against my chest again.

"I thought you didn't want me to see Lilah," I said. "You told me if I ever came near your house, you'd send me to the…uh…shittiest, most vile prison you could find on this side of the Mississippi." He laughed again.

"I did say that."

"That was before I was a good guy."

"Nope," he said. He shook his head and looked down. He took another drag then looked back up to me. "Being a good guy means you do it for free."

"Fuck no," I said. "I'm risking my damn life for you, you shit-head." He chuckled. "You do it for free??"

"Fuck no," he said. "I risk my damn life every day." He took a hit and leaned back in his chair. "I was going to invite you to dinner." My heart started pounding again.

"At your house?" I asked.

"Yeah. Would you like to come to dinner at my house?"

"Man," I said. "I don't know."

"Why don't you know? Lilah and I talked about it."

"I have to come sober, don't I?" I asked. He smiled.

"Well, yeah," he said. "But Isabel is planning to do martini flights so you won't be sober for long."

"Isabel," I said. "I'd forgotten about that bitch."

"She's not that bad," he said. "She's all about protecting Lilah."

"How does she feel about you?" I asked curiously.

"She hated my guts at first but she's better now. I don't think she'd think twice about shooting me, though, if it came down to that."

"No joke," I said. I inhaled and held it, blew it back out. "She's a pistol."

"You could bring a date if it would make you feel better," he suggested and grinned. "I'm sure Desiree would love to accompany you."

"That hoe?" I asked and we both laughed again. "Yeah, okay." Adrian stood up.

"Saturday night at seven," he said. He pointed at me as he took one last hit. "You know where I live."

"I might be high," I told him.

"Well, that'll make two of us," he said. He put out his cigarette in the ashtray on the table. "Thanks for the ganja."

"Yep."

I watched him as he hopped down the steps to the sidewalk. The alarm on his car went off when he hit the key fob. He got inside and started it. He took off like a bolt of lightning, shifted into second, and floored it through the red light one block down the hill.

I was where I was right now because of Lilah. I let her influence every decision I made when we were together and even afterward, I thought about what she would do before I made a final call on anything. I could still hear my name coming out of her mouth when we made love.

My whole entire life had revolved around her and our son.

Woodlawn

Isabel

I don't know what Lilah is thinking when it comes to this dinner party. What I do know is she seemed cool as a cucumber. She wasn't. This is what Lilah does. She pretends to be in whatever mood she wants to be in even though she's not in it. She fools a lot of people that way. But not me. Her biggest dilemma right now? What to wear. She'd already gone through her closet. Now she was going through mine.

"I want to look sophisticated but sexy," she said as she took my red Valentino dress out and looked at it.

"Hell, no," I said as I laid across my bed. "You are not wearing that."

"Why not?"

"Because that is not the type of dress you wear for an informal dinner party. That's more like I'm going to get crazy laid tonight but I want to look like a lady before it happens."

"True." She put it back and pulled out a mint green angora sweater dress. Well, it was a sweater dress in the front with a cut out back. "What about this one?"

"Yeah," I said and shrugged. "It's super sexy but conservative at the same time. You probably need to wear some kind of undergarment though, and it has to be backless. Look at the back." She turned it around.

"Well, what do you *think* I'm going to wear, Isabel?" she asked. "You think I'm going to be buck naked under it?"

"I didn't mean underwear, dufus. I meant like.... uh..."

"A girdle??" she asked surprised. "What exactly are you saying??"

"What I'm saying is you can see everything through that dress." She laughed.

"I should go braless," she said. "McCain always loved my boobs and they're twice the size they used to be."

"Well, you have great boobs," I told her. "But you don't want him to see your hard nipples and if you don't wear a bra he will."

"What makes you think my nipples are going to be hard?" she asked and laughed again.

"I don't know," I said. "My nipples are always hard."

"Big surprise."

She took the dress off the hanger and began to remove her clothes. She slipped the dress over her head and looked at herself in the floor mirror. She rubbed her hands over her stomach.

"Hmm...Does it look like I'm pregnant?"

"You can't tell yet," I assured her.

"Well, that's good because the last thing I want McCain to know is that I'm pregnant. Do you have something I can wear under it?"

"Well, if you wear stockings, you'll have your garter."

"Adrian loves it when I wear stockings with a garter belt," she told me.

"Every man loves it when you wear a garter belt," I said and looked to the ceiling. She rubbed her hand over her stomach again.

"I bet you can see the straps of my garter through this, though."

"Well, then, wear regular panty hose."

"Eeww," she said. "Who wears that shit?"

"Lots of women wear that shit."

"Do you??" she asked.

"When I'm cold," I admitted.

"I feel like I'm wearing kiddie tights when I wear them," she said. "I cannot feel sexy in panty hose. It's a contradiction in terms."

"I had a guy take off my pantyhose once," I told her. "It was weird. I felt like he was changing my diaper." She waved her hand at me and laughed.

"Lord, Isabel."

"It's true."

"So, what am I going to wear under this?" she asked. I got up and dug through my lingerie drawer. I had to dump it out on the bed to find what I was looking for. I held it up. It was a backless teddy combined with a wired bra.

"This."

"Woo…. that's cute," she said. "Where did you get that?"

"Tom gave it to me for our anniversary one year," I said as I looked at it longingly. "We had a lot of good sex when I was wearing this."

"I'm assuming you've washed it," she said.

"Well, yeah. Eeww." I threw it to her and she caught it. She held it up and turned it around.

"Is this thong going to go up my ass in a good way or a bad way?"

"What does that mean?" I asked and chuckled.

"Well, sometimes they go up your ass and get lost so you feel nothing and sometimes they make you feel like you got a 2x4 up in there."

"The disappearing kind," I said. "But don't get drunk and pee through it like I did once."

"Oh, my god," she said. "Remember the time we went on the double date with those twin guys??"

"Oh yeah," I said, laughing. "The time you shit yourself." She pointed at me.

"Life lesson: Always have a spare pair of panties in your bag." I held out my hand and she high-fived me.

"Or have a friend who does," I added.

We both burst into laughter just as Matt stuck his head into the door.

"Hey," he said. "Can I drive the Rover?"

"I still can't believe you have a driver's license," Lilah said. "You're not old enough to drive."

"I am," he said and smiled. "Mom?"

"Please tell me you aren't going to let him drive the Range Rover."

"Man," Matt said. "Thanks a lot, Lilah. Don't you have more trust in me than that?"

"I don't even trust my own kids. Have you seen Ben drive??" Lilah asked. Matt shrugged.

"Well, I don't drive like Ben. I promise." I picked up my keys off my bedside table and threw them in his direction.

"Dinner party at Lilah's house at seven," I reminded him. "You need to be there at six-thirty."

"Why??" he asked. "I was going to take Eden to the movies."

"Woo," Lilah said as she glanced in my direction. "She's sexy."

"Don't tell him that," I told Lilah but she ignored me.

"She *is* sexy," Matt said as he pulled his phone out of his pocket. "Look at this." He handed Lilah his phone.

"Oh, my god, Matt. She's naked."

"Give me that," I said as I took it out of Lilah's hands.

"She sent you a naked picture of herself??" I asked unbelievingly. "Are you serious? What kind of girl does that?"

"She's cute," Lilah added. I gave her the evil eye.

"Mom," Matt said. "Chill out. All the girls do it. It's not a big deal."

"All the girls do it??"

"Yeah," he assured me. I looked over to Lilah.

"All the girls do it," I repeated.

"Does Vonnie do it?" Lilah asked Matt.

"Gross. How would I know??"

"Maybe I should send one of myself to your Dad," I said to Matt.

"Couldn't hurt," Lilah commented.

"Ya'll are disgusting," Matt said.

"Did you send this girl a picture of your dick??" I asked him.

"NO!!"

"Well, I just thought maybe ya'll traded pics," I said as I looked down to his phone again.

"No," he said. "We did not."

"You promise?" I asked as I looked up.

"I promise," he said.

"Well, bring her to Lilah's for dinner," I told him as I handed his phone back to him. "Then go to a late movie."

"Isabel!" Lilah said. "Do you know how many people we have already?"

"What's one more??" I asked. "We can put the leaf in the table."

"At the rate we're going we're going to need both leaves in the table." I shrugged.

"What are we having?" Matt asked. I narrowed my eyes at him. I had always told my kids beggars can't be choosers. "I mean, it doesn't matter. I'm just curious."

"I'm doing sherried doves."

"Awesome," Matt said.

"You are??" Lilah asked me.

"Yeah."

She ran across the room and hugged me, pushed me back on the bed, and fell on top of me.

"Ya'll are weird," Matt said as he shut the door.

"Six-thirty," I yelled after him. I pushed Lilah off me. "Get up. You weirdo."

"Where did you get doves?" she asked as she got off the bed.

"Tom's mom called me yesterday and asked me if I wanted some," I said. "His dad went dove hunting and she had beaucoup of them. The boys love them so every year she sends me some."

"Aw, that's sweet," Lilah said. "I love those little birdies."

"Wrong," I said and laughed. "Just wrong."

"Well, that's what they are," she said. "Do you think everyone will like the doves? I mean, I know we all do but some people might be weird about it."

"Do you think I give a shit about that?? You can't store doves. They have to be cooked fresh and I am not about to waste them. They're delicious."

"Okay," she said as she pulled my dress over her head. She took off her bra and panties and pulled on the teddy I'd given her then grabbed the dress and put it back on.

"Well?" she asked as she looked in the mirror once more. "What do you think?" I sat back on the bed and she turned to me.

"I think McCain is going to wish you were still his," I said.

Lilah

Me: Are you nervous?

McCain: Yes

Me: Don't be. Everything will be fine.

McCain: Easy for you to say.

Me: Are you going to kidnap me? LOL

McCain: I wish.

Me: I would send you a heart emoji but I don't know how.

McCain: LOL. So, I guess I'll see you later tonight.

Me: Okay.

McCain: Ttyl

Me: What does that mean?

McCain: LOL. Talk to you later.

Me: Oh. Okay. Ttyl.

Damn it. Isabel was going to beat my ass when I told her I was talking to McCain.

If I told her I was talking to McCain.

Isabel

"Yoo-hoo! Lilah!"

It was Lilah's mom coming through her front door.

"Good gracious," Lilah said to me. "What is she doing here?"

"Lilah!" I chastised as I walked toward the door to greet Loretta. "Your mama loves you to death."

"Too much," she mumbled.

I took Loretta back into the kitchen and she walked over to Lilah and wrapped her arm around her waist, kissed her cheek. She sat her grocery basket on the table. Loretta was the only person I'd ever known who carried groceries in a basket. She said paper bags were tacky.

"I brought you a fruit cocktail cake, baby doll," she said. "And one of my roasted herb chickens."

"Oh? Thanks, Mom. That was sweet. What's the occasion?"

"Adrian told me you were having a dinner party tonight," she said as she took the cake and chicken out of the basket. She sat them on the kitchen table. "And I thought maybe you might need some help. I know how things like this overwhelm you sometimes."

"When did you talk to Adrian?" Lilah asked her mother as she smiled at me.

"Why, honey, I talk to him every day."

"You do?" Lilah asked. She looked over to me once more and I shrugged. "Why do you talk to him every day?"

"He calls me," she said. "He loves me. Sometimes more than you do."

"Oh Lord," Lilah said. "You've seduced him into believing I don't love you as much as I should, haven't you?"

"Me?" Loretta asked as she brought her hand to her chest. "Sweet, little me?"

"Mom."

"No, honey. I have done nothing of the sort."

"Well, speak of the devil," I said as Adrian came into the kitchen. He went over to Lilah and laid his hand on her waist. She turned to him and they kissed.

"Hey, baby," he said.

"Hi," she said sheepishly.

Lilah still acted like her and Adrian were completely innocent when she was around her mother but I knew differently. Boy, did I know differently. Blowjobs in the pantry. Wonder what Loretta would think about that?

"And my second favorite woman in the world," Adrian said as he walked over to Loretta. He kissed her cheek. "Are you staying for our dinner party tonight?"

"Oh, good gracious no, honey. Mr. Winston and I are going to the club tonight."

"You and Mr. W going clubbin'?" Adrian asked and chuckled.

"The country club," Lilah said. "You goofball."

"You need to go to the ABC store," I told Adrian. "Here's a list." He took it from me and read it.

"Damn," he said as he looked up to me. "What the hell are we doing tonight?"

"Martini flights," I reminded him. "Remember?"

"Ah, yes." He turned to Lilah. "Sharla and Terrence just got in. I think they're settling in at the hotel now but I told Sharla to come over here and hang with you guys. You will love her. I've known Sharla since high school."

"That's good," Lilah said as she looked over to me. "We've been wanting to meet Sharla."

"We have," I added. "If we have enough martinis tonight maybe we'll all end up in the hot tub with Sharla."

"And Terrence," I added and winked.

"I don't think Sharla and Terrence are into that kind of thing," Adrian said and laughed.

"What kind of thing?" Mrs. Winston asked.

"They're not water people," Lilah said. Adrian and I looked at each other. He shook his head and tried not to laugh. I laughed out loud.

"I'll probably get Terrence to go to the ABC store with me," Adrian told us trying to change the subject. He looked over to me. "Because this list makes me look like I'm an alcoholic."

"Professional drinker," I told him. "Don't get the two confused." He walked up behind Lilah and grabbed her from behind around her shoulders, dipped her backward and kissed her deeply.

"Oh, sorry, Loretta," he said when he stood Lilah back up. "That was disrespectful. I apologize." Loretta laughed and waved her hand at him.

"It's nice to see the two of you so in love," Loretta said. "But get it while the getting's good. Before my little grandbaby gets here." She looked over to me. "Because we all know you won't be having any good sex for a while after that happens."

"Mom!" Lilah chastised and Adrian laughed.

"I have a feeling Adrian could commit a murder and your mom would be able to justify it somehow," I told Lilah.

"For sure," she said and laughed. "I think she likes him better than me."

"You are silly," Loretta said to her daughter. "I gotta get out of here. I need to take your Daddy shoe shopping. What a dreadful chore. Enjoy the fruit cocktail cake. These yankees need some good old-fashioned Southern cooking. Have Maria ready around four. I'll come get her. Okay, sweetie?"

"Okay," Lilah said as she walked over and hugged her mother. "Thank you, Mama."

"See ya, Mama #2," I told her as I leaned up against the counter. I had been calling Lilah's mom Mama # 2 since high school.

"Don't do anything I wouldn't do," Loretta said as she pointed her finger at me. "You hear me, Isabel?"

"You got it," I said as I pointed back to her.

I had a feeling we were all going to do a lot of things Mama #2 wouldn't do. Some of them would be illegal (Isaac's stash, letting our kids drink). I hoped things wouldn't get too out of hand because when our two families got together things sometimes got out of hand. It wasn't because our children were bad. They were just mischievous and loved playing jokes on one another. Throw in a little alcohol and you had a recipe for a wild night. With any luck there would be no fights or fires or dares to run across the lawn naked at three o'clock in the morning. Hopefully no one would fall off a roof or end up downtown peeing on the railroad tracks. But there would be drinking games and shots. There were always shots. All I could do was pray Roy was the one on duty.

Dinner Party

Isabel's Sherried Doves

Loretta's Herb Roasted Chicken

Zucchini "Crab cakes"

Chestnut Cornbread Stuffing

High Street Potatoes

Asparagus Casserole

Mandarin Orange Salad

Baked Carrots and Apples

Pastel Ice

Blueberry Pie

Lilah's Chocolate Éclair Pie

Loretta's Fruit Cocktail Cake

Isabel's Rum Cake

It was six-forty-five when the doorbell rang. Everyone was present except McCain. All the children apart from Ben. Tiffany had arrived along with Vonnie's Hunter and Matt with Eden, who was gorgeous even with her clothes on. Terrence and Sharla. I saw Lilah stiffen as Adrian went to answer the door. I walked over to her and took her hand in mine. Her palms were sweaty.

"It's gonna be fine," I whispered in her ear. I heard Adrian in the foyer.

"Good to see you, McCain," he said.

"You, too, man. Thanks for the invite."

"Sure. You look nice, Desiree."

"I clean up good," she said. "You didn't get that cup of sugar yet."

"We have to talk about the sugar later," Adrian said and chuckled.

"We can do three if you want," she said. "You know I can give your girlfriend sugar, too."

"Damn, Desiree," McCain said. "Can you act like you have a little bit of class?? I looked to Lilah.

"He brought a date," I told her.

"Who, apparently, wants to give me some sugar, whatever that is," Lilah said.

"I'm getting in on that," I whispered. "Don't you leave me out."

"You don't even know what it is yet," Lilah told me.

"I'm imagining it."

Lilah slapped me on my arm and McCain came into the living room. Everyone fell silent, like you could hear a pin drop silent. Adrian led him and his date (who it was clear to see was streetside) directly over to Lilah. They stood in front of us.

"Lilah," Adrian said. "I don't think I have to introduce you two, do I?"

"No," Lilah said quietly. She offered her hand to McCain.

"Aw, come on, Lilah," he said. "Give me a hug." She looked over to me.

"Well, hug the son-of a bitch," I told her.

"Good to see you, too, Isabel," McCain said. I smiled.

I couldn't say I was glad to see him as well because I wanted to tie him to the back of my Range Rover and drag him down the interstate. He reached for Lilah and she let him take her into his arms. I looked around the room.

"Hi," she said quietly.

"It's been a while," he said when they parted.

"Yeah," she said. "A while."

"Are these all your kids??" he asked.

"No," she told him. "Some of them are Isabel's. Let me introduce everyone." She pointed everyone out. Except Ben. He was missing. Where the hell was he?

"Where is Ben?" I asked Adrian. "Do you know?"

"Yeah," Adrian said. "He'll be here soon. He had a few things to do."

"What things?" I asked.

"Well," Adrian said, ignoring me. "Let's get everyone something to drink."

"Let the martini flights begin," Lilah said as I headed over the makeshift bar we'd made on the buffet.

"Yeah," Adrian said and smiled. "Let's get this party started."

"I've placed everyone's name on their plate," I told everyone.

"What if I don't want to sit by who you put me by?" Michael asked.

"Too bad," I told him.

I always put the adults at one end and gradually moved everyone down the table by age. It works out better that way.

"So, McCain," Adrian said once we'd been seated at the table. "Tell everyone what you've been doing lately."

"Thanks," he said and laughed. "Way to put me on the spot."

"Well, you should be proud of what you do now."

"Yeah," he said. "I guess."

"He's a traitor," Desiree said. "But don't worry, Boo." She bumped her shoulder into his. "I ain't trippin' over it. It your life." She looked over to Lilah. "I need to talk to you, girl."

"Oh?" Lilah said.

"It's the threesome," I leaned over and whispered in Lilah's ear. She pinched my leg under the table.

"Ow."

"Dis man you got," Desiree said as she looked over to Adrian. "It okay with you I give him a cup of sugar?? I don't usually ask but you cool, girl."

"What's a cup of sugar?" Vonnie asked.

Leave it to Vonnie to ask the questions no one else wanted to ask.

"It's what you give him," Desiree said as she pointed to Hunter. "Don't lie, girl. I know you fucking him."

"Desiree!" McCain chastised. "Damn."

Vonnie put her hands over her eyes. I can honestly say I've never seen Vonnie embarrassed over anything but I watched as red crept up her neck to her cheeks.

"Aw, I sorry, girl," Desiree said. "I didn't mean to embarrass you. I sorry."

"It's okay," Vonnie said as she took her hands down.

"If I can butt in here," Isaac said, very calm and collected. Very Isaac.

"Isaac," Tiffany started but he shushed her.

"I think if Adrian doesn't want the sugar," he said. "I'll take it." I burst out laughing. So did Lilah. Adrian tried not to laugh. Tiffany smacked Isaac on his arm.

"You pervert," she said. It was the perfect way to break the ice. Leave it to Isaac to bring everything together when it started to fall apart.

"Me, too," Matt said.

"And me," Michael added.

"Oh my god," Vonnie said as she turned to Hunter. "You better keep your mouth shut."

He held up his hands up in surrender. That was his best option. You can do two things with Vonnie. Surrender and live or maintain your position and suffer the consequences. It was clear to see Hunter had already learned that lesson.

"I give all ya'll a cup a sugar," Desiree said and smiled.

"No, you won't," I said and Adrian laughed. "Nope."

"I just kiddin,' girl," Desiree said to me. "I ain't gone take your boys purrity."

"She means purity," McCain said and laughed.

"They are far from pure," I said as I leaned around the table to look at them.

"That is true," Ben said from the kitchen doorway.

We all turned around to look at him. He was wearing a ragged t-shirt and a pair of baggy sweatpants. It was easy to see he had been at the gym working out. He crossed his arms over his chest.

"Ben," Lilah said. "Didn't I tell you to be here at six-thirty??"

"I'm not having dinner with that motherfucker," he said nodding to McCain.

"Ben!!" Lilah chastised. "That is uncalled for."

Ben walked into the dining room and before anyone could do anything, flipped the table with all the desserts on it upside down.

"Ben!!" Lilah standing up. "Stop it!!"

"Damn it," Michael said. "Grandma's fruit cocktail cake."

"And the éclair pie," Vonnie added. I stood up beside Lilah and Ben pointed to McCain from across the table.

"That asshole shouldn't be in this house," Ben said. "You need to get the hell out of my house."

"Okay, that's it," Adrian said as he stood up. He walked over to Ben and grabbed his arm and not in a friendly way. "Let's go outside."

"Fuck, no," Ben sad as he tried to jerk away from Adrian but Adrian held onto him tightly. "Get the hell off me."

"We're going outside," Adrian said. "Whether you want to or not."

Ben turned and tried to punch Adrian in the face but Adrian grabbed his arm. Terrence pushed his chair back and went over to them.

"Let's all take a breath," Terrence said.

Ben struggled to get away from Adrian but Adrian grabbed both of his arms and pulled them behind his back as he began to drag him to the back door.

"Damn," Desiree said.

"Mom," Ben said. "You gonna let him do this to me??" Lilah didn't answer. "Huh?? Come on, Mom."

"Stay here," I told Lilah. "Let Adrian handle it. Ben will get over it." Terrence opened the back door and they all went outside.

"McCain," Lilah said. "I am so sorry. I don't even know what to say."

"It's okay," he said. "I get it."

He gets it?? How did he get it? Did he know Ben was his? Had Lilah told him and not told me she told him? No, she wouldn't have done that without consulting me first. Did Ben know McCain was his father? And if he did, how the hell did he find out? Because I was certain Lilah hadn't told him. Did Adrian tell him?

"Well," Vonnie said and clapped her hands together. "Shall we continue dinner?"

"Somebody pass the stuffing, would you?" Isaac asked. We all looked to him and he smiled. "What?? I'm hungry." He turned to Vonnie. "Aren't you hungry, Von?"

"Yeah," she said. "I've been looking forward to this food all day long. Why let Ben screw it up?"

Thank you, Isaac and Vonnie.

"It ain't a party 'til there's a fight," Desiree added and laughed. She picked up her fork and began eating again then looked to McCain. "Right, Boo?"

———

I took off and headed for the back porch before Lilah could stop me.

"Isabel!" she said. "What are you doing?"

"I'll be right back," I said as I turned around. "Vonnie, organize the clean-up. You can probably save the éclair thing since the top is still on it." I pointed to the two cakes upside down on the floor but with the plastic wrap still over them. "And the cakes."

I walked through the kitchen and out the back door. Ben was leaning up against the porch railing with Adrian and Terrence standing in front of him. I pushed through them both and grabbed Ben by the neck of his shirt.

"What the hell is wrong with you??" I asked him. "Why would you do that to your mother?" He was silent. "WHY???"

Terrence reached for me and I heard Adrian say, "Not a good idea."

"I don't want that motherfucker in my house," Ben said as he tried to shrug me away. "Get off me." I twisted the neck of his t-shirt tighter in my fist and backhanded him across his cheek with my other hand.

"Ow!" he said. "Isabel! What was that for??"

"Damn, Isabel," Adrian said. "I didn't know you had that in you."

"Don't forget I have this in me," I told him. He chuckled and stuck his hands into his pockets. "You wanna know what it's for?" I asked Ben. "It's because your Mama isn't out here to do it herself because I can guarantee you if she could get her hands on you right now it'd be a lot more than a slap in your face."

"I'm not afraid of her," Ben spat.

"Yes, you are," I said. "I know you are. Because you know what she's capable of. She would have you on your knees right now and you'd be begging her to let you go. Wouldn't you?"

"Probably," he admitted.

"Would she?" I heard Terrence ask Adrian.

"Oh, yeah. No doubt."

"Wow," Terrence said.

"Tell me what your problem is with McCain, Ben," I said to Ben. "Because I'm failing to see how it warranted your bad behavior."

"He's a fucking idiot," Ben said. "I know what he did to Mama when they were in college and I can't believe you guys even let him in this goddamn house."

"That was my idea," Adrian said.

"Why??" Ben asked. "After you told me how he was dangerous and now you bring him into our house with Mama?"

"I don't believe I said dangerous," Adrian said calmly.

"Well, you implied it."

"I did," Adrian admitted. "You are correct. But if you had gotten your act together like I told you and shown up when your mother told you to, you'd know that McCain is trying to get his act together. I like to help people who are trying to help themselves. That is what McCain is doing. If I find out differently things will change but right now, I'm giving him the benefit of the doubt."

"Why…." Ben started.

"Stop talking," I told him.

"He's been helping me with some things here in Woodlawn," Adrian continued. "The case I had here?" Adrian pointed down. "When I was Tristan? The root of that operation was being partially manned by McCain."

"Are you kidding…." Ben started again. I had let go of his shirt but I hadn't backed up.

"Listen to Adrian!" I shouted into his face.

"I originally thought McCain was the pin but he's not," Adrian told him. "There's a chain of command I wasn't even aware of until after McCain started helping me. So, you should probably be thanking him instead of treating him like shit."

"Let me tell you what's going to happen next," I said to Ben. "You are going to go in there and apologize to your mother. Aren't you?" No answer. "Ben," I warned.

"Okay," he said.

"As far as I'm concerned this is not about McCain," I said as I put my hands on his biceps. They were bigger than they used to be. Much bigger. I wanted to shake some sense into him but I didn't. "This is about your mother. It doesn't matter what the reason is that McCain is here, you respect your mother's decisions." He looked down. "Okay??"

"Okay."

"And one more thing while I'm at it," I said. "You're nineteen years old. You need to start acting like you're nineteen years old." I motioned back inside the house. "That little temper tantrum you just pitched?? Not acceptable. You're an adult and you need to exercise some self-control."

"Okay."

"You have the freedom to pursue your life in whatever direction you want to take it," Adrian told him. "But you have to remember that along with that freedom comes responsibilities. You can't expect to be treated like an adult unless you act like one."

"I…"

"Nope," I said still holding onto his arms. "I'm still not done. I can guarantee you your mother is in there right now excusing your bad behavior. She shouldn't be. She should be telling everyone what a jackass you are most of the time."

"He's gotten better," Adrian added.

"Thanks, man," Ben said.

"When Adrian isn't here you agreed to take care of her," I said. "What you just did is not taking care of her."

"I know."

"I just want to make sure we're clear on those two things," I continued. "Respect. Not being a jackass. Can you do that??" Adrian chuckled and unbelievingly so did Ben.

"Yeah."

This is what happens when Adrian is part of a conversation. He turns it around without you even knowing he's turning it around. It's like walking through a damn enchanted forest. By the you get to the other side you're charmed and all is mysteriously well. Except all wasn't mysteriously well but Ben didn't need to know that. Not yet.

Lilah

Me: I'm sorry about what happened last night.

McCain: Don't worry about it.

I wanted to tell him about Ben but I couldn't. Not over text.

Me: Ben has a bad temper.

McCain: Seriously. I understand. I have a bad temper, too. LOL.

Me: You do.

McCain: Did we ever fight?

Me: I don't think so.

McCain: I always loved that about us.

Me: Yeah. You're too complacent.

Had I told Adrian that? Was that why I loved Adrian's cool calmness so much? Because of my relationship with McCain?

McCain: Me??? Are you joking? You've seen me clear a room many times.

Me: Not with me, though.

McCain: True

Me: How come?

McCain: Because I loved you.

Me: Do you still love me???

McCain: Yes.

Amityville

Adrian

"Adrian!!" Serena called as she came through the back door with Renaldo. Estela followed her.

"Hi," I said as she crawled up into my lap. Estela came over and stood beside me. Lorelei smiled.

Serena had never crawled up into my lap. I'm not sure if she knew what role I played in her mother's life or if she'd ever wondered. She turned around to me and I grabbed her around her waist to prevent her from tumbling onto the floor.

"Thank you for my kitten!!" she said excitedly and she kissed my cheek. I looked over to Lorelei and she raised her eyebrows.

"Well, you're welcome," I said. "Do you like him??"

"I love him," she said as she looked back over her shoulder to her mother. "But Mamma won't let him sleep with me yet."

"No?" I asked. I looked to Lorelei and smiled. "Why not, Mamma??"

"Yeah," Serena said. "Why not, Mamma??"

"Why not, Mamma?" Estela asked. I wondered if she knew what it meant or if she was just mimicking Serena.

"You," Lorelei said pointing at me. "Are getting yourself into trouble."

"Me?" I motioned to myself. "I'm getting *myself* into trouble?"

"You are," she said as she stood up.

"They haven't eaten," Renaldo said and he looked to me. "How're you doing, Adrian?"

"Good," I said. "And you?"

"Oh, I think I'm going to make it although these two…" He motioned to Serena and Estela. "…are going to be the death of me, I'm sure."

"I've heard they're quite fond of you," I told him.

"And I of them," he said and laughed. "They're a mess, though. I do not believe the language barrier has made either one of them any less mischievous."

"I'll bet."

"Renaldo and me and Estela had tea at four!!" Serena announced. Lora smiled and walked over to the stove.

"Hot tea?" I asked, surprised.

"Teatime," Renaldo clarified. "We had some petit-fours and I had tea. The girls had cola."

"Ah," I said.

It surprised me Lorelei let the girls drink cola with Renaldo but then she allowed a lot of things when it came to him and the girls. He was like a grandfather to them.

"I just made this chicken," she told Renaldo. "Would you like me to fix you a plate?"

"I'd love one," he replied. "Thank you, Miss." Lorelei made him a plate and wrapped it in foil, handed it to him. "Thank you, Miss," Renaldo said again as he opened the back door.

"You're certainly welcome," Lora said. "I won't need you any more tonight if you want to retire for the evening."

"I appreciate that, Miss, but I'd rather clean the kitchen tonight as opposed to in the morning."

"Oh, don't worry about that," Lorelei said. "Adrian is going to clean the kitchen."

"I am??" I asked and Serena laughed.

"Very well, then," Renaldo said. "Good night."

"I'm going to clean the kitchen?" I asked when Renaldo shut the door.

"You and Serena," Lorelei said looking to her daughter. "Since you guys are partners in crime now."

"Mamma!!" Serena whined. "That's not fair!!"

"Don't worry," I told Serena. "I'll do it. You know what comes on television tonight?" I asked her and Estela. Lorelei glared at me.

"What?!" Serena asked excitedly.

"What??" Estela asked.

"The real Cinderella movie comes on tonight!" I only knew this because Maria had been talking about it for weeks.

"La veritable pel·lícula de Ventafocs arriba aquesta nit," Lorelei told Estela. Estela laughed and jumped up and down excitedly.

"What's the real Cinderella?" Serena asked.

"Yeah," Lora said. "What's the real Cinderella?"

"It's Cinderella with real people instead of cartoon people." Serena's eyes widened.

"Truly??" she asked.

"Truly," I told her. "Go upstairs and get ready for bed while I clean the kitchen then we'll watch it together."

"Pugeu a la planta de dalt i prepareu-vos per dormir mentre netejo la cuina, i després la vigilarem," Lora said to Estela.

"Yay!!" they both said as Serena jumped down out of my lap. They ran up the back stairs.

"Adrian," Lorelei said as she leaned up against the counter. She crossed her arms across her chest. "This is not a war you want to start with me." I laughed.

"There's a war??"

"You know I don't let the girls watch television."

"Oh, good grief, Lora. You act like it's a tool of Satan."

"It can be," she said. "Have you ever watched *The Ring*??"

"Anyone who has ever watched that movie knows it's fictitious."

"Anyone who grows up around magic every day knowing their mother talks to Spirits does not know it's fictitious. Serena does not need to know there truly are Spirits out there like that. I know and you know but she is not old enough to know. Do you understand what I'm saying?"

"Kind of."

"Kind of?" she asked, exasperated. "I'm going to be dealing with this for the rest of my life, aren't I?"

"What? Me?"

"Your loose Spiritual morals," she said.

"Loose morals??" I stood up and walked over to her. "Loose morals??" I started to tickle her waist and she bent over.

"Stop!!" she shouted but I didn't. "Stop!! Oh, my god."

"Say you'll help me clean the kitchen," I said as I continued tickling her.

"No," she managed. I kept tickling her and pulled her into me so she couldn't get away.

"Say it," I demanded.

"Okay, okay!!"

She gave in and I let her go. She took a deep breath and tried to gain her composure. I leaned up against the counter beside her.

"Loose morals, huh?" I said.

"Watching television is one," she told me breathlessly. "And the other day you brought them that huge chocolate bar."

"That they never got," I reminded her.

"They would've been climbing the walls if I'd given it to them," she insisted. She ran her hands through her hair to straighten it. "Look what you did to my hair."

"Let them be kids, Lora."

"See??" she asked me. "This is what I'm talking about." She tucked some of her hair behind her ears. "When we have our own baby, you'll be even worse."

"I didn't have an opportunity to spoil Stef," I explained. "Are you not going to let me spoil our baby?"

"You can spoil it," she said. "Just not to its detriment."

Serena and Estela came flying down the back stairs in their matching Cinderella nightgowns.

"I'm ready!!" Serena said.

"I'm ready!!" Estela repeated. I reached down and picked up Estela.

"Can you translate?" I asked Lora.

"Sure."

"You know," I told her. "Watching Cinderella on television tonight is a treat. You don't get to watch television every night. This isn't the beginning of a new trend."

"Ja ho sabeu" Lorelei said. "Veure la Ventafocs a la televisió aquesta nit és una delícia. No arribareu a veure la televisió totes les nits. Aquest no és el començament d'una nova tendència. Digues a Adrian que ho entenguis." *(Seeing the Cinderella on television tonight is a delight. You will not get to watch television every night. This is not the beginning of a new trend. Tell Adrian you understand.)*

"Yes," Estela said to me.

"Mamma doesn't let us watch television," Serena explained.

"I know," I said. "She just fussed at me." Serena laughed.

"Aren't you and Mamma friends?" she asked.

"Yes," I answered. "We are."

"Did you know I have a big brother?" I looked up to Lora and she smiled.

"Tell me about him," I prompted as I put Estela down.

"I haven't seen him in a while," she admitted. "Have I, Mamma?"

"No, darling."

"Do you know where he is?" I asked Serena.

"No," she said. "But Mamma said he'll be back really soon."

"He will," I assured her.

"Do you know him?"

"No," I said and smiled. "But I'm hoping I can meet him once he comes home."

"I like him," she said. "Even though he's a boy." Lorelei and I both laughed.

"Well, that's good."

"I like you, too, Adrian."

"I like you as well, Serena." I leaned down and picked her up. I kissed her cheek. "If I tell you a secret, will you promise not to tell anyone else??"

"Si us dic un secret, em prometeu que no digueu a ningú més?" Lora said to Estela.

"I love secrets," Serena said excitedly.

"Yes," Estela said. Serena grinned as she looked over to her mother.

"Don't I, Mamma??"

"Oh, yeah," Lora agreed.

"Your Mamma is planning to have a baby," I said.

"Vull tenir un nadó," Lora said to Estela. *(I want to have a baby.)*

Estela's eyes widened and Serena brought her hands to her face and peeked through her fingers at me. She was such a dramatic child. I couldn't imagine who she got it from. Lora and I laughed.

"Truly?" she asked her mother.

"Truly," Lorelei verified. Serena reached for Lora and she took her from me.

"I'm so excited, Mamma!!" She kissed Lorelei's cheek and Lora kissed her in return.

"Me, too!"

"Who's going to be the Patri?" she asked. She looked back and forth between me and her mother and Lora pointed to me.

"You!!" she said almost as if it were an accusation.

"Yep," I said. "Me. Do you still love me?"

"You're going to have sex with Mamma," she said and Lora widened her eyes. "Right, Mamma?"

"Uh…" Lora started. "I…" She looked to me then back to Serena. "Who told you that?"

"What?" Serena asked innocently.

"About sex?"

"Kylie. Her Mamma is going to have a baby and she said it's because her Mamma and Patri had sex."

"Oh, boy," I said and laughed.

"Holy Jesus," Lora said. "How does Kylie know this?"

"That her Mamma and Patri had sex?" Serena inquired.

"Yes."

"She saw it on the television." I laughed. I probably shouldn't have but I couldn't help myself.

"A tool of Satan," I managed. Lora narrowed her eyes at me.

"Well, don't listen to Kylie," Lora said as she sat Serena down. "She doesn't know what she's talking about. You and Estela go with Adrian. He's going to let you guys watch Cinderella."

"Què dius tots?" Estela asked Lorelei. *(What are all of you saying?)*

"El bebè serà meu i el nadó d'Adrian," she told Estela. *(The baby will be mine and Adrian's baby.)*

"Estàs casant?" Estela asked. *(Are you getting married?)* Lora looked over to me.

"She just asked me if we were getting married," she said. I didn't know what to say so I didn't say anything.

"No carinyo. Però esperem que algun dia." *(No, honey. But hopefully one day.)* Estela smiled.

I had no idea what Lora told her. Serena came over to me and I took her hand.

"Come on," I said as I reached for Estela's hand. "Let's go turn on the devil's box."

"I swear to you, Adrian," Lorelei called as I walked out of the kitchen. "We're going to rumble after this." I poked my head back around the kitchen doorway.

"Rumble?" I asked and grinned.

"Yes!!" she insisted as she motioned back and forth between us. "You and me, after the girls go to bed."

"…can have sex," Serena finished.

When Ari opened her front door, she was holding Roger in her arms.

"I'm afraid Rajah will kill him," she explained and I laughed.

"It's not funny, Adrian," she said.

"He's a kitten," I told her. "What could he possibly do?" She looked over to Rajah as Lorelei sat him down on the carpet.

"He's a huge kitten," Ari pointed out. I shrugged. He was. "He's bigger than Roger."

"Thank you for doing this, Ari," Lorelei said.

Ari ushered me and Lora, Serena, Estela and Rajah into the living room. Rajah walked around and smelled everything while I sat all the girl's belongings at the bottom of the stairs. He was still technically a kitten but he looked like a full-grown housecat.

"How long are you guys staying?" Ari asked the girls as she looked over all their things. "Three weeks??" Lora told Estela what Ari had said and she and Serena laughed. "You do realize I do not know this strange language."

"It will be fine," Lorelei told her. "Serena can translate."

"Since when did Serena learn Catalan??" Ari asked, surprised.

"Oh, she doesn't know Catalan," Lorelei said. "But her and Serena have developed a sort of sign language so Serena can tell you what she's saying for the most part or if she needs anything."

"The most part," Ari repeated then she punched me in the arm.

"What?" I asked as I rubbed my hand over my arm.

"This is all your fault," she said.

"Noies,"(*Girls)* Lorelei said. "Puja al pis i porta les maletes a la teva habitació.(*Go upstairs and take your suitcases to your room.)* Go upstairs, Serena. Take your things. Okay?"

"Okay," Serena said.

"Okay," Estela repeated and they headed for the stairs.

"Take the pink room," Ari called after them. She looked back to us. "I am seriously telling you guys. Don't leave me with these girls for a long time while you go off and party."

"It's a birthday dinner," Lora said. "Jeez, Ari."

"Uh-huh. You forget I know both of you." She turned around to see Rajah sitting on the back of her sofa. "And that thing looks like he'll take my head off if I move the wrong way."

"He's watching you," I told Ari. "He sees everything you do."

"Shut up, Adrian!!" she said and I laughed. She pointed at me then turned around again to look at Rajah who was still sitting in the same place, in the exact same position, watching her.

"See?" I said. "I told you. He's just waiting to get you alone."

"*Shut...up,*" Ari said and she tried to hit me again but I backed away.

"He's sweet," Lorelei told her. "He won't bother you but he likes to sleep in the bed."

"He does?" I asked. "Is this why he can't sleep with Serena? Because he sleeps with you?"

"Guilty," Lora admitted.

"He's not sleeping with *me*," Ari said.

"He'll find you in the middle of the night," I teased Ari. "Don't worry."

"I am going to kill you!!" she told me. "Shut the hell up!"

"Give me Roger," I instructed. "Go over and see Rajah."

"I'm afraid," she said as she handed Roger to me.

"Just say 'here kitty kitty,'" I offered and Lorelei slapped my arm. Ari ignored me.

"Hi, pretty boy," she said as she sat down on the sofa in front of him. He hissed.

"Don't move," Lora coached. "Let him know you're serious."

"About what?" Ari asked

"Just let him know you want to be friends," Lora said. "Reach out to him."

"I swear to you," Ari said. "If he takes my hand off..."

Roger looked up to me.

"Your mother is getting ready to die," I whispered to him.

"Why is he like this?" Ari asked. "I thought you told me he was nice."

"He is nice," Lorelei said. "He's a domesticated wildcat."

"I am the one who told you that!!" Ari reminded Lora.

"He's just really protective over me and the girls."

"Yet you're going to leave him alone with me."

"Once he sees how sweet you are to the girls everything will be fine."

"Until then, watch your back," I said and chuckled.

"Fuck you, Adrian."

"Language!"I chastised.

"Don't say that word in front of the girls," Lora told Ari.

"Well, duh," Ari said. "Come on, Rajah, let me pet you. Can I pet you? I bought a treat for you."

"I hope it's a small animal," I told her. "That's what he eats for snacks." She ignored me but Lora looked over to me and mouthed, 'Stop it.'

"He's looking at me weird," Ari said. Lorelei walked over and sat down on the sofa beside Ari. Rajah looked to her and swished his tail back and forth.

"Be friends with Ari," she pleaded with Rajah. "She's my best friend. See?" She leaned over and gave Ari a hug. As soon as she did Rajah jumped down off the back of the sofa between them.

"He's smart," Ari said.

"He also has x-ray vision at night," I whispered to Roger but loud enough for Ari to hear. "So, when it's dark he can see you. You just can't see him."

"Shut up, Adrian," Ari and Lorelei said at the same time.

"I'm talking to Roger," I said defending myself. "Stay out of our personal conversation."

I watched then as Rajah rubbed his body up against Ari. He sat down beside her and began to purr. He purred louder than any cat I have ever known. Like a lion. Now it made complete sense to me why those cats were in the basement of that drug house. As if the rottweilers weren't enough.

"Okay," Lora said as she stood up. "We're good to go." She walked over to the foot of the stairs and left Ari and I in the livingroom. "Girls! Come tell Mamma good bye."

"Is Estela calling her Mamma?" Ari leaned over and asked me.

"Yes."

"That's not good."

"Why not?" I asked as Serena and Estela came bounding down the stairs. "She loves Lorelei."

"Well, yeah. But Lorelei is not her Mamma and soon she's going to be taken away from her."

"Lora told me she was thinking of adopting her," I confided.

"I give up," Ari said. "She's lost her goddamn mind." I handed Roger back to her.

"Ari," I said. "Lorelei is lonely."

"I hardly think another child is going to fill that void."

"She's happy. Let her be happy."

"Is big daddy, Tony, gonna pay for this child, too?"

"Big daddy, Tony, gives his Angel anything she wants," I reminded her.

"Except her son," Ari whispered.

There was a good reason Lorelei didn't have her son right now but I couldn't tell that to Ari. She wouldn't have understood it anyway. Rarely did *The Empire* do anything that made sense to anyone except themselves. We walked over to Lorelei and the girls in the foyer.

"They want to give you a hug before we leave," Lorelei explained to me. I squatted down and opened my arms.

"Well, come on," I said. "Give me a hug." They both giggled and wrapped their arms around my neck.

"Go show him to Rajah," Ari said as she handed Roger to Serena. "Tell Rajah to be nice."

"Okay," Serena said happily as she skipped off with Estela.

"Thanks, Ari," Lora said. "I owe you one."

"You owe me more than one," Ari told her. I walked toward the front door and ushered Lorelei outside.

"Bye, Ari," I said as I leaned over and kissed her cheek. She pulled on my arm. "Thanks for doing this."

"You know why she's so happy?" she asked quietly as she held open the screen door. Lorelei walked toward the car.

"Tell me. I can hardly wait." I looked back over my shoulder to Lorelei. "You're driving."

"No, I'm not," she shouted.

"Tell me," I said to Ari.

"Because this whole thing you've got going on..." She waved her hand around in front of me.

"What whole thing?"

"You and her, and Serena and Estela, and that damn furball in there. It's a family. It's what she's always wanted with you."

"It's not a family," I said.

"In her mind it is."

"Okay."

"Don't go to the Hamptons and ressurect your old love life," she told me.

"That will never happen," I assured her. "It's a birthday dinner."

"Famous last words," she said as I walked toward the car.

The Hamptons

Adrian

"You're driving," I said again when I got to the car.

"No, I'm not," Lorelei said.

"Yes, you are," I told her as I opened the driver's side door. "Get in."

"Adrian."

"What?" I asked. "You were dying to drive it before and now, no?"

"That was three blocks!" she said. I shrugged.

She shook her head, smiled and threw her bag on the front seat. Unlike Lilah, Lorelei loved to drive. She loved to drive fast. Four tickets in one summer fast. We got in and put on our seatbelts. She put the keys in the ignition and started it. The dashboard came to life.

"What if I wreck it?" she asked. I looked at her sideways as she put on her sunglasses.

"What if I say you got kidnapped in the Hamptons?"

"Oh ha, ha." She shifted into reverse. "I don't think I would've gotten this dark red. I would've gotten that forest green color."

"Let me guess," I said as I looked behind us. You could never be too careful with Lorelei. "It goes better with your hair."

"Exactly."

She stopped in the street and looked over to the dashboard again. Fortunately, there wasn't a lot of traffic and even though everyone in the village knew my car I doubted whoever saw us would be surprised to see Lorelei driving it or that she had stopped in the middle of the street. I had pretty much given up on the rumors circling Amityville about us. I'd rather people talk about what they saw as opposed to what they imagined. I've learned the general population thrives on secrets as a form of entertainment. I refuse to be entertainment. That's what HBO is for.

"Can I put the top down?" Lorelei asked. I couldn't resist the temptation.

"I don't know?" I asked. "Can you?" She stuck out her tongue at me and pressed the button.

"May I remind you of the temperature outside?" I asked. She reached over to the temperature dials and turned them up as high as they would go.

"That's what the heat is for," she informed me. "Woo...you have seater heaters." She pressed the buttons to turn them on.

"Seater heaters??" I asked and laughed.

"That's what Serena calls them in my car," she said. "We need music." I punched the password into the touchscreen.

"You have a password?" she asked as she looked down.

"Nope. Keep your eyes on the road."

"We're not moving," she said.

"Then go." She shifted into first.

"You have a playlist for me, don't you?" She knew me so well.

"I do. Put your turn signal on," I said as she pulled up to the stop sign.

"Adrian, I know how to drive. If you're going to be a backseat driver then let's trade seats now." I raised my eyebrows. "I'm serious." I mimicked zipping my lips.

She was right. She did know how to drive. She knew how to drive too well. All my fault, I thought. All my fault. The surround sound system took over and Ed Sheeran's *Beautiful People* filled the interior of the car.

"I love this song!" Lorelei declared.

"I thought you might."

"Doesn't Khalid sing this with him?"

"Wow," I said. "And I thought I was the music guru."

She smiled as she took the exit onto the highway. We hit the interstate and she flew into the fast lane as she shifted into fifth, sixth, seventh, weaving in and out of traffic. She glanced over to me to see my reaction. I mimicked zipping my lips again. I leaned over closer to her.

"Can I just say one thing?" I shouted over the music. She smiled. "If you get a ticket, I'm not getting you out of it."

"You will."

"No, I won't."

"Yes, you will," she assured me. "Are we going straight to Angelic Manor?" I turned the radio down.

"Did you have something else in mind?"

"Not really."

"It's *your* birthday," I said. "Oh, wait. I have an idea."

"What?"

"Let's go to that French restaurant you told me about." She looked over to me briefly.

"Adrian, we could never get in there. You have to make reservations weeks ahead of time to get a table there. Plus…" she motioned down to her clothes and then mine. "We're not dressed for dinner there."

"Hmm…" I raised my eyebrows.

"Adrian…what did you do?" she asked.

"I might as well tell you."

"You might as well."

"We have a table at nine." She looked over to me. "Keep your eyes on the road."

"Are you kidding me?" I shook my head. "Oh my god, Adrian. What the hell am I going to wear??" I laughed.

"You're welcome."

"No, seriously. What am I going to wear?"

"I bought you a dress." She looked over to me again and I grabbed the steering wheel. "Drive. I'll talk. You listen, but drive." She nodded. "We have to go pick up your dress – and you should probably try it on, but we have plenty of time. It's only one-thirty. We'll go to Angelic Manor and drop off our things…"

"Oh…my…god…please tell me you're kidding."

"Do you want me to be kidding? Because if you do, I'm about to lose a lot of money."

"I know but I'm thinking about where we'll go and what I'll wear. I packed for a cold walk on the beach and pizza."

"You thought your birthday dinner would be pizza??" I asked, astonished. She shrugged.

"It's just me and you," she said. "I wasn't thinking we'd have a formal dinner."

"You told me there were really nice restaurants," I reminded her. "Did you not think I might take you to one?"

"I never know with you," she said as she glanced over to me.

"Look at the road!"

"I am!!" she told me. "But what am I going to wear?"

"Well, you already have a dress for tonight."

"But I need shoes."

"Shoes," I said. "It's all about the shoes."

"It is."

"You know that little boutique on the corner, the one with the blue and lavender awning?" I asked.

"Yeah."

"That's where your dress is," I informed her.

"Adrian," she said. "Everything inside that boutique is outrageous."

"Coming from you?? The girl who has about forty pairs of Christian Louboutin shoes?"

"The one who can't pay her electric bill," she said and smiled.

"Yeah. Her." She looked over to me briefly.

"We'll have to turn on the heat at Angelic. It's probably freezing in there."

"Then we can go pick up your dress," I said. "Find a good place for happy hour then go back to the house and change for dinner."

"Okay," she said.

She smiled and I could tell I'd already made one birthday wish come true. When we pulled up to the ornate black iron gates in front of Angelic Manor I was in awe. You couldn't see the house from the gate but you could see the manicured lawn and tall sycamore trees. You could see the angel statues that populated the extensive gardens and meandering through it all a pale-yellow path of pea gravel.

I'd only been to Angelic Manor once. Lorelei and I were in high school and we'd snuck off on a Sunday morning. We spent the entire day there in the big oak canopy bed of the master bedroom. It may have been the only room I remembered if we hadn't used the blue and white marble countertop in the kitchen for a brief mid-afternoon interlude. I had taken pictures of Lora that day laying on the counter laughing. Completely naked. I took a deep breath.

"Damn," I said as she dug through her bag for the gate key.

"What?" she asked as she found the key.

"I just had a flashback of you naked on the kitchen countertop."

"Oh, my god…what happened to those pictures??" she asked.

"I don't know," I said. "Nana probably confiscated them." Lorelei brought her hand to her heart.

"You think Nana saw those pictures??" she asked. I shrugged.

"Maybe. Probably."

"Holy shit, Adrian," she said. She looked down to her lap. "Oh, wow."

"What?" I asked. She looked up to me and laid her hand on my arm.

"I just thought, well…I was thinking about how I'd never be able to look Nana in the eyes again…" I bowed my head. "…and then I remembered she's not here." I ran my hand over my mouth, shook my head slightly.

"I do that all the time," I admitted. "I think about how I want to tell her something. I even picked up my phone the other day before I realized I couldn't call her." Lorelei rubbed my arm.

"I'm so sorry, Adrian." I took a deep breath.

"You know what she would've said?" I asked Lora.

"What's that?"

"About the pictures, I mean." Lorelei smiled. "Not then. Like if she saw you now and remembered it."

"Well, she had a mind like a steel trap so I'm sure she would have remembered it." I chuckled.

"Oh, yeah. Definitely."

"What would she have said?" she asked.

"She would have told you that you should've had a better photographer." We laughed together. "And then she would have given you a speech about how you are a beautiful and intelligent woman and how you should be careful because not all guys are sweet like me."

"And a Bible verse," Lora added. I laughed.

"Yep."

"She was such an amazing woman, Adrian. I'm so sorry you lost her."

"Yeah."

"I love you," Lora said and she leaned over and kissed my cheek. She ran her hand over my hair. "Nana was so proud of you. You've done everything you told her you were going to do."

"Yeah." She rubbed my arm again then opened the car door, hopped out. She couldn't get the gate open so I got out and walked in front of the car.

"Here," I said. "Let me try." She gave me the key and I jiggled it in the lock, turned it.

"How did you do that?" she asked. I shrugged.

She grabbed ahold of one side of the gate and I took the other and we rolled them open. I hopped back in the car and drove through then got out to help her shut them again.

"They insist the gate always be locked," Lorelei told me as we got back into the car.

"All I want to know is when they're going to make it into the next century."

"Oh," she said as I drove down the driveway. "You mean the rollers on the gates?"

"Nonna Elene insisted they stay that way and I think it's sentimentality."

That made perfect sense to me. I knew there were a lot of things at Fairy Tale that could be modernized but neither Tiffany nor I wanted to change any of it.

"Wasn't Angelic called something else at one point? Nana used to call it something different but I can't remember what it was."

"Yeah," Lorelei acknowledged. "Before I was born it was called Summerview but Nonna Elene changed it afterward because I was the first grandchild."

"Angel – Angelic."

"Yeah," she said. "It's kind of embarrassing."

"I think it's cool," I told her. "I'd love to have a mansion named after me."

"Yeah, well, my cousins don't like it very much."

"Understandable."

The driveway of Angelic Manor wove around through trees and gardens toward the house. A straight driveway would have taken a few minutes. The maze we drove through now took fifteen.

"Was this curving pea gravel driveway Nonna Elene's idea, too?" I asked.

"Of course," Lorelei said. "She said it was so people couldn't speed."

"Funny," I said as I held up my pointer finger. "But effective."

"I know, right?"

I pulled up to the house underneath the white stone portico. She dug through her bag to find the house keys. I got out and retrieved our bags from the car as she walked up the steps to the front door. The fountain on the other side of the driveway spewed high into the air and fell elegantly back into the crystal-clear water beneath it. The smell of evergreen and seasoned firewood lingered in the air. She unlocked the door and entered the code into the alarm system on the wall as I shut it behind us.

"Jeez, it feels like it's forty degrees in here."

"See?" she said as she stood in front of me. "I told you." I reached over and rubbed my hands up and down her upper arms.

"Are you trying to warm up me or yourself?" she asked and laughed.

"Both," I answered. "It gets like this at Fairy Tale, too, if you don't keep fires burning in all the rooms downstairs." She reached for me then and wrapped her arms around my neck. She laid her head up against my chest.

"Thank you," she said quietly. She looked up to me and I kissed her forehead.

"Happy Birthday, Lora."

"Why are you so sweet to me?" she asked.

"Because I'm afraid," I teased.

"Would you stop saying that!?!"

She grabbed my hand and I followed her into the living room. It was the whitest room I've ever seen in my life with gray tufted sofas and chairs and turquoise and pale-yellow velvet pillows. A crystal chandelier that could have easily killed ten people if it fell hung over us. Across the room a gigantic stone fireplace towered from floor to ceiling. No hearth. You could literally walk through this fireplace into the dining room on the other side if there was no fire. And in the far corner, a grand piano. I walked over to it. This wasn't just any grand piano.

This was a digital grand piano. This was my dream piano. I pushed the bench back and turned it on. Lorelei pulled open the gray and yellow brocade curtains on the French doors across the back of the room.

"No!" she said when she looked over to me. "We don't have time for that!"

"What?" I asked as I turned it on.

"I know you can't help yourself when you're near a piano."

"I can't," I said as I began to play.

"Adrian!" Lora chastised, then she realized what I was playing.

"What?" I asked and smiled. "You don't like this song?"

"Adrian," she said again, but this time in reverence and awe. Not chastisement.

"You know, Nana always told me I had to sit down to correctly play the piano. Think I should sit down?"

Lorelei bowed her head. I continued playing and she listened. My composition of Journey's *Open Arms*. I'd written it, recorded it, and mailed it to her along with my letter when she was in Sicily.

"I was in Sicily," she said.

"Yeah."

"You memorized it," she said thoughtfully.

"I wrote it," I said. "It's hard to not remember one of your own compositions."

"*Open Arms*," she said.

"Yes."

And before I knew it, she had brought her hands to her face. She cried. Not a whimper or a few simple tears. Full-fledged crying. Her shoulders shook. I stopped playing and walked over to her.

"Oh, Lora," I said as I wrapped my arms around her. "I didn't mean to make you cry. I'm sorry." I rubbed my hand over her hair then pulled away. I took her upper arms in my hands. She hung her head and continued crying. "Hey, look at me."

She looked up as tears ran down her cheeks. I wiped them away and grabbed her hand. I led her over to the French doors and stood behind her, rubbed my hands up and down her arms again. The Ocean. Dark blue water topped with white rolls of cascading waves. Solace for the most troubled of hearts.

"It's beautiful."

"I know," she said. "Every time I come up here and stand at these doors it takes my breath away." I wrapped my arms around her again.

"Let's have some champagne," I said and kissed her cheek. "I know there is champagne here. Whoever heard of an Empire compound without champagne??" She laughed, sort of. "Then we have to go get your dress."

"Okay."

"You go get the champagne and I'll turn on the heat."

Angelic Manor was heated by water filled radiators. Probably another thing Nonna Elene had insisted stay in place. I wasn't complaining. The heat that came through those kinds of radiators could inundate a room in minutes.

"Which ones do you want me to turn on?" I asked.

"Uh…" she turned around to face me. "The main rooms down here. I'll do the kitchen. And my bedroom upstairs, whatever room you want to sleep in."

"What room do you want me to sleep in?" I asked.

"You choose," she said and smiled.

I turned on the radiators downstairs and heard the hissing of the water filling them. The downstairs rooms would be toasty in no time. I climbed the grand staircase. It wasn't as grand as Fairy Tale's staircase but then I didn't know of many staircases that were. When I came back down Lorelei had the champagne, two glasses and a towel. She held onto the glasses and handed the bottle and towel to me. I unscrewed the wire and wrapped the towel around it, popped it open. Champagne went everywhere.

"Holy shit," I said as I held it away from me and Lorelei laughed. "Did you shake it up?" She nodded and laughed. "What is wrong with you?"

"Pour us some," she said as she held out the glasses.

"If there's any left," I joked and filled them both with champagne. I held up my glass. "To us."

"And our night together," she said as she tinged her glass against it. "Because it's going to be unforgettable."

"Is that a cautionary statement or your accomplished intuition?" I asked. She laughed and winked at me.

"You tell me," she answered and smiled.

There was no parking lot for the boutique so when we drove past it, I pointed to a space on the other side of the street.

"Make a U-turn at the light," I told her.

"How much you wanna bet I can park this car in one move?"

"Fifty dollars," I said. She laughed.

"Oh, ye of little faith."

She pulled past the spot, put one hand on the back of my seat and turned the steering wheel with the other. Perfect parallel parking in one smooth move. She turned off the ignition and looked over to me, held out her hand.

"You owe me fifty bucks," she said. I pointed to the boutique up the street.

"There is a dress in there for you and it was a hell of lot more than fifty bucks." She laughed and opened her car door, walked around to the sidewalk and handed me the keys.

"Look at me," she said as she looked down to her clothes. "I'm not sure I'm dressed appropriately."

She had on a pair of ragged jeans rolled at the ankles, a silk jade blouse with a cream fur vest and a pair of five-inch cream-colored sandals adorned with jade rhinestones across her toes. Bright pink polish on her toes and nails. Oh, and Ari's white fur coat. But she didn't know that yet.

"You're dressed fine," I said. She put her hand on her hip disgustedly.

"Coming from the man wearing dress pants and a jacket."

"Nana," I said and laughed. "She once told me never to come to The Hamptons without a jacket."

"Smart woman," Lorelei commented. I nodded.

Nana always said the well-dressed men got all the beautiful women. She was right. As usual. But then I don't think I ever saw Dada in anything other than a dress shirt and pants. He was kind of like Lilah's mom. Always ready in case there was company to entertain and, at Fairy Tale, there was always company to entertain.

"Was Ari in on this whole trip, dress, dinner thing?"

"Of course," I said. "You don't think I could've accomplished all of this by myself, do you?"

"I'm going to kiss her when we get back home."

"Can I watch?" I joked. She smacked at me and we walked toward the boutique. One of the clerks greeted her as soon as we walked inside.

"Miss. Vallario."

Not Anastasio. Vallario. Everyone on Long Island knew Lorelei belonged to Gianni Vallario. If Charles knew Gianni and Lorelei were no longer married, he didn't indicate it in any way. The Empire allowed divorces but they did not recognize them. Lorelei would always be Gianni Vallario's 'wife.'

"Charles," Lorelei said.

"I haven't seen you for a while, Ma'am," he said.

"I haven't been up here in ages," Lora told him. She turned to me. "Do you know Adrian?"

"I don't think so, Ma'am."

"This is Adrian Bennett," Lorelei introduced us. "Adrian, Charles Meadow."

"Forgive me, Sir, but did your mother own Fairy Tale?"

"My grandmother. Yes."

"I'm so sorry to hear of her passing, Sir. She was a remarkable woman. My condolences."

"She was," I said. "Thank you." I put my hand on Lorelei's back. "Do you have a dress for Miss. Anastasio?"

Charles smiled and turned knowing exactly what the change of name I gave implied.

"I do." Lorelei punched me when he walked away.

"Stop it," she warned but she was smiling.

"I don't like it," I said when she came out of the dressing room a little while later.

"You picked it!" she exclaimed.

"Well, I know but it looked better on the model." She held up her middle finger and Charles snickered. "No, just the color." I looked over to him. "Does it come in another color?"

"No, Sir." Lorelei rolled her eyes. "If you don't mind, Sir, I can pick a few dresses for Miss. Anastasio?" Lora pointed at him.

"Yes!" He smiled.

"I shall return," he said as he walked away.

"What's wrong with this color?" Lorelei asked me.

"It's just blah."

"Tan is usually blah."

"I know. I thought it would look good with your skin tone but it really doesn't."

"I'm going to take that as compliment, regardless."

"You should."

Charles returned with three dresses. Hot pink. Violet. Strawberry red. He held them on his finger and turned to me.

"If you don't mind, Sir, I can help her with accessories and shoes." Lorelei smiled and I held up my hands.

"Of course."

He handed the dresses to Lorelei and she turned to go back into the dressing room.

"May I offer you something to drink, Sir?" Charles asked me.

"You're good at this," I said and he smiled. "What are my choices?" He put his hands behind his back.

"Champagne, bourbon and, I believe today we have scotch as well."

"Bourbon."

"On the rocks, Sir?"

"Thank you."

"Shall I retrieve something for Miss. Anastasio as well?" We might not need a happy hour after all.

"Champagne," I requested.

Lorelei came out in the hot pink dress. She was stunning. She held up her hair with her hands on top of her head and twirled around. I shook my head and smiled.

"Up to you," I said when she faced me.

"That's all I get?" I took a deep breath and smiled.

"You look beautiful. Try the others."

Charles came back with our drinks and another clerk who held several boxes of shoes and a tray of jewelry. Lorelei took the champagne and winked at Charles. He blushed.

"Stunning," he said to me. I nodded.

A few moments later, strawberry red.

"No," I said as soon as I saw her. She put her hands on her hips.

"I thought you said it was up to me."

"Well, it is, but I'm just telling you I don't like that one."

"What's wrong with it?"

"I don't know," I said. I gestured toward her. "It just has that poochy thing in the front."

"What poochy thing?" she asked looking down. "My stomach??"

Women.

"No, not at all. It just doesn't fit you well. You have a beautiful body. You should show it off." She smiled. "Try the next one."

"Okay," she said and turned back into the dressing rooms.

"That was a marvelous recoup, Sir," Charles told me.

"I had to say something," I said and shrugged. "She looked like I'd just told her Saks Fifth Avenue burned down."

Charles chuckled and Lorelei came out in the violet dress. There should have been a moment of silence. It fit her perfectly, tightly across her hips then flouncing out at the bottom to the floor. The sheer layers of fabric sparkled with violet sequins. She turned around. Spaghetti straps that crisscrossed her back. It was cut so low in the back I could see the bottom of her backbone between her hips. Her olive skin made the color pop even more. She turned back around. Her eyes sparkled.

"Do you like it?" she asked as she held out her hands to the side. She turned around again and the bottom of the dress swirled around her.

"It's gorgeous," I said. I took a sip of my bourbon.

Not harsh. Perfectly aged bourbon. Perfectly balanced.

"Shoes?" she inquired and the clerk handed her a perfectly matched pair of violet sandals. With feathers.

What kind of bird has violet feathers??? I had never seen shoes with violet feathers but I had a feeling it wasn't fake feathers and that I was about to spend hundreds of dollars on a pair of what was probably dyed bird shoes. She slipped one over her foot and adjusted the strap at her heel. She stood, perfectly balanced, as she placed the matching shoe on her other foot. Another woman walked up to the clerk's desk.

"That is a beautiful dress," she said to Lorelei.

"Thank you," Lora said but the happy go lucky look on her face changed slightly. The woman looked over to me.

"I hope you're going somewhere special if she's wearing that." I looked back to Lorelei and smiled.

"Oh, we are."

Another clerk appeared with a cupcake adorned with a lit candle.

"Happy Birthday, Miss. Anastasio." Lora looked at me and smiled. I shook my head.

"Give it to Mr. Bennett," she said.

"Oh Ma'am, you must first make a wish and blow out your candle."

"You should," I agreed and the clerk walked over to her.

She looked upward then closed her eyes, blew out the candle. Somehow, we had attracted several other clients who stood watching her. They all clapped when she opened her eyes. It felt like a dream but it wasn't. The woman who had complimented her walked over to me.

"I assume you know what you're getting yourself into?"

"I know," I said and smiled. She sat down in the chair next to mine. "She's very beautiful. I should be careful, right?" I wasn't about to admit anything else. No one else would understand anyhow and my response was the only expected response.

"So, she's yours?"

A pointed question I couldn't avoid.

"Yes."

"Does she know that?" I nodded.

"She does."

"Does Gianni?"

Lorelei

As we left the boutique together that afternoon I grabbed ahold of Adrian's hand. He let me take it which surprised me a little. I swung our arms back and forth between us.

"What's wrong?" I asked him. "You look like you're in another world." He looked off into the distance but he didn't answer me for a minute.

"What?" he finally said as he looked over to me.

"What's wrong?" I asked again.

"Oh, nothing. I'm fine." He didn't seem fine.

"Are you sure?" I asked. He let go of my hand and wrapped his arm around my shoulder, pulled me into him.

"Yes, absolutely. Where do you want to go for drinks?"

"How about The Lavender Room?" I suggested.

"Isn't that a martini bar?"

"Yeah," I said. "Don't you think it would be fun?"

"Well, let's do it!" he said as put the packages in the car.

He escorted me around to the passenger side and opened my door. When we got closer to the bar, we realized there was very long line. People were scattered everywhere.

"Wow," he said. "Popular destination."

"There's a parking lot right over there," I said as I pointed down the street. He put his four-way flashers on.

"Hop out and get in line," he said.

"Great idea," I told him.

Ten minutes later he walked up to me as I stood in line. It had barely moved.

"I'll be right back," he said and kissed my cheek quickly.

"You're leaving me?!" I exclaimed. He smiled as he backed away, held out his hands like he had no choice.

"Give me a minute," he called. The guy in front of me turned around to me.

"Is he leaving you?"

"Doubtful," I said.

"Well, let me know if he does, okay? I know the bartender. I can get us some free drinks." I nodded.

"Okay. Thanks."

"Lora!" Adrian called from the front of line as the doorman unlocked the velvet rope and beckoned me. I winked at the guy in front of me.

"Apparently my connections are better than yours."

"Aw, come on, dude," another guy called.

"Have a good evening, Ma'am," the doorman said to me as he ushered me through the ropes.

"What did you do?" I asked, narrowing my eyes at Adrian. We walked down the brick steps together. He smiled and squeezed my hand.

"I can't give away my secrets."

I knew his secret. It was called DEA credentials. He'd probably told them this was an undercover operation. We were stopped at the landing by another doorman.

"One moment, please," he said. I looked over to Adrian and he shrugged. For no apparent reason we were then escorted further down the steps.

"Have a wonderful evening, Ma'am, Sir."

We rounded the corner at the bottom of the staircase where there was a closed door with a brass placard on the front.

The Lavender Room Rules

You must silence your cell phone. A jacket does not 'dress up' a t-shirt. No t-shirts. No baseball caps. No reservations. No special bar requests. Your server will bring your drinks to you. No 'O' bombs or Jager-bombs. No bombs of any kind. No Jell-O shooters. No Budweiser. No light beer. No cosmopolitans. No daiquiris. No frozen drinks of any kind. Please treat all women like you would want another man to treat your sister. Please do not bring anyone into The Lavender Room you would not take to mother's house for Sunday dinner. Welcome!

"Holey jeans," I said to Adrian as I looked down.

"You're a beautiful woman," he said as he touched the collar of my shirt. "And you're wearing a jade, silk blouse, a cream fur vest and five-inch heels. I think you're good."

"I'm impressed," I said. "That notice was very tasteful."

"I'm almost afraid to go inside," he told me and I laughed.

"I'm sure you're one of the best dressed men in there," I told him and he looked over to me.

"Sure I am."

Adrian has exquisite taste in clothes. Actually, Nana had exquisite taste in clothes because I knew she bought most of his. Undoubtedly along the way she had somehow passed her exquisite taste down to him. Tonight, he wore slim-fit black pants and a cream dress shirt with a black jacket. It sounds so simple but didn't look simple at all. His hair was a lot thicker than I remembered and tonight he'd pulled the front back behind his head with a thin black hair band. Unless you were close to him, you'd never know it was there. He'd cut the underside over his ears, which made it much more sophisticated. It reminded me he wasn't a kid anymore. Neither was I.

The door opened in front of us and a girl in a purple velvet jacket ushered us inside. The room was bathed in violet light with deep purple carpet and zebra print chairs.

"This way," she said as she led us to a table in the far-left corner. She pulled out my chair as Adrian sat down in his. She handed both of us cream colored cards with a list of cocktails on them.

"I highly recommend our Lavender Martini," she said. Adrian took my card and handed them back to her.

"Sounds good. We'll take two."

"Excellent."

"Did you read what was in them?" I asked Adrian as the waitress walked away. He shook his head.

"I don't think it said and I'm afraid to ask."

When our server returned with our drinks a little later, she asked if we had dinner reservations anywhere. Adrian told her of our plans.

"Fine," she said. "I will confirm them and arrange a car for you."

"Oh, we drove," he said. "We don't need a car."

"And we need to change as well," I said as I gestured to my jeans.

"This is only my suggestion," she said. "If you don't mind?"

"No," Adrian said. "Of course not."

"It will be very difficult to find a parking space anywhere near the Bistro this evening and…" She gestured to both of us. "I think you both look stunning." Adrian and I exchanged glances.

"Totally up to you," he said to me.

"I actually have my dress in the car," I told him and he smiled.

"I remember," he said. "That was…" He looked upward. "Eight hundred and thirty-seven dollars ago." Our server laughed softly.

"We were at Alannah's Boutique before we came over here." I explained, embarrassed.

"As I stated," the server said. "You look stunning but if you'd like to change you are more than welcome to use our private glamour room."

"I might do that," I said. "Thank you very much."

"Of course," she said. "Just let me know."

"What is a glamour room?" Adrian asked when she walked away.

"A magical room that makes you glamourous." He raised his eyebrows and I laughed. "I'm just kidding. I don't know."

"Is this really happening?" he asked.

"I think so," I said and smiled. "It's probably so you won't get trashed and miss dinner."

"Why do they care?"

"It's the Hamptons," I said. "Why do they do anything they do?"

"Remember that bar in the City that had the hot tubs in them?" he asked. I laughed.

"Yeah. That didn't last very long."

"This is classy, though," he said. "It's a very well thought out plan."

"Until someone disagrees," I pointed out.

"I have a feeling the people here don't care whether you disagree," he commented.

"Very true."

The server returned with our drinks. Of course, they were lavender. Perfectly clear lavender. No garnishments. They looked soothing, but dangerous.

"May I get you two anything else?"

"No," Adrian said. "I think we're good for now."

"If you aren't opposed, I will bring you another drink in about fifteen minutes." She handed us the cocktail card back. "If you'd like to try another cocktail instead of your current one just let me know." Adrian thanked her.

"Fifteen minutes," I said. "That's a little presumptuous. Don't you think?"

"Not for a place like this." He took a sip of his martini. "Damn. That's straight vodka."

"Aren't martinis always straight vodka?" I hesitated. "Or gin?"

"Well, yeah," he said. "But now a lot of bars have all those fruity concoctions. Not too long ago I had a kiwi-watermelon martini."

"Eeww," I said. "How was that?"

"It was eeww," he said and laughed.

Four lavender martinis later we were summoned for dinner. We were a little drunk. Okay, maybe more than a little drunk. Now I understood their offer for a driver.

"Oh, my dress," I said to Adrian. "I forgot."

"Ma'am," our server said. "I did not forget. You have plenty of time."

"I'll go get it," Adrian said as he stood up.

"And the shoes," I said.

"And the shoes," he repeated.

"Do you think you can find your way back?" I asked teasingly. He pointed at me.

"I am not as drunk as you, Miss. Anastasio."

I smiled as he turned for the door. It had been a long time since I'd felt this good. Adrian was like a drug to me but one that could not be duplicated by anything or anyone else. There was no generic brand for Adrian Bennett. He may have belonged to Lilah but tonight he was mine. When I came out of the glamour room a little while later, he was leaned up against the opposite wall looking at his phone. He looked up to me as I shut the door behind me.

"Wow," he said. We just watched one another for a minute. He had a white mink coat draped over his arm.

"Yeah?" I asked as I walked toward him. I laid my hand on his chest and kissed his cheek.

"Is this Ari's coat?" He smiled.

"Yes. She was afraid you would get cold. She said you'd forget your coat."

"I did," I admitted.

"Uh-huh," he said as he held it up for me.

"I love her so much!" He laughed and I slipped my arms into it.

Our server, Charlotte, led us out a back door and up another set of steps to a waiting black town car. The driver opened the door for us and ushered us inside.

"Music preference?" he asked as he got inside the car with us.

"This is fine," Adrian said. It was Bach. Adrian and his classical music.

"You could probably play this better than him," I whispered in his ear.

"Maybe," he said and chuckled.

When we walked into the restaurant later, the maitre'd welcomed us.

"Miss. Vallario," he said. "How nice to see you. May I take your coat?"

"Yes, thank you." He slipped Ari's coat off my shoulders and handed it to the clerk at the front desk.

"Right this way."

It was darker than I remembered, the atmosphere serene. Seashell pink and gold everything. Votive candles lighted each table. We were escorted to leather tufted booth with pink velvet buttons. An enormous pink glass chandelier hovered over us. A waiter immediately brought us a glass of champagne (pink) and presented us with the evening's menu.

"Happy Birthday, Miss. Vallario. We will begin serving at your request."

"Thank you."

"Did you tell them it was my birthday?" I asked Adrian as the waiter walked away. He smiled.

"Maybe."

First Course
Trio of Baked Oysters
Rockefeller/Sauce Francaise/Champagne Mousseline
Second Course
Oxtail Consomme
Third Course
Intermezzo of House-Made Sorbet
Fourth Course
Lobster-Stuffed Wellington
With Pommes William, Baby Carrots, and Truffle Demi-Glace
Fifth Course
Cheese Plate
Cabot Clothbound Cheddar & Classic Stilton with Profiteroles and House-Made Jams
Sixth Course
Charlotte Russe

"Well, this takes the wonder out of the selection process, doesn't it?" Adrian asked.

"It does," I said as I perused the menu. "Are you ready for Oxtail?"

"Do I have a choice?" he asked and chuckled. "What is a profiterole?"

"Usually a cream puff of some kind," I told him.

"Think they'd let me have that first?"

"Doubtful," I answered.

I smiled and looked across the table at him. This handsome, incredibly kind and giving man. I wanted him to still be mine and not just tonight. Forever. I hadn't lost him because of another woman yet I should have known that would be the inevitable outcome. I had lost him because of *The Empire.* I reached across the table for his hand. He looked back to me, his eyes searching mine. He knew me better than anyone.

"Thank you, Adrian," I said. "You have no idea how much this means to me."

"I think I do," he said as he squeezed my fingers. "You think I don't remember but I do." I smiled and looked down. "Hey." I looked back up to him. He knew what I was thinking. "You know I'm going to bring Stef back to you, don't you?"

He would. If anyone could, it would be him. I nodded because I couldn't speak. Just the mention of Stef's name tonight brought tears. Adrian saw them before I had the chance to wipe them away.

"Do you believe me?" he asked.

"Yes," I said tearfully. I pulled my hand away and dabbed my eyes with my napkin.

He reached into his coat pocket and pulled out a small blue box. He handed it to me from across the table. Tiffany blue. Of course, it was Tiffany blue. Fairy Tale always gave Tiffany gifts just like Palazzo

Cremisi always gave Gucci. Well, I guess I shouldn't say only Palazzo Cremisi. *The Empire.*

"Happy Birthday."

"Really?" I asked as I brought my hand to my chest.

"Uh-huh." I took it from him, untied the white satin ribbon and lifted off the top carefully. Inside was a black velvet pouch.

"What is it?" I asked. He shrugged.

"Open it and find out." I loosened the strings and turned it upside down. A rose gold ring fell out into the palm of my hand. In script, **Love.**

"Paloma Picasso," I said.

"Yeah."

"How did you know I wanted this?" He reached into his pocket again and pulled out a magazine page. He unfolded it and showed it to me.

"Did you take that out of my datebook?" I asked unbelievingly. He chuckled.

"Uh-huh."

"Adrian! I can't believe you went through my datebook!! What is wrong with you?"

"Want me to take the ring back??" he asked. I sighed.

"Did you read my notes?"

"On?" he asked and grinned.

"Oh, never mind."

"Take off all those other rings," he said. I looked down at my hands. "Give them to me." I smiled and took them off. All but one.

"I can't take this one off," I said.

He watched me for a moment. I thought he was going to ask me about it but he didn't. I handed the rest of my rings to him. He put them into his coat pocket. "Give me the *Love* ring."

"No!" I said and laughed. "You gave it to me. I'm not giving it back."

"Give it to me," he insisted so I handed it to him. I always gave in with Adrian. He might not have been able to say no to me but I couldn't say no to him either. "Hand." I held out my hand and he slipped it on the middle finger of my left hand. I looked down to it. It fit perfectly.

"Wrong finger," I teased. He smiled.

"Close enough?" he asked. I wiped another tear from my cheek and nodded.

"Mm-hmm."

"I will always take care of you, Lora," he assured me. "Whenever you feel like you're alone I want you to look down at this ring because you never will be." I didn't know what to say so I held out my hand and looked at the ring he'd just put on my finger.

"Thank you, Adrian," I said softly.

"You're welcome." He motioned to the ring on my other hand. The one I refused to take off. "Now tell me about that other ring." I looked down to the middle finger of my right hand. I held it out and he looked at it. It was a gold monogram ring, one letter delicately woven into another.

"Your initials?" he asked.

"No."

"Okay," he said. "I have to admit I've never been good with the fancy cursive letters."

"Look at it closely," I told him. He took my hand and looked a little more intently then shrugged.

"I admit defeat," he said and smiled.

"SBA."

"I'm supposed to know what that means, aren't I?" he asked looking up to me. I shrugged.

"Probably not but you always put the initial of your last name in the middle."

"B?"

"Yes."

"Bennett?" he asked carefully. I smiled.

"Yeah."

"SA," he said thoughtfully.

"Yes," I said and he smiled.

It had been a long time since I'd seen him smile that way. He smiled that way the morning after we first made love. He smiled that way when I gave him the violet polo shirt for his birthday, and the day he gave me Bluebell for mine. I imagined he smiled that way the first time he saw a picture of our son.

"For real?"

"Mamma did it," I explained to him. "I didn't even know until after he was born. She did it as a surprise for me."

"He has my name," he said thoughtfully.

"Yeah."

"Does Gianni know?"

"Are you kidding?" I asked and laughed. "He doesn't even know his middle name. I'm not even sure he knows it's Stefan and not just Stef."

"I can't believe your Mamma did that."

385

"She made it happen," I said. "For us."

"Wow."

"Remember after I left Amityville and she told you she was always on my side? And that my side was you?"

"Yeah," he said. "I never really knew what that meant."

He looked down. It was almost as if he couldn't believe what I was telling him. Not that Stef had his name but that my mother had so cleverly crafted a plan in such a conspiring way. So conspiring that it was outside the realm of *The Empire.*

"Your mother," he said as he looked up to me. "Is such a perceptive woman. I remember once someone telling me back then when you were my girlfriend…" He hesitated. "…that I should be careful because Roslyn Anastasio was a formidable woman."

"That she is," I agreed. "When she makes up her mind about something no one can change it."

"I'm glad I'm on her good side," he said and chuckled.

"You are," I assured him.

I wanted to tell him how my mother's plans went far beyond what he could even imagine but tonight wasn't the right time to reveal the blueprint she'd designed for us. I wasn't sure when that time would be or if it would ever be. If Mamma's plans didn't perfectly align with everything else happening in *The Empire,* I might end up taking all her secrets to my grave. Adrian wasn't just on Mamma's good side. Adrian was the only side she had.

Adrian

"Man, it's cold out there," I said as we came into the darkened foyer. I shut the door behind me.

"That chilly sea breeze," Lora explained. She grabbed ahold of my arm. "I am so drunk. Are you drunk?"

"Sort of," I admitted.

In truth I was so drunk we had to take a cab back to the house. I probably could have driven back to Angelic but getting a DUI was not an option. Randy had gotten a DUI not too long ago and Jenny had put him on desk duty for three months. The cabbie almost seemed afraid to go through Angelic's gates once Lora unlocked them but then she'd presented him with her driver's license.

"Do you know who I am??" she asked a little disgustedly. "I'm Tony's daughter. I can call him if you'd like (she couldn't) but I'm thinking that won't be necessary. Will it?"

I'm not sure if that calmed the cabbie's fears or made him even more fearful but he proceeded through the gates, nonetheless. As we walked through the front door, I helped Lorelei out of Ari's coat then laid it over the curved railing at the bottom of the stairs.

"Lights?" I asked because other than the moonlight coming through the French doors the house was dark.

A few obscure shadows flitted in and out of the darkness. My mother would have called them shadow people but I knew differently.

At least I knew differently at Angelic Manor. Not so much at Fairy Tale where shadows moved around the rooms like orbs. Lora turned on the foyer light and the chandelier came to life but this chandelier wasn't your typical everyday chandelier. It was a massive chandelier that glowed with tiny blue lights, the only lights in the house now. They did nothing to overcome the shadows but they were beautiful.

"Watch this," Lora said as she turned on another switch. Another set of lights came on in a light, fairy pink.

"Nice," I said as I stuck my hands in my pockets. "Nothing is too decadent for *The Empire*."

"More," she said. She continued turning what appeared to be a dimmer switch and the pink lights glittered amongst the blue. A further turn and the blue lights begin glittering with them. They gleamed across the marble floor like a disco ball in Studio 54.

"Stay right there," she said. She pointed at me and stumbled down the foyer steps.

"Be careful," I said and laughed.

"Because I want you to hear something."

Angelic Manor has a surround sound music system that reverberates throughout the entire house. I knew this because that day in high school when we'd snuck away to come here to make love, we'd listened to an entire soundtrack Lora had created just for us. No matter where we went in the house that day the music had followed us. Now the foyer filled with music and Lorelei peeked her head around the corner.

"You know this song?" she called over the music.

Of course, I knew this song. It was *September* by Earth, Wind and Fire.

"Ah…memories," I said because this was the song Roslyn used to teach me how to waltz. I'll never forget it because dancing with Roslyn was a dream come true and a living hell all at once.

"Take off your shoes," she said. "Dance with me."

"Why do I have to take off my shoes?" I asked as I took her hand but I put one foot behind the other and slipped my shoes off at the heels, shoved them up closer to the wall. I looked down. "How about your shoes?"

"Nuh-uh," she said as she began dancing in front of me. "I can't dance barefoot. I have to have on my heels."

"You will break my toes if you step on my feet with those shoes," I pointed out. She smiled.

"Twelve years of dance," she reminded me. "Remember?"

"How could I forget? Your space and my space," I said before she could. I placed my hand on her waist.

"Do you remember how to do this?" she asked and smiled.

"What? Waltz??"

"Yeah."

"Maybe," I said. "It's been a while."

"It's like riding a bike. It will come back to you."

We moved around the darkened foyer underneath the blue and pink sparkling lights. She let go of my hand and took my fingers as she twirled underneath my arm. I placed my hand on her waist and guided her through and we continued across the floor.

"See?" she said. "You remember."

"This is a much faster song than I remember," I said and laughed.

"It's good for your cardiovascular system," she said as I pulled her back into me. I wrapped my arm around her and she looked over her shoulder to me. I held her there then spun her around quickly. "You sure are out of breath for someone so physically fit."

We danced to *September*. It is one long-ass song. In fact, I can't think of a longer song apart from *Mozart Sonata 11* and I have never had to dance to that song. Thank God. Lorelei stopped.

"Okay," she said as she let go of my hand. She went around the corner and I leaned down with my hands on my knees. I was a little dizzy. "You better know this one."

"The pressure," I said bringing my hand to my forehead. "Am I gonna have to dance to this one?"

"Of course."

"Are you trying to kill me?" She only smiled and laughed. "I may not be able to walk tomorrow," I told her. "I'm getting old."

"Just listen," she instructed.

I listened as she walked toward me. It was a song we had danced to many times. "*Get Outta My Dreams. Get Into My Car*. Billy Ocean. The Gala. The night I lost my virginity. She smiled and grabbed my fingers but quickly let them go. I felt them trail across my waist as she moved past me and back again. I guided her with my hand on her waist. She didn't need it but it connected the dance and we flowed together as we moved across the floor. The lights, the music, the dancing.

I watched Lora's hair trail behind her. She smiled again. She was happy. Really happy. I wanted to give her everything I knew she wanted but was too ashamed to admit. She moved past me and trailed her fingers across my cheek. I caught ahold of it and pulled her back to me.

"Aha!" I said. "You thought you'd trick me, didn't you?"

"I can't believe you remember this," she said.

"I can't believe you do," I countered. She moved past me once more. "Do you remember our lift?" I asked as I pulled her into me again. She nodded as she twirled beneath my arm. I followed her across the floor, me still in my sock feet, her still in her stiletto's. "I'll take that as a yes."

"I might weigh more," she warned me.

"No," I said. "I don't think so. Are you ready?"

"Yes."

She backed away from me, held onto the tips of my fingers. Whether she was ready or not was unknown. She didn't move. I wasn't sure what ready meant to her when she was this drunk. I wasn't even sure what it meant to me.

"What?" I said and she laughed.

"I don't know if I can do this, Adrian," she said as she backed further away from me. "Wait! I have to take off my shoes." I laughed. "You're going to catch me??"

"Of course, I am." She pointed her finger at me.

"You better catch me, Adrian!!"

"I'm gonna catch you, Lorelei!!" I said and pointed back.

At least, I hoped I would. She backed up even further, probably about twelve feet or so away. We both started laughing because whether I could catch her when I was this drunk was questionable but when you're drunk those kinds of possibilities are funny. You're not thinking about the risk of falling on a marble floor and breaking your neck.

"Wait!" I said as I leaned down to take off my socks. "If I try to catch you with my socks on, I'm going to slide across the foyer and we'll both end up on the floor."

"That might be fun," she said and giggled.

"Maybe," I said and laughed with her. "But I doubt it." I steadied myself and looked back up to her. "Are you ready?"

"Yes!!" she exclaimed.

"On three," I told her. She nodded. "One, two, …" And she ran. "I said three!!" I shouted as I prepared to catch her.

When she got closer, she jumped toward me. This was not the way the original dance went. Originally, she was not this far away and she certainly didn't need to jump. I grabbed her by her hips as soon as she reached me. Her feet left the floor. I'd learned back then it wasn't truly her waist I was grabbing. It was her hips and fortunately now I remembered that technicality. I lifted her above me, further than I'd ever lifted her before, and we turned in a circle. She raised her hands from my shoulders.

"Not sure if that's a good idea," I said, and she laughed.

I brought her back down and she slid down my body just like she had that night at the Gala only now she was much more voluptuous. I felt every dip and curve of her body against mine.

It doesn't matter how in love you are with someone. If another woman's body touches you the way Lorelei's had just touched mine it gives you an instant high. I was pretty sure I could feel the testosterone moving through my body at lightning speed. When Lorelei's feet touched the floor again, I brought my hands to her neck. I felt her hands hesitantly on my upper arms as I touched my lips to hers. It wasn't a perfect kiss. Our lips parted and my bottom lip went into her open ones. We separated for a moment then kissed again as the music continued to play. We watched one another for a moment.

"This is what you want, isn't it?" I finally asked.

"Yes," she said breathlessly.

I woke up on my side the next morning in the enormous king size bed inside the master suite. Lorelei was nestled behind me with her arm across my hip. My head pounded with an unrelenting pain. An intrinsic consciousness told me I was undeniably naked. I turned over and raised my arm over my head onto the pillows behind me. Lorelei snuggled closer to me and laid her head on my chest. That was when I realized I wasn't the only one naked.

I closed my eyes and tried to remember what had happened but I could only remember bits and pieces. Stumbling through the front door. Dancing under the glistening lights of the foyer. Shots in the kitchen. A roaring fire in the fireplace. Shit. I jumped up and grabbed my pants because my boxers were nowhere in sight. I slipped them on and ran out the bedroom door to the baluster over the foyer. I peered into the living room. There was no fire in the fireplace but there were pillows scattered across the floor. And feathers. Feathers everywhere. The French doors to the terrace were open, the sheer light blue curtains blowing in the frigid morning air.

I descended the stairs and walked across the foyer to the living room and over to the terrace doors. The same pain I felt in my head moved across the rest of my body with a throbbing heaviness. The cold air hit my bare chest as I grabbed the curtains and pulled the doors shut behind them. It took every ounce of energy I had to make it back to the top of the stairs. When I walked into the bedroom Lorelei was face down in her pillows. The blue and gold embroidered comforter was in a tangled mess at the foot of the bed. I sat on the edge and propped my head in my hands, swallowed my nausea.

"What's wrong?" she mumbled from underneath her pillow.

"The French doors were open," I told her.

"Is that why it's so cold in here?" I reached down to the bottom of the bed and pulled the comforter up over her. She rolled over and looked up to me.

"Yeah."

"Turn the radiator up," she instructed so I got up and knelt beside it. I turned the handle. "Shut the door." I shut the bedroom door. "Get back in bed."

"Anything else, your Highness?" I asked as I pulled the covers back. I crawled underneath of them. The radiator hissed into existence.

"Why are you getting in bed with your pants on?"

"Because I can't find my boxers."

She held up the covers and looked under them. There lay my boxers along with her pink lace underwear. She handed my boxers to me then raised her hips and slipped on her panties.

"Did we?" she asked as I took off my pants and slipped on my boxers.

I got under the covers and pulled them up close around me. It was freezing in the room but the radiator was warming it up slowly. I laid back against my pillows and ran my hand through my hair.

"I'm not sure," I said. I took a deep breath and blew it back out. "My head is throbbing."

"Mine, too," she said as she sat up. "I'm going to throw up." She got up and ran into the bathroom.

I heard her retching into the sink. I laid in bed thinking, 'I am not going to throw up. I am not going to throw up.' I didn't realize it at the time but we weren't totally hungover yet which became evident later in the day as our symptoms worsened. We may have even still been a little drunk because I don't think the consequences of what we'd done had fully registered with us yet. Lorelei came back into the bedroom

"We were naked," she said as she wrapped the tie around her robe.

"Yeah," I acknowledged. She got back into the bed.

"Adrian…" she started and I turned to her.

"Hey," I said as I laid my hand on her arm. "Let's just not talk about it. We're going to pretend like it never happened. I don't remember it. Do you remember it?"

"Some of it. Not much."

"Forget whatever you remember," I told her.

"Adrian, it's not that easy."

"Why not?"

"Because it's just not."

"Why can't we pretend like it didn't happen?" I asked as I fell back against my pillows again. "It's not like anyone else was here."

"Because it did," she said.

"You just said you didn't remember much of it. Try not to remember the rest."

"Adrian, look at me." I turned to her. "I could be pregnant right now."

"You could be pregnant right now anyway."

"Well, I know that but…"

"What difference does it make?" I asked. "It's going to be mine either way. Why fret over it? If you're pregnant there is no way we'll ever know one way or the other." She just stared at me. "Is there?"

"No."

"Perfect."

"Oh my god," she said sitting up in the bed. "Oh, my fucking god."

"What??"

"The cameras," she said as she ran her hands over her hair.

"What cameras?" I asked, alarmed. I sat up beside her.

"The security cameras," she said. "They're all over the entire house."

"Who sees them?" I asked.

"No one unless they turn them on at the other end."

"Who's they?" I asked.

"Everyone."

"Like everyone in the 'family' everyone?" She nodded.

"Everyone."

"Can *we* watch it?" I asked.

"Yeah," she said. "But I don't know how."

"I can figure it out," I told her as I stood up. "I've confiscated hundreds of them over the years." I pulled on my pants and looked around the room for my shirt, found it on the desk chair across the room. I slipped it on and began buttoning it.

"Confiscate as in get rid of?" she asked.

"Yeah," I said. "After I watch it."

"Do you want to watch it?"

"I don't know," I said as I reached for her hand. I pulled her up off the bed. "Maybe. Where's the control room?"

"In the basement but I can't get into it. This place is locked down like Ft. Knox." I turned to her.

"Who are you talking to?" I asked as we went down the stairs together. "Do you know how many security systems I've disarmed over the years?"

"Have you ever disarmed an Empire security system?" she asked. "Because I'm not sure what happens when you do that."

"I don't care what happens," I said as we walked across the living room toward the kitchen. "I'm confiscating that footage."

"The police might come," she warned. I stopped and turned to her.

"The police?" I asked. "Are you kidding me?"

"No," she said seriously.

"You think the police is going to come 'rescue' *The Empire?*"

"Maybe." I took her hands in mine.

"Okay, first, trust me when I say the police are not coming."

"How do you know?"

"I just do," I answered. "Secondly, I am the police."

"But the police up here are different, Adrian."

"Lora," I said. "I am a federal agent. I have authority over pretty much anyone." She didn't look convinced so I put my arms around her and pulled her into me.

"When have I ever let anything bad happen to you?" I said into her hair. "Huh?"

"Never," she answered.

"Never," I repeated.

The kitchen was a disaster. Several cans of whipped cream. Empty, of course. Liquor 43. Empty, of course. On the counter: Vodka, Malibu Rum and Basil Hayden. Not empty, but close. A bottle of hot sauce and a jar of maraschino cherries. Lorelei pulled me toward the basement door. I followed her down the stairs. It was nearly pitch-black dark at the bottom. She introduced me to the security keypad. I reached out to hit the star key.

"What are you doing??" she asked when it lit up.

"Lighting it up?? Chill out." I hit the disarm button and it blinked red three times.

"Holy shit, Adrian."

"Chill," I told her again. "I can't disarm it without a code."

"No one gets notified??" she asked.

"Not unless I enter the wrong code too many times."

"How many times is too many times?"

"I don't know," I answered. "But usually three."

"So, you only have three chances to get it right?"

"Would you chill out??" I asked. "Sit on the steps."

"Ugh," she said as she sat down behind me.

"What is the chance this code is the same as the front door code?" I asked her.

"None."

"And you're sure about that?" I asked as I turned around to her.

"It's *The Empire*, Adrian. What do you think?" I turned back around to the keypad.

"There are two basic master codes," I told her. "1111 or 1234. 1234 is the most common." I punched in 1234. Nope. "Well, it's not 1234."

"Adrian, you're making me nervous."

"I'm making myself nervous," I said and laughed. I punched in 1111. Nope. "Okay," I said. "So, it's neither of those which makes me think they have their own master code or are using the installer code."

"Jesus," Lorelei said from behind me. "I'm going to have a nervous breakdown."

"No, you're not," I told her. "Stop it. My gut instinct is telling me it's an installer code because only *The Empire* installs Empire security systems and they probably have the same installer for all the compounds." I turned around to her. "Don't you think?"

"Who knows," she said.

"This is a 2GIG system."

"I have no idea what that means," she said.

"Do you have your phone?" I asked.

"No."

"Go get mine. I think I saw it laying on the kitchen counter."

"Okay."

I laid my head back against the brick wall behind me and ran my hands over my face. I should have known something like this would happen. I should have taken Ari's warning a little more seriously.

"Is it dead?" I asked as she handed it to me.

"No."

I called Terrence because I knew he had memorized all the installer codes for every security system known to man. I could've looked it up but this was much easier.

"Hey," I said when he answered. "I need the installer code for a 2GIG home security system."

"Where are you?" he asked suspiciously.

"I can't answer that right now."

"6978."

"How many chances do I have to get this right because I've already used two."

"Usually three," he said.

"Awesome. Will it lock up or go on alert?"

"It depends on how they set it up."

"Even more awesome."

"May the force be with you," he said and laughed.

"Yep."

"Hey, try 6978 before we hang up. I have another idea if the whole house doesn't explode when 6978 is wrong."

"I love it when you try to console me."

"I try."

I punched in 6978. Nothing.

"What happened?" he asked.

"Nothing."

"Do it backwards but you only have one minute to enter it on the pad inside or the system will revert and go on alert."

"Whatever 'alert' means," I said.

"Always expect the unexpected," Terrence told me.

I punched in 8796 and the keypad lit up yellow, the latch unlatched, and I yanked on the door. The alarm that sounds until you enter the code again on the inside went off which scared Lorelei to death.

"Oh my god," she said as she stood up.

"I'm in," I told Terrence. "Thanks."

"Dinner on you next time," he told me.

"Yep." I held the door open for Lora.

"Look for the pad in here," I said as I flipped on the lights. "We have one minute."

"Shit," she said as she rounded the room then, "I found it!"

I ran over to the pad and punched in the code again. The alarm stopped immediately. Lora leaned over with her arms on the huge mahogany table.

"That glass cubicle has all the security camera stuff in it," she said as she laid her head in her hands. "I think I'm having a mild heart attack."

I walked around to the other side of the table and leaned up against it. I examined the set-up. This wasn't just for the security cameras. This was the electrical panel for the entire house. I watched all the lights blinking on and off. There didn't seem to be any rhyme or reason to it.

"Well?" she asked me.

"Give me a minute," I said.

I reached over and flipped the main power switch. A whir of activity and then...nothing. The lights went out and everything in the entire house shut down. Lorelei and I stood in pitch black darkness. Like, I couldn't even see my hand in front of my face darkness.

"Shit, Adrian!!"

"It's fine," I said. "Relax. There's a flashlight behind you on the counter. Get it, will you?"

"What?? Where??"

"Right behind you," I said. "Feel around."

"No, there's not."

"There is," I insisted. "I saw it when we came down through the door."

"Here," she said disgustedly a moment later. I turned on the flashlight and shined it toward the cabinet in front of me.

I started turning on individual power switches. The lights and heat pump came back to life and then the phone rang. It was the landline attached to an old red rotary-style phone sitting on the table behind me.

"Well, answer it," I said.

"Are you serious right now??"

"You want me to do it??" I asked and shrugged.

"Hello," Lorelei answered. "It's Lorelei, Sir... Yes, Sir... Uh...It's fine. We're okay. Uh...well, can you hold on a minute?" She put her hand over the receiver. "He wants to know who is here with me."

"Who is it?" I asked as I ran my hand through my hair. She rolled her eyes.

"It's Sam Corleone." I brought my hands to my chest.

"*The* Sam Corleone? Wow. I'm so flattered."

"Adrian!!!"

"Give me the phone," I said as I reached for it. She widened her eyes in disbelief but she handed it to me.

"Are you kidding me??" she mouthed with her hand on her hip.

"Sam," I said. "Hey. It's Adrian Bennett." Lorelei brought her hands to her face, pressed her fingers into her eye sockets. "Yeah," I said into the phone. "Well, Lorelei needed a little getaway. I'm sure you understand. You know how women are...yeah...I know, right? Well, yeah. Haven't we always??" I laughed. "She is." Lorelei looked at me and held out her hands.

"What???" she mouthed.

"No," I said into the phone. "Don't worry about it...Yeah, she's fine... I'll tell her." I looked to Lora and smiled. "Sam said he loves you."

She flipped me off with both hands. I raised my eyebrows and widened my eyes, shrugged.

"Well, I think there might be some sensitive information on the cameras," I said and laughed again. I held the phone on my shoulder as I turned the alarm system back on. "I know. I'll turn them off next time." I chuckled. "Now that I know how."

Next time. There wouldn't be a next time but Sam didn't need to know that right now. In fact, him thinking otherwise was probably to my advantage. Lorelei's eyes widened and she held up her hands.

"Well, this needs to stay between us," I said. "You know how that goes... Yeah... I've never been able to say no to Lorelei." Lora paced around the basement. "I know, right?" I laughed again. "I'll take care of her. You know I will. Of course."

And then, "I just want to make sure Stef is safe," Sam said.

"He is," I assured him.

Holy shit, I thought. Tiffany was right. *The Empire* had chosen the DEA as a haven for Stef. We were the solution to their war within. If only I knew what that war within entailed. Because there was no doubt in my mind there was a lot more involved to this than just a nasty custody battle between the Anastasios and the Vallarios. At least I knew the Montenaris were on mine and Lora's side. The rest of *The Empire* was still questionable.

"Thank you for everything you've done, Adrian," Sam said. "I am eternally grateful."

Sam Corleone. Eternally grateful to *me*.

"You're welcome, Sir."

"I'll be in touch," Sam said.

Click. I handed the receiver back to Lorelei. She brought it to her ear and held out her arms and shrugged.

"He hung up," I said. "It's fine."

"It is not fine!!!" she yelled at me.

"It is," I assured her.

"I can't believe you're just sitting there like that."

"Like what?" I asked.

"Like everything is fine!!!"

"Everything *is* fine."

"Adrian, he is going to tell Papa everything!!" I shrugged.

"Okay."

"Are you serious right now??" she asked. I got up from the table and walked over to her and placed my hands on her upper arms. She was shaking.

"Everything is okay," I told her. "I promise."

"You keep telling me that," she cried.

"Well, don't cry. You're too pretty for that."

"Stop trying to pacify me!!" she said angrily.

"I'm not trying to pacify you," I said. "Evidently, Sam trusts me. So, cheer up."

"Sam trusts no one," she told me.

"We'll see," I said as I leaned over and kissed her cheek. "But I think you're wrong."

—

Once I'd confiscated the security camera tape and made sure it was not accessible to the entire Empire family Lorelei and I took a bath. Well, she took a bath. I took a shower. I told her it might help her feel better. When I got out of the shower, I wrapped a towel around my waist and went over to the tub. I sat on the edge. It was the biggest bathtub I'd ever seen surrounded by windows that looked out over the beach.

"Feel any better?" I asked.

"I don't know," she said as she laid her head back against the tub. "I feel like I want to shoot myself."

"Give it a little bit of time," I said. "You'll feel better soon."

"Not just that," she said of her hangover. "The tape or video or whatever the hell it is and Sam…and eventually Papa, if not already."

"I told you. It's fine."

"I think it was a good idea on Sam's part for us to stay another night. Isn't that what he said?"

"Yes. He suggested we stay another night."

"Why?"

"I don't know."

"I need more time to recuperate. Don't you?"

"I'll be okay either way."

"Are we staying another night?" she asked.

"Up to you. It's your birthday." She looked up to me.

"Well, I think my birthday has gone seriously downhill."

"We've had a few bumps in the road."

"A few??"

"Just relax," I told her. She laid her head back against the tub again and closed her eyes.

"Should we watch the tape?" she asked.

"I'm going back and forth with that," I said. "If we watch it then we will know what we did. If we don't then we won't. Which do you prefer?"

"We already know what we did," she said. "That's not a question."

"You know what I mean. Do you really want to watch us having drunk sex?" She opened her eyes and looked up to me, smiled.

"What if you tied me up or something?" she asked. "What if we did something really twisted?" I laughed even though I shouldn't have. "Why are you laughing?"

"Because I think that is highly unlikely."

"Did you turn the security cameras off?" she asked.

"Well, I turned the security alarm back on but not the cameras. Why?"

"Good," she said and she yanked on my arm.

When she did, I lost my balance and fell over into the tub with her. The water was so deep I briefly went underwater. When I surfaced, she was laughing.

"You are in so much trouble now," I said and pointed at her.

"Bring it," she said.

———

"Hello?" Tiffany answered.

"You got a minute?" I asked as I walked toward the beach. Lorelei was still feeling a little ragged. When I left the house, she was fast asleep on the sofa in front of the fire I'd built.

"Where the hell are you?" Tiff asked.

"I'm at Angelic."

"With her??"

"Would you just listen to me??" I asked. She took a deep breath and blew it back out again.

"I'm listening."

"You were right," I said.

"About?"

"*The Empire* and Stef."

"What do you mean?"

"Well…" I hesitated. "I had a conversation with Sam this morning."

"Corleone??" she asked. I could tell she was not only in awe but somewhat troubled. "What did you do?"

"I shut the power down here trying to bypass the security system."

"Why on earth would you do that??"

"It doesn't matter," I told her. "Just listen. So, he calls because I shut the power down. I'm sure he gets an immediate notification of some kind when that happens at any of the compounds."

"Well, yeah," Tiff said. "Duh."

"We talked about why I was here, how he knew Lora loved me, if I would promise to take care of her, that her safety was important to him. I needed to confiscate the security system footage so I had to explain to him why."

"Why?" Tiff asked. I held my breath.

"It doesn't matter. That's not the point."

"It does matter," she said. "Tell me."

"I brought Lora here for her birthday."

"I know that," she said. "Against my better judgment."

"Well, yeah. But we got kind of trashed and…"

"Adrian," she warned. "Please tell me you're not telling me what I think you're telling me."

"It happens," I said. "It's happened to you before." And when she said nothing. "More than once."

"There is no comparison between having a drunken one-night stand and you cheating on the woman you're supposed to be marrying. Are you still marrying Lilah? Or did Lorelei convince you to marry her instead??"

"Tiff…"

"So, just when I thought the Long Island Lorelei may have reformed herself, she finally completes her mission of getting into your pants."

"Tiff…"

"Tell me it is never going to happen again."

"It won't."

"Ever."

"Ever," I repeated. "It's fine."

"It is NOT fine," Tiffany said. "At least when it happened to me it wasn't recorded on an Empire security system."

"Which has been confiscated with a blessing from Sam."

"Who cares??" she asked. "You are engaged. Practically married, might I add. That is a commitment, Adrian. You do love, Lilah, don't you?"

"Why are you asking me that?" I asked. "Of course, I love Lilah."

"People who love one another don't cheat on each other with an old girlfriend," she told me.

"I was drunk!" I explained. I was beginning to lose my temper. "What else do you want me to do?"

"I don't know," she said dismissively.

"Can we not just leave this alone? It's over. It's done. There's nothing I can do about it."

"There are repercussions for that kind of behavior," Tiffany said.

"I get it, Tiff. Okay??"

"You better make sure that tape gets destroyed."

"Do you think I'm stupid??"

"I'm questioning that at this point."

"Are you done?" I asked.

"Jenny is going to beat your ass," Tiff said.

"Why?" I asked. "She likes it when I get friendly with the enemy."

"This is not just the enemy, Adrian. This is *The Empire*. You know that and she already told you not to sleep with Lorelei."

"Yeah, I know but she doesn't need to know about that. Sam told me he was eternally grateful to me."

"For what?"

"Stef, I guess. I think he trusts me."

"Sam trusts no one," Tiffany said.

"That's what Lorelei said."

"I can't believe Long Island Lorelei and I actually agree on something."

"Who would've thought?" I asked facetiously.

"Go on."

"While I was on the phone with him about the security system, he asked me if Stef was safe."

"What?"

"He asked me if Stef was safe."

"He asked you this in front of Lorelei?"

"No," I said. "We were on the phone so she couldn't hear his end of the conversation."

"What did you tell him?"

"I told him he was."

"You're an idiot," she said.

"Wow."

"Oh my god, Adrian. You might have just given *The Empire* DEA classified information. Did you think about that?"

"I don't think that's what it was about," I said. "He wasn't fishing for information. He was concerned about Lora so obviously he would be concerned about Stef."

"As he's thinking to himself, 'Hmm...I wonder if Adrian knows where Stef is...'"

"No," I said. "Trust me. That was not what it was. How long have I been doing this, Tiff?"

"I don't know."

"I can read people even over the phone. That is not what this was about. This was about Sam verifying we had taken Stef and that he was safe."

"Don't you think given the wealth of information Sam is privy to that he would already know where Stef is and if he were safe??"

"What I think is he wanted me to know it was his idea."

"The whole set-up thing, you mean?"

"Yes," I said. "I think it was Sam's way of telling me the DEA having Stef was not the DEA's idea. It was his idea. He wants to make sure I know he is still in control."

"Is he?" Tiffany asked.

"If he wants to be, yes."

"Have you told Jenny any of this?"

"Not yet."

"I still think she's going to beat your ass," Tiff informed me. I didn't say anything. "Because if you're thinking you can be best buddies with Sam Corleone you need therapy."

Lorelei

Adrian and I slept in the same bed our final night at Angelic but we didn't make love or anything even close to it. He held me but when it comes to me and Adrian that is the equivalent of a handshake. I fell asleep easily in his arms even though I thought I wouldn't be able to sleep at all. I woke in the middle of the night to an empty bed.

I got up and went into the bathroom and stood in front of the mirror. I looked at myself. How had I gotten here? Why wasn't I with the only man I'd ever truly loved? Why had our son been taken from me? Was karma that cruel? And if it was, what had I done to deserve it? What lesson was I supposed to take away from this? The fear inside of me rose and fell in my chest and I began to cry. I sunk down to the floor and leaned over on my knees.

There was only one other time I could remember crying this way and that was when I found out I was pregnant with Stef. It was when I realized I'd probably never see Adrian again and that the baby growing inside of me would never know his real father, that instead he would be raised within *The Empire* by a man who only believed he was his son. Now I cried for the drunken mistake Adrian and I had made. I cried for what it meant, our son, for all the times I'd wished for Stef, for all the times I knew Adrian was lost to me. I stood up and picked up the hand towel off the counter, brought it to my face. I looked in the mirror again. Black mascara ringed my eyes so I wiped underneath of them with my fingers.

411

"No!" I said out loud. "Stop it!"

I turned from the sink and walked back out into the bedroom. I grabbed my robe off the foot of the bed and wrapped it around myself. I needed to find Adrian. When I opened the bedroom door, I heard the piano. No one ever played it. I'm not even sure why we had it but now Adrian was playing it. I smiled. I couldn't help but smile. I tiptoed over to the baluster and peeked over the edge. The clock that hung on the stone wall over the fireplace read three twenty-five.

There was a floor lamp sitting next to the piano but other than that the living room was dark. I watched for a moment as Adrian's hands moved over the keys. Chill bumps erupted over my skin because whenever Adrian plays from memory there are no musical notations he must follow, only whatever flows from his mind through his fingers to the keys.

Now he played Beyoncé's *Halo*. It was his song for me when we were in school because he said I was *his* Angel but I had never heard him play it on the piano. I didn't even know he could play it on the piano. Tonight, it resonated with me so deeply tears ran down my cheeks once more and my shoulders shook. I listened as the music changed from one delicate sonata into another. *Endless Love.* He'd played that song for me the morning after we first made love. It was the first time I'd ever watched him play; the first time I'd watched his fingers move magically over the keys.

When the music changed again it changed from *Endless Love* to *Forever.* Doesn't seem like much of a difference, does it? *Endless Love* should be *Forever,* shouldn't it? But, trust me, it's two completely different songs. A simple piano medley that after a quiet pause changed to a much more sophisticated sound. It was an electronic composition capable of changing the most doubtful of lovers into believing again.

I watched Adrian's fingers flip from one mode to another and when he did, so did his demeanor. This song excited him and I could tell playing it made him incredibly happy. *Forever*, a song hinting of dance but everyone knows is about so much more. An unassuming turn on the dance floor changes a day of rhythm into a night of pleasure. Dance *Forever* just like Chris Brown said to do.

It was then I realized that is exactly what Adrian was doing with Lilah. Dancing, leading her from one move to another. Moving from our dance to theirs. This morning it happened on a keyboard in a manner of minutes but I knew in life it had taken much longer. It wasn't as if Adrian had skipped any beats. He'd rested and he'd rested quite a while. Now he was ready to begin playing again. Forever. With Lilah. No rests. Not anymore. I watched him play.

He played sincerely. No one could ever accuse Adrian of not having talent. He had an ability not many musicians possessed. He had a reverence for music – every kind of music - which made his ability magical. Now I knew without a doubt he was in love. I could see it on his face. I watched him dance. Without me.

With her.

The next evening, I closed Angelic and set the alarms at the front door while Adrian took our bags out to the car. It had been a beautiful day. Not as cold as when we'd arrived. It was still quite chilly in the shade but when I stood in the setting sun, I could feel its warmth on my skin. I sat my bag down on the portico as I struggled with the deadbolt. The doors at Angelic had always been uneven with the latches. I yanked it and finally got the key to turn in the lock. I grabbed my bag and hopped down the front steps.

"Got everything?" I asked Adrian.

"I certainly hope so," he answered.

I walked over to him as he leaned over the car and bumped my hip into his. He stumbled sideways but then he picked me up and hoisted me over his shoulder. My bag fell onto the ground.

"Adrian!!" I shouted and pointed behind him. "Stop it! Look! My lip gloss is rolling down the driveway."

"Oh no!!" he teased as he ran around the side of the house with me on his shoulder. "Your lip gloss! What a travesty!"

"I paid $59 for that lip gloss!" I exclaimed. "Where are you taking me??" He ran through the pine trees surrounding the backside of the house onto the terrace. He sat me down.

"Turn around," he told me. "Look."

"I know what the ocean looks like, goofy," I said.

"No," he told me. "This."

It was one of the most beautiful sunsets I'd ever seen.

"Oh, wow."

"Do you know how much I love you?" he asked from behind me as he tried to catch his breath.

This, I knew, was Adrian's way of telling me something he knew I didn't want to hear. He always went about it in a way that gave me another option than the bad news he was about to deliver. Like, if you don't like what I'm going to say, here's something else to think about instead.

"Yeah."

"You are so amazing and so beautiful and smart." He took my hands in his.

"Adrian," I said. "Stop." He turned me around.

"Lora, I can't be the man you want me to be." He hesitated. "I want to be but I can't." I looked down.

"We lost it," I said quietly.

"You are going to find someone who can give you everything I can't." He took my chin in his hand, tilted my face toward him. "You know that, right?"

"Yeah."

"You will always be a part of my life. Not just because we have children together. Just because you're that amazing." He kissed my forehead.

"Children?? As in the plural form of child??" I asked. He smiled.

"Yeah." The ocean air blew my hair into my face and he reached up to push it off my forehead. "You're going to miss it," he told me so I turned around to face the water again.

We watched the final flecks of pink, yellow and orange move over the surface of the water as the sunlight seeped behind the evening clouds. Dusk settled over the beach and he came around and stood in front of me. He took my face in his hands then leaned over and kissed me. It was, and probably still is, one of the softest and most gentle kisses I've ever received. It wasn't sensual but it was full of love. I don't know why but afterward we both smiled. As if the kiss was the last chapter at the end of a very good book. I knew I would always hold a special place in his heart just like he knew he would always hold a special place in mine. And maybe in another life he could give me everything he was giving Lilah now.

"That's our last kiss," I said as I looked up to him. "Isn't it?"

"Yeah," he said softly. "For now."

"For now??" I asked, hopeful. He smiled again and put his hands on my waist.

"Well, remember we said if we were single at fifty, we were going to marry one another."

"I might be able to make that happen," I said as I laid my arms on his shoulders.

"Oh yeah?"

"Sure."

"Does it involve a magic wand??" he asked.

"And your Batman decoder ring."

"I should probably get that back from Terrence then."

"Probably," I said and we both laughed.

Amityville

Adrian

The following morning, I poked my head around the corner into Jenny's office.

"I heard you wanted to talk to me?"

"Water cooler talk?" she asked.

"Karen."

"Uh-huh. Come in here and shut the door." I walked inside her office as I motioned to myself.

"Am I in trouble?"

"Yes," she said. "Sit down."

Shit.

"How is Estela doing?" she asked.

"Good, I guess."

Please God, tell me Jenny does not know Lora and I left Serena and Estela with Ari while we went to the Hamptons.

"You guess??" she asked. "Have you not seen her lately?"

"Uh, well, I see her when I go over to Lorelei's," I said. "She's happy if that's what you're asking."

"That's not what I'm asking," she said. "I was just wondering why you and Lorelei left her and Serena with Ari while you both skirted off to the Hamptons?"

Shit.

"Jenny, it's not what you think."

"Tell me what it is, then."

"I took Lora out for dinner for her birthday," I explained.

"What part did you miss when I told you not to sleep with her??" Jenny asked.

How could she possibly know Lora and I slept together? Shit.

"Why do you think we slept together?" I asked.

"Adrian," she said. "I have always wondered how you manage to fool so many people with your intimidation and bullshit when you can't even look me in the eye if I ask you a pointed question. Maybe you and Lorelei shouldn't have had a conversation about it in her kitchen."

"Shit," I said. This time out loud. How could I so easily forget Lorelei's house was bugged? Better yet, how could she forget??

"What is it with you lately?" she asked. "You're not thinking."

"I know."

"Is it Lilah? Because she's the only thing that's changed in your life."

"She's the only thing that's changed in my life??" I asked, unbelievingly. "Everything has changed in my life, Jenny. The woman I adored, loved, trusted, needed…is gone."

"Nana," Jenny verified.

"Yeah, and then there's the woman I've loved my whole life here…" I pointed down. "Right here in Amityville."

"Lorelei."

"Yeah. And in Woodlawn, a woman I never thought I could love the way I love her."

"Lilah."

"Yeah. Then, I finally get to meet my son and all I can do is think about what my life and his would have been like if I'd met him a lot sooner."

"Yeah," Jenny said as she leaned back in her chair.

"And now I have an even bigger problem."

"Lay it on me," she said. I leaned forward with my elbows on my knees.

"I had a woman approach me at Alannah's boutique when I took Lora there to buy her a birthday dress." I hesitated and Jenny motioned for me to go on. "She asked me if Lorelei was mine," I said. "I don't know who she was. Never seen her before in my life. When I told her yes, she asked me if Gianni knew."

"I'm guessing Carlotta Lanza," Jenny said. "She lives there. "Ring a bell?"

"Lanza," I repeated. "An Empire family."

"You got it," Jenny said. She leaned forward on her desk. "Angeline Vallario's sister."

"Shit."

"Yeah, that's what I'm thinking, too."

"Damn it," I said as I ran my hands through my hair. "Sam called while we were at Angelic."

"You went to Angelic??" Jenny asked as she leaned over her desk toward me.

"It's where Lora wanted to go," I told her.

"I honestly thought you were smarter than that."

"It wasn't a big deal," I said. "Everything is under control. Just trust me."

"Adrian," she said. "You are pushing me further than you've ever pushed me before. Do you realize that??"

"Yeah."

"What do you think I should do about it?" she asked. I shook my head.

"Fire me??" I asked as I looked up to her.

"Right, like that's going to help." She looked over my head, bit her lip. She was thinking. "Have you seen the paperwork that came with Stef when we took him?"

"Is it in the Montenari case file?"

"Yeah."

"No," I said. "I just asked Karen to retrieve it for me. That's when she told me you wanted to talk to me."

"You just asked her for it??" Jenny asked appalled. "Don't you think you should have asked for it before now?"

"Well, yeah. But I have everything I need in *my* case file. I didn't think there was anything relevant in the Montenari one. I mean, you told me pretty much everything about it I needed to know."

"Do you know what's in that file?"

"Uh…not to sound sarcastic…but yes, Jenny. Yes, I do. That's why I asked for it." She smiled. "What?? How the hell am I supposed to know exactly what's in it if I haven't seen it yet??"

"Stef has two birth certificates," Jenny said as she held up her fingers "The original one states his name as Stefan Antonio Vallario. You want to tell me what the other one says??"

"It says Stefan Antonio Bennett," I told her.

"Oh??? Wow, you must be psychic! I thought you hadn't seen it yet."

"I haven't. Lora told me about it."

"Let me guess, while you were lying in bed in the afterglow."

"Come on, Jenny." I took a deep breath and blew it back out. She motioned for me to go on. "Roslyn did an application for correction of Stef's birth certificate soon after he was born. I guess she kept the original one along with it."

"Well, when I first got all the papers from the Montenaris, which, by the way, were in perfect order, thanks to Roslyn."

"Roslyn left all Stef's important documents with the Montenaris to make sure I would get them," I said thoughtfully.

"Well, you're his father. Anyhow, I went through it this weekend just perusing it to see if anything stuck out to me that might help with your case."

"And?"

"There is a manila envelope in it with birth certificate printed on the front. I'd never thought to look inside because it seemed pretty cut and dried but I opened it this weekend. There was a folder with two pockets inside. On one side is the birth certificate with the Vallario name on it. Roslyn labeled it Vallario. On the other side which she labeled Bennett was nothing. It was gone. Someone took it out of the folder before we gained possession of it, probably even before the Montenaris gained possession of it."

"Gianni."

"Gianni," she confirmed.

"So, how did he get ahold of Stef's papers? Lora would have never given him access to them."

"He's a clever man. I'm sure he figured it out."

"But he didn't know about the correction," I said. "At least I can't imagine he did."

"I'm sure he was shocked to see the birth certificate with your name on it and wanted to verify it so he took it."

"Verify it with whom??" I asked. Jenny was silent while she waited for me to catch up. "Ah...Vital Statistics."

"Yes, but does the Department of Vital Statistics keep paper copies anymore? Do they even have the original one with the Vallario name on it??"

"I'm sure they have the correction application filed somewhere."

"They do," Jenny said. "That is verifiable."

"But not by the general public. Only government authorities."

"Like us," she said.

"So, all of Stef's paperwork with the exception of the corrected birth certificate has Vallario on it even though it's not his real name."

"Correct."

"So, now Gianni knows for certain I am Stef's father even though Stef has his name."

"Bingo."

"The original birth certificate with the Vallario name on it must have disappeared from Vital Statistics," I said thoughtfully. "Who could make that happen?" I asked but I already knew the answer. "Roslyn."

"I love it when you answer your own questions," Jenny said. I smiled. "But here's another question."

"What's that?"

"In order to file a correction for a birth certificate you have to be related to the child. Some states require one signature. Some two. New York requires two." She held up two fingers. "Roslyn signed for Lorelei probably because, at the time, Lorelei was a minor."

"Makes sense."

"Guess who signed for your side of the family?"

"I have no idea."

"Elizabeth Montenari," Jenny told me.

"Isn't she the current registrar of Vital Statistics?" I asked. "Or did she die?"

"She should have died," Jenny said and laughed. "She's got to be at least ninety. But no, she's still alive and still the registrar."

"So, she signed her part…" I hesitated. "…as the registrar *and* for my side of the family?"

"You got it."

"Isn't that illegal??" I asked.

"Not unless she's not your family."

"Well, of course, she's not my family," I said. I thought for a moment. "That's why Sam put Stef with the Montenaris when he sent him away."

"Logical conclusion to come to," Jenny said. "The Montenaris are Stef's supposed family."

"How are the Montenaris my family??" I asked.

Then, I thought, Ana. The spirit of the little girl who wouldn't leave me alone. Family.

"I gotta go," I said standing up.

"Why?" Jenny said as she stood up with me. She came around her desk. "Where are you going?"

"I have to find out Ana's last name," I said as I opened her office door.

"Who is Ana?" she asked, perplexed.

"She's the little girl who won't leave me alone," I told her as I walked backward.

"What??" Jenny asked. "What are you talking about?"

"Just trust me."

"I've never trusted you."

"Trust me now." I pointed at her. "Because I think I just figured it out."

"Adrian!" she called after me. "Don't you go and do something I can't get you out of. I'm warning you." Terrence laughed as I ran past his desk.

"When has a warning ever meant anything to Adrian?" he asked.

"Damn it," Jenny said.

I ran into the Inn and slammed the door behind me. I don't know why but I was immediately drawn to Nana's old Victorian desk. I started opening all the tiny drawers across the back of it. There must have been at least twenty of them. One of them had pictures of Nana as a child. I knew this because she had shown them to me and Tiffany many times. Tiffany walked out of the kitchen and over to me.

"What are you looking for?" she asked.

"Remember all those pictures Nana had of herself when she was little?"

"Yeah."

"Where are they?"

"I have no idea," Tiff said. "Why?"

"Aren't they in one of these drawers??"

"Maybe. What is going on?"

"I don't know," I admitted as I leaned back in the desk chair.

I ran my hands through my hair. Maybe I was wrong. I was new to this listening inside your mind thing. How did I know what was legitimate and what wasn't?? How did I know whether one thought followed by another random thought had any kind of valid correlation? Mary Angela used to tell me one day I was going to realize there aren't any coincidences in this world, only the magic we carry inside ourselves.

"You're acting weird," Tiff told me as she walked over to the rolling globe. "Want a drink?"

"Sure."

I decided then and there I wasn't going to tell Tiffany about my suspicions regarding Ana. It would make me sound like a crazy person and maybe one day I would be like Lorelei and not care if I sounded like a crazy person but for right now, I did.

"You're becoming Lilah and Isabel," I told Tiff when she handed me my drink.

"Why, thank you!" She said and laughed.

"Next thing I know you'll be handing me a cigarette."

"Ha."

"Liquor is not the answer to every problem you have, you know," I warned. She winked at me as she walked away.

"Of course, it is," she said.

Lorelei

Adrian didn't go with me when I went for my third treatment. He never said he couldn't go. I just didn't ask him. I knew he wanted to go back to Woodlawn to be with Lilah. I'm guessing the sooner he got back to her the sooner he could ease his guilt over us. Ari once told me when she was having an affair with a married man, she felt no guilt whatsoever. I'm not sure if what I'm feeling is guilt. It's not regret because I don't believe you should ever regret anything you do. You always learn *something* from it. What I wanted to learn now was that I was right about my body - that it preferred actual sexual intercourse over a needleless syringe. Dr. Sherrill walked into the exam room.

"Well, hello Miss. Lorelei!" she said cheerfully.

"Hi," I said.

"Are you ready to try this again?"

"I'm ready," I said.

And then, the tears came. It wasn't because I hadn't gotten pregnant yet even though I'm sure that is what Dr. Sherrill thought. She sat down on the stool in the room and rolled over to me, put her hand on my knee. It reminded me of the day Dr. Lee told me I was pregnant with Stef. When she said, 'Adrian isn't for you.'

"Remember when I told you we might have to do this more than once?"

"Yes," I said. "But I didn't think it would take this long."

"Well, you know I told you it might not happen right away. The odds of a woman getting pregnant from the first procedure is unlikely. It could've happened given your and Adrian's..."

"But it didn't," I interrupted as I wiped a tear from my cheek.

"No," she said. "It didn't but that doesn't mean it won't happen at all."

"It didn't happen last time either."

"Once again," she said. "It doesn't mean it won't happen at all." She hesitated. "I don't usually delve into my patient's private lives. If they want to talk about it, I do. But I never ask questions. Not usually. But I have a question for you. You don't have to answer it if you don't want."

"Okay."

"Why aren't you and Adrian doing this the conventional way? It seems he cares about you greatly. I would go as far as saying it appears he loves you."

"He does love me."

It was at that point I wanted to tell Dr. Sherrill about what had happened over the weekend but I couldn't. Adrian and I had agreed not to tell anyone and pretend it never happened. I've never understood what happens with me and Adrian when we're together. It's like there is a magnetic force that pulls us together whenever we're close. Like it's not even our choice. Like the Spirits are doing me a favor. One I didn't even ask for.

"So, why not?" Dr. Sherrill asked.

"It's complicated," I admitted.

"Do you want to tell me why?" I took a deep breath.

"Adrian was my first love," I said. "We fell in love in high school. We lost our virginity to each other."

"Hence your obvious emotional connection," she surmised.

"Yeah, but we were separated. I don't really want to get into all that."

"Okay."

"Anyhow, after we were separated, I found out I was pregnant."

"Your first pregnancy."

"Yes, and I had Stef."

"Ah, another reason for the emotional connection," Dr. Sherrill said.

"Yes." I looked down, noticed my hands were shaking so I locked my fingers together, hoping Dr. Sherrill wouldn't notice.

"Another personal question," she said. I nodded. "Is he married to someone else?"

"No," I said. "Engaged."

"Ah…and might I ask why the two of you decided to do this?"

"Because I asked him to," I told her.

"Why?"

"I have to go back a few years," I said.

"I have all afternoon," she said and smiled. "You're my last appointment today."

"After Adrian and I were separated I had Stef and then I went to college and ended up overseas."

"Why did you go overseas?"

"I've always been intrigued by other languages," I said tearfully. "And I wanted a degree in linguistics." I sniffed and she reached behind her and grabbed a tissue, handed it to me. "I had an opportunity to get my undergraduate degree and my masters if I went overseas for the advanced program." I wiped my eyes then my nose. "I wanted to teach people about how all languages fit together. How we all speak the same language, just in a different way."

"Oh wow," Dr. Sherrill said. "That's amazing."

"Anyhow, while I was overseas Adrian finished his undergraduate degree and became a DEA agent."

Dr. Sherrill pushed her chair back a little and widened her eyes.

"Adrian is a DEA agent?" she asked.

"Yes," I said and dabbed my eyes again.

"You think he could talk to my children about the dangers of drugs?" she asked and laughed. I laughed, too.

"I'm not sure he'd give a good speech," I said. "He smokes pot almost every day."

"Maybe not," she agreed.

"When his Nana died, he came back here and well, we got back in touch."

"And decided to have a baby," she concluded. I nodded. "What does his fiancée think of this?"

"He hasn't told her," I admitted.

"Oh, wow."

"I know, right?"

"Why hasn't he told her?"

"I don't know," I said. "It has something to do with his current case and he's not allowed to talk about it."

"Understandable. But, forgive me for asking, what does you and him having a baby have to do with his current case?"

"You have all afternoon?" I asked and laughed. She looked at her watch.

"I have until four," she said. "Then we need to do your procedure and I have to go pick up my son from basketball practice."

"Stef…"

"Your and Adrian's son?" she confirmed.

"Yeah. He isn't with me and I can't tell you why."

I brought my hands to my face and began crying again. Dr. Sherrill rolled back closer to me and put her hand on my knee. She didn't say anything for a few moments and my cries turned into a sob. She stood up and put her arms around me.

"Oh Lorelei," she said. "I'm so sorry."

"I…" I started. "I wanted another baby with Adrian." I sniffed and brought the tissue to my face again. "I ask him and he agreed."

"Because he can't say no to you," she said and smiled.

"Did he tell you that?" I asked looking up.

"He told me the day you guys first came in," she said. "That it was a sickness." She laughed.

"Oh, that's right," I said. "He always says that."

"*Has* he ever said no to you?" Dr. Sherrill asked curiously. I thought for a moment.

"I think he did say no once and I threw a brass candelabra at him."

"That's a good reason to never say no again," she said and smiled.

"Yeah," I said. "He still has a scar on his forehead."

"Oh wow," she said. "You actually hit him?"

"Yep."

"And he didn't break up with you after that?" she asked.

"Surprisingly, no."

"He must *really* love you."

"Just not enough," I said and looked down.

"What is that supposed to mean?"

"He's in love with someone else," I told her.

"But you're still in love with him," she concluded. I nodded and begin to cry again.

"I love him so much," I sobbed. "I thought...I thought...I wasn't."
I brought the tissues to my face once more. "But then I saw him and the
feelings...they...they just came back." Dr. Sherrill took a deep breath.

"Does he know this?" she asked. I shrugged.

"Maybe," I admitted. "I haven't verbally told him I'm in love with
him. He knows I love him but I'm not sure he knows how much I love
him, that I'm still in love with him."

"Don't you think you should tell him?"

"What if..." I paused. "What if he...I mess up what he has
with Lilah?"

"Who's Lilah?"

"His fiancée."

"How would that mess up his relationship with her?" Dr. Sherrill
asked.

Our past weekend at Angelic Manor flooded my mind once again.
I've heard people say when you're drunk you tell the truth about
your life. Did that apply to what happened between me and Adrian?
Did he make love to me because he was drunk and that was what he
truly wanted?

"What if when I do, he realizes he's still in love with me, too?"

"Is that a hope or a worry?" she asked and smiled.

"A little of both, I guess."

"I think you should tell him" she said. "His reaction isn't your
responsibility. You realize this, do you not?"

"I know he loves Lilah," I said. "He's told me how much he
loves Lilah."

"I think the human heart can hold a lot more love than you're
giving it credit for."

"You can't be in love with two people at the same time," I pointed out.

"No," she agreed. "But you can love two people equally."

"You think he might love me just as much as he loves Lilah?" I asked.

"What I think is that he loves you a lot more than you believe."

"I'm here!"

It was Ari. She always said that when she came through my back door as if I'd invited her over and was expecting her at any moment. I was in the kitchen with all the ingredients for my Cocoa-Mint Brownies spread across the counter.

"Whatcha making Layla girl?"

This was Ari's nickname for me. She said everyone had a nickname for me except her. Most people got my name wrong the majority of the time but my mother had insisted it be pronounced Lora-lay not Lora-lie. She said everyone in the states had it all wrong. I seriously doubted her claim until I went to Spain where they do, in fact, pronounce it Lora-lay. Obviously when I was there, I was thrilled everyone called me Lora-lay without me having to correct them. Hence, Ari lovingly called me Layla.

"Would you stop calling me that?" I asked as I stirred the brownie batter. "Cocoa-mint brownies." She walked over and grabbed me around my neck, kissed my cheek, then stuck her finger into the batter. I smacked her hand.

"I love those," she said. She stuck her finger into her mouth.

"Stop it!"

"Why are you in such a bad mood?"

"I'm not in a bad mood."

"Yes, you are," she said as she hopped up onto the counter beside me.

"Why are you here?" I asked as I turned around to preheat the oven.

"See? Perfect example of you being in a bad mood." I turned around to face her.

"You are way too cheerful this morning."

"Why shouldn't I be?" she asked. "It's a new day full of promise and hope."

"You slept with a new man last night," I resolved. She grinned and widened her eyes.

"Maybe."

"You did."

"Okay," she said jumping down off the counter. "You just need a hug." I gave in and let her hug me. I tried not to cry but I couldn't hold back the tears. When I sniffed, she pulled back from me and put her hands on my shoulders.

"Spill it," she said. I bit my lip but I said nothing. "Tell me."

"Dr. Sherrill told me Adrian loves me," I told her. Tears rolled down my cheeks.

"When was this?"

"My last treatment."

"Well, Adrian does love you," she confirmed. "I think that's more than obvious."

"Not like that," I said. "He loves Lilah."

"Yeah, he loves her, too."

"That's what Dr. Sherrill told me," I said as I reached up to wipe away my tears.

"And this is a problem why??" she asked. I pulled away from her.

"I can't tell you," I said as I walked over to the refrigerator. I pulled out a beer and handed it to her. She stared at me but she took the beer and grabbed the bottle opener off the side of the fridge.

"Do I want to know why you have beer in your refrigerator?" I didn't answer. "Ah…Adrian." She held up her beer and looked at it then took a taste. "Gross. What the hell is this?"

"I don't know," I said. "Some weird beer he likes. Give it to me. I'll drink it. Have some wine." She handed it to me and I took a swallow. When I turned up my nose, Ari laughed.

"See?"

"Okay," I said and smiled. "Yeah. This is going down the sink."

"That's better," she said. "I haven't seen you smile for a while, Layla girl."

"Would you stop calling me that???"

"Why? I've been calling you that forever," she said. "And now, suddenly, you don't like it?"

"It sounds too much like Lilah," I admitted. Ari pointed to me.

"Aha! Finally, the truth."

I leaned back against the counter and the temperature timer on the stove went off so I turned around and poured the brownie batter in the pan, stuck it in the oven.

"Lilah sounds like…"

"An angel that just descended from heaven," Ari finished.

"Wow," I said. "Thanks, Ari. Way to make me feel shittier than I already do."

"Why do you feel shitty?"

"I don't know," I said as I looked to the ceiling. "You tell me. It just seems like she's perfect."

"I doubt she's perfect," Ari supposed. "She's probably as far from perfect as you can get."

"Why would you say that?"

"I just can't see Adrian with a Miss. Goody Too-Shoes," she said.

"Adrian talks about her like she's the eighth wonder of the world."

"He's in love with her," Ari said. "Of course, he does. But that doesn't mean she's perfect. It just means he…"

"Thinks she's perfect."

"Oh jeez, Lay. Let's change the subject. How was your appointment? You never told me how it went."

"That's when Dr. Sherrill told me Adrian loves me," I told her.

"Other than *that*, how was your appointment?"

"It was an appointment," I said. "Except it's my last one." I pulled a wine glass off the rack under the counter, poured myself a glass from the Pinot Noir Ari had taken off the shelf. "You know this wine is supposed to be for my beef Bourguignon. "

"I'm sure there's plenty more in the cellar," she said. I nodded. "I think you need a new hobby." I scrunched up my nose.

"Why?"

"Because your obsession with having Adrian's baby is taking over your life."

"No, it's not."

"It is."

"IT IS NOT," I insisted as I slammed my wine glass down on the counter. Ari took a step back.

"Okay," she said holding up her hands. "You need to tell me what the hell is going on because this is not the Lorelei I know. This is some mutant woman who's on the verge of losing her mind."

"Wow," I said. "Thanks." I took a deep breath and leaned against the counter again.

"The truth hurts."

"You know how Adrian and I went to Angelic this past week for my birthday?"

"Well, I helped him plan it, against my better judgement."

"Thank you for that."

"Uh-huh."

I held out my hand with the *Love* ring on it.

"Oh, wow," Ari said as she took my hand in hers. "That's beautiful." She looked up to me and smiled. "Wrong finger."

"That's what I said."

"But you're smiling."

"Alannah's," I said. "A Versace dress. Christian Louboutin shoes."

"By the way," she interjected. "Where is my fur coat?"

"It's upstairs."

"Ah…" She held up her pointer finger. "Good to know."

"We went to Jasmin's Bistro for dinner." Ari started counting on her fingers.

"Okay," she said. "I'm up to about two thousand dollars. And you're telling me he doesn't love you?"

"I never said he didn't love me," I said. "He loves me. He just doesn't love me the way I want him to love me."

"You know," she said. "I just got this mental image of Adrian walking a tightrope between you and Lilah. She's sitting on a cloud with a harp and you're on the other side in a slinky red dress."

I picked up an egg out of the carton on the counter and threw it at her. It hit her right between her boobs and she came after me, chased me around the kitchen island until I stopped and turned to her. She stuck her finger in the egg yolk on her shirt and wiped it down my nose and onto my lips.

"Ugh," I said as I backed up. "You're disgusting." I spit into the sink and grabbed a paper towel.

"I love you," she said as she took my paper towel and wiped the front of her shirt. "But seriously, Lay...you've got to chill out with Adrian, okay?"

"We had sex," I blurted out.

Ari stood perfectly still. She stood so still it seemed she was frozen. I knew she was breathing but it didn't look like it. She looked deep into my eyes and tilted her head to the side.

"At Angelic?" she said motioning over her shoulder.

"Yeah."

"Are you screwing with me right now?"

"No," I said. "Why would I be?"

"Because you're losing your goddamn mind, that's why."

"What do you think? I dreamt it or something??" She turned her head from one side to another.

"Did you?"

"No."

"Are you sure?" she asked.

"Yes!! I'm sure." I waited for her to say something else but she didn't. "He told me not to tell you...or anyone else, for that matter."

"Of course, he did," she said as she moved closer to me. She took my hand in hers. "Lorelei, tell me the truth. Did it really happen or are you fantasizing?" I jerked away from her.

"You act like I'm some crazy lunatic or something."

"Eh…"

"Like I would lie to *you*," I said disgustedly. Ari took a deep breath.

"Well, you could be lying to yourself."

"I'm not," I told her.

"Did he use a condom?"

"No. It was kind of spontaneous."

"Were you drunk?" she asked.

"Mm-hmm." She grabbed the bottle of wine and my hand.

"Get your glass," she instructed. "Come on." I took her hand and followed her down the hall to the living room.

"I never use this room, Ari."

"I know but we are today."

"I loved Nonna but I hate this furniture," I said as I looked around. "It's so…."

"Victorian…" Ari finished. She sat down in Nana's old Henry VIII chair and I settled on the velvet settee.

"That chair is extremely uncomfortable," I said, so she moved over to the matching velvet sofa beside me.

"Did you get Adrian drunk and seduce him?" Ari asked.

"No," I said and took a sip of my wine. "Well, we were both drunk but I didn't try to seduce him."

"Did he seduce you?"

"Like he would have to do that," I said.

"Very true," she said. She threw her feet up in front of her on the ottoman. "Before I start the lecture, tell me how many times you did it."

"Why do you assume it was more than once?" She stared at me; eyes wide. "I don't know. We were drunk. I think he felt sorry for me."

"People don't have sex when they feel sorry for each other."

"The magnetic force field, then."

"That is much more believable," she said and took a sip of her wine.

"Does Lilah even know you exist?" Ari asked me.

"Adrian said she wants to meet me."

"Holy shit," Ari said. She slapped her hand on her leg. "I wanna be here for that. Can I be here for that?"

"You're sick."

"Don't you want to meet her?" she asked.

"I'm not sure."

"What do you mean 'you're not sure?' You should be dying to meet her."

"Why?"

"To see if you're prettier than she is," she said and laughed. I threw a pillow at her. "What are your feelings about Lilah?"

"What do you mean?"

"Have you talked to the Spirits about her?" she asked.

"No."

"Why the hell not?"

"I don't know," I said. "I guess I just haven't thought about it. I mean, they told me before she and Adrian were in love."

"Don't you want to know more than just that? Or are you afraid of what they might tell you?" She motioned to herself. "Because I would be afraid of what they might tell me."

"I don't know."

"When will you know?" she asked.

"Know what?"

"Whether you're pregnant?"

"Uh…" I thought for a moment. "Well, my period is due on the twenty-fourth but it varies, so a week after that. If I haven't had one by then I'll do a pregnancy test."

"Will you promise me something?" Ari asked.

"What's that?"

"That you're not going to be crazy if you have his baby."

"What are you talking about?"

"I don't think you should broadcast who the father is – in vitro or not."

"I'm not going to do that," I said, shaking my head.

"And don't go all gaga on me and obsess over it, either. Like don't constantly suppose because of the baby Adrian will one day be yours. And please don't treat it like it's a porcelain doll or constantly call him every time it does something cute or is sick or whatever. Be responsible about it."

"Are you done?" I asked, aggravated.

"Yes."

"I told Adrian about Mamma giving Stef his last name." Ari stared at me.

"How did he respond to that information?"

"He was floored."

"In a good way or a bad way?" Ari asked.

"Good, I think."

"Lora!!"

Ari and I looked at one another as the back door opened and closed.

"Knight in shining armor," she said. I rolled my eyes.

I honestly believed he'd scurry off to Virginia as soon as we returned from Angelic. Apparently, I was wrong. Maybe he didn't feel as guilty as I thought.

"We're in the living room," I called back.

Adrian appeared in the archway between the foyer and the living room, propped his hand against the wall beside him. He was wearing holey jeans and a gray and black Chanel sweater with PARIS written across the chest, interlocking C's across his six-pack. He pushed the sleeves of the sweater up his arms. He smelled like the inside of a florist's shop. You know that green smell, the one you always want to capture but can never find?

"Hello, lover," Ari said.

"You told her, didn't you?" he asked me as he ran his hand through his hair.

"I…" I started. He looked over to Ari.

"She told you, didn't she?"

"She's my best friend!!" I said, trying to defend myself.

"The **Love** ring is beautiful," Ari said. "I knew it would happen. I told you it would happen."

"Holy cow," he said as he turned and walked back toward the kitchen. "Beer??"

"In the refrigerator door," I called back to him.

"More than one?" he shouted.

"Yep."

I heard the refrigerator door close and he appeared at the archway to the living room again with a beer in his hand.

"You smell like the Garden of Eden," Ari told him. "Has anyone ever told you that?"

"I'm not kidding, Ari," he said.

"So serious," she said. "Jeez, Adrian. Of course, I'm not telling anyone. How long have we been friends?"

"Too long," he said. He took a sip of his beer.

"Why are you wearing a Chanel sweater?" she asked him. He brought his hands to his chest and looked down.

"It's my Halloween costume," he said facetiously. "I'm going as a Chanel runway model."

"Oh, ha-ha." Ari laughed. "You're funny." Adrian laughed, too.

"It was in my dresser drawer."

"Nana," I explained.

The oven alarm went off and Rajah sneaked in. At least he thought he sneaked in. He often did, then appeared out of nowhere and scared the living daylights out of me. Even so he always made amends. Now he majestically slipped around the corner behind the sofa.

"Will you get that?" I asked Adrian.

"Yeah."

"Brownies??" he shouted as he walked back toward the kitchen. "Are they for me?"

"Of course," I called back. They weren't because I didn't even know he was still in Amityville but he didn't need to know that.

"Ah!!" I heard him say. "Mint brownies. My favorite!"

Ari winked at me and I rolled my eyes. Rajah leapt onto the back of the sofa and rubbed against the back of Ari's head. She nearly jumped out of her skin.

"Holy shit!" she exclaimed as she reached around to pet him. She rubbed her hand over his head and he hopped down beside her. "Rajah!! You scared me to death, you evil cat."

It almost appeared as if Rajah were smiling. He was smart and he loved playing jokes on people. Usually me. When Adrian came back into the living room, he had a half-eaten apple in his hand. He walked over to me and kissed the top of my head.

"You're amazing," he told me. "You made my favorite brownies when you didn't even know I was coming over here."

"Seriously?" I asked as I looked up to him. "You think I didn't know you were coming?" He smiled and shrugged.

"I should know better by now."

"You should," I told him. He looked to Ari.

"If Lora told you about what happened at Angelic, she also told you about telling me Stef's last name. Didn't she?" Ari nodded and Adrian motioned across his mouth with his fingers.

"Zip it," he said. "That is confidential information that could affect us in a negative way."

"Do you know how long I've known Stef has your last name?" Ari asked.

"I'm serious, Ari."

"I know!!" she yelled at him.

"Well, don't yell," Adrian said. "Just be conservative in your thoughts with this information."

"I've been conservative in my thoughts with this information for years," she told him.

"I can't believe you didn't tell me before now," Adrian said to Ari. He looked over to me. "I can't believe neither one of you told me before now."

"How were we supposed to give you this information?" Ari asked. "Carrier pigeon? Through a secret courier service? Because no one ever knew where you were."

"You know where I am right now," Adrian said smartly.

"Well, yeah, but for the last ten years you've been…" Ari stumbled for the correct word.

"…incognito," I finished.

"Yeah," Ari said. "That."

"That's the life I've chosen," he said as he leaned up against the doorframe. He took a bite of his apple. "It's what I do."

"Why don't you quit and just be a piano teacher or something?" I asked.

"Me?" He motioned to himself. "A piano teacher?? You think that would fulfill the need I have for making the world a better place?"

"One piano at a time," Ari commented.

Woodlawn

Adrian

I had been back in Woodlawn for three days since my drunken deba-cle with Lorelei and all I could think about was what had happened between us. I couldn't think about either of my cases. I couldn't think about me and Lilah. I couldn't even make love to Lilah.

I have never in my life not been able to get it up. Ever. Lilah told me not to worry about it, that all men had this problem every now and then. I told her, 'maybe some men, but not me.' She laughed and told me it sucked getting older but I knew the only way I was going to have any peace in my life ever again – and be able to get it up - was to talk through what had happened with me and Lora with someone else.

Most times talking to Tiffany put my mind at ease when I had a problem. She understood me but I'd already talked to her about this so I knew how she felt. Talking to her about it again would only generate another lecture and I didn't need another lecture. I needed understand-ing. Talking to a woman is a different kind of therapy anyhow. Talking to another guy usually involves less drama, if any drama at all. It's just facts, questions, and answers. Direct questions. Straight up answers.

I have never had a best friend. Ever. But Isaac was about as close to a best friend as I'd ever had. Isaac was logical and level-headed and what he said always made sense. It surprised me sometimes because guys his age usually don't make any sense at all. They are usually caught up in girls and partying and how they can get out of whatever it is they are supposed to be doing. Isaac did those things but he didn't let it overcome his rational thinking. Isaac was different. Tiffany said he had an old soul.

"Hey man," I said when he answered the phone.

"Hey," he said. "What's up?"

"What's the chance you can meet me at the diner for lunch today?" I asked him.

"Sure. Is everything okay?"

"Maybe but don't tell your Mom or Lilah you're coming, please."

"Okay. No big deal. You want me to come now? I can meet you in about thirty minutes."

"Yeah. That's good."

I went back and forth inside my head about the two ways this conversation could go. Isaac could understand and somehow help me get through the mess I'd gotten myself into or Isaac could tell me what an asshole I was and then tell Isabel everything I'd said. Somehow, I was betting on him understanding. He was sitting in a booth at the back of the diner when I got there. I walked over and sat down across from him.

"I don't think I've ever seen you upset," he said. "But you look upset."

"I'm not upset."

Lexie, a girl from my World Studies class at school, walked over with an order pad in her hand.

"Oh hey, Tristan!" She reached down to hug me and I let her. People still called me Tristan. It didn't bother me. They'll get it right eventually. "Lisa and Trace told me you were back here! Are you here for good?"

"For now."

"Wow, you know I have a hard time not thinking of you as Tristan." She laughed. "Can I still call you Tristan?"

"If you want."

Isaac raised his eyebrows and chuckled. Lexie leaned over close to my ear but, apparently, that wasn't good enough because she shoved me over and sat on the edge of the booth beside me. "You're doing undercover work now, aren't you?"

"Something like that." She widened her eyes.

"Is it here??"

"Uh…I'm not really allowed to talk about my cases." I motioned to Isaac. "This is Isaac, by the way. Isaac, Lexie."

"We've met," Isaac said but Lexie didn't acknowledge his presence.

"You know," she said to me. "I've never known anyone who did undercover work. It's cool, right?"

"Sometimes."

"You should definitely play piano or something on the side. Like… uh…" She snapped her fingers. Now she acknowledged Isaac. "Who is it?" Isaac raised his eyebrows. "The famous piano guy?"

"Uh…" Isaac pondered.

"The composer??" Lexie asked impatiently.

"Mm…Mozart??" Isaac answered. She snapped her fingers again. "Yes!"

"I'm not quite that talented." She bumped her shoulder into mine.

"Yes, you are! I heard you play at the talent show."

"Thanks."

"So, you're dating Vonnie's mom, right?" I looked to Isaac.

"Yes."

"You know she kicked her husband out. Was it because of you?"

"Uh…that's kind of a personal question," I said. She leaned a little closer to me.

"Did you know she's going to have a baby?"

"I did."

"Is it yours?"

"Also, a personal question," I pointed out and Isaac laughed again.

"Lexie!" a guy from the kitchen called. "Get over here!" She stood up.

"I'm coming!" she called back.

"Sorry," she said. "I gotta go but we'll talk soon. Okay?"

"Yep. Can we get two beers?"

"Just water," Isaac called after her.

"Oh sorry," she said. "Of course."

"Wow," Isaac said when she walked away. "You're like a local celebrity."

"Apparently."

"So, tell me what's going on."

"I…uh…" I hesitated. "Okay. I'm just going to be completely frank with you." Isaac raised his eyebrows.

"Okay."

"My high school girlfriend is living in Amityville again."

"You've seen her?"

"I've talked to her," I told him.

"Name?"

"Lorelei. She came to Nana's funeral."

"Ah."

"We kind of started seeing each other…"

"Whoa…" he said holding up his hand. "What??"

"That was probably the wrong way to say it. Not romantically. Just like catching up." Lexie brought our drinks.

"Food?" she asked.

"In a minute," I said and she walked away. "But Lorelei is kind of still in love with me, I think."

"Wow."

"Look, Isaac. I'm not going to get mushy on you or anything but you're the closest thing to a best friend I've ever had." He smiled.

"Aw…I like you too, Adrian."

"I need to confide something in you," I said. "I need you to promise me no matter how shocked you are that you won't tell anyone else."

"Okaay…"

"I love Lorelei."

"Okay."

"One day you are going to fall in love with someone – like really fall in love and either you know what I mean right now or you don't. If you don't know what I mean then it hasn't happened yet. Ideally it's the same girl you lose your virginity with because you shouldn't have sex with a girl you don't love."

"Okay, Dad." I took a deep breath.

"You know what I mean."

"Yes."

"Lilah is that girl for me."

"You lost your virginity with Lilah???"

"No!!"

"Well, you're not being clear here." I sighed.

"Okay, I lost my virginity with Lorelei. Not that it matters but we've kind of gotten off track."

"You're the only one talking," he reminded me.

"Right. So, the only two women I've ever loved – been *in love* with - are Lorelei and Lilah. I still love Lorelei. I am not *in* love with her. Does that make sense?"

"Perfect."

"Okay – so, I lost Lorelei and I don't want to get into that right now but ever since I saw her at the funeral, well, she's the type of person you can just pick up where you left off – no matter how long it's been. And I don't mean the sex…just the friendship we had, however many years ago it's been."

"Okay." Isaac shifted in the booth. "I feel like I might need that beer after all."

"You might." I motioned to Lexie and she walked over. I pointed at Isaac. "Beer." She held out her hand.

"I.D?"

"Lexie," I interrupted. That's all I had to say. She walked over to the bar and came directly back with a beer for Isaac.

"You owe me one," she said to him. I shook my head.

"Anyhow," I continued. "I didn't know that then, but apparently, when Lorelei and I separated back then, she was pregnant." I thought that would shock Isaac but it didn't so I kept talking. "That's not really relevant here but it's a factor. Kind of."

"Just to be clear," Isaac said. "Your baby?" I nodded.

"I did something I can't undo."

"What did you do?"

"Lorelei and I made a decision and I can't undo it." I stopped and Isaac just watched me. "She lost Stef."

"Who's Stef?"

"Our son."

"Wait," he said. "She lost him?? Did he die?"

"No. It's a long story but suffice it to say that she doesn't have custody of him right now."

"Why not? What did she do?"

This was a lot more complicated than I thought. At least trying to explain it to Isaac was a lot more complicated than I thought.

"She didn't do anything." I hesitated. "She went overseas for school and she got pregnant."

"So, she has two kids? Yours and someone else's?"

"Yes." I hesitated. "And now, she has another little girl I think she's getting ready to adopt but that is also irrelevant."

"She must love children," Isaac commented.

"Seems that way, huh?" I hesitated. "I can't get into the details but she has a very close-knit family. Strict. Lots of rules."

That was an understatement but it would have to suffice for now.

"Are you saying she doesn't have either of her kids?"

"No," I said. "She has her daughter, Serena, and the little girl, Estela."

"Serena is the one who's not yours?" He took a sip of his beer.

"Yeah, and the fact she doesn't have Stef with her has been…well, fairly debilitating."

"Is she, like, sick?" Isaac asked. I took a deep breath.

"No," I said shaking my head. "She's just very sad."

"Well, yeah," Isaac said. "I can only imagine."

"Okay, I'm just going to say it."

"Alright."

"Lorelei wanted another baby and I have the ability to give it to her."

"Any man has the ability to give it to her," Isaac commented. "I can give it to her."

"Ha." Sometimes Isaac was so logical it was funny.

"Is she pregnant?" he asked. "Is that what you're telling me?"

"No."

"Okay," he said. "I am totally confused but I'm hoping you're going to clear all of this up for me."

"This is why I asked you to come to lunch." Isaac took another sip of his beer. "She's not pregnant yet but I'm sure she will be any day now."

"Hold up," Isaac said again. "You're sleeping together on a regular basis so she can get pregnant?"

"No," I said.

"Go on."

"Okay. So, Lorelei's birthday was back in…well, it doesn't matter… and I promised her I'd take her out to dinner for her birthday but we didn't go because of everything that's been happening with my case here."

"Taking an old girlfriend who is still in love with you out to dinner for her birthday when you're engaged to another woman sounds perfectly logical to me."

"Are you being facetious?"

"Yep." He pointed to himself. "Is it my turn to talk or yours?"

"You."

"Well, given I have limited information right now I'm wondering what the hell you were thinking while you were in Amityville and

Lilah was here having a nervous breakdown over you." I could tell he was angry.

"It's not what you think," I said. He scratched his forehead.

"I'm waiting."

"Here's a concise explanation," I said. I laid my hands on the table. "Lorelei wanted a baby with me." I hesitated. "Just me."

"Sounds dangerous."

"We did artificial insemination." Isaac lowered his eyes then looked back up to me.

"Like in a test tube?"

"No. Like I gave her a…."

"Contribution?"

"Yes," I said. "And then they put it inside of her." Isaac fell back against his seat.

"Holy shit."

"Yeah."

"Does Lilah know about all this?'

"No."

"Wow."

"I know."

"Why haven't you told her?"

"Because when I got back to Woodlawn all that stuff was going on with Vonnie. It wasn't the right time and I waited and then it just became harder and harder. I told Lilah I was going back and forth between here and Amityville because of my new case and to work on the Inn….and I was…but part of the time I was with Lorelei."

"You haven't had sex with her at all?"

"Well, that's kind of why I wanted to talk to you."

453

"So, you have." Lexie arrived at the table.

"Food?"

"Uh…bring us two cheeseburgers, fries and more beer," Isaac said, probably because he knew I was temporarily mute.

"Awesome," Lexie said and she took our menus.

"Have you?" Isaac asked as she walked away.

"The birthday dinner," I explained. He pointed to me.

"See? I told you. Dangerous. Is she hot?" I shook my head and smiled. I knew I could count on Isaac for understanding.

"Yeah. Pretty hot." I pointed back to him. "But that doesn't make it okay."

"No," he said.

"So, you see where I'm at right now?'

"I don't envy you, man."

"I love Lilah."

"I know. You don't have to tell me that."

"No. I mean I love her a lot. More than I've ever loved any woman and I have screwed everything up so bad. If I had just told her about it all in the beginning."

"You probably should have talked to her before you gave the contribution."

"No shit. It sounds crazy but it wasn't a well thought out plan. I mean, the insemination thing was but not the birthday thing…but Lora was so down."

"Wait, who?"

"Lora – Lorelei. I call her Lora."

"You should not call her Lora in front of Lilah." He hesitated. "Or Mom."

"I know. Anyhow, we talked about it and just the thought of it made her so happy. I couldn't say no and now she's obsessed with getting pregnant."

"By you?"

"Yeah."

"You know I hate to say this but I'm going to. This almost sounds like that old movie, Fatal Attraction. Like Lorelei is going to kill an animal and string it up on the beach before this is over."

"You and Tiffany definitely belong together," I said and laughed. He smiled.

"Why?"

"Because that is exactly what she said."

"That Lorelei is going to kill an animal??"

"No, just the Fatal Attraction reference."

"Oh."

"So, now when Lorelei gets pregnant, we won't know if it's from the artificial insemination or from when we had sex for her birthday."

"I love birthday sex," he said. "Birthday sex is great."

"Isaac," I said and smiled. "That is not what I need to hear right now."

"Look, man," he said. "I see where you're at with all this. I mean, I'm not Mr. Perfect, you know. Before I fell in love with Tiff, I used to sleep with three or four girls at a time."

"I didn't need to know that." He laughed.

"So, what are you going to do?"

"I don't know," I said. "I just needed to talk to you, to tell you what's going on. What do *you* think I should do?" He took a deep breath and looked to the ceiling then leaned forward with his elbows on the table.

"I think…" He hesitated. "I don't know what I think, honestly. I think I need to think about it some more."

"So, you don't think I should do anything right now?"

"I think I need to think about it some more," he repeated. "Let me think about it."

"Look, I know Lilah is like a second mom to you."

"She is."

"Do you think I'm a horrible person?" I asked.

"No," he said. "Not at all. I think you made a mistake. We all make mistakes. Some are harder to get out of than others…like this one. But I'm going to go home and think about it from your perspective because I can't do that here."

"Okay. Thanks, man."

"Yep."

"Do you think Lilah will hate my guts afterward?"

"After you tell her?" he asked.

"Yeah."

"I'm not sure you should tell her," he said. "I mean, I don't think you should lie to her about it. Maybe you should think about telling her on a need to know basis. Like, what does she need to know right now?"

"You tell me."

"For one, Lorelei's not pregnant so talking about her pregnancy–however it happens -is not necessary at this point. Secondly, there is no need to tell Lilah another woman is in love with you. When she meets Lorelei if she comes to that conclusion herself and wants to talk about it then talk about it but why bring it up if it's not even a question?"

"True."

"And three, well, I'm going back and forth between you telling Lilah…" Lexie brought our cheeseburgers.

"Thanks," I said.

"Anything else?" she asked.

"I think we're good for now."

"Awesome." She turned and went back toward the kitchen.

"What purpose does it serve to tell Lilah you made a mistake??" I ran my hands through my hair.

"I don't know."

"I don't think you should lie to her, that's not what I'm saying. I just…you know how Lilah is."

"Yeah."

"I mean, if you think there's any chance she'd find out on her own then yes, definitely, you should tell her. But, if there's not…why upset her for no reason?"

"You've become your mother," I commented. He smiled.

"Maybe. Let me think about it some more, though. Okay?"

"Yeah."

"But, for now, I think we should put it on the back burner."

"We?" I asked and smiled.

"Yeah," Isaac said. He held up his hand for a fist bump. "We."

Isaac smiled and looked behind me. Tiffany walked over in front of our table.

"What are you doing here??" he asked surprised.

"I missed you," she said as she leaned down and kissed him.

"How did you know I was here?"

"Uh…I saw your Mom's Rover parked out front."

"Ah…"

"What are the two of you up to?" She slid into the booth beside Isaac then took his hand in hers and brought it to her mouth, kissed it.

Lexie came running over to our table.

"Tiffany!" she said. "Oh my…jeez, girl. Stand up, give me a hug!" Tiffany stood up and hugged Lexie. She looked over Lexie's shoulder to me and mouthed 'What?' I shook my head and shrugged. "It's so good to see you," Lexie said. "Are you back here for good, too??"

"Well, for a little while," Tiff answered. Lexie pointed back and forth between Tiffany and Isaac.

"And the two of you are together??"

"Yeah," I answered. "Isaac is off the market." Isaac laughed.

"Holy shit," Lexie said. She pointed her pen at Isaac. "I knew this would happen. Lindsey is going to be devastated."

"Why is it I don't miss the drama of high school?" I asked Isaac and he smiled then looked back to Lexie.

"Lindsey and I broke up months ago," he told her.

"Well, yeah," she said. "I know but it doesn't mean she doesn't still love you."

"I don't think it was love," Tiffany said.

Isaac and I both raised our eyebrows because we know what Lexie doesn't. Tiffany has no issue with putting people in their place if she deems it necessary.

"No?" Lexie said. "What do you think it was?"

"I don't think Lindsey knows what love is, honestly," Tiff said.

"Jesus," Isaac said, somewhat under his breath.

"Oh yeah?" Lexie asked. "Why is that?" Tiffany didn't hesitate.

"Because you can't be in love with one person and sleep with other people at the same time. Can you, Adrian?" Lexie sucked in her breath and I glared at her. "Would you get me a beer, please?" I looked to the ceiling and Lexie walked away. Tiffany was never going to let me forget what I'd done to Lilah.

"Did you have to do that, Tiff?" Isaac asked.

"Why not? Sometimes people need to be educated on relationship rules. It is evident to me there are a lot of girls around Woodlawn who are confused about those rules."

"Relationship rules," Isaac said to me and I narrowed my eyes at him. Lexie brought Tiffany a beer and sat it down on the table in front of her.

"Anything else?" she asked Tiff.

"Hmm…" She reached over and picked up a French fry off Isaac's plate and popped it into her mouth. "What is your soup today?"

"Tomato Bisque," Lexie answered.

"Perfect," Tiff said. "I'll have that and a grilled cheese sandwich."

"Yep," Lexie said and turned but then she stopped. "Hey, Tiff?"

"Hmm?"

"Are you undercover, too?" We all laughed but Lexie didn't seem to think it was funny.

"Not hardly," I offered.

"What do you do?" Lexie asked. "Or are you unemployed??"

"I swim with dolphins," Tiffany answered. Lexie walked back over to our table.

"Like, you work with the dolphins at the dolphin show?"

"I wish," Tiffany said and laughed. "But no. I work at a lab on Long Island. I'm a marine biologist."

"Get out," Lexie said.

"It's true," I told Lexie. "She makes more money than I do." Lexie looked back and forth between us.

"You are twins, aren't you? Or was that just pretend?"

"Lies," Isaac said. "Can't trust anything either of them say. All lies." Tiffany slapped him on his arm and shook her head. She looked back to Lexie.

"We actually are twins," Tiffany said. "But I was born first." Lexie looked confused.

"I'm the only one who can see dead people, though," I added, and Tiffany widened her eyes at me. Isaac looked at me like he thought I'd lost my mind and Lexie's mouth fell open.

"Are you for real?" she asked.

"No," I said. "I'm just kidding. I'm just screwing with you."

"That's not funny, Adrian," Tiffany said as she looked across the table to me. "Not funny at all."

"It was a joke," I said, defending myself. "Jeez, doesn't anyone around here have a sense of humor anymore?"

Lilah

I rarely have hard liquor in my house because Isabel has every liquor known to man at hers. I have never seen another home bar with as much alcohol as the one at Isabel's house. We had two things to talk about at Happy Hour today. McCain and Lorelei. Isabel arrived with raspberry liqueur, vodka, and the banana liqueur she was still trying to get rid of. She came through my back door carrying all of them in her school briefcase. I laughed.

"Why are you carrying all that liquor around in your school bag?" I asked.

"Because Roy told me I couldn't carry open containers of liquor in my car and this was the only thing I had to put them in, plus I have thirty physics tests to grade."

"Since when have you ever listened to Roy?"

"Since he's running radar across the road from my house," she said holding up her bag. "This is the only thing I had to hide it in."

"You don't have any paper bags?" I asked as I sat down at the kitchen table.

"Well, that's kind of obvious, don't you think?" she asked as she plopped everything down on the table in front of me. "Shit."

"What?" I asked as I peered into her bag with her.

"The raspberry liqueur leaked out onto all the kids' tests." I laughed. I couldn't help it.

"I ought to smack you," she said. "It's not funny."

"It is," I said. "Move out of the way and let me handle it."

"What are you doing to do?" she asked as she stepped back. I pulled out all the bottles and sat them on the table. The tests underneath of them were sticky and stained red.

"Shit," she said.

"Okay," I said. "First off, let's separate all of them before they stick together." I peeled half of them apart and handed them to her.

"This would only happen to me," she said as we spread the papers across the kitchen table. Vonnie walked into the kitchen.

"What are ya'll doing?" she asked as she walked to the refrigerator. She grabbed a lime Perrier and came over to the table, looked over my shoulder.

"Isabel spilled raspberry liqueur on all the physics tests, so we have to separate them before they stick together."

"Ya'll are hilarious," Vonnie said and laughed.

"Hey," Isabel said. "Take these bottles and make me a drink."

Vonnie picked them all up and sat them on the counter then went over to corner cabinet to get the shaker. She got ice out of the freezer and put some into the shaker.

"Ready?" Isabel asked.

"Yep," Vonnie said. "Go."

"You know Social Services would probably take us away if they knew you were letting your seventeen-year-old daughter shake cocktails," Ben said as he leaned up against doorway. He was holding a bottle of Wesson oil in his hand.

"Kiss my ass, Ben," Isabel said and he laughed.

"Why do you have my Wesson oil?" I asked him.

"I don't know," he said. "I was cleaning my room."

"You're disgusting," Vonnie said. "You do, too, know why. Misty."

"Shut up, Vonnie," Ben said.

"Who's Misty?" I asked.

"It's not Misty," Ben said. "It's Mistelle."

"She's the biggest hoe at school," Vonnie said. She looked to Ben. "You probably have chlamydia."

"I'm gonna pee in my pants," Isabel managed as she bent over laughing. Ben handed the oil to me.

"Well, I don't want it back," I told him. "Eeww." He laughed.

"Go," Vonnie said to Isabel. "The ice is melting."

"Two ounces of vodka…"

"Hey, hold up," Ben said to Vonnie. "That is way more than two ounces."

"It doesn't matter," she said as he walked toward her. "It's just Isabel. I'm not bartending for Applebee's."

"One ounce of the Raspberry," Isabel continued. "One ounce of the Banana."

"Woo," Vonnie said. "This banana smells like bubble gum."

"I know, right?" I asked. "It smells like Adrian."

"It does," Vonnie agreed.

"Orange Juice," Isabel said. I started wiping the physics tests off with wet paper towels.

"The pink isn't coming off," I told Isabel. "They won't be sticky but they'll be pink." Ben picked one up.

"And smell like raspberries," he said and laughed. Isabel pointed to him.

"Ben, I swear, if you tell anyone about this I will…"

"You will what?" he asked as he opened the refrigerator. "Can I have this beer?"

"Only if it's not the last one," I told him. "Adrian will not be happy if he comes home and you've drank all his beer."

"Shake it, Vonnie," Isabel said. Vonnie shook the shaker over her head and grabbed a martini glass out of the corner cabinet. She poured the contents of the shaker into the glass.

"What's this called?" she asked. "It smells delicious."

"You can have a sip," Isabel said. Vonnie picked up the glass and brought it to her mouth.

"Mmm…"

"It's called a Wet Dream," Isabel said absentmindedly. Vonnie gagged and sprayed everything in her mouth across the room including over all the physics tests.

"Oh my god," she said. "That's so disgusting!!"

"Damn it," Isabel said looking over the tests on the table. "Damn it all to hell. I give up."

"What's wrong, Vonnie?" Ben asked. "You don't swallow?"

"I'm gonna fucking kill you," Vonnie said as she grabbed a pot out of the dish drainer by the sink. She chased Ben into the living room with it in her hand.

"Hey!!" I called. "Knock it off."

"Dirty word jar," Isabel called. I picked up the martini and motioned to Isabel.

"Come on," I said. "Let the tests lay there and dry and then I'll help you grade them. Let's go in the living room and sit down."

"Well," Isabel said as she plopped down on the sofa. I sat down beside her and handed her drink to her. "On another note, I found Miss. Magic. Where's your iPad?"

"It's on the table right there," I said as I pointed to it.

"Wanna see what she looks like?" Isabel asked as she turned it on.

"I don't know. Do I?"

"She has a Facebook page," Isabel said. "And everything is set to public so you can look at it all."

"Who does that?" I asked.

"What?"

"Set everything to public."

"Technologically challenged people like you," Isabel informed me. "Look."

There she was. Lorelei Anastasio Vallario. She was beautiful. She smiled with her eyes. Her long dark hair nearly reached her waist. She was wearing an off the shoulder sweater with tassels around the neckline. You couldn't tell what color because the photo was in black and white. Someone had made her laugh and snapped the photograph. I wondered if it had been Adrian.

She had a lot of photographs Isabel and I scrolled through but no captions so you didn't know the identity of anyone. Two adorable little girls. A best friend, apparently, since there were many pictures of them together. A full moon over the bay. Blooming roses on a trellis. A very large unusual looking cat on top of an antique organ. And the one photograph that did have a caption: Palazzo Cremisi – a red Victorian house with the setting sun behind it.

"Is this her house?" I asked Isabel as I pointed to it.

"Yes."

"Scroll down," I told her. "Let's look at her posts."

There's a full moon tonight!! on a black background. *Do you dare?*

"What does a full moon mean?" I asked Isabel.

"If I was pregnant it would mean I'm going into labor," Isabel said. "But other than that, I have no idea."

Need a little pick-me-up? on a flowered background. *Our all-natural elixirs are made to enhance your weary spirit. Why poison your system with alcohol when my spiritual elixir is truly the answer?*

"Does she not drink?" I asked.

"How would I know?" Isabel said. "Didn't Adrian say she did herbal stuff and shit?"

"She's an apothecarist."

"Is she one of those new age weirdos who doesn't believe in modern medicine?" Isabel asked.

"Maybe," I said. "Keep going."

Selene laid eggs! on a Facebook background of a dove with an olive leaf. I looked over to Isabel.

"A bird?" I asked. She shrugged once more. "What else lays eggs?"

"Uh, lots of things. Birds, snakes, frogs, I don't know.

"You teach biology and you don't know??" I asked looking over to her.

"Well, I know," she said. "But I didn't know you wanted a comprehensive list. Keep going." I She scrolled down further.

Overheard at market: All girls are into astrology now. And all that witch stuff. It's supposed to scare people but I'm not afraid. It's stupid.

Me: You're right. There's no reason to be afraid of witches. We only devour lost souls when there's a full moon at summer solstice.

"Wow," Isabel said.

"What does that even mean?" I asked.

"It means she practices magic."

"What kind of magic?"

"The kind of magic you'd be scared of," Isabel said. "Apparently."

"Nuh-uh," I said and slapped Isabel's arm. "Quit it." She laughed and scrolled down a little further.

"I didn't scroll this far before," she said.

Then, there it was.

> *#tbt – 2007 – Forest Secondary School Junior Prom - Remember this?*

A prom picture with three couples.

> Tagged: *Adrian Bennett, Ariana Acosta, Justin Hill, Terrence Mason, Sharla Johnston*

"That's Terrence," Isabel said as she pointed to his picture.

"And Adrian," I said.

"Oh, my goodness," Isabel said pointing to Adrian. "Look at him. He was so cute. It doesn't even look like he needed to shave." She laughed. "And he's so skinny."

"Are you being serious right now?" I asked as I turned to her.

"Why? You don't think he was cute??"

"Well, of course, I think he was cute," I said. "But he's with her."

"That was over ten years ago," Isabel told me. "Ten years, Lilah. You already knew she was his high school girlfriend. It's a cute picture." I said nothing. "You know I'm right. Aren't I?"

"Yeah," I said begrudgingly. "I guess." I turned to Isabel. "Why doesn't this show up on Adrian's Facebook page?"

"Because you can set up your account so all the things you're tagged in won't show up on your page until you approve them first."

"So, he didn't approve it?" I asked.

"Right."

"But why would he do that? I mean, I know they're still friends. He told me they were."

"Lilah, honey," Isabel said. "You're the reason."

"Why would I be the reason??" I asked as I brought my hand to my chest.

"Because he doesn't want to have to explain it to you and he knows you'll ask."

"Well, now I'm going to ask anyway," I said.

"No, you're not."

"Why not?"

"Because then he'll know you've stalked her page," Isabel told me.

"Oh, wow. You're right."

"Hot pink," she said as she pointed to Lorelei. "Look at that dress. Wonder how she talked Adrian into wearing hot pink?"

"I doubt it was very hard," I said. "I mean, look at her."

"Okay," she said as she laid my iPad in her lap. "We're done. Do you feel better or worse?"

"I don't know."

"You feel better," she said picking up my hand and weaving her fingers through mine. She squeezed them.

"Ow," I said. "You weirdo."

"You feel better because if you hadn't seen her, you'd want to see her, and it would have driven you crazy."

"No," I said. "It would not have driven me crazy. It would've driven *you* crazy."

"Okay," she admitted. "So, it was me."

"Yeah."

"Cheers," she said picking up her martini glass. "To stalking old girlfriends."

"I don't have anything to cheer you with," I said.

"Oh, sorry."

"You know how I told you Adrian wanted us to go to the Inn for summer vacation?"

"Woo!" Isabel said widening her eyes. "We can meet Little Miss. Magic."

"Maybe, but have you asked Tom about it? So, the boys can go, too?"

"I'm sure he'll be fine with it," she said. "He hates me but not them."

"Isabel, Tom does not hate you. He loves you."

"He has a funny way of showing it."

"Are you joking?" I asked. "He wants you back. You just need to behave."

Ben came up behind us and kissed me on the top of my head.

"Yeah, Isabel," he said teasingly. "You just need to behave."

"Shut up, Ben," she retorted.

"I'm going out with Mistelle," he said to me.

"Need some Wesson oil?" Isabel asked as she looked up to him. Ben pointed at her.

"You're hilarious." He looked down to the iPad. "Holy shit. Who is that?"

"That's Adrian's high school girlfriend, Lorelei," I answered.

"Then or now??" he asked.

"Now," Isabel said.

"Damn." He turned. "I'm outta here."

"Well, great," I said. "Just great. My own son thinks Adrian's high school girlfriend is hot."

"He didn't say she was hot," Isabel told me. "He just said 'damn.'"

"That means she's hot."

"Okay," she said, suddenly serious. "Since Ben just left, we need to talk about some important things."

"Like what?"

"Like the whole situation with him and McCain."

"I think I'm just going to let it go, Isabel," I said. "Adrian and I have talked about it."

"Adrian said to let it go?"

"No."

"Well, then, we need to talk about it," she said. I turned to her and laid my hand on her knee.

"Okay," I said. "I have a confession to make."

"Lilah, whenever you lay your hand on my knee it means you've done something bad. What have you done?"

"Promise you won't get mad???" I asked.

"No. I am not promising anything. I am reserving the right to protest."

"Holy cow," I said. I took a deep breath. "Okay. Are you ready?"

"I'm ready," Isabel said as she crossed her arms over her chest.

"I've been talking to McCain." Isabel bit her lip and narrowed her eyes at me.

"And the purpose of this is?" she asked.

"I'm pretty sure he knows."

"He knows what? Like what I think you're saying he knows??"

"Yes."

"Okay," she said as she held up her pointer finger. "Here's the most important question."

"What?"

"Does Adrian know you're talking to him?" I looked down to the floor then back up to Isabel. "He doesn't, does he?" she asked.

"No," I said quietly.

———

I woke in the middle of the night to Adrian tossing and turning in bed. It wasn't just any tossing and turning. He was having a bad dream.

"Stop!" he said out loud as he sat up. He woke himself up so I didn't have to.

"What's wrong?" I asked as I sat up beside him. "Were you having a nightmare?" He ran his hands through his hair and shook his head back and forth.

"Yeah," he said. "I guess so." He fell back against his pillows. "Holy shit." I moved over against him and he put his arm around me. I laid my hand on his chest. His heart was beating so fast.

"What were you dreaming?" I asked. He didn't say anything so I added, "You don't have to tell me if you don't want."

"No, no," he said. "It's not that. I'm just trying to gather my thoughts. I…" He hesitated. "…I was on this road. Like walking. It was a dirt road and it seemed like it was a long time ago."

"When?"

"I don't know," he said. I rubbed my hand across his chest. "Maybe like the twenties or thirties?"

"Okay."

"I look across this field and I see this house burning."

471

"Oh, wow."

"So, I'm running down the road trying to get to it, to help them."
He hesitated and I waited. "I finally got there and there's this man and
woman…that's how I know it was the twenties or thirties, by what they
were wearing."

"Okay."

"It was a huge house with these big columns in the front," he said
holding up his hands to frame it. "Kind of like Tara in *Gone with the
Wind* and it's burning. Fire coming out of all the windows. There is no
way this house is going to be standing for much longer."

"There were people inside? Was the fire department there?"

"A man and a woman were standing outside. I could hear the fire
trucks coming but they weren't there yet. The woman starts telling me
her daughter is inside and pleading with me to go get her. I wanted
to…." He hesitated and looked over to me. "But it was so bad, Lilah.
Like I would have died."

"Yeah."

"It was horrible."

"I'm sorry, baby," I said as I ran my hand over his chest once more.
I patted him and got up.

"Where are you going?" he asked.

"To get you some water."

I went into the bathroom and ran him a glass of cool water and
took it back to him. He drank the whole thing and sat it on his bedside
table then turned to me again.

"The woman started calling the little girl's name and took off
toward the house. I was yelling at her to stop and then I woke up."

"What was her name?"

"Who?" Adrian asked.

"The little girl?"

"Giovanna."

"That's a beautiful name."

"It is," he agreed. He thought for a moment. "It's weird but I feel like I should know who this little girl was."

"You have no idea?" I asked.

"None," he answered.

Adrian

When I woke the next morning, my throat was on fire. Every intake of air rendered me breathless and left behind it a wave a nausea that overtook all my senses. Lilah had already gotten up and left me to my own devices. I liked to think she had no idea I felt like I was going to die. I looked over to the bedside table and stared at the clock, finally realizing it was after nine in the morning. Holy shit, I thought. I sat up thinking I was certainly late for work and would be fired although I highly doubt Jenny would fire me for being an hour late. Then I realized it was Sunday and I was at home in Woodlawn. I fell back against my pillows as Lilah came through our bedroom door.

"Well, good morning, sleepy head."

"Hi," I croaked. She came over and sat beside me on the bed.

"You sound horrible," she said leaning over to kiss me. I wanted to stop her but I didn't have enough energy. She put her hand on my forehead. "And you're burning up." She wiped a strand of hair off my face. "Do you feel bad?"

"Yes," I barely whispered.

"Oh, honey," she leaned over again and kissed my forehead. "What's wrong? Is your throat sore? Does your head hurt?"

"Yes…"

I coughed and a burning sensation made its way from the back of my throat up through my nose, which I didn't even know was possible.

I grabbed a tissue off the nightstand and brought it to my face, sneezing several times as I watched Lilah walk toward our bathroom. She came back with a thermometer, a bottle of green cold medicine and some other bottle with a spray top. It was red.

"I have to get up," I said sitting up. "I don't have time for this. I have a million things to do."

"Lay down," she said so I did. Mainly because I did not have the wherewithal to disagree. She sat beside me again as she put all her supplies on the bedside table. "Do you want the good news first or the bad news?"

"I didn't know there was *any* news."

"Abe has strep throat."

"Awesome."

"Matt has what may be the flu but Isabel says it's just a cold and Vonnie told me a little while ago her head hurt so bad, she wanted to shoot herself which is probably a sinus infection."

"Even more awesome."

"It doesn't mean you have any of those things. It could just be a coincidence."

"Right." I grabbed another tissue off the nightstand and sneezed into it. She tucked some of my hair behind my ear.

"You need to rest. Open your mouth." Before I got it completely open, she stuck the thermometer inside. "How did you feel yesterday?"

I motioned to the thermometer indicating I couldn't really answer her at the moment. She poured some of the green medicine into the little cup attached to the bottle and handed it to me as she pulled the thermometer out of my mouth.

"Yeah, that's what I thought," she said looking at it.

"This is medicine for nighttime, Lilah."

"I know." She waved her hand at me. "Just take it."

"It will make me sleep all day," I protested.

"Well, that's what you need to do. Your temperature is 102.3."

"Great. And here's an observation." She turned to look at me because I was still holding the cup in my hand. "If I take this and sleep all day I'm not going to sleep tonight." She looked at me like I was crazy. "Am I missing something here?"

"No. I'll just give you another dose tonight. Just take it."

"It can't be good to drug yourself so you'll sleep for two days."

"It won't be two days. Don't be ridiculous. Just take it."

I usually did whatever Lilah told me to do because as much as I hated to admit it, she was most often right. I sat up. I already knew what this stuff tasted like so I tried to down it like a shot. That didn't work very well and I put my hand over my mouth.

"Swallow," Lilah said. I widened my eyes because I was about to spit it across the bed. "Swallow." I shook my head back and forth. "Just do it." I somehow managed to swallow although afterward I thought I was going to cough up my lungs. "Yay!" she said cheerfully, patting my back. "You did it!"

"I'm not 10," I commented. She took the cup from me and fluffed my pillows.

"Go back to sleep," she said. "When you wake up, I'll check your temperature and see how you feel but if you're not better by tomorrow you'll have to go to the doctor."

"Oh, no," I said. "Adrian Bennett does not go to the doctor." She stood up.

"Adrian Bennett does whatever I tell him to do." She pulled the sheets up around me, like she was tucking in a child at night. I grabbed her arm as she turned to walk away.

"What?"

"Thank you."

"For what?"

"For taking care of me."

"It's my job to take care of you," she said as she ran her fingers down the side of my face. "I love you."

"You know you're going to be sick," I said as she walked toward the door. She turned around, her hand on the knob.

"No, I'm not. I have built up an immunity over the years."

"From what?"

"From everything." She smiled as if she was amused. "It's called living with kids."

That night I coughed until my throat was raw. I kept telling Lilah I was fine and she let me suffer for about an hour. Probably to convince me that next time I needed to listen to her. She finally got up and went into the bathroom. She came back with what she called vapor rub – whatever the hell that is. She rubbed it on my chest and laid a washcloth over it then she crawled in bed beside me and propped me up with pillows across her lap. I fell asleep as she massaged my neck and shoulders. I'm not sure if she slept at all but she made sure I did.

It took me over a week to get over that sickness and two weeks afterward to stop coughing. I'm still not sure what I had but Lilah took care of me the entire time. She sat in bed with me all day every day. She read. I slept. Whenever I woke up, I would look over to her and she'd smile and run her hand over my hair, lay her cool fingers against my hot cheek.

"I love you," she whispered every single time.

This woman I love put everything aside to stay by my side. I didn't need her to stay by my side but she did. She even sent Ben to the pharmacy to buy more medicine so she didn't have to leave me alone. And, as usual, she was right.

She never caught it.

Vonnie

I have been fascinated with the afterlife for as long as I can remember. I think the idea of talking to people who have passed over is cool as shit. I believe they have important things to tell us. I also believe they are as excited to talk to us as we are to talk to them.

I don't think anyone else in my family believes those things. Maybe Isabel because she is the craziest person I know. I know for a fact if I told Grandma Loretta I believed in Spirits, she'd take me to church for an exorcism. She wouldn't recognize the difference between me saying I believed in them and me saying I believed there was one inside of me. To her those two things are probably the same.

I remember this one time when Isabel thought Ben had a demon inside of him, which is a perfectly reasonable assumption given Ben's behavior most of the time, so who knows what Isabel thinks. I know for certain Matt's girlfriend, Eden, believes it because we've talked about it. The only problem is that we don't know any Spiritualists because I can guarantee you if we did, we'd have already visited them.

When I found out Adrian's high school girlfriend talked to dead people I was intrigued. I wanted to know more about her and what she did so I asked Tiffany about her. She had come into town for the weekend but Isaac had to work so she was spending the day with me. We were having lunch at the diner in town, and I decided now was as good a time as any other.

"She talks to dead people," Tiffany told me.

"Seriously?" I asked as I swiped a fry into the ketchup on my plate.

"Yep."

"Do you believe her?"

"That she can do it?"

Tiffany wasn't eating an unhealthy cheeseburger and fries like me. She was eating chicken salad with celery and carrots. I told her she was a health nut. She told me if I ate healthier maybe I could fit into my size zero jeans again. Bam. Tiffany is not one to hold anything back. It's one of the things I love most about her.

"I mean, I guess," she said now about Lorelei. "Her grandmother did it."

"So, it's like inherited?"

"I have no idea," she said. "That's what Adrian tells me."

"How does he know?" She looked off into the distance for a moment like she was trying to decide how to answer.

"I guess she told him. He believes pretty much anything she says."

"Still?"

"Oh, yeah."

"What kind of relationship do they have now?" I asked. Tiffany smiled.

"Are you asking for yourself or for your mom?"

"Me," I said.

"You're not going to tell Lilah if I tell you, are you?"

"No."

"You promise?"

"Pinky swear," I said as I held out my hand and we locked pinkies.

"They're friends." She hesitated.

"That's it?" I laughed. "That's all I get for a pinky swear?"

"Okay," she said holding up her finger. She took a bite of her chicken salad then washed it down with some fruity mineral water. "They've always been weird with one another."

"What do you mean?"

"Like super protective, like they have secrets no one else knows about."

"Do they?"

"Nah," she said. "Adrian would've told me. He tells me everything."

"Do you think he still loves her?"

"Sure," she said.

"What???" Are you kidding?"

"Not like that," she said and laughed. "Like friend love. They've known each other for so long."

"Do you like her?"

"Eh," she said moving her hand back and forth. "She's okay."

"You don't like her," I concluded.

"I think she's still in love with Adrian. In fact, I don't think she ever fell out of love with him." I took a sip of my coke and the waitress took my plate.

"Dessert?" she asked.

"Yes," I answered.

"No, thank you," Tiffany said. "But a coffee would be good. Decaf."

"You got it," the waitress said. She turned around halfway back to the counter and pointed at Tiff. "Cream and sugar?"

"Just cream."

"Do you ever eat anything that has sugar in it?" I teased.

"Birthday cake," she told me. "On birthdays."

"So, you think Lorelei is still in love with Adrian? After all these years?"

"Yep."

"He's not in love with her," I said. "He's in love with Mom."

"Yep," she agreed. "But I will tell you something else that needs to stay between us because the general population would think I was nuts if I admitted it to them."

"What?"

"Lorelei has many talents," she started. "Talking to dead people is only one of them."

Our waitress returned with the dessert menu.

"Need a minute?"

"Please," I said.

I was much more interested in hearing what Lorelei's other talents were than I was in picking out a dessert. Although the chocolate meringue pie was calling my name.

"First off," Tiffany said. "I like to give credit when credit is due because I don't want you to think I'm talking shit about Lorelei."

"Okay."

"She is highly intelligent," Tiff told me. "Like super smart. Smarter than anyone I've ever known. She has a master's in linguistics and…"

"What's linguistics?"

"It's the study of speech, like how different languages develop and fit together, their varying sentence structure, I don't know. A bunch of stuff."

"Wow."

"Yeah. So, she has that, and she speaks a bunch of different languages."

"And she's talking to dead people for a living??"

"I know. I wonder about that, too. She's also an apothecarist."

"What is an apothecarist?" I asked Tiffany as the waitress walked up to the table.

"Decisions?" she asked.

"Chocolate pie," I told her as she poured Tiffany a cup of coffee and sat the cream on the table.

"You got it."

"An apothecarist is like a natural pharmacist," Tiffany explained as she poured cream into her coffee. "She does cures and potions and all kinds of stuff like that. Lots of people in Amityville go to her instead of a regular doctor."

"Has she killed anyone yet?" I asked jokingly. Tiff laughed.

"Not that I know of," she said. "But it wouldn't surprise me."

"Seriously?"

"You never know with Lorelei," she confided. "I think she has a lot more power than most people think."

"What do you mean 'power?'"

"Okay, here's what I wanted to tell you. The pinky swear?"

"Yeah."

"I think Adrian is obsessed with her." I scrunched up my nose.

"Seriously? Like stalker obsessed?"

"No," she said. "Just regular obsessed. Like not a bad obsession. Just obsessed. I don't know how to explain it." She held up her pointer finger and leaned closer to me. "I think Lorelei cast a spell over him." I leaned back.

"Nuh-huh," I said shaking my head. "No, you don't."

"I do."

"Why?"

"Because Adrian is not an obsessive person. In fact, he is as far from being obsessive as you can get. You know him. He is direct. When he has something to say, he says it. He doesn't hold back and if he doesn't want to do something, he's not afraid to say no to you."

"Like you," I said and laughed.

"Right. But here's the thing. He has never, not even once, been able to say no to Lorelei."

"To what questions?"

"Every question, every plea, every want, every desire, anything."

"I need examples," I said.

"Hmm...okay. You know how weird Adrian is about his car? He doesn't let anyone drive it. No one. He won't even let me drive it and I'm his twin sister. Guess who he does let drive it?"

"Her."

"Yep. He has a meeting for work but she wants him to stay and eat dinner. Guess what he does?"

"Blows off the meeting to eat dinner with her."

"Yep."

"She wants to go shopping; he takes her shopping. She's upset over something, but he's supposed to be driving back to Woodlawn so he stays until she's not upset anymore. She'll call him at the weirdest times and ask him to come over to her house and no matter what he's doing he always drops it and goes over there."

"You think they're having sex??" I asked.

"Mmm..." she said.

"They are, aren't they?" She didn't answer. "I think Mom heard him talking to her on the phone. I mean, I didn't hear what he was saying but I was only joking when he came back inside..."

"Where was he?"

"On the back porch." Tiffany nodded. "Anyhow, when he came back inside, I asked him if he was a player. I was halfway joking."

"What did he say?" she asked. She took a sip of her coffee.

"He acted like he didn't know what to say."

"Sounds about right. He's very guarded when it comes to their relationship."

"Why?"

"I don't know," she admitted.

"I want to meet her," I said. Tiffany ran her hands through her hair and sat back in the booth.

"Everyone who doesn't know Lorelei wants to meet her." She picked up her coffee and held it in her hands. "She's like an enigma in Amityville. She has very few friends."

"What about all the people who go to her for medicine??"

"Do you know about the personal life of your doctor??" Tiffany asked. She took a sip of her coffee.

"No."

"Well, no one knows anything about Lorelei either. Except maybe her best friend, Ari."

"I thought you said she didn't have any friends."

"She has one friend," Tiff explained as she held up her pointer finger. "Ari."

"Does Ari talk to dead people?" I asked. Tiffany laughed.

"No," she said. "She's studying to be a doctor."

"Oh, wow. That's amazing."

"Yeah. I like Ari. She's a good friend to me and Adrian, too. But when it comes to Lorelei, she is very private."

"Like Mom and Isabel."

"Pretty much."

"I just don't get it, though," I said.

"Get what?"

"Why Lorelei doesn't have any friends. I mean, I know the deal with her and Adrian but for the most part she seems like a really cool person."

"Most people are scared of Lorelei," Tiff said and laughed. "Including Adrian."

"Is that why he never says no to her?" I asked.

"Probably. That or the spell."

"You really think she can cast spells over people??"

Tiffany shrugged and the waitress brought my pie. She reached across the table with her fork and took off a little piece off it.

"Holy shit," she said after she ate it. "That's like a taste of heaven.

"I know, right??" I asked and we laughed.

"You wanna know about Lorelei?" she asked.

"Well, yeah."

"Look her up," she suggested. "She has a website."

"No joke??" I asked excitedly. "Really?"

"Yeah."

"What is it?" I asked. "Wait." I pulled a pen out of my bag and grabbed a napkin. "I gotta write this down." Tiffany laughed.

"I don't think you need to write it down," she said. "It's pretty easy to remember."

"What is it?"

"Amityvillemagic.com."

"Simple and to the point."

"Yeah," Tiff said. "Unlike the subject within."

—

I called Eden before I went to bed.

"Hey," she said. "What's up?"

"What are you doing?" I asked.

"I'm having sex with Matt."

"Oh my god, Eden," I said. "Why did you answer your phone if you're having sex?? I could've left you a voicemail."

"Because I'm done," she said. "I'm just waiting on him."

"Holy cow, Ede. I didn't need to know that." She laughed.

"Hmm…shit," I heard Matt say in the background.

"It was good, wasn't it?" Eden said to him and I heard them kiss.

"Yeah," he said and I heard them kiss again. Apparently, Matt kept kissing her because she said, "Stop! I'm trying to talk to Vonnie."

"Eden!!!"

"What???"

"I know a Spiritualist."

"Really?? Who?"

"Well, I don't know her but she was Adrian's high school girlfriend. She practices in Amityville."

"What good does that do us?" she asked.

"She has a website," I told her." And I want you to come over and look at it with me."

"What does it say? I'm putting on my panties."

"I haven't looked it up yet. I want you to do it with me."

"I'm putting on my bra."

"Are you coming??"

"Yep. Be there in ten."

Ten minutes later she burst into my room. The scent of sex followed her. I'd given the code to everyone. We all had. Adrian would kill us if he knew.

"You smell like sex," I said as she shut my bedroom door.

"I just had sex," she told me and grinned.

"Oh, my god. Just come over here." I slid up against the pillows on my bed and she came and sat next to me.

"You truly smell like sex," I said as I looked over to her. I opened my laptop.

"What does sex smell like?" she asked and laughed.

"I don't know, it's a mixture of sweat…semen and…" I paused and looked upward.

"Patchouli?"

"Yes," I agreed. "That's it. Okay. Let's do this."

I typed amityvillemagic into my browser. I couldn't take my eyes off the screen. Neither could Eden. Before us was one of the most beautiful women I'd ever seen. She was like a cross between Mila Kunis and Angelina Jolie. We both stared at her picture.

"Wow," Eden said.

"Adrian's doing her," I said. "He has to be." Eden swatted at my arm.

"No, he's not." I turned to her.

"You just told me a few months ago, before you knew who he was, he was probably doing every girl on campus," I reminded her.

"Well, yeah. But that's when I thought he was a sexy drug dealer with no morals," she said. I rolled my eyes. "Scroll down." She pointed to the screen. "Click on that."

It said, 'What is it like on the Other Side?'

"What happens after death?" Eden read. "Life is everlasting and does not end when we die. Life is forever. On the other side there is no adjudication…"

"What is adjudication?" I asked.

"Beats me," Eden said.

She kept reading:

"… or chastisement as many believe yet there is always perfect justice."

"What does that mean?" I asked. "Perfect justice?"

"I have no idea."

She went on to read:

"The radiance of mysticism exists within all of us and this realization removes the trepidation of the unknown regarding death. Our souls are connected to a superior mindfulness that continues to lie in spirit form in another dimension. A kingdom of unconditional love. This love is yours. So is the kingdom."

Beneath this description: 'Consultations by appointment only.' Eden and I looked at one another.

"What are you thinking?" I asked.

"I'm thinking I want to go to this fucking kingdom."

"You want to die??"

"Of course not!!! Why would you ask me that?"

"Because that's what she means when she says kingdom. Like heaven."

"Oh…"

I went back to the home page.

'Apothecary'

I clicked on it.

"In medieval times an apothecarist was simply another term for a general practitioner," I read. "The Anastasio family has operated apothecaries for centuries. Our practices are renowned for our expertise in herbal medicine. We believe this planet contains a remedy for every malady on earth. We combine spices and herbs from around the world to create all-natural medicines and tonics. Our naturopathic elixirs combine science and erudition to create sophisticated antidotes. Our apothecary is located on the corner of Fox and Azalea streets inside historic Palazzo Cremisi. Apothecary hours vary so we urge you to make an appointment. However, emergencies are always met with immediate care."

"What kind of emergencies?" Eden asked.

"Who knows," I answered.

"She's weird," Eden concluded.

"You think? I think she's cool as shit."

"Okay, well maybe eccentric is a better word."

"Agreed."

I kept scrolling down and reading. At the very bottom: 'Favors upon request.' I pointed to it.

"What's a favor?" I asked and Eden laughed.

"Maybe it's like a cup of sugar."

"You think??" I asked.

"No," she said. "It can't be. Ask Tiffany. If she's a hoe, Tiff will tell you."

"True."

"Hey," I said. "Mom told me we're going to Amityville for the summer. Are you in?"

"Hell yeah!!" Eden said. "Do I get to sleep with Matt?"

"Maybe." I shrugged. "If you don't you can always sneak into his room after everyone has gone to bed."

"Very true."

"So, let's plan on going to see Lorelei."

"Little Miss. Magic?" Eden asked.

"Where did you hear that?"

"I didn't. I just made it up. Why?"

"Because that's what Isabel calls her, too," I said. Eden smiled.

"Maybe we're intuitively connected."

"Who?" I asked. "You and Isabel?"

"No, me and Lorelei."

"You're a nutjob," I told her. She laughed.

"Hey, do you have any condoms?"

"Buy your own condoms," I told her.

"I can't."

"Why not?" I asked.

"Because I smell like sex and I can't go in the pharmacy smelling like sweat, semen and patchouli." I just stared at her. "Please. Matt is waiting for me."

"Are you serious??" I asked. "You left him there??"

"He told me by the time I got back he'd be ready to do it again."

"Oh, my god," I said. I reached inside my bedside table drawer.

"I neeeeed," she begged.

"Well, that makes two of us," I told her, and we laughed. "Cherry or spearmint?"

"Flavored condoms??" she asked as I searched through the drawer. "Cherry."

"I know," I said. "Cool, right? Hunter gave them to me because I told him I wasn't giving him a blowjob unless he was wearing a condom."

"Smart," she agreed.

"Yeah, I need to make him go to the clinic and get tested so we don't have to do that shit anymore." She held up her hand for a high-five and I slapped it.

"Safety first!" she said.

Amityville

Adrian

When I got back from Woodlawn the following weekend, I turned on the lights in the front foyer, the grand staircase and the living room all at the same time. I always turn on all the lights right away because I don't want to see all the orbs floating around the room. When I asked Lorelei about them, she told me they were just Spirits who wanted to talk to me but hadn't gotten up enough nerve to approach me yet. Hence, turning on all the lights as soon as I walked through the door was necessary because I didn't like to think about how many of them there were. And then, there was Ana. I walked straight over to the rolling globe and pulled a glass off the rack on the outside of it. The ice bucket was full. That meant Tiffany was home, too. She came out of the kitchen.

"I always know when you are home because you turn on every light there is."

"Well, yeah. If you saw what I did, so would you."

"Rough day?" she asked as she walked over to me.

"You could say that," I answered. I grabbed the bottle of gin and poured it over my ice. Tiffany took one of the cucumbers out of her drink and slipped it into mine.

"You need a garnish," she said when I smiled.

"I need more than a garnish," I told her. I walked over to the sofa and sat down.

"Tell me about it," she said as she sat in the leather chair across from me.

"You know the little girl that won't leave me alone?" I asked her.

"Yeah," she said. "Ana?"

"Yeah. I need to talk to her."

"I didn't realize you had that capability," she said as she leaned back in her chair. She crossed her leg and stuck her finger into her drink, pulled it back out and stuck it into her mouth.

"I don't," I said. "That's what so fucked up about this whole situation."

"Adrian!" she exclaimed. "Language."

"I'm frustrated," I told her. I ran my hand through my hair. "Initially I wanted to get rid of her then I talked to Lorelei and she said Ana had something to tell me so I started entertaining her more. She's not talking to me but she's communicating with me if that makes sense."

"Okay," Tiff said. "Like when she wrote her name on the mirror, you mean."

"Yeah."

"Why do you want to talk to her? Did something happen?"

"Gianni has the copy of Stef's birth certificate with my name on it."

"Fuck," Tiffany said.

"Language!!" I chastised as I pointed to her and she stuck her tongue out at me. "He took it from the paperwork Roslyn sent to the Montenaris."

"Why would they give it to him??"

"Nobody gave it to him. He just took it. Probably before the Montenaris even had it."

"Lorelei would have never given it to him."

"I know. I mean, who knows how he managed to get it. He's *The Empire*. How do they manage half the things they do?"

"Is that why he is so pissed?"

"Who knows why Gianni is pissed. Gianni has been pissed ever since the first time I met him."

"Where is the birth certificate with his name on it?" Tiff asked.

"There's one with Stef's personal papers but I'm not sure about Vital Statistics. I mean, did they change the birth certificate when Roslyn filed the correction or just make a new one and throw the old one away?"

"I'm sure they didn't throw it away. They're Vital Statistics. Unless someone told them to throw it away. Who does Roslyn know in Vital Statistics?"

"That was my question. Jenny said Elizabeth Montenari. She's the registrar for the Department of Vital Statistics in the state of New York. She's old as dirt but she didn't just sign as the registrar. She signed for my side of the family as well."

"But that's our family," Tiffany said. "Why would she pretend to be us?? I don't understand."

"Well, me neither but that's what brings me back to Ana. "What if that is what Ana is trying to tell me?"

"That Elizabeth is pretending to be us?"

"Or something like that," I said.

"Is that why you were looking for Nana's pictures before you left for Woodlawn?"

"Yeah."

"So, what is Ana's last name?" Tiff asked. I pointed at her.

"You always amaze me with your insight," I said. "That's exactly what I want to know. Do you think it's a possibility Ana might be a Montenari?"

"Well, anything is possible," she said. "But it makes sense."

"Lorelei told me to talk to Ana tonight."

"When did you see her?"

"I haven't. I talked to her on the phone."

"You didn't tell her about your suspicions, did you?"

"Do you think I'm stupid??"

"Given your behavior with her in the Hamptons I'm wondering about that."

"I'm gonna let that go but only because I don't want to hear another lecture from you." Tiffany rolled her eyes. "I told Lora I needed to talk to Ana. I didn't tell her why and she didn't ask. She said I should try to invoke her."

"I am not having a séance with you. That's where I draw the line."

"I'm not having a séance, Tiff. Jeez." I stood up and walked around the room. "But I need you to be with me. Lora said Spirits are more apt to talk to people who are the same sex as them."

"I can't talk to her," Tiffany said. "I don't have your gift."

"You can't have a conversation with her but she can still hear you. She can hear anyone. It's just a chosen few that can hear her in return."

"Lucky you."

"I know, right?"

"Well, I hate to be the bearer of bad news but I have a date tonight."

"With whom?" I asked, surprised.

"Levi."

"Who the hell is Levi?"

"He just started working at the lab. He asked me to dinner and I said yes."

"Is this work or pleasure?" I asked as the doorbell rang.

"Maybe both," Tiff said. She stood up. "I guess I'm about to find out."

"You're not wearing what you're wearing right now," I said.

"Yes, I am."

"No, you're not," I told her. She turned to me.

"What is wrong with what I have on?" she asked looking down.

"You can't wear leather pants on a first date." She laughed as she went up the foyer steps.

"This is not a first date, Adrian. Jeez. I'm not like you. I don't cheat on my significant other."

"Screw you." I plopped back down on the sofa and ran my hands through my hair. "Damn it," I said to myself.

"Come in," I heard Tiffany say. "Meet my brother."

What is the last thing I wanted to be doing tonight?? Interviewing one of Tiffany's vast collection of admirers. She came down the stone steps into the living room with Levi following behind her. Like a puppy.

"Levi," she said as she gestured toward me. "This is my brother, Adrian." I stood but not because I wanted to. I walked toward him and extended my hand.

"Adrian Bennett," I said. "Nice to meet you." I took my gun out of the back of my jeans and laid it on the table beside me.

"Really?" Tiffany mouthed to me. I smiled.

"You, too," Levi replied as he stared at it. He looked around the room. "This place is amazing."

"It was our grandparent's home," Tiffany told him. "We grew up here."

"Wow," he said. "What was that like?" Tiffany and I looked to each other.

"It was fun," Tiffany answered.

"If you like haunted castles," I said and Tiffany gave me the evil eye.

"This place is haunted?" Levi asked.

Just as he did the gold and purple chandelier above us dropped about three feet. Plaster fell off the ceiling around it. The lights flickered but then came back on.

"There's Ana," Tiffany told me and smiled.

"Who's Ana?" Levi asked as he looked around.

"Family," Tiffany explained. "But don't worry. She's harmless."

"At least we think so," I added.

After Tiffany left on her "date" I made myself another drink. Ana had heard me. She knew I wanted to talk to her and it would only be a matter of time before she presented herself. I opened the French doors and walked out into the courtyard. I looked around. Nana would be so disappointed. The tiki lights had burned out a long time ago and needed to be replaced. The trellis needed to be repaired. And the pool? The pool.

I remember when I was little, I always thought the pool was a pond. The inside had been painted black back then so when you dove into the water you couldn't see anything. It scared most everyone but Nana had a way of reassuring people. Especially our guests. She told them it was because she wanted it to look like a natural cove and not an artificial one. People happily accepted that explanation. Tiffany and

I always considered it an adventure. We used to pretend there were sea monsters at the bottom except they weren't scary sea monsters. They were nice sea monsters. Like our friends. I guess when we had all the Spirits, like the ones we had floating around Fairy Tale, sea monsters were the least of our worries.

Soon after Nana closed the Inn all my uncles repainted the pool a sky blue then used it for parties and family get togethers. Get togethers Tiffany and I were never invited to. I was going to paint it black again, fill it with water and put lights inside of it. I was thinking a light incandescent glow would make the black waters a little less intimidating. When I finished renovating the Inn it was going to look just like it did when Tiffany and I were children. Maybe in the process I would figure out how to turn the Guardians of Fairy Tale on and off.

"Adrian..." I heard in my mind.

I turned and just like I expected Ana was there. She beckoned me with her finger and I walked toward her.

"I'm so glad to see you," I told her and she smiled. "I truly hope your day was better than mine."

When I said it, she laughed. It was the first time I'd seen her laugh. She was happy although I didn't know why. I liked to think it was because I was finally acknowledging her. I walked back through the French doors and closed them behind me. Ana hovered over Nana's Victorian desk.

"Come," I heard in my mind.

"What is it, Ana?" I asked, and she motioned to Nana's desk. I must have been right, I thought. "You want me to sit down?"

She smiled. That meant yes. I don't know how I knew that's what she wanted. I just did. I went over to Nana's desk and sat down in Nana's velvet chair. It was the only chair in the room that matched nothing else. Dada had given it to her on her fiftieth birthday because she said she always wanted a leopard print chair. It had never been a comfortable chair so I'm not sure why Nana loved it so much. Ana motioned to the nooks above the desk. She was trying to show me something so I looked through all of them. In one there was an old skeleton key. Lora was right. You just knew. Not because the Spirit told you. You just knew.

"The key?" I asked Ana and she smiled again. "What does it go to?"

"Come," I heard in my mind.

I followed Ana up the grand staircase and to Nana's room. Once inside she led me over to Nana's bedside table drawer – the one where Nana had her Tiffany diamond ring. The drawer that, as she grew older, held her most precious possessions. Her diamond. Her journal. Ana motioned to it.

"I don't need this key," I told her. "It's not locked."

"Open," I heard in my mind so I opened the drawer.

The drawer was filled with photographs, newspaper clippings and Nana's vast collection of lipsticks. Even as Nana got older there was never a time you saw her when she wasn't wearing one her lipsticks.

"You want me to put some of these on?" I asked as I held one up.

Ana laughed again and motioned to the drawer again. I reached my hand as far back in the drawer as I could, past all the photographs and newspaper clippings. A small wooden box. I pulled it out and showed it to Ana. She nodded. It was padlocked with a small gold lock.

"Open it," I heard in my mind.

I stuck the key into the lock. Of course, it fit perfectly and I turned it. When I turned the key, the lock popped open. Ana hovered over me but as I took out the photos inside, she came down and stood behind me on the bed. She put her hands on my shoulders. It felt like someone had draped a warm blanket over me.

"You're freaking me out, Ana," I said. Once again, she laughed.

"I love you," I heard in my mind.

I felt no fear whatsoever then. If anything, I felt love and security. Never in a million years would anyone have been capable of telling me a Spirit could comfort me. But that is exactly what I felt. Comfort and protection. And trust. I felt trust. Ana trusted me. Why??

I flipped through the pictures. They were all photos of Nana when she was younger. Her years in the city with Dada before they bought the Inn, every birth of every child her and Dada had, including my mother. In that photo a dark shadow hung over the room.

"See?" Ana said in my mind. "Your mother. Deceptive."

"No joke," I said out loud.

"The next picture," I heard.

I flipped to the next photo. Nana with another woman and a little girl. Nana and the woman looked to be very young. Maybe late teens or early twenties. They were on the beach. Here? Nothing in the photo was familiar to me except Nana and I only knew it was Nana because of the pictures she'd shown me of herself when she was younger. She'd shown them to me and Tiffany many times.

"Turn it over," Ana said in my mind. She pulled me closer. "It's okay. Don't worry."

I flipped the picture over. On the back of the photo, in Nana's handwriting: Me, Elizabeth & Giovanna.

"You're the little girl?" I asked Ana.

"Yes," she said.

The next day I went to Lorelei's. I'd bought her a baby gift. She hadn't told me she was pregnant yet but she was. I have no idea how I knew. I just did.

Before I could knock on the door, she flung it open and grabbed me around the neck. She almost knocked me backward down the porch steps.

"Whoa," I said. "Are you happy to see me?" She lifted her feet and I grabbed her around the waist with one arm.

"I'm pregnant," she said, kissing my cheek. "I'm pregnant!!"

"Oh," I said. "Okay. That's good…" She let go of me and stood back.

"Good?"

"Yeah," I said hesitantly. "Is it not good?" She slapped me on my chest.

"Oh my god…what planet have you been on? They've only done this like sixteen times." I held up my fingers.

"Three times."

"Only three?" she asked. I nodded. "I thought we were going to have to go back in and get you to do it again." I didn't know this.

"Oh, damn it…. I wanted to do that again. So bad. I love giving strange women a cup with my semen in it. The way they look at you -like you've just laid an Easter egg…. it's the most amazing feeling in the entire world." She turned and walked back inside the house.

"I hate you. You should be happy."

"I'm just kidding, Lorelei…I'm happy. Of course, I'm happy. You know I'm happy, right?" I handed her the shopping bag I was carrying.

"What is this?" she asked.

"It's what you wanted."

"What did I want?" she asked opening the bag. She put her hand over her mouth. "Oh, no. You didn't." A tiny tear slipped out of the corner of her eye.

"What? I thought it was good." She pulled out the baby monitor.

"This is the one I wanted."

"I know."

"But you didn't know I was pregnant yet."

"I knew you would be soon." She grabbed me around my neck again and hugged me tightly.

"Oh, Adrian. You shouldn't have done this. It's too expensive."

"You said you wanted to be able to see the baby while you were on the porch and in the Spirit room." She turned the box over and looked at all the options.

"Well, I didn't mean a home security system." I laughed and we walked inside the house.

"Well, you got one." She reached to hug me again and I wrapped my arm around her waist. "You think I'm not going to take of you. Of course, I am." She began to cry. This was pregnancy, I'd heard. I shut the front door behind us.

"You're not alone," I reassured her. "I promise."

She pulled away from me and rubbed her hand across my cheek.

"You are so handsome," she said as she wiped the tears off her cheek with her other hand.

"I know," I admitted. She slapped my chest then led me into the kitchen.

"How was your time in Woodlawn?"

"I was sick as a dog while I was in Woodlawn," I said as I walked to her refrigerator.

"Why?"

"I don't know." I pulled out a bottle of V-8. Lorelei didn't drink them. She only bought them for me. Like the beer. I coughed. "Something the kids had." I took a gulp of my juice. "The flu, maybe." I coughed again. "I'm still coughing up my lungs."

"Oh," she said as she leaned up against the counter island. "I'm sorry. Do you need a remedy? I can make you some of my lemon and honey cough syrup."

"That would be awesome," I said and she smiled. "I am so tired of coughing."

"Do you want me to put the whiskey in it?" I laughed.

"That shouldn't even be a question." She smiled.

"What else is on your mind?" she asked. "I know it's something."

"Lora, I had an experience with Ana last night."

"Oh good!" she said excitedly. "How did it go?"

"I'm not sure." I handed her the picture of Nana and Elizabeth Montenari with Ana.

"What is this?"

"Turn it over."

She did and read, 'Me, Elizabeth & Giovanna.'

"Where was this?"

"In Nana's bedside table drawer. Ana told me the little girl in the picture was her."

"That's weird."

"Tell me about it." I took another drink of my juice. "What do you think it means?" She grabbed my hand and pulled me with her into the Spirit room. "Please tell me you aren't going to read my palm again." She laughed.

"I'm not," she assured me. "Sit." I sat down in the velvet chair across from her desk. "I just get better responses from Spirits in here and I feel like someone wants to talk to me about this."

"Who?"

"I want you to think about Ana."

"Why?"

"Remember how I told you Spirits are apt to talk to people of the same sex?"

"Yeah."

"Well, maybe Ana will talk to us together."

"As in we can invoke her?"

"Maybe. Think about her. Think about what you want to know."

She closed her eyes so I closed mine too. Honestly, I was desperate at this point. I didn't have much patience when it came to things I wanted to know. Not knowing anything about Ana's identity was driving me crazy.

"Ana," Lorelei said. "Can you hear me? Adrian is here. We want to talk to you."

Here's my issue with this. I absolutely believe Lorelei has this power. I'm just not sure *how* much power. I opened my eyes. I probably shouldn't have but something told me to open them. Ana was standing in the corner behind Lorelei.

"Lora," I said quietly. She kept her eyes closed.

"Concentrate."

"Ana is standing behind you." Lora opened her eyes slowly but she didn't turn around. "You don't believe me?"

"I believe you but I don't want to startle her. Ask her to come to you."

"Out loud?" I asked.

"Yes."

"Ana," I said. "You were the little girl in my dream, weren't you?"

"That is not what I told you to say," Lora chastised.

"It's what she wants me to ask her. You told me I'd just know. I just know."

"Okay."

"You died in that fire, didn't you?" I asked.

"Yes."

"Tell me who you are," I said out loud. Lorelei squeezed my hand. "Are you a Montenari?"

"I'm yours," she said. Only this time she said it out loud. Lorelei heard her just as clearly as I did. "What do you mean, Ana?" I asked. "How are you mine?" She smiled and came over to me. Lorelei sucked in her breath and brought her hand to her mouth.

"I can see her," she said as Ana came around the desk toward me. She walked over to me and took my hand. I looked to Lorelei. She was mesmerized.

"Hold me," I heard Ana say in my mind.

"Can you hold a Spirit?" I asked Lorelei.

"I like to think I know the answers to most Spiritual questions but I have no idea."

"She asked me to hold her," I told Lora. "What should I do? Can you still see her?"

"Yes," Lora answered.

"What should I do?" I asked again.

"Try to pick her up," she said. "Like you would Serena or Estela."

I reached down, picked up Ana and sat her in my lap. She felt just like any other little girl. Like Serena. Like Estela. Like Maria.

"This is blowing my mind," Lorelei said.

"Yours??" I asked. "How do you think I feel right now??"

Ana laid her head on my shoulder while Lora and I sat in astonishment.

"Tell her how you feel right now," Lorelei suggested.

"Okay." I rubbed my hand over Ana's hair. "I love you," I told her because I really did.

"I love you, too, Patri," she answered. Lora and I stared at one another.

"Who is your Mamma?" she asked Ana. Ana got down out of my lap and walked over to Lorelei. "She just asked me to hold her," Lora told me when Ana got to her.

"Well, do it," I said.

Lora reached out and Ana crawled up in her lap. She put her arm around Lorelei's neck.

"I am so freaked out right now," Lorelei said. "I have never had anything like this happen to me. Ever."

"You're welcome," I said and smiled.

"I love her," Ana said to me as she looked to Lorelei. Lorelei looked to me.

"She loves me."

"I heard her," I said and smiled.

"Ana…" I started but before I could get anything else out, she disappeared right in front of our eyes.

Later that afternoon when I got back to the Inn, I fixed myself a drink and called Tiffany.

"Hello?" she answered.

"Hey," I said. "Come home."

"I'm at the lab."

"So?"

"I have responsibilities," she told me. "What do you need?"

"Wow," I said as I took a sip of my drink. "But, okay. I have something to tell you that is going to surprise you."

"Let me guess," she pondered. "Lorelei is having twins."

"How did you know??" I asked.

"Are you serious?"

"No," I said and laughed. "But that would be fun. She is pregnant, though."

"You're a glutton for punishment," she told me. "Is she really?"

"Yes."

"Ugh. Okay. Let me finish up with my babies and I'll be home."

"Alright."

Lorelei's pregnancy wasn't the reason I wanted Tiffany to come home but she didn't need to know that yet.

"Want me to pick up a pizza?"

"Nah," I said. "I'm making Tandoori chicken."

"You're making Tandoori chicken??"

"Yeah."

"Nuh-uh."

"I found Nana's recipe file. I'm doing it on the grill."

"That sounds like a catastrophe," she warned. "Nana did not do it on the grill. She did it under the broiler."

"Well, I know that. But I'm going to do it on the grill."

"Did you marinate the chicken?" she asked. "Because you have to marinate the chicken and I'm just not seeing you do that."

"I did," I said. "Thank you very much. It's been marinating all day."

"Holy cow," she said and laughed. "Are you wearing an apron??" I laughed, too.

"No," I said. "But I can put one on if you need a picture for Instagram."

"Funny. "I'll see you in a little bit."

"Okay. Love you."

"Love you."

Tiffany and I always said 'love you' to each other when we parted whether it was on the phone or in person. Lilah thought it was cute. It burned Lorelei to the core.

I walked out into the courtyard. I needed to get a move on with everything. I needed to find someone to paint the pool. I looked around. The tiki lights. The trellis, too. There was so much work to be done. I couldn't wait to get the guys up here to help me with it all. There was one thing, however, that didn't need any work and that was the summer kitchen. I had cleaned the racks of the grill and cleared all the debris out of the fireplace and the stone oven. My favorite thing about the summer kitchen was that you could spray it down with the hose after you used it. I had done that, too.

Tiffany had no idea what I had up my sleeve and Jenny was going to kill me but she'd get over it. I'd been walking a thin line for a while, Jenny said. And if I didn't get my act together, she was sending me to The Wall. Yeah. Like Border Control. I was pretty sure she was kidding. Even so, I probably wouldn't have done what I did if I hadn't already known Ari was taking Lorelei into the city for dinner and a spa day tomorrow. She said Lorelei needed to get away from Amityville without me. She emphasized 'without me.' I didn't disagree. I put the charcoal into the grill and lit it then went back inside to get the chicken.

I needed to tell Tiffany about the encounter Lorelei and I had with Ana but sometimes when things are overwhelming for me, I need time to process them before I share them with someone else. I had no doubt Tiffany would have some insight on my experience with Ana. She most often had insight on everything that happened to me. In the meantime, I needed a distraction. So, I went to pick up my son. No matter what was going in my life he could always make me laugh. I decided it was time for Tiffany to meet Stef. He came down the back stairs.

"Patri!" he said excitedly as he ran over to me.

"What's up, dude? Did you take your shower?"

"Yes, Sir." I tussled his hair. It was wet so I knew he was telling me the truth. "Miss. Jenny told me Nana had a jacuzzi." I laughed.

"Well, it's not exactly a jacuzzi," I said. I took his hand as I led him out to the courtyard. "But come over here." He looked out the French doors and took in the enormous pool, hot tub, trellis, and the summer kitchen with the stacked stone fireplace.

"Wow," he said in awe.

"It's a mess," I told him. "You gonna help me clean it up??" He looked up to me.

"Sure. We need to put water in the pool," he suggested. I chuckled.

"Yeah, but we gotta clean it first."

"Can we swim in it afterward?"

"Of course," I told him. "You know I used to swim in this pool when I was little. I learned to swim in this pool."

"You did?"

"Yeah. You know how I learned how to swim??"

"You took lessons," he said smartly.

"No, Dada threw me in when I was six months old."

"Oh no!!" Stef said as he brought his hand to his mouth. "On purpose?"

"Well, yeah. He knew I'd swim instinctively."

"What's instinkfully?" he asked. I laughed.

"In – stinc – tive – ly." He repeated what I'd said. "It means by nature, like I just knew it when I was born. No one had to teach it to me."

"Did you??" Stef asked.

"Yeah, I swam back up to the top."

"Do you remember it??" he asked.

"No."

"That's probably a good thing," he concluded.

"Probably," I agreed and laughed.

"You lived here when you were little, too? In this house?" He looked back inside the living room doors.

"Uh-huh."

"Did you ever get lost?" he asked. I chuckled again.

"Nah," I told him. "It's not as big as you think."

"It's humongous!"

"You know who's going to be here soon?" I asked as I walked back inside the doors and toward the kitchen.

"Who?" he asked, following me.

"Your Aunt Tiffany."

"She's your sister, right?"

"Yes," I told him as I got the chicken out of the refrigerator. I took down a plate to put it on and grabbed the grilling utensils. "My twin sister."

"You can't be twins," he said matter-of- factly.

Another thing I'd learned about children with my job: never question anything they say until you know what context they're saying it in.

"Why not?" I asked.

"Because you're a boy and she's a girl." I laughed.

"Well…" I hesitated. I was going to have to give the sex talk soon. "Let's go cook this chicken."

"Okay," he said. "Can we get a cat?"

"What?" I asked and laughed again. He made me laugh a lot and it felt so good. "Why?"

"Miss. Jenny has a cat," he said.

"Yeah, I know."

"It's really big," he said. "I want a cat like that."

"Well, that cat is a special kind of cat," I told him. I put the chicken on the grill and it sizzled. "You have to have a special license to have that cat."

"How come?"

"Because those cats are half wild."

"Simba isn't wild," he said. "He sleeps with me." I turned the chicken.

"Well, I didn't mean his demeanor. I meant his breed."

"What's breed?" he asked. I laughed once more.

"It's about who his mother and father are." Tiffany came through the front door and threw her keys into the basket on the hall table. "Go surprise your Aunt Tiffany," I told him.

"Will she be nice?" he asked.

"Why would you ask me that? Of course, she'll be nice."

"Not everyone is nice," he said.

I was going to kill Gianni, Lorelei's Papa, and anybody else that could potentially get in the way of me reuniting this child with his mother. If having Stef here at the Inn didn't get me banished to The Wall, killing all of them would.

"Adrian!" Tiff called as she came through the living room doors. She brought her hand to her heart.

"Oh, my goodness," she said. I turned to Stef as I placed my hand on his back.

"Stef, meet your Aunt Tiffany."

"Why didn't you tell me?" she asked as she squatted down to the floor. I just smiled. "Well, come here," she said to Stef. "Give me a hug." He ran to her. Yeah. He literally ran.

"Hi," he said excitedly as he hugged her. "You know what Patri told me?"

"What's that?" she asked.

"He said we could fill the pool with water!!"

"Did he now?" she asked as she stood up. "Did he tell you we had to clean it first?"

"Yes Ma'am."

"Yes Ma'am," she repeated. "Very good manners."

"Are you talking about him or me?" I asked and grinned. "It's not because of me."

I moved the chicken from the hot side of the grill to the cooler side and closed the lid.

"Lorelei," Tiffany said. I nodded.

"Or Roslyn. Or both."

"Did you know my Mamma can speak seven languages?" Stef asked Tiffany.

"I do know that about your Mamma."

"Isn't that cool?" he asked.

"It isn't just cool," Tiffany said as she pulled him into her. "It is super cool." He grinned from ear to ear.

"Did you know my Mamma?" he asked her.

"I did," Tiffany said.

"Do you know where she is?" he asked. He asked everyone he met this question. It broke my heart. Fortunately, everyone he asked thought he was Jenny's nephew.

"No, honey," Tiffany said and she opened her arms. "But your Patri is going to find her."

"He's taking too long," Stef said and I laughed.

"Hey," I said jokingly to him. "I'm working on it, okay?"

"Do you work on it every day?" he asked. "Because you should."

Now, Tiffany and I both laughed.

"I do," I assured him.

"Hey, you know what?" Tiffany asked him. "Guess what I have? You get ten questions."

Stef's eyes lit up. Tiffany has always been good with children. She somehow knows what will excite them most. Maybe it was just a female gene.

"Is it alive?" he asked. She pointed to him.

"You're good! Yes, it is alive."

"Is it a person?" he asked. Tiffany smiled.

"No."

"Is it an animal?" he asked.

"Yes."

"Can you keep it in the house?" he asked.

"He is really good at this," Tiffany said to me as she widened her eyes.

"Of course, he is. He's mine." Stef beamed.

"You cannot keep it in the house," Tiff answered.

"Um…" Stef brought his finger to his lips, thinking. "Can it walk?"

"Where did he come from??" Tiffany asked and laughed. "Seriously??"

"I told you. He's mine."

"Tell me, Aunt Tiffany!" Stef said impatiently.

"No," she said. "It cannot walk."

"Can it swim?" Tiffany shook her head.

"This is unbelievable," she said to no one in particular.

"I'm smart," Stef said. I chuckled.

"It can swim," Tiff verified.

"Is it a fish?" Stef asked. Tiffany looked up to me.

"I got him now," she said.

"I wouldn't bet on it," I told her.

"Is it??" Stef asked, excitedly.

"No," Tiffany said.

"Does it have legs?" Tiffany and I both laughed again.

"No," she said holding up her fingers. "You only have two questions left!"

"I know!!" he said. "Let me think." Then, "Do you know, Patri?"

"I do," I answered.

"Um…Is it big?" he asked me.

"Relatively speaking, I would say, yes, it is big."

"Well, it can't be an octopus because they have legs."

515

"Right," Tiffany said.

"Does it live in the ocean?" he asked.

"Most of the time," Tiffany answered. Stef smiled.

"I think I know!!!" he said excitedly.

"Well, tell her," I encouraged him.

"I want to be sure," he said. "Can I ask just one more question?" Tiffany looked to me then back to Stef.

"Yes, but only because you're my nephew."

"Is it friendly??" Stef asked with a grin on his face.

"Yes," Tiffany confirmed.

"A dolphin!!" he said, jumping up and down.

"Unbelievable," Tiffany said to me. I laughed and shrugged.

"You have a dolphin???" Stef asked. "Tell me!!"

"Well, I don't own him but I take care of him."

"Can I see him?"

"You can," Tiffany told him. "You think I'd tell you I had a dolphin and then not let you see him??" Stef laughed.

"I hope not!!"

I lifted the grill lid and took the chicken off and put it onto a clean plate.

"That smells delicious," Tiffany said.

"I'm not wearing an apron," I teased.

"Did you make rice?"

"Of course not. I did soak the rice, though."

"You are becoming Martha Stewart," Tiffany joked.

"Lilah makes me cook," I told her. "So, I'm learning."

"Lilah makes you cook??" she asked and laughed.

"We cook together."

"Of course, you do," she said. "So, I'll make some Indian rice. It won't take long since you've already soaked it." We all headed toward the kitchen.

"She's nice," Stef said to me. I laughed.

"I kind of like her," I agreed.

"I know why you and Aunt Tiffany are twins."

"Oh yeah? Why?"

"Because you were born at the same time. Weren't you?"

"Yes," I said. "We were born at the same time."

"You have the same Mamma though," he said. "Right?"

"Yes."

"Where is she?" he asked me, and Tiffany turned from the counter. We exchanged glances.

"She lives somewhere else," Tiffany said.

I'm sure she thought that was a sufficient answer for a ten-year-old but Stef was mine.

"Is she nice?" he asked.

Richmond

Lilah

Isabel drove around the block a third time.

"Isabel," I said. "Clearly, you can see there is no parking lot anywhere and I am not walking ten blocks just so you can park in one."

"You're not even walking one block," she told me. "This is one of the most dangerous areas in Richmond."

"Oh, it is not."

"It is," Isabel said. "You know what Roy told me?"

"Roy??" I said. "Are you serious?"

"He knows," she said. "He's been a cop for over twenty years."

"In Woodlawn," I reminded her. "Not Richmond."

"Well, he still knows."

She stopped in the middle of the street and put on her four-way flashers. Oddly enough cars didn't blare their horns like they did in Woodlawn. They just simply went around us.

"What is up with this traffic?" she asked.

"Get out of the car," I said. "So, I can park."

We both got out and I walked around to the driver's side and got back inside. I took the four-way flashers off and drove up a little further until I found a spot on the street.

"Watch this," I said as I put my hand on the back of her seat. "It's easy."

I turned the wheel and easily backed into the parking space. Not perfectly so I pulled forward and backed up again until I was flush with the rest of the cars.

"Damn you," Isabel said.

"One day when you swallow your pride, you're going to allow me to teach you how to do it."

"I don't need to know how to do it." She smiled. "I have you." I put the car into neutral, pulled the parking brake and turned off the key.

"You should never leave your car in neutral," she said. "Put it into first and pull the parking brake."

"Shut up," I said as I turned to her. "This is my Jeep. I've been driving it for over five years now. I think I know how to drive it."

"No," she said. "You don't or you would've put it in first."

"What is wrong with you?"

"Okay," she said as she crossed her arms over her chest. "I didn't tell you this before but I think this is a horrible idea."

"Why?" I asked.

"Because I think you're…I don't know…playing with fire."

"That's what you told me about Adrian," I said and laughed.

"This is not funny, Lilah. You are toying with the lives of…" she counted on her fingers. "One, two, three, four…a lot of people. Do you realize that? And the fact you're assuming he knows about Ben is crazy to me."

"I think I know McCain well enough to know he knows," I said as I laid my hands on the steering wheel. "I saw it in his eyes at dinner when Ben walked into the room. So, trust me. He knows. This is a simple visit."

"It is far from a simple visit," Isabel informed me.

"I could've lied to you and come by myself." She pointed at me.

"If you ever do anything like that…lie to me about something this important…our friendship is over."

"Oh, good grief," I said. "Don't be so dramatic."

"I'll tell you how dramatic I am. Roy told me crime on Hollyhock Road is so abundant…" I laughed.

"Roy used the word abundant??"

"Listen to me, Lilah," she said. "Please."

"Okay. Okay."

"He said the pizza places around here refuse to deliver to this neighborhood."

"Okay."

"He also said some areas of Hollyhock are so rough the police refuse to patrol between dusk and dawn and ambulances refuse to enter."

"Are you serious??" I asked.

"You think I'd make it up?? Call him."

"Who?? Roy??"

"No, you re-re," she said. "McCain. Tell him to come get you."

"No."

"Yes."

"Isabel…"

"Do it," she said. I pulled my phone out of my purse and scrolled through to my recent calls. I looked over to Isabel. "Do it or we're leaving."

"Holy cow," I said as I waited for McCain to answer.

"Put it on speaker phone."

"Shut up," I said as I hit the speaker button.

"Hello?"

"Hi," I said.

"Hey. Are you bailing on me?" McCain asked and laughed.

"No," I said. "I'm here. I just…well…" I looked over to Isabel and narrowed my eyes. "…I'm kind of concerned about this neighborhood."

"Are you kidding me?" he asked and laughed. "After the neighborhood we lived in??"

Now Isabel narrowed her eyes at me.

"It's been a while," I said as I stuck out my tongue at Isabel.

"Okay," he said. "I'll come get you, babe. You driving your Jeep?"

"Yeah."

"Okay," he said. "I'm on my way."

Click.

"Babe???" Isabel asked as soon as I clicked off.

"What? I didn't tell him to call me that."

"Are you even serious right now?" Clearly, she was not amused. "I wanna smack you so hard."

"Jeez, Louise." I handed her the keys. "Chill out."

"Listen to me," she said as she grabbed my arm. "Just because he was on his best behavior at dinner the other night does not mean he is like that all the time. Have you thought about that??"

"Yes."

"You do realize he could get you in there and try to rape you or God only knows what else."

"He is not going to do that," I said.

"How do you know?"

A knock on my window and I jumped. I opened the door. McCain was wearing black jeans with a black t-shirt that had D.A.R.E. in free-style script across the front, and in a smaller font, 'To keep kids off drugs.'

"Well, hello Isabel," McCain said as I got out of the car. "I didn't know you were joining us."

"She's not," I said. "She has somewhere to go. Don't you, Isabel??"

"Yep." She got out and walked around to the driver's side and McCain and I walked up onto the sidewalk. She put down the window. "Hey!"

"What?"

"Call me."

"Okay," I said.

"Soon!!!"

"Okaay…" I said. "I get it."

McCain put his arm around my neck and pulled me into him as we walked down the sidewalk. I didn't want him to but I didn't say so.

"You like my neighborhood?" he asked and chuckled.

"I heard you can't even get pizza here."

"Oh, we have a guy," he said and laughed again.

"Yeah?"

"Yeah…" he said as he looked down to me. "This is it."

We walked up the cement steps to a jalousie porch. He had all the windows open but it didn't help any. I could smell old grease, asphalt and popcorn. The outdoor air might have even made it worse.

"Do you rent this?" I asked as he opened the front door.

"Yeah," he said.

The inside was sparse but immaculate. McCain had always been a neat freak. I remember I used to leave the toothpaste in the sink and he'd fuss at me about it.

"How long have you been here?" I asked as he directed me to a seat.

"Um…about a month. You wanna drink?"

"Whatcha got?" I asked.

"Anything."

"Just fix me something," I told him and smiled. "You're better at making drinks than I am."

"I don't know how to make all those fancy drinks," he said as he leaned up against the kitchen doorway with his arm over his head.

"What makes you think I drink fancy drinks?" I asked and smiled. He motioned to me.

"Well, look at you."

I looked down to my clothes. I didn't think I was dressed up. I had on a pair of Guess jeans, a white silk t-shirt and a brown plaid jacket, brown leather boots. I'd put my hair up into a loose Chignon but just because I was too lazy to curl it. Okay, that's a lie. I put it up that way because I knew that was the way McCain liked it.

"You know me, McCain," I said casually. "I'll drink anything at least once." He laughed.

"True."

He went into the kitchen and I looked around me. A light blue corduroy recliner. A brown flowered sofa and a brown pleather ottoman. A round side table with a digital clock and a picture of a woman. I got up to look at it. His mother. I'd only met her once. She'd only spoken broken English then. McCain came out from the kitchen with two drinks. He handed one to me.

"Ah," he said. "Mam." I took my drink and looked up to him.

"How is she?" I asked.

"She passed away last year," he said as he looked down.

"Oh, McCain," I said as I reached for his arm. "I'm so sorry."

"It's okay," he told me. "You had no way of knowing. Sit down." I went back over and sat down by the window.

"You like that chair?" he said and laughed.

"Gold velvet," I said and smiled. "How can you not like gold velvet?"

"I know, right??" he said. "I only paid fifteen dollars for it at the thrift shop down the road. It's missing a couple of buttons."

"I don't think anyone would notice that," I said.

I took a sip of my drink. Straight whiskey. Now or never. And what if I was wrong? What if that little voice inside of me was deceiving me? It wasn't. He knew.

"Look, McCain, I didn't keep Ben from you. That wasn't my intention."

"You don't have to apologize."

Thank you, Jesus. I was right.

"He doesn't know you're his father."

"I figured after his little temper tantrum at dinner the other night," he said. "Man, he thinks he's a bad ass, doesn't he?"

"To a fault," I said. "Kind of like you."

"That would be a true statement," he agreed.

"I've tried to beat it out of him but so far it hasn't worked." I laughed and he laughed with me.

"Yeah. I hear you can get rather fierce with your children."

"Is that so?" I asked.

"Vonnie told me you put her in a headlock on the floor one night." He smiled. "Did you?"

"She called me a fucking bitch," I told him. "So, yes." He leaned up with his fist extended to me. I didn't know what it meant.

"Fist bump," he explained.

"Oh," I said and laughed. I put my fist against his.

"Damn," he said. "Look at that ring."

I looked down to my lap. He'd embarrassed me. Here he was with a fifteen-dollar chair from a thrift store drinking out of a plastic cup and I'm wearing a fifty-thousand-dollar ring. I held out my hand even though I didn't want to.

"Yeah," was all I could manage.

"Adrian rolling in the big dough, huh?" he asked.

Did I tell McCain it was Nana's? No.

"He has good taste," I said.

"I'll say." He leaned forward with his elbows on his knees, held his drink in his hand. "What is that? Three or four carats?"

I briefly wondered if Isabel was right. Would he try to take it from me? No. McCain would never do anything even close to that.

"Something like that."

"About Ben," he said. "You gave him my name."

How the hell did he know that?? Play it cool, I told myself.

"I did," I answered.

"Why?" I took a deep breath.

"Honestly?"

"Yeah."

"I don't really know," I confessed. "I...you know...right after you have a baby, you are kind of in a state of bliss."

"You associate me with a state of bliss?" he asked and grinned.

"That's not what I meant...."

"I know." He chuckled.

"I meant…I mean…I gave him my name, too. It's Benjamin Winston McCain. Well, now it's Benjamin Winston Trenton but McCain is what is on his birth certificate."

"You want to fix that?"

"Well, I don't need to fix it," I explained. "I mean, I changed it when Eric and I got married because he adopted Ben but Ben doesn't know Trenton isn't his real name."

"But McCain is on his birth certificate?" he verified.

"That's right."

"Do you want me to fix it?"

"What do you mean?"

"I can fix it for you…if that's what you want. I have connections for that kind of thing."

"McCain…I'm just so…." I looked down to my lap. "I don't know what I want."

"I get it," he said. "Don't think I don't. If you don't want Ben to know I'm his father then neither do I. I can get a birth certificate for him with your name on it. It won't be the one filed at Vital Statistics but it will be one you can give him. It'll suffice for pretty much anything he needs it for." I brought my hands to my face and he got up and came over to me.

"Stand up," he said. I stood up and he wrapped his arms around me and I began to cry.

"McCain…"

"Please don't cry, Lilah. It breaks my heart."

It broke his heart?? It broke mine, too. I had so many emotions floating around inside of me. Feelings I hadn't felt in years. It was a mix of uncertainty and fear but amidst them was a strange sense of gratefulness. Tenderness, even. McCain ran his fingers up and down my back. He pulled away from me.

"We'll figure it out," he told me and he put his hands on my neck. "Don't worry about it, okay? Whatever you want to do is what we'll do. Okay?"

"Yeah." I looked down.

"Hey."

I looked back up to him. We watched each other for a moment then I closed my eyes. I took a deep breath and the musky scent that emanated from McCain's skin surrounded me. He moved closer to me and I felt his lips touch mine. He tasted like whiskey. I didn't want to give in but I did and I kissed him back. He moved his hands from my neck to my waist and I leaned into him. Our bodies against one another's. I felt his tongue inside my mouth. What did I want?? He started to pull my shirt out of my jeans. Shit.

"I love you," he whispered into my ear then kissed me once more. "Maybe I should lock the door? What do you think?"

"Maybe," I said and he smiled.

Damn it. Fuck. Sex with McCain had always been incredible. I'd never had anyone make love to me like he did until I made love with Adrian. Could I lie to Adrian? Could I lie to Isabel?? Shit. Fuck. McCain walked to the door but before he could lock it someone pushed their way inside the house. Desiree.

"Well, well, well," she said as she pointed her gun at me. "What do we have here?" She looked to McCain. "Little Miss. Rich Girl."

"Well, well, well," Isabel said from behind her as she held her gun to Desiree's head. "What do we have here? Little twenty-five-dollar whore."

"Isabel," McCain said as he stepped in front of me. "Don't do something stupid."

"Shut the fuck up, McCain! Do you think I give a rat's ass what you think right now?" Isabel yelled.

"Don't shoot that gun," he said. "Desiree, put down your gun."

"Fuck no," she said. Isabel took the safety off hers.

"You better drop that gun right now or I'm gonna blow your head off."

"You won't," Desiree said. "You probably don't even know how to shoot that gun."

"Wanna bet?" Isabel said and before anyone could do anything else, she had shot the lightbulb out of the ceiling fan above us. She put it back to Desiree's head. "Still think I don't know how to shoot it??"

"Isabel," I said thinking I could calm her down.

"What did I tell you, Lilah??" she asked. "The most dangerous part of Richmond. 'Oh no, Isabel. Everything is a white picket fence around here.' Desiree, if you don't drop your gun, you'll be the next fatality."

Adrian, where are you when I need you? I thought. Desiree threw her gun on the floor in front of her.

"Happy now, bitch?" she asked as she turned to face Isabel.

Isabel stepped forward and handed me her gun. I handed it to McCain. I probably shouldn't have but it was my first thought. He wanted to protect me, right? So, why wouldn't I? What happened next is still unbelievable to me. Isabel pushed Desiree back onto the brown flowered sofa, got on top of her with one knee and held her down. Desiree tried to fight her but Isabel had her pinned so she couldn't move.

"Wow," McCain said to me.

"No one calls me a bitch," Isabel screamed in Desiree's face. "You little whore, selling your sorry self just to get some more crack. Where is your dignity? Where is your self-respect? Nowhere. It's nowhere because you've given up on yourself."

"My life ain't none your business," Desiree said. "Get the fuck off me."

"How old are you??" Isabel asked.

"Get the fuck off me," Desiree screamed. Isabel slapped her in the face.

"Answer the goddamn question. How the fuck old are you??" Desiree said nothing. Isabel grabbed her around her neck and shook her. "TELL ME."

"Twenty," Desiree said quietly.

"You think this is all you're worth, don't you? You couldn't be any more wrong. Why are you wasting away your life like this?"

Isabel stood up but Desiree didn't move. She pointed to me then looked back to Desiree.

"You see that??? That woman standing there with the silk shirt and the brown leather boots? Looks like she stepped off the set of the Young and the Restless, doesn't she?"

"Is that supposed to be a compliment?" McCain whispered in my ear.

"I'm not sure," I answered.

"SHE WAS YOU!!!" Isabel screamed. "That little rich girl got her act together. She took back her self-respect and changed her life." Desiree just stared at her. "You are fucking beautiful. What the hell is wrong with you??? That can be YOU!"

She picked up Desiree's gun off the floor and handed it back to her.

"Go ahead," Isabel said. "Shoot me now. I dare you."

Amityville

Adrian

I slept hard that night. When I woke up, I knew Gianni was back from Sicily. When I got to the office, the first thing I did was forage through the airline records from the past week. No Gianni. But that didn't really mean anything. It just meant he'd gotten smarter. He'd used a fictitious name. Just like I did.

I didn't think he was on Long Island. He'd gone into the City somewhere. He knew I could easily find him on Long Island. I could find him in the City, too. It would just take a little longer. He was buying time but eventually his clock was going to strike twelve.

When Tiffany and I were little Nana used to take us to Our Lady of the Seas on Clover Street after she got groceries so we could hear the church bells ring. She always timed it just right so we got there right before noon. Tiff and I used to count one through twelve. In fact, I think that's probably *how* we learned to count. Now as I sat at my desk, I could hear the church bells of Our Lady of the Seas ringing because the church was right across the street from the office. I stopped to count. I put my head in my hand and closed my eyes as I often did when I was doing any kind of critical thinking. Jenny walked up behind me. She was famous for walking up behind people when they least expected it.

"Boo!" she said. I nearly jumped out of my skin.

"Holy shit, Jenny!!" I said as I turned around. "You just scared the living daylights out of me."

"What are you thinking about so intently?"

"I wasn't thinking. I was counting."

"What are you counting?" she asked. "How many lives you have left?"

"Funny," I said as I leaned back in my chair. "I was counting the church bells."

"What church bells?" she asked as she sat down on the corner of my desk. I chuckled.

"The ones that just rang??"

"Oh," she said. "Our Lady of the Seas."

"Yes."

"Do I want to know why?" she asked.

"Old time sake," I said and smiled.

"Ah...hey listen, I need you to go to Oceanside."

"For what?" I asked.

"Sam Corleone has requested your presence."

My heart pounded. Sam Corleone. The only person other than me and Lora who knew about the security system footage. Well, Tiffany knew but she didn't really count. It couldn't possibly be about that, though. Could it?

"What does he want?" I asked. Jenny shrugged.

"Didn't say," she said. "Sam Corleone rarely gives a reason for anything."

"True," I said as I stood up. I blew out a deep breath. "Okay."

"He's at Lakeland. You know where that is, right?"

"Jenny," I said as I put on my jacket. "Everyone knows where Lakeland is." She widened her eyes.

"Yet few have ever seen it. Have you ever seen it?" she asked. I dug my car keys out of my pocket.

"In pictures," I admitted.

"Well, you're about to see it in person. Maybe *you* should take some pictures."

"I'm thinking that is totally against their code of conduct."

"That's good thinking," she said.

"Yep." She stood up beside me.

"He said there's someone there he wants you to see."

"Do you have any idea who it is?" I asked.

"None."

"Shit, I hate going into unknown territory. You know once I get in there I only come back out if they want me to."

"Very well aware of that," she said as she crossed her arms over her chest. "When was the last time you ran the obstacle course?"

"Out back?" I asked. I shut my computer down and locked my desk.

"Yeah."

"The last time you made me run it," I said and smiled. We walked toward the front door. "Are you inferring I need to do it again or what?"

"I was just wondering if you were physically able to flee Lakeland on foot should that need arise."

"You're hilarious."

"Are you?"

"Of course, I am, Jenny. I run four of five miles every morning."

"Yeah," she said and grinned. "But you might have obstacles."

"Shut up," I said and we laughed. "Alright. I'm outta here." I punched in the code and opened the front door. "If you don't hear from me by seven, just assume I'm dead."

"I don't think it's that kind of visit but it's always smart to be prepared," she said and winked.

Sam and I only have one thing in common. Well, two. My son and my son's mother. I pressed the phone icon on my steering wheel as I took the exit for the highway.

"Call Lorelei."

"Hey," she said as an answer. "What's up? You never call me anymore."

"I don't need to call you anymore. I can just stop by."

"Then why are you calling me?"

"First off, you okay?"

"Yeah. Yeah. I'm fine."

"Sam Corleone wants to meet with me at Lakeland." I thought I'd get an immediate response but I only got silence. "Do you have any idea why?"

"None," she said. "Unless it has to do with the video."

"That's what I thought but it couldn't possibly be about that, could it? I mean, he wouldn't have called Jenny if it was about that."

"He called Jenny?" she asked, surprised.

"Yeah."

"Wow."

"Why would he call Jenny and not me?"

"Because he wants a record of your visit," she informed me. "He wants to make it official."

I got ready to tell her he said he had someone there he wanted me to see but thought better of it. There were so many things I wanted to tell Lora but couldn't.

"Alright, well, I guess I'll find out."

"Please call me as soon as you leave," she said.

"Okay."

"Promise?"

"Promise."

"I love you."

Lorelei Anastasio is the only woman besides Lilah and Tiff I tell I love on a regular basis. Nearly every day, in fact.

"I love you, too," I said.

When I pulled up to the gates at Lakeland, they opened immediately which meant someone was waiting for me. Lakeland was another of *The Empire* compounds and so far, it seemed very similar to Angelic Manor.

I drove through gardens past several fountains, a pool and then, a replica of the Statue of Liberty on a stacked stone platform. Well, New York *was* the Empire state but I'm pretty sure most people don't assimilate the Statue of Liberty with *The Empire*. It seemed a bold statement to make on *The Empire's* part, but then it was *The Empire*, and while most people would probably consider a replica of the Statue of Liberty inferring anything other than America's freedom as being disrespectful, I'm sure *The Empire* thought the same thing about the United States of America. I finally saw the house in the distance. Boy, did I see the house.

The lake that Lakeland sits on is a manmade lake but that doesn't make it any less beautiful. There are rolling hills with perfectly manicured lawns and in the center of it all: the house. It almost seems as if the house is built into the hills. Maybe it was. I've never seen anything like it and I probably never will again. It was a series of floors, all with floor to ceiling windows but placed at just the right angle to make the house appear as if it melts into the field behind it. There were three sections to this house. The main part of it was brick with old stone interspersed throughout the exterior of the first and second floors. The two side sections of the house were dark brown wood, also interspersed with old stone. The mullioned windows created a multi-dimensional effect to the many rooflines. I pulled up underneath of the stone portico at the front door.

The front door. Remember the little cottage door of Bilbo Baggins house in *The Hobbit*? That's the door except it's huge. It is also banked by two humongous tree trunks that make it seem as if you're walking into a forest. I'm not sure how an architect would make that happen but now I knew what I would talk to Tom about when I finally got to meet him because he probably knew the answer to that question. Before I got to the door, it opened.

I was expecting to see Sam. Of course, I was expecting to see Sam. He was the one who'd ask for me, right? He was the one who'd called Jenny. An official record, Lorelei said. I walked toward the door and she held out her arms. I smiled and wrapped my arms around her, picked her up and twirled her around just like I used to. She laughed as I sat her down. Lorelei's mother. Roslyn.

"Adrian," she said as she put her hands on my cheeks. "I'm so happy to see you."

Lorelei

When a Spirit gives me unsolicited information, I implore them for more. The Spirit who continually gave me information about Ana had a mission. And now it wasn't only giving me information about Ana. It was giving me information about Adrian's past. Were the two somehow related?

My first question was 'Who is Ana?' And why is she so important? What message did Ana have to give Adrian? Why did the Spirit give me the name Cristiano? And for that matter, why did it tell me Caris knew? What did she know exactly?? Did she just know the answer to the mystery of Adrian's name? And if she did, where the hell was she?

Spirits sometimes hide, I thought. Especially if they are watching you. Caris was watching me. She'd always watched people. She did it here on earth so no doubt she would do it in the Spirit world as well. I hadn't heard from or seen Caris since my dream with her, but that dream wasn't a one-way dream. Two people were involved in that dream. I just had to figure out where the other one was.

"Where are you, Caris?" I said out loud as I sat at the kitchen table with my cup of coffee. It was meant to be a rhetorical question. Even so the curtains at the window above the sink fluttered as if a breeze had blown through, but the window was closed.

"Where are you, Caris?" I asked again. I looked upward. "Someone tell me where she is."

Adrian could probably help me figure it out but as far as I knew Adrian didn't know his mother had passed to the other side. The only difference between me and Adrian when it comes to solving mysteries is that he thinks he can only solve them through people here on earth. He'd use earthly resources to find out about Ana. After all, she had already showed him the picture of her with Nana so I was sure there were other palpable clues. But I didn't need palpable clues. I only needed Caris. Suddenly a thought popped into my head.

I have learned over the years to never underestimate anything I hear in my mind no matter how obscure or ridiculous it may seem. So, I asked Caris a question she would least expect.

"If you hadn't been able to convince Raymond to marry you," I started. "What last name would you have given Adrian?"

Rajah walked into the kitchen and jumped up onto the table in front of me.

"Uh...I think not." I pointed to the floor. "You know and good and well you don't get on this table."

He jumped down. He was a good cat. He could be stubborn but for the most part he listened when I talked to him. I watched him as he jumped up onto the counter.

"Rajah!" He ignored me and walked over to the huge farmhouse sink. He stepped down into it. "What are you up to?" He stood up on his hind feet and pressed his front paws against the windowpane. "What's out there, boy?" I asked as I got up from the table and walked up behind him. I leaned closer to him and pulled back the curtain. I peered outside into the dark. Rajah rubbed his chin against mine. He wasn't purring like he normally did when he gave me love. "I don't see anything." We stood there for a few minutes gazing out the window together and Rajah began to growl. He saw something. He swished his tail back and forth and hissed.

'You may not see me,' I heard in my mind 'But don't let your blindness fool you, Lorelei. I'm here.'

Caris.

Woodlawn

Lilah

Me: I am so sorry

McCain: Why are you sorry?

Me: I just feel like everything that happened is all my fault.

McCain: It's not.

Me: But still.

McCain: Hey, don't worry about it. Okay?

Me: Okay.

McCain: You promise?

Me: Yeah

McCain: You know seeing each other probably isn't a good idea. At least, for now.

Me: I know.

McCain: I hope I didn't cause any problems between you and Adrian.

Me: Everything is okay.

McCain: Okay. Good. Can we still talk every now and then?

Me: Yes.

McCain: Should I hide my number if I call? LOL.

Me: Not a bad idea.

McCain: It will either say 'private' or 'anonymous.'

Me: How do you know this??
McCain: WHO are you talking to??
Me: LOL

Amityville

Adrian

"Please, come in," Roslyn said as she led me through the door. "Look at you. You're so handsome!" She reached out and touched one of my biceps. "Oh, my goodness, those arms."

"Thanks," I said as I looked down to my arm and laughed.

"How's my boy?" she asked.

"Me or Stef?" I asked teasingly.

"Oh, stop it," she said as she tapped my arm. "Give me another hug." I reached down and picked her up and twirled her around again. She was just as tiny as Lora.

"Better?" I asked when I sat her down the second time.

"You smell so good," she admitted. "Like a Tahitian sunset."

"Are you hitting on me?" I asked and smiled. She waved her hand at me.

"Of course not. You silly boy. Come into the sitting room with me. Tell me how Stef is doing."

I sat down on a green tufted ottoman in front of a green and purple plaid chair. The red and gold oriental carpet beneath my feet would have looked odd in any other home but here it just looked like classic

541

American royalty. I looked up over the stone fireplace. A picture of *The Empire*. The entire Empire.

"Nice picture," I said as I gestured to it. "The founding families?"

"Yes. You know how that goes."

"I do." We watched each other for a moment. "Stef is doing good. He loves being with Jenny."

"I guess you can imagine how much I miss him," she said as she sat down across from me in a leather wingback chair.

"As does your daughter," I said.

"She adores him," Roslyn said.

"He adores her."

"You know, Adrian. We only do what we feel is necessary. Sometimes Angel doesn't understand it all."

"I never understand it all," I said as I leaned forward on my knees. "What can I do for you? I know you summoned me for a reason. Is Sam here?"

"No," she said.

"Mr. Anastasio?"

"No," she said. "He has much more important things to attend to. Well, at least he deems them more important. Not so much me." I nodded. "You have no idea how much it means to us that Stef is with you."

"So, I was right."

"About?"

"Stef was at the Montenaris on purpose." Roslyn nodded. "Tony knew the drug raid was coming."

"Of course," she admitted and smiled. "*The Empire* is connected in many ways and there are so many politics involved. And I don't mean The Hill in Washington." She laughed.

"I get it."

"Adrian," she said. "You and Angel have a beautiful little boy. He is so precious."

"Yes."

"Have you had an opportunity to get to know him?" she asked. "I know that's what Angel wants."

"Yeah. I introduced him to Tiffany last week."

"That's awesome," she said. "I bet he loves her, doesn't he?"

"Yeah. She's going to take him to the lab to see the dolphins," I said. "He'll probably be in the pool with her before it's over."

"He will love that."

"Yeah."

"Is the water cold this time of year?" Roslyn asked.

"If the heaters aren't on," I admitted. "But Tiffany will outfit him before she throws him in." Roslyn laughed.

"Well, that's good." She hesitated. "As I was saying, you and Angel have a precious child."

"We do."

"It is my understanding Serena has taken quite a liking to you."

"How do you know that?" I asked.

"We're *The Empire*," she said. "We know everything."

"I guess you also know about Estela, then?"

"She is adorable," Roslyn said.

"She is," I agreed. "Lora has been a godsend to that child. I'm not sure what would have happened to her otherwise."

"I can't wait to meet her."

"Lora wants to adopt her," I told Roslyn.

"That doesn't surprise me."

"What do you think about that?" I asked.

"I think if it makes Angel happy, she should do it."

"That's what I told her, too."

"Well, she has our blessing," Roslyn assured me.

"That's good to know."

"You know I also know my daughter is pregnant with your child?" she asked.

"I did not know," I said. "But I am not surprised. She has no idea you're here. Aren't you afraid she'll show up at some point?"

"Of course not," Roslyn said as she stood up. "You think *The Empire* takes those kinds of chances?" She walked over to the mullioned windows. "That lake is full of Angel's tears. This house has nothing but bad memories for her."

"Why?" I asked. She turned to me.

"Because this is where we came when we left Amityville."

"You were here?" I asked pointing down.

"Yes."

"This close."

It wasn't a question.

"Yes."

"I didn't even know Lakeland existed back then," I told her.

"I know."

"I did some crazy things when you took Lora from me." Roslyn brought her hand to her heart as she walked toward me.

"Oh, Adrian, you must know it wasn't me."

"Yeah. I do."

"You've always been like a son to me," she said. "I've always loved you."

"I know," I said as I stood up in front of her.

She walked back across the room to the leather chair where she'd been sitting as she motioned to the liquor cart by the window.

"Well, take a shot, because I have something important to tell you."

"I need a shot?" I asked and chuckled. I walked that way.

"You do."

I picked up one of the crystal decanters. It had a silver chain around it with a placard that read 'Whiskey.' Every decanter had a silver chain around it. 'Vodka.' 'Gin.' 'Rum.'

"You know what kind of whiskey this is?" I asked.

"The best kind," she said and smiled.

"Of course. I think I'll do it on the rocks if that's okay with you."

"Whatever you want," she said.

"Shall I fix something for you?"

"Vodka on the rocks," she said. "If you don't mind. Give me a little bit of lime."

"Sure."

I fixed her drink and walked over to her, gave it to her. I returned to my seat on the ottoman. She took a sip of her vodka.

"Adrian," she said. "Practically speaking, you and Angel will be raising four children together soon."

"Is that how you see it?" I asked and smiled.

"Yes." She leaned forward with her drink in her hand. "I have something very important to tell you."

"You've mentioned that."

"It is between me and you, okay?

"And *The Empire*?" I asked and laughed.

"If you can figure out how to disarm *The Empire* security system don't you think an Empire wife can, too?"

"You sly cat," I said and she grinned. "You know about the tape."

"I do," she admitted. "I'm sure you won't be surprised to hear me say I hope that is when Angel conceived but it has nothing to do with what we're talking about today."

"Did you watch it??" I asked, appalled. My face flooded red. She laughed.

"Some of it," she confessed. "But don't worry. I fast-forwarded through that part."

"That's good," I said and laughed, too. "Because the idea of my girlfriend's mother seeing me naked elicits an emotion I can't quite identify."

"Your girlfriend?" Roslyn asked and smiled. "Do you still consider Angel to be your girlfriend?"

I hadn't even realized I'd referred to Lora that way.

"Sometimes," I admitted. "It's weird." She took a sip of her vodka.

"I understand."

"Quick question," I said changing the subject. "Why did Sam call Jenny if this was just about me and you?"

"Because I told him to," she said simply.

"No explanation?" I asked. She smiled.

"Politics."

"Ah…"

"Adrian," she said. "Did Sicily ever tell you about her mother, your great-grandmother?"

"Yes," I said. "Anne."

"Anne," she repeated. "A beautiful woman."

"You knew her?" I asked, surprised.

"Oh no," she said waving her hand at me. "But I've heard so much about her. What did Sicily tell you about her?"

"Hmm…she told me she came over here from India without any family." Roslyn nodded.

"Have you ever seen a picture of her?" she asked, standing up.

"No," I said. "I don't think so. Nana never showed me any pictures of her mother." She walked over to a chest-of-drawers and pulled out a picture album.

"I want to show you something," she said as she brought it over to me. "Scoot over."

I scooted over on the ottoman and she sat beside me, spread the album out over our legs. She pointed to a picture of a girl. An Indian girl.

"That's your great-grandmother," she said. "Anjali Anand." I bent over and looked at it closely.

"Wow," I said. "I've never seen her before. Anjali? That was her real name?"

"Yes. I'm sure she changed it because no one could pronounce it correctly."

"Yeah, probably." I looked at the picture more closely.

"She was really beautiful."

"Like your mother," Roslyn said and I looked over to her. "Your mother looks exactly like Anjali. Do you disagree?"

"Uh...I guess not."

"Did Sicily ever talk to you about her father? Your great-grandfather?"

"Not really. I know she said she never knew him."

Roslyn closed the picture album and sat it on the chair behind us then she took my hand in hers and pulled me to a standing position. She pointed to the photograph over the stone fireplace.

"You see that man?" she asked. "The one on the third row back??"

"Uh...I'm not sure which one you're referring to."

We walked closer and Roslyn put one hand on my shoulder and pointed to the picture again with the other.

"That man right there. The one with the long dark hair?"

"Yes."

"That is Cristiano Montenari," she said. "He is your grandfather. And that little girl he's holding? That is his daughter, Giovanna."

My grandfather. A Montenari. Jesus. It was what Ana had been trying to tell me.

"She was killed in a fire when she was five years old," I managed. Roslyn turned to me.

"Yes," she said but she didn't seem surprised I knew about it. "She would have been your great aunt. Sicily's little sister."

"The Empire has a lot of secrets," I managed. I took a sip of my whiskey. "I'm guessing I'm not the only one."

"Oh, sweetheart," she said as she laid her head against my arm. "You have no idea."

"Does Lora know?"

"What do you think?" Roslyn asked. She looked up to me and I shrugged. "Adrian, Angel tells you everything. If she'd known, so would you."

My phone rang and I pulled it out of my pocket. Jenny.

"I'm sorry, Roslyn. I need to take this call. Do you mind?"

"Of course not," she said waving her hand at me. "Take your time."

"Hello?"

Roslyn took me by the arm and led me into another room. She went back out into the sitting room and shut the double doors behind her. It appeared she wanted to give me my privacy but I didn't take that for granted. Even if Roslyn couldn't hear me, I'm sure someone else could.

"Are you still at Lakeland?"

"Well, yeah," I said. "I just got here. Why?"

"You need to wrap it up. I just got off the phone with Tina at the office in Richmond. It seems your little girlfriend has gotten herself into trouble."

"What??" I asked disbelievingly. "What are you talking about?"

"Apparently, she and Isabel – her crazy friend…" She hesitated. "Well, it seems they went over to the East Side to see McCain."

"What?? Are you screwing with me right now??"

"No," Jenny said. "But I kind of wish I was."

"What happened? Are they okay?"

"They're fine. Lilah went into McCain's apartment while Isabel waited for her, I guess. And another woman came in and held Lilah at gunpoint." I ran my hand through my hair, paced back and forth.

"Are you joking?"

"No," Jenny said and laughed. "Jeez, Adrian. If this were a joke it would be in very poor taste. Don't you think?"

"To say the least," I agreed.

"Anyhow, I guess Isabel had a gun? Does she own a gun?"

"She shouldn't," I said. "But yes."

"Well, in this particular instance you should be glad she does because she went into McCain's apartment after the other woman did and put her gun to the woman's head."

"Oh, my god. Please tell me she didn't shoot her."

"No," Jenny said. "No fatalities but Lilah is a little shaken up. I guess it won't surprise you to hear Isabel isn't shaken up at all. She's just mad as a hornet. You need to get down there and get this straightened out. Jeez, Adrian. Do something."

"What the hell do you want me to do?"

"Well, first off, console your fiancée then put the fear of God into her and Isabel because I don't want anything like this ever happening again. Ever. Secondly, you need to get Isabel's charges dismissed. Thirdly, you need to talk to McCain and find out what the hell is going on." I already knew what was going on. Ben.

"Where is the other woman?" I asked. "The one that pulled her gun on Lilah?"

"She's in jail where she should be. She had some other outstanding warrants so she'll be in the system for a while. I'm sure McCain isn't happy about it or maybe he is. Who knows?"

"Is Isabel in jail?"

"She was but after I talked to Tina, they let her go."

"Shit."

"Yeah, so get your ass down there. What's going on at Lakeland? What did Sam want?"

"Not Sam," I said. "Roslyn."

"Is there???" Jenny asked appalled.

"Yep."

"Well, damn if this hasn't been a day."

"You can say that again," I said.

"What did she want?"

"I have no idea," I lied. "We had just made a cocktail."

"Will she let you go?" Jenny asked.

"Of course, she'll let me go," I said. "What do you think she's going to do? Hold me hostage?"

"You never know with *The Empire*."

"Roslyn loves me. I'll just tell her there's been an emergency and I need to go back to Virginia. She'll understand."

"You're sure about that?" Jenny asked. "Because the last thing we need to do right now is piss off *The Empire*."

"I'm positive but she did confirm they placed Stef at the Montenaris on purpose so we'd take him."

"You were right."

Actually, Tiffany was right.

"I'm always right," I said.

"Get your ass to Richmond," she told me. "You should fly. My gift to you."

"A gift from you to me. Have you ever given me a gift before?" I asked and chuckled.

"Uh…your birthday??"

"You mean the Starbucks gift card I gave to Lilah because I don't drink coffee?" She ignored me.

"Hey, I'm looking at the flight schedules right now. I can get you on the four-thirty flight but you'll have to sit in coach."

"As long as it's not a middle seat," I said.

"It is," she affirmed. "But don't blame me. This trip isn't for me. This trip is for your philandering girlfriend."

Woodlawn

Lilah

Isabel says I always want more than I have. That I am never satisfied with anything. She is most likely right. She is famous for telling me to just be happy. Stop thinking about everything you don't have and be thankful for what you do have. Maybe this is partially the reason I went to see McCain. It was supposed to be about Ben but now I had to ask myself, 'Was it solely about Ben or was it about me, too?' And, if it was partially about me, what was I expecting? What did I want?

Growing up with parents who were old enough to be my grandparents made me vain, selfish and impatient. Of course, that wasn't my parents' intention. And while I wasn't an only child I might as well have been. My brother was twenty years older than me so he was gone before I was even born. I was unexpected but a miracle child, cherished, spoiled completely rotten, given everything I wanted whenever I wanted it.

Let me tell you right now that going into adulthood with those expectations gives you nothing but disappointment. The world doesn't work that way and once I had children, I learned very quickly putting yourself first didn't work anymore. I still have issues with it to this day but I'm getting better. Isabel and I offset each other. She and her three sisters were all within a year of one another. Isabel wasn't deprived by any means but she had to wait her turn. I have never had to wait my turn. I have never had to wait for anything. Daddy told Eric when he gave me away if Eric didn't plan on spoiling me the way he did the marriage would never work. Eric must have taken that advice – or maybe it was a warning – to heart because he did, for the most part, spoil me the way my Daddy did. The only problem with this was I took complete advantage of that quality in Eric. I had to learn the hard way that always wanting more was a horrible way to live.

Adrian usually called to tell me he was coming home but not every time. Every now and then he would just show up out of the blue. I'm not complaining because his arms always made everything better especially if I was having a bad day. This time, however, I *was* expecting him. He had called me and told me he was on his way and he didn't sound happy about it. It was the first time in my relationship with Adrian I thought he might just be mad at me. He'd never been mad at me before – over anything. The thought of it now made my heart sink.

I was sitting on the living room couch reading a new novel when someone punched in the code to the front door. I wasn't truly reading it. I was pretending to read it because I didn't want anyone to know I was a nervous wreck. I'd asked Isabel to be here with me when Adrian got home, but she told me I needed to do this on my own. She was most likely right, but I was going to smack her later anyway. Adrian opened the door. The love of my life. Everything I'd ever wanted. The man of my dreams. The one I thought for the longest time didn't exist.

The first time I saw Adrian, before I admitted to Isabel what I thought of him, I remember thinking about how there must be something wrong with me. Here I was a thirty-something year old woman and I was having fantasies about a high school kid. I thought there must be a disorder for what I felt and that, more than likely, there was a drug out there that could fix it. In the past there has always been a drug that could fix it. Adrian threw his keys into the key basket by the front door and I hopped up off the sofa. I ran into his arms, nearly knocked him over. He was holding a bunch of roses in his hand.

"Hi," he said and smiled. He enveloped me into his arms. "Did you miss me?"

"Yeah," I said as I wrapped my arms around his waist.

I buried my face into his shirt. A soft, blue chambray I grasped in my hands behind his back as I pulled him into me. Still bubblegum and cookies. He sat his bag down on the foyer floor and ran his hand over my hair.

"I brought you roses," he whispered into my ear.

"Thank you," I said but I didn't let go of him. He chuckled.

"Baby." He kissed my temple. "I wasn't even gone that long."

"I know," I whimpered as I began to cry.

"Sweetheart," he said trying to pull away. "Look at me."

"No." I buried my face further into him.

"Did you think I'd be mad?" he asked running his hand over my hair again. "Why would I be mad? Yes, you did something you probably shouldn't have but you didn't plan it to turn out the way it did. What happened wasn't your fault."

Who was this man? And how in the hell did I ever manage to make him mine?

"I need you here with me," was all I could get out before I broke into tears again.

He leaned over and laid the roses on the foyer table and picked me up with his arm under my knees. He pulled me closer to him. He kissed my temple again and carried me up the stairs.

"You need a little pampering?" he asked as he carried me down the hall to our bedroom.

Our bedroom.

"Mmm-hmm."

I could smell the outdoors on him. I reached up and ran my hand through his hair, let it fall back to his shoulders. He smiled as he laid me down on the bed. He leaned over me, his hands on either side of my head. His smile. It was like a drug to me. That feeling when the heroin first hits your vein. He laid down on top of me, propped himself up on his elbows. We were both fully dressed but it didn't matter. He was this close to me. He wasn't in Amityville. He was here. Not with her. With me.

"Hey," he said as he tucked a piece of my hair behind my ear. "Your hair is getting so long. It's so beautiful."

She had long hair. Dark and wavy. The kind of hair that always looked good. The kind with corkscrew curls down her back. Not curls she had to create. Natural curls.

I reached down to the hem of his shirt and pulled it up his chest.

"You know, this shirt buttons up the front," he said. He raised his chest and I slipped it over his shoulders anyway. His hand went to my waist underneath my shirt. "What are you wearing?"

"It's a bodysuit," I said.

Cream. Lace. Underneath a see-through light pink blouse. He started unbuttoning it.

"Were you expecting company?" he asked and grinned.

"You," I told him. He kissed my décolletage, trailed his tongue down between my breasts. I brought my legs up on either side of him onto the bed.

"You always taste so sweet," he said into my skin. He pushed my blouse back off my shoulders then unbuttoned it the rest of the way and pulled it from underneath me. He looked down at my stomach and shook his head.

"What?" I asked.

"You have entirely too many clothes on," he said. "How to solve this problem?"

He reached down and unbuttoned my jeans, ran his hand down inside of them, laid it on my stomach. The warmth of his hand pulsed through my body like a river of warm chocolate. I shifted my hips and he helped me pull off my jeans. He stood up as he pulled them off my legs. I waved my legs in the air and smiled. He grabbed my foot and kissed the top of it.

"You used to kiss the bottom of my feet," I said teasingly.

"Until I discovered you never wear shoes and who knows what might be on the bottom of them."

"You're so smart," I said and pointed to him.

"Uh-huh." He laughed and unbuttoned his jeans. One swift pull with one hand. Pop. Pop. Pop. "Music?"

"Sure," I said.

He pulled his phone out of his back pocket and scrolled through his playlist. I watched him standing there. This man. Faded button-fly jeans. Nothing but faded button-fly jeans. Dark hair that fell softly onto his shoulders. Dark, full eyelashes that surrounded his sable eyes. He smiled and laid his phone down on my dresser. It automatically connected to the Bluetooth speaker I never used sitting on top of my bookcase across the room. I'd forgotten it was even there. He took off his jeans. Navy blue and dark green plaid boxers against his dark skin.

"How about this?" he asked.

I Knew I Loved You, Savage Garden

"Did you know?" I asked and smiled.

"Before I met you?"

"Uh-huh."

"Yeah," he said. "No doubt. The first time I saw you I thought, 'I'm going to make that woman fall in love with me.'" I smiled. With my mouth. With my eyes. My heart. With everything I possessed.

"You did not," I said. He brought his hands to his chest.

"I did," he insisted. "I promise you I did."

"I can't believe you know this song," I said. He pointed at me.

"You have so much to learn about me."

"Still?" I asked.

"For the rest of your life," he assured me as he raised his arms over his head and stretched.

"Is that so?"

He leaned down over me and began singing the song into my ear. If you know the words to this song you know this was the most romantic moment of my life thus far. My heart melted.

"Every word," he said when he stopped singing. "Every single word." He raised up to look at me, ran his hand down the side of my face. "I love you, Lilah." I pressed my lips together to keep from crying again. You are not supposed to cry when you are making love. But this was a good cry. A sweet cry. A thankful cry. An 'I can't believe this man is mine' cry.

"Well, don't cry," he said and chuckled. He wiped the tiny tear trickling down my cheek with his fingers. "Do you love me?"

"Mmm-hmm."

"Are you going to marry me?" he asked.

"Mmm-hmm."

"I want us to get married on the beach behind the Inn," he said. "Can we do that?"

"Mmm-hmm."

"You want to ride off on a white horse afterward?" he asked and smiled.

"Yes."

"Well, then, I guess I better start looking for one."

"Isabel had a white horse," I managed. He raised up.

"Are you serious?"

"Yeah. Her name was Royal Destiny."

"Wow. Isabel has all kind of fascinating talents."

"She does," I answered.

"Does she ride?"

"Yep. Her and her boys."

"We are way off topic here," he said as I shoved his boxers down his legs with my feet. I leaned up and kissed him. He slipped his fingers into the bottom of my bodysuit and the snaps popped open. "Woo! No panties." I laughed.

"You don't wear panties under a bodysuit," I told him. He lowered his mouth to my neck.

"No?"

"No." He ran his hands up my ribs pulling the bodysuit with him. I raised my arms and he pulled it over my head.

"No bra, either?" he asked and smiled as he lowered his mouth to my breast.

"No," I breathed as I ran my hands through his hair again. His hair. I couldn't keep my hands out of it and I had tried. Many times.

"You were waiting for me," he said as he raised up. "Weren't you?"

"Well, I figured I was in trouble so I prepared for that possibility."

"Were you planning on seducing me out of my anger?" he asked and laughed.

"Oh, yeah."

"This is your plan most of the time," he said. "Isn't it? This is how you always get your way."

"It works," I admitted and smiled.

"For the most part."

"For the most part," I repeated.

He lowered his face to mine, traced his tongue across my lips. My entire body trembled. Whenever he touched me this way my body trembled. His touch was magic to me. It calmed and excited me at the same time. I felt his hips grind against mine but he didn't enter me. He teased me. I grabbed ahold of him and tried to pull him into me but he was stronger than me. Of course, he was. I moved my hands to his biceps. I ran my hand over his new tattoo.

"I love this tattoo," I said. "It's so perfect for you."

"Yeah. My fairy tale life with you." He kissed the tip of my nose.

"When are you going to get my name tattooed on you?" I asked jokingly.

"Is that what you want? You want to brand me? So, everyone knows I'm yours?"

"Yep." He ran his hands across my shoulders and down my arms. I felt him hard against my thigh. He rubbed against me then shoved himself inside of me. I sucked in my breath.

"You want your name on me?" he whispered in my ear as he moved against me.

"Uh-huh."

"Where?" he asked. I ran my hand down his stomach to that little dip in between it and his hip. I traced my finger across it.

"Right here," I told him.

"Oh yeah?" he asked.

"Uh-huh."

"Do you want it in freestyle script? Block print? Times-Roman?"

"Ha-ha."

"You want me to put a heart around it?"

"Yeah." He moved against me again and I tightened my muscles around him.

"Ah," he said as he buried his face into my shoulder. "That's crazy good."

"Yeah?"

"Yeah."

"What does it feel like?" I asked.

"It feels like a warm hug, like you're extremely happy to see me."

"I *am* happy to see you," I told him and laughed.

He pushed himself further into me and grasped my wrists in his hands. The weight of his body on mine held me in place. It was that line between pleasure and pain when the innermost part of him connected with the innermost part of me. The perfect spot. The one that made me lose my mind.

"Ah…" I managed. "Mmm…." He kissed my neck then my chin then my lips.

We moved together, our lips against one another's with our mouths open. He exhaled his breath into me and I took it in then breathed it back out to him. He talked into the most intimate part of me.

"I love you," he said.

I closed my eyes and wrapped my legs around his waist. He pulled my hips up off the bed as he moved over me. I tasted the perspiration of his chest and he raised my hands over my head. His mouth went to my shoulder, my breasts, my stomach, past my bellybutton as he trailed his hands down my arms to my shoulders. He traced his tongue across my hip and I opened my body to him. My heart beat fast against my chest and I put my hands on his shoulders as I raised my body to meet him. I grasped the comforter beneath me because we weren't under the covers. We were on top of the covers. With the blinds open. If Mrs. Cole walked by, she'd probably call me later and tell me how irresponsible I was. If she did, I was going to tell her about:

Ocean currents. How the waves cross over you. How you float through them and try not to go under but then realize going under is your best option. How you hold your breath and let the whitecaps move over you. How you hope when you break through on the other side the rest of the ocean is still there. I didn't expect it to be there. I expected to open my eyes and be in Oz. Maybe I could click my heels and end up in Shangri-La. No, it was the Garden of Eden. He raised up.

"Stay with me, Lilah," he said.

Now it was a beach off the coast of Fiji. I was in the blue-green waters. The waves lapped against my thighs as I drifted out further into the sea. The warmness of the water overtook me and I sank further down into it.

"I'm…"

I couldn't get anything else out. I felt his hands firmly on the back of my thighs. My heart beat wildly and I grabbed his head in my hands, held him firmly in place. He raised up when I released my grip on him, came up my body and pressed himself into me once more. His mouth covered mine. The dual effect of what had just happened and him moving against me was surreal. I dipped down into the warm Fijian waters again, let them flow up to my shoulders and over my back. I tasted the salt of the ocean on his lips. It was salty-sweet. It was flowers.

He shoved his hips into mine further. It was his turn now. He deserved it. He settled his face into my neck and I felt his body stiffen then relax against mine. Again. One more time. He pulled out of me.

"Turn over," he said as he raised his body off mine.

"What?"

"Turn over," he repeated. "Put your hands on the headboard."

I got up onto my knees and leaned against the back of the bed, my head down. He put one hand above me and pulled my hair over my shoulder with the other. He leaned down, touching his lips to the back of my neck. I could feel him hard against my thigh. He moved his hand from my shoulder to my waist and I felt his fingers graze against my ribcage. He shoved himself inside of me. I sucked in my breath.

"Oh…" I managed. I held my breath. Mmm…"

"Is this too hard?" he asked as he shoved himself deeper into me. Again, and again. I didn't answer. "Lilah?"

"Yes," I breathed. Now he grabbed my hair in his hand and pulled my head backward.

"Is this too hard?" he asked, his lips against my cheek.

"A…a little…"

"No, it's not," he said and he pushed himself into me once more. I gasped.

He thrust his hips into mine one last time and I felt the warmth of him surge through me. It was the most extraordinary feeling on earth because it wasn't just his body against mine. It was the essence of him. It was the secret part of him, the best part, and I was the only one who got it. No one else got this private part of Adrian except me. No one. Not even her. He put his hands over mine on the headboard as he struggled to catch his breath. He spoke into my ear.

"Do not…ever…go to McCain's apartment again," he said as he grabbed ahold of my wrists tightly. Too tightly. "Do you understand me?"

He kissed the back of my neck, ran his fingers down my arms and up again. He put his hands over mine then entwined our fingers together. He squeezed them tightly. Too tightly.

"Adrian," I murmured. "You're hurting me."

"You…are…mine," he whispered, ignoring my plea. "Are you mine?"

I knew I loved you before I met you…

"Yes," I managed. He let go of my fingers and brought his hands down to my waist. I turned back to him and he kissed my lips.

"Do you think I love you?" he asked as I wrapped my arm around the back of his neck.

"Yes."

"How much?"

"A lot," I answered, mainly because I thought that was what he wanted to hear. It wasn't untrue. I did believe he loved me a lot. I just…

"Don't make me have to remind you again," he whispered before I could finish my thought.

The next day at Happy Hour I told Isabel what had happened.

"*That* is what you got as a punishment??" she asked unbelievingly.

"It was a little rough," I admitted. "I mean, it kind of hurt." She stared at me.

"Are you even kidding me right now?"

"No."

"Lilah," she said. "I would pay someone to do that to me." I laughed.

"You would not."

"I would. I promise you."

"Didn't you and Tom ever have rough sex?" I asked. She stared into the distance.

"Hmm…not really. Tom is a complete gentleman in bed. I mean, I had to teach him how to go down on me."

"Are you kidding?" I asked. "I can't believe you've never told me that." She shrugged.

"It was kind of embarrassing," she said. "I was in love with a guy who didn't know how to get me off with his tongue."

"Doesn't it say in the Bible that cunnilingus is a sin?"

"Uh…I don't think it's the Bible," she said. "I think it's the law."

"Fellatio *is* illegal in some states," I told her.

"Well, damn. We should be under the jail by now." We howled in laughter and Isabel slapped my leg. I held up my wine just as Adrian walked through the back door.

"To fellatio," I said and Isabel and I touched glasses.

"To fellatio," she repeated.

"Nice cheer," he said and grinned. He leaned back against the counter. "Ya'll can both do me if you want." He started unbuttoning his jeans. "When one of you gets tired the other one of you can take over." I picked up a pencil that was laying on the kitchen table and threw it at him. "Hey," he said as he caught it. "You could put my eye out with that thing." He laid it on the counter and buttoned his jeans back up.

"Is oral sex illegal?" Isabel asked.

"Do I look like an authority on fellatio?" Adrian asked gesturing to himself.

"You're an authority on almost everything else," Lilah commented.

"Thanks, baby." He smiled. "Actually…."

"See?" Isabel said. "I knew he'd know."

"It is illegal in Louisiana and North Carolina to have oral intercourse," he told us.

"Is that it?" Isabel asked. "Just those two?"

"Apparently, we wouldn't be under the jail," I said as I raised my eyebrows.

"Well, it's also illegal in Oklahoma and Kansas but only between consenting gay or lesbian partners."

"How does that make any sense?" Isabel asked. He shrugged.

"You asked."

"So, if I lived in Oklahoma, I could go down on you but not Lilah." He smiled.

"Right. But you can do a dead person there if you want. They allow that."

"Gross," I said.

"For the record," Adrian continued. "Nebraska, Vermont and New Mexico also allow you to do a corpse but they're good with sodomy, too, so at least they're consistent.".

"We live in a sick world," Isabel stated.

"We do," I agreed.

"So," Ben said as he poked his head around the corner. "What I've learned today." We all stared at him. "I should mark NC State and LSU off my college picks."

Vonnie came down the back stairs into the kitchen.

"Why?" she asked. "I was thinking about LSU. That's a really cool school."

"No," Isabel said. "You'll get arrested."

Amityville

Lorelei

I walked toward the front door with the bowl of candy in my arms with Serena hanging onto one leg and Estela on the other. I'd promised the girls I'd take them trick-or-treating but so far, the doorbell would not stop ringing. Everyone wanted to come to Palazzo Cremisi on Halloween night because...wait for this...that is where the witch lives.

"Mamma!" Serena protested. "You said only one more trick or treater and then you'd take us!!"

"Well, this is the last one," I told her as I opened the door. "I promise."

There was a lady standing on the other side. Slim black pants, black turtleneck, shiny high heeled black boots wearing a long, black trench coat. Red lipstick and nails. She had a thin, white cigarette between her lips and was stunningly beautiful. Movie star beautiful. Take your breath away beautiful.

"May I help you?" I asked.

"I heard I was being summoned," she said.

"Excuse me??" I asked as the girls held onto my legs.

"Was it you or my son?"

"I'm sorry, Ma'am," I said. "I think you must be at the wrong house."

566

"Oh, no," she said. "I'm at the right house. Palazzo Cremisi. You're Lorelei." The girls had moved behind me. If I'd had someone to move behind I would've, too. I said nothing. "You *are* Lorelei, yes?" she asked, her dark eyes sparkling.

"Yes," I said. "I'm Lorelei."

"I can totally see why he is so taken with you."

"Pardon?" I asked.

She took a puff off her cigarette and blew the smoke upward into the dark, night air. She peeked around me to look at Serena and Estela. "They're not Adrian's, are they?"

"No."

A sudden chill coursed down my spine and I shivered. This was the mysterious woman I'd wanted to meet my entire life. The one I had unknowingly summoned with a simple question. The one everyone in Amityville warned me would one day return. She looked nothing like she did in the dream. She was younger. More vibrant. Full of life.

"Caris," I said cautiously.

She smiled coolly and reached her hand into the bowl of candy I held in my arms.

"Trick or treat," she said.

"Enter through the narrow gate. For wide is the gate and broad is the road that leads to destruction, and many enter through it."

Matthew 7: 13 (NIV)

Continue the journey with
Lilah and Adrian in

Happily Ever After

A Magical Tale

Coming *very* soon!

SPECIAL THANKS TO:

Jonathan Caleb – for helping me realize that even if your mothering skills are a little subpar ("you are NOT good with teenagers") you can still turn out amazing kids who end up being your best friends

My editor, Amy Laabs Pope – for being a dear friend and an incredible sounding board- who I plan to have multiple drinks with when we finally meet

Deborah G. – for teaching me that a woman's true power lies within, that magic is not a myth and that every day is a good day for a little belladonna tea

And the town in the Center of the Universe

(we really are…look it up)

Ashland, Virginia

Because everyone knows that's where Woodlawn is…

ABOUT THE AUTHOR AND HER FAMILY

Renay Jordan is the mother of four incorrigible children. Along with her best friend, Melanie, they've attempted to raise their nine children the best way they know how: lots of love, trial and error, and the occasional wild party when they momentarily gave up.

They've celebrated each other's birthdays and survived the birthday parties they've thrown for their kids. They've weathered divorces and now, grandchildren, who they plan to tell all about their parent's errant behavior the first chance they get. They've survived hometown rumors (Mel is not an alcoholic and Renay did not have an affair with a teenager – even though she thought about it), old boyfriends, pregnancy tests (once in a drugstore bathroom) and every now and then a little illicit behavior they will never admit, much less reveal.

Renay and Melanie have fought, made up and made out (no, just kidding on the last one) although they have considered getting rid of their men and buying a llama farm. (Llamas are mild-mannered, clean, intelligent and less likely to cause heartache.)

THE PAGES IN BETWEEN SERIES began a journey for them that exposed their irresponsibility in life and discredited them as parents which initially embarrassed everyone but has become a bond that ties them all together even tighter.

Their motto: Family always comes first. Screw everyone else.

Note: Lola (the little chihuhua/pug) is NOT for sale. Neither are the grandchildren.
(Some of the children are, though.)

Melanie & Renay (before the cocktails)

Photo credits: Brooke Hallock Photography

More photos of 'the family' in party mode in Happily Ever After, A Magical Tale. We didn't do anything illegal (that I know of) but no one's talking about what happened after the photographer left. 😉